THE ANGLER WHO LANDED A PRIZE CATCH!

There was a knock at the surgery door. Before I'd
time to say 'Come in', in walked a big man,
wearing a tweed hat, anorak, and tweed trousers
tucked into a pair of wellington boots. He walked
stiffly, with his right hand clutched to the
corresponding buttock.

'I'll have to shake hands with me left, doctor,'
he said as I greeted him.

'Fine by me,' I said. 'Won't you sit down?'

'If it's all the same to you,' he said, wincing
slightly, 'I'd rather stand.'

It was John Denton, River Authority head bailiff
on the Tadchester end of the River Tad.

He turned around and lifted his anorak. There,
dangling from the seat of his pants, was a large
piece of pink metal. 'It's a Devon minnow,' said
John – a salmon lure. It was dangling from a
vicious triangular hook which had obviously gone
in much further than the tweed.

Also by Dr Robert Clifford in Sphere Books:

LOOK OUT, DOCTOR!
OH DEAR, DOCTOR!
SURELY NOT, DOCTOR!

DR ROBERT CLIFFORD

Three Times A Day Doctor?

Just Here, Doctor
Not There, Doctor
What Next, Doctor?

SPHERE BOOKS LIMITED

A *Sphere* Book

Just Here, Doctor copyright © Robert D. Clifford 1977, 1978
First published in Great Britain by White Lion Publishers Ltd 1977
Published by Sphere Books Ltd 1979
Reprinted 1980 (twice), 1981, 1983, 1985, 1986, 1987, 1988
Not There, Doctor copyright © Robert D. Clifford 1978
First published in Great Britain by Pelham Books Ltd 1978
Published by Sphere Books Ltd 1980
Reprinted 1981 (twice), 1984, 1986, 1987, 1988
What Next, Doctor? copyright © Robert D. Clifford 1979
First published in Great Britain by Pelham Books Ltd 1979
Published by Sphere Books Ltd 1981
Reprinted 1985, 1986, 1987, 1988

This omnibus edition published by Sphere Books Ltd 1991

The right of Robert D. Clifford to be identified as author of this
work has been asserted by him in accordance with the Copyright,
Designs and Patents Act 1988.

ISBN 0 7474 0758 4

Printed and bound in Great Britain by
BPCC Hazell Books
Aylesbury, Bucks, England
Member of BPCC Ltd.

Sphere Books Ltd
A Division of
Macdonald & Co (Publishers) Ltd
Orbit House
1 New Fetter Lane
London EC4A 1AR
A member of Maxwell Macmillan Pergamon Publishing Corporation

Just Here, Doctor

Illustrated by Bill Martin
(*Sunday Express*)

To my wife, Pam

Prologue

Life is a tragedy, for we are all born eventually to die. We survive our tragedies by laughing at them.

'*A friend once told me that when he was under the influence of ether he dreamed he was turning over the pages of a great book, in which he knew he would find, on the last page, the meaning of life.*

'*The pages of the book were alternately tragic and comic, and he turned page after page, his excitement growing, not only because he was approaching the answer but because he couldn't know, until he arrived, on which side of the book the final page would be. At last it came: the universe opened up to him in a hundred words: and they were uproariously funny.*

'*He came back to consciousness crying with laughter, remembering everything. He opened his lips to speak. It was then that the great and comic answer plunged back out of his reach.*'

Christopher Fry

Contents

1	In Need of Practice	11
2	A Town like Tadchester	16
3	All Things to All Men	28
4	Pork and Means	38
5	Ways of Life and Death	49
6	Miraculous Draughts	58
7	All in the Mind	70
8	Curious Cures	80
9	Formulae for Survival	91
10	Down the Mine	100
11	The Nightmare	112
12	Miracles and Malingerers	116
13	Birth of a Doctor	128
14	Come Quickly, Doctor	138
15	Thick Ears in the Sunset	147
16	Swings and Roundabouts	158
17	Friends and Neighbours	170
18	After the Ball	180
	Postscript	190

I

In Need of Practice

I had begun to hate Winchcombe Hospital. I had nothing against the place itself, but I had been doing residential hospital jobs for three and a half years and was fed up with lack of sleep, lack of time off, and endless, tasteless hospital meals.

I had come to Winchcombe because I had hoped to go into general practice in the area, but here I was with just one month of my year's appointment to go, and no sign of anything on the horizon. Thirty-seven interviews for various practices had seen me on the short list of only six, and each time I had been turned down in favour of a married doctor.

The fact that I had come to Winchcombe after a failed romance did not in any way sweeten my bitter cup.

However, there was still hope. A practice in Tadchester had asked me to come and see them on Sunday. They did not give details, but I knew them all vaguely as I had treated some of their patients. This was hopeful certainly – or would it be another fruitless interview with my precious Sunday off wasted?

There was no direct bus service from Winchcombe to Tadchester on a Sunday, and I had not been able to afford a car on my measly hospital pay, but one of the consultants, John Bowler, kindly lent me his wife's car for the day. I drove off in plenty of time for my three o'clock appointment.

The second half of the drive was along the coast road, and I was watching some yachts out at sea as I drove along.

My reverie was interrupted by a screeching of brakes and the shattering of glass. Oh God! I slammed on my brakes and jumped out of the car to find an irate woman of about thirty-five examining the side of her car. I had drifted into her as she was about to pass me, and taken the side almost completely off.

She was furious.

'You damned fool,' she shouted. 'Were you asleep? Don't you ever look out of your rear mirror?'

We exchanged names and addresses. She was a Mrs Jean Hart of Tadchester. Fortunately both cars were still roadworthy, and I drove on, shaken, wondering how I was going to tell John Bowler about the crumpled wing and battered sidelight of his car. It just didn't look like being my day.

I reached Tadchester at about 2.30, parked outside the surgery of Drs Maxwell, Johnson and Hart, and rang the bell. There was no reply, so I sat in the car waiting for somebody to open up.

By three o'clock nobody had appeared. I got out and walked round the surgery to the back where there were living quarters, and saw a caretaker's bell which I pressed. Again there was no reply, so I went back to the car and fished out the letter confirming their phone call. The address right enough, was 'Drs Maxwell, Johnson and Hart, The Surgery, Tadchester'. Then my heart sank. The letter said that the appointment would be at Dr Johnson's house, Hillsborough House, The Hill, Tadchester.

I leapt into the car, asked directions from a passer-by, and eventually – at 3.45 – arrived at a huge house at the top of the hill, the other side of the River Tad from where I had been waiting at the surgery.

I ran to the door, out of breath. I was met by a very tall, thin, gruff man, whose greeting was 'You are late. I am Dr Johnson. Come in. We have been waiting for you.'

I was taken in and introduced to the other two doctors, both of whom looked stern and impatient. The shorter one I gathered was Dr Maxwell, and the red-haired one was Dr Hart.

Dr Maxwell, who seemed a kindly man, said, 'We have

interviewed twelve people in the last two days: you are the only one who has kept us waiting.'

My heart dropped. Twelve. And I bet they were all married. What chance did I stand?

They asked a few perfunctory questions. I thought they were just going through a few polite motions before they turfed me out. They did seem to know quite a bit about me, and we discussed some of their cases I had coped with at Winchcombe Hospital. They obviously knew John Bowler, my physician, very well.

The tension that had been in the room earlier lessened. We were chatting amicably about cases when Dr Maxwell, with a smile on his face, said, 'Now is the hardest part of the interview. Come and meet the partners' wives. There are only two; I, like yourself, have remained independent.'

There was one of those awkward pauses when all four of us

were standing back to let the others go through the door first. Eventually, I stepped forward and pushed the door open. It hit something and there was the most resounding crash. On the floor behind the door was a lady and the wreckage of a tray of tea. I helped her up, apologising profusely, and vaguely aware that I recognised her.

'My God,' she said, 'it's the maniac driver! What the hell are you doing here?'

This was all I needed.

The name 'Hart' should have rung a bell. Of all the people I could have crashed into in my reverie I had to choose the wife of one of the men who were interviewing me. I daren't look at the cups and saucers on the floor – they were bound to be part of a best bone china set that had been in the family for two hundred years.

My slight hope of being selected flew out of the window.

Another lady, obviously Mrs Johnson, came out to help clear up and organise a further tea.

The three partners and I sat waiting for the two ladies in a gloomy silence. Dr Maxwell tried to make light conversation, but nobody took him up.

Eventually the ladies joined us and tea was conducted in a chilly silence. Mrs Johnson, the wife of the tall, thin man, was obviously very refined. She questioned me about my school and background, neither of which appeared to impress her over-much. I had been to grammar school, not a public school. I did not ride, had no money, and was badly dressed.

Somehow we got through tea. Dr Maxwell, whom I liked best, saw me to the door and said, 'We have one or two more candidates to see, but we'll be in touch.'

I had heard all this before. Sadly I got into the battered car and drove back to Winchcombe.

John Bowler laughed when I told him my experiences.

'Don't you worry, Bob,' he said, 'I think the job is yours. And don't worry about the car: it's covered by insurance.' I just couldn't believe him.

Two days later I was rung by Dr Johnson saying that I had been selected and that they wanted me to start next week as an assistant for six months with a view to partnership. At last I had found a practice.

I told him I would be delighted to join them but had one further month to do of my hospital appointment to complete it, then I would be able to start on the first of the next month.

Dr Johnson replied very sternly, 'You either come next week or not at all,' and slammed the phone down.

I was furious. Going into partnership was like getting married. I would probably spend the rest of my life with these people. How could he speak to me like this? And what would the hospital do? They wouldn't release me. I had to serve my time out.

I took all my troubles to John Bowler.

'Bob,' he said, 'take my advice. These are fine doctors. They are at their wits' end in the middle of a 'flu epidemic. They have had all sorts of partner trouble which I won't go into, but I wouldn't be advising you to go unless I thought they were a good practice.

'They are worn out, they are weary – and they need you. Leave it to me to sort things out with the hospital. My advice is go – if you have problems you can always come over and weep on my shoulder.'

So I was to go into practice at last. I didn't really believe it, and the circumstances could have been better, but I trusted John Bowler. I sorted out my duties as best I could with my fellow housemen, packed what few belongings I had, and made arrangements to buy my own car.

I knew very little about Tadchester. My only visit had been that disastrous interview. I wondered what Tadchester was going to think of me.

15

2

A Town like Tadchester

Tadchester is a small town (population 6,500) on the estuary of the River Tad in one of the most beautiful parts of the Somerset coast. It is a Jack-of-all-trades market town, with some fishing, some light industry and a lot of farming.

Six miles north is Thudrock Colliery, known locally as Siberia, where the town's unfortunates are sent by the Labour Exchange if they can't find any other job. As well as the Labour Exchange conscripts, Thudrock employs a good number of men from the town who are miners by choice and heritage.

Tadchester is also a seasonal holiday town and is invaded by holidaymakers from all over the country, particularly from the north. It is 200 miles from London, far enough for people to feel they have really got away. Some of the locals obviously hibernate during the winter, as the summer months bring forth a crop of Tadchester characters who disappear completely once the weather starts to deteriorate.

The town is split in two by the River Tad, and further split by the large hill which dominates one side of the river. The other side is flat pastureland stretching off to marshes and the sea coast. You are not just a Tadchester resident, you are either 'Up the Hill' or 'Down the Hill'.

There is no strict social division between Up the Hill and Down the Hill, but the majority of the down-the-hillers are the

Haves, and the majority of the up-the-hillers are the Have-nots.

The bridge joining the opposite sides of the river is the famous old Tadchester Bridge. People come from miles to walk the bridge and enjoy the view from it, which is one of the best in the area. Quite often the lifeboat from the nearby seaside village of Sanford-on-Sea has actually to come inland to rescue inquisitive children who have toppled over the parapet into the depths of the Tad. In fact, holidaymakers are the only people one ever sees on the bridge – any inhabitant of Tadchester who is seen to cross from one side to the other is immediately branded as a traitor by his neighbours. Old Mr Clegg, who had lived Up the Hill all his life, was once seen by watchful fishermen to sneak across to the Down the Hill side late at night for some undoubtedly furtive reason. His papers and mail weren't delivered for a week.

Luckily, doctors were given carte blanche as far as the bridge was concerned, and I was at liberty to spend the whole day crossing from one side to the other without fear of having my essential services cut off.

By the time I actually did arrive in the practice the 'flu epidemic was past its peak and life had settled to its normal hectic pace.

I liked the look of my three partners: Dr Steve Maxwell, Dr Henry Johnson, and Dr Jack Hart. They were all different. The senior partner, Steve Maxwell, was a saint of a man, a bachelor, and I have never met his equal. His whole life was medicine. There was never too little time for him to go and see anyone or to attend to someone. Whereas we had a rota for weekends off, he worked every Sunday. He was a good listener, thought my jokes were uproarious, could tell some very good yarns of his own (all of which I took with a pinch of salt), and was never far away when help and counselling were needed.

The only time I ever knew Steve other than his usual cheerful self was when a professional lady cellist in her late sixties returned to Tadchester. I gathered she had given him trouble before she had left the area. She pursued Steve from dawn till dusk. If she was going out, she would ring and tell him so; when she got there, she would ring to say that she had arrived, for no particular reason, presumably just to keep in touch. Poor Steve appeared to wilt before us; I had never seen him in this sombre mood before. We were at a loss about how to deal with it.

We had made it a ritual for all four of us to meet every morning for coffee. These were good-humoured gatherings and served a useful purpose, allowing us to blow off steam and share our worries and discuss medical problems. It had become my lot to tell some new outrageous story each day.

Coffee breaks were not the same with Steve in this sort of mood, which seemed to be going on and on. One morning as he stared gloomily into his coffee, I dared to ask, 'How's the cello going, Steve?' He grunted, not looking up.

'You know the real problem,' I said. 'She wants you to pluck her G string.'

Steve collapsed in a fit of laughter that I thought might have developed into hysterics, but it restored his balance, and he was with us once more.

My second partner, Henry Johnson, was the most unflappable man I have ever met; he was also one of the tallest and thinnest. He did the surgery at the local cottage hospital and combined his practice with surgical out-patients' sessions, surgical lists and, in the summer, seemed to live almost day and night at the hospital, dealing with road traffic accidents and the many mishaps that befell the visitors.

Henry had one weakness – he was prone to attacks of crippling lumbago. In his stubborn, dogmatic way, he refused to let it interfere with his work. One afternoon he hobbled painfully in to conduct his ante-natal clinic in spite of our protests that he should be at home in bed. 'Go on,' he growled, 'I can manage.'

The first patient he interviewed comfortably from his desk, telling her to slip behind the screen and prepare for examination. As he got up from his chair to conduct his examination, he twisted, slipped, and fell on the floor. He couldn't move.

'Quick. Help me!' he shouted.

The young lady patient dashed from behind the screen and the two of them struggled, wrestling together to get him up off the floor. It seemed to go on for ages. Eventually they managed to get him sitting on the edge of the examination couch.

'Thank you,' said Henry, the sweat streaming down his face.

At that moment he turned to look properly at his anxious helper, to find that she was absolutely stark naked. They looked at each other and both burst out laughing.

Jack Hart was my third partner. He was a soft-spoken Scot, had a great sense of humour, and did most of the anaesthetics at the hospital. The only time he gave me any cause for concern was on one rare occasion when he was sick and I was looking after him. He had a very painful renal colic; that is, he had a small stone in his kidney. His pain was so great that I gave him an injection of pethidine.

His wife was out at the time but there was no cause for alarm. A kidney stone is a mechanical condition which usually rights itself, and he could come to no harm. My complacency was shattered by a hysterical phone call half an hour later from his wife, Jean, who had just got back from a meeting.

'Where is Jack?' she asked. 'He isn't in the house and his dressing gown is still here.'

Oh God, I thought – he has reacted to his injection and flipped.

I rushed round to his house, to find the wanderer returned and Jean sobbing in the chair; I couldn't tell whether they were sobs of grief, relief or joy. Eventually she recovered sufficiently to explain.

Having put down the phone after speaking to me, she had looked out of the window to see Jack walking up the drive in the rain, in his gumboots and pyjamas, flashing a torch. She feared then that he had really gone. But what had happened was that Jack's next-door neighbour had come knocking frantically at the door. His child had swallowed a penny and was choking: could Jack come straight away? Jack had jumped out of bed straight into his wellies, and rushed round, grabbing his torch en route, to give first aid in his pyjamas.

Jean had recovered by now so we celebrated Jack's return from cuckoo-land with a tot of whisky each. Jack, smiling and quite unperturbed, said, 'I think I have passed my stone. Do you think we have found a new cure?'

I acted as house surgeon when Henry Johnson had his gall bladder out. He didn't really trust any other surgeon except himself and I think he would really have liked to have done it himself with a spinal anaesthetic and a mirror. He made an uninterrupted recovery from his operation until he was convalescing in Spain. While he was out swimming, his stitches burst, and he had to be rescued by the local life guards.

'Lot of rubbish,' said Henry. 'I wouldn't have sunk – I had my finger over the hole.'

I came to the practice armed to the teeth with knowledge of the latest procedures – I was determined to show my colleagues how good and up to date I was. It took only a few weeks in practice to disillusion me completely. All my newly learnt techniques and modern methods were of no avail; my patients had a medical folklore of their own and it was I who had to do the relearning and readjust my way of thinking.

One of the first cases was a man with severe diarrhoea. To the amazement of my partners I was bustling around, sending samples off to laboratories, doing blood tests, determined to make a show of this, my first real test. They watched with interest.

All my tests came back negative. My patient, after a few really stormy and dehydrating days, recovered and went back to work. It was only some months later, when I got to know his wife, that I learnt the true cause of the diarrhoea.

The couple had only been married a few weeks when I was first called to the husband. They were still in a state of bliss, getting to know each òther, still somewhat shy, and both wary of saying or doing anything indelicate.

The wife knew the husband was severely constipated, but this was far too delicate a condition to discuss together. Trying to do her best for her man, she fed him with a chocolate laxative in the back row of the cinema. She became so engrossed in the film that she gave him three whole bars and even had a couple of pieces herself. He, poor lad, thought he was enjoying the genuine plain dark bitter.

The wife begged me to keep her secret, and this was one of many confidences I had to tuck away.

After a few months in practice I wondered how my partners had managed to cope before I came. There was no doubt that the patients wanted my services: their appreciation was marked by the flow of goods and produce – eggs, chickens, clothes, joints of meat, and drink – that were showered on the surgery doorstep for me.

It was only later that I realised that any new face appearing was always a sign for all the old lags to come and pour out their endless symptoms which my senior partners had got tired of listening to. The showers of gifts were not because they thought I was such a good doctor but because I looked so hard-up and undernourished, which was a fairly accurate diagnosis.

I had come from being a penniless student to being a penniless doctor with a car to buy, accommodation to find, as well as having to put some money into a share of the practice equipment. This did not leave any cash for the replacement of my frayed shirts, tattered trousers and jackets, very much worn down at the elbows.

I reminded my grandfather that ten years previously he had said that, if I ever became a doctor, he would lend me some money to buy a car. Otherwise I would have been doing my visits on a bicycle. Grandfather had made this promise in the perfect confidence that I would never qualify at anything, and required a lot of cajoling before he actually came up with the goods.

My impoverishment was highlighted when, for a time, we had an assistant. Although he was just as poor as I was, he had inherited a very smart black overcoat from his father. On his first visit, with a flashy case and his smart coat, he was answered at the door with 'Not today, thank you – we have got somebody ill in here.'

Nobody gave him anything. He was envious of the piles of

goodies that I seemed to accumulate all the time. At last, one day, he came in triumphant, with a single egg clasped in his right hand like the torch of the Olympic runner.

'You see, I *am* wanted,' he cried.

'Who gave you that?' I asked, jealous of his success.

'Nobody,' answered our assistant. 'There was a bowl of eggs on the table at my last visit and I pinched one.'

Medical school had not prepared me for most of the conditions I had to deal with, and I found it very difficult to communicate with my patients. A young Irish girl came in, obviously seven or eight months gone, complaining of a swollen stomach.

'What do you think it is, doctor?'

'Is there any chance that you could be pregnant?' I asked.

'I was,' said the girl, blushing, 'but I killed the baby.'

She pulled up her dress to show a piece of Elastoplast stuck across her navel.

'I stopped it breathing.'

She did not appear again, but six months later I had a piece of christening cake with an Eire stamp on the packet. The enclosed card said 'With love from Kathleen'. Obviously her faith in Elastoplast had been dispelled.

My Irish girl's lack of knowledge was surpassed only by another lady who arrived, excited, at my ante-natal clinic, having been threatening to come for several weeks, saying she was pregnant. Before examining her I was trying to work out when she was likely to be due.

'When was your last period?' I asked.

'Oh, I've got one now, doctor,' she said. 'You won't be able to examine me until it has stopped ...'

I was once nearly electrocuted by a delightful old vicar who lived with his sister at the far end of the practice. He was lying in bed at home when I saw him for the first time. When I touched his wrist to take his pulse, I had what felt very much like an electric shock. And every time the metal end of my stethoscope got within an inch of his chest, sparks began to fly across the intervening space.

'Whatever else is wrong with you,' I said, 'you are full of electricity. I will have to earth you before I can examine you.'

There had been no mention of this situation during my medical training. I got a piece of wire from his workshop, tied it round his ankle, took the other end out of the window and stuck it in the ground round a six-inch nail. I completed my examination without electrical interference and then took the earth wire off. As soon as I had removed the wire, I got a shock again whenever I touched him. Not only was he the most electric man I had ever come across, but he seemed to be an expert at recharging his own batteries.

I had to call in the Electricity Board for a second opinion. A brisk man in a deerstalker cap assessed the situation and said, 'The explanation is quite simple. He is lying on an electric blanket that has been wired round the wrong way. Even when it has been turned off it acts as a condenser.'

I took the precaution from then on of wearing rubber-soled shoes whenever I went visiting.

I had become very friendly with Eric Martin, the proprietor of the Tadchester Electrical Services. He had a shop in Bridge Street, just 200 yards from the river. We used to go about a lot together and often, on a Wednesday when we both had the afternoon off, would go in search of a rugby match. A few days after my electrical excitement with the vicar, he produced an electronic screwdriver.

'Just the thing for your medical case,' he said. 'If you find any more electric patients, touch them with this and the handle should light up.'

I had only a few weeks to wait to use it. One crusty, retired, old Army officer, Colonel Langston – a private patient – had been in bed for a week with bronchitis. He spent the whole week roasting, with his electric blanket turned full on. He was too comfortable. He had a TV set at the foot of the bed, he smoked incessantly (spilled ash all over the sheets), and I thought we would never get him up.

I had an odd tingle when I examined him, and thought that

23

this was the time to try out my new instrument. First I examined his chest with my stethoscope. It was absolutely clear, but I did allow myself a 'tut-tut'.

'What is it?' he asked. 'I thought I was improving.'

I reached into my bag, pulled out my screwdriver and put the point on his chest. To my delight, the fluorescent tube in the handle glowed. I repeated this about six times, with the Colonel's eyes almost popping out of his head.

'You are getting too much electricity,' I said. 'You will have to get up.'

He was out of bed and beginning to get dressed before I had finished packing my medical case.

I had an odd tingle on one other occasion, when called to visit the local beauty queen – Gwendoline Jacobs – who was complaining of tonsillitis.

She met me at the door in the smallest bikini I have seen, and lay on a black satin-covered couch for me to conduct my examination. I got the same shock when I touched her, but no sparks when I pulled out my stethoscope.

'What a pity,' said my beaming patient, 'that your stethoscope doesn't have shorter tubes.'

'Roll over,' I said quickly, and plunged a syringe full of penicillin into a bronze buttock. I had the feeling that if I were not careful my rubber-soled shoes were going to let me down.

Gwendoline rubbed her buttock ruefully. 'I would like a good over-haul, doctor,' she said, 'a really full check-up.'

'I am afraid we don't have time to do that on the National Health Service,' I replied. 'The only time we do full examinations of fit people is for insurance companies.'

I grabbed my case and bolted.

Gwendoline came off the couch at speed to detain me, but her penicillin-filled bottom pulled her up with a jolt.

I made the front door safely. Gwendoline was left standing, with one hand on the couch taking the weight off her puncture.

'Can you recommend a good insurance company?' she shouted.

I closed the front door behind me.

* * *

I was called to see Mrs Southern, the wife of a local solicitor. Mr Southern was a precise, meticulous man who liked everything in order and wanted everything explained in detail. The fact that he did not understand medicine meant nothing to him: he was quite prepared for me to spend an hour explaining to him in detail exactly what might be wrong with him or his wife, and all the possible permutations of what it could be, what it might be, and what it could lead to. 'I have a right to know, doctor,' he would say.

I was puzzled by Mrs Southern, who was obviously dominated by her husband. She had giddy attacks and occasionally would collapse. She needed quite some rousing after one of her collapses, which were attended by spells of sleepiness that I could find no explanation for. I did routine blood tests and routine urine tests. There was no sign of her being diabetic. I thought she was rather thin and wondered whether she ate enough, but just could not pin down what might be wrong with her.

Her illness was episodic. She might be perfectly well all day, then I would be called by her husband in the evening to another of her attacks.

He was getting more and more impatient with my failure to diagnose, and made the observation that during her attacks, when she was slurry and confused, there was often a strong formalin-like smell about her.

I looked round their tidy house, precise and clean, like Mr Southern's shirt and tie, the row of Bibles on the shelf (they were staunch churchgoers) and wondered if she could possibly be drinking too much.

I ventured to question Mr Southern about this possibility and was met with an indignant blast of rage – how dare I suggest such a thing! Neither he nor his wife ever touched a drop: there was, in fact, no drink in the house.

I was called twice more to see Mrs Southern, in what I now called a 'slurry attack' where she could hardly stand up and was sleepy and muddled.

'Well,' I said, 'when she has her next attack, I want you to collect a specimen of her urine during her attack or as close to it as possible, and bring it round to the surgery.'

The police were very good at estimating the amount of alcohol in people's urine: why shouldn't I be?

A few days later Mr Southern came round with a specimen.

'She has had one of her attacks again, doctor. I am extremely worried, and I do hope you find something from whatever tests you are doing on her water.'

I sent her specimen to the Winchcombe Path. Lab., asking for a urine alcohol estimation as soon as possible.

The pathology technician rang me back a few hours later. My suspicion was right. Her urine was full of alcohol. She was a secret drinker. As the cheery technician said on the telephone, 'I shouldn't stand with a lighted match too close to anyone passing this stuff, doctor – they are likely to blow up.'

I had to go to the Southerns, take Mr Southern out on his own and gently explain to him that there was no doubt that his wife was drinking a lot of alcohol. He was absolutely flabbergasted and just couldn't believe it. He was also deeply hurt and upset, and I comforted him as best I could.

'I know she can't be drinking, doctor,' he said. 'There just isn't any drink anywhere.'

'Let me know one day when she is out,' I said, 'and we'll search the house together.'

Southern consented. 'This sounds awful – going behind my wife's back – but her health's at risk. She is getting steadily worse.'

A few days later his wife was out and together we ransacked the house. Mr Southern found the treasure trove: at the back of the airing cupboard there were twenty-seven empty cooking-sherry bottles.

Mrs Southern was the first of many lonely housewives I found who comforted themselves with sherry that only too often became consumed in increasing quantities.

In those days you could get cooking sherry for about five shillings a bottle, and you didn't have to go to a wine shop or pub to buy it. Cooking sherry could always be put on the grocer's bill, and this was the hidden source from which it came.

We had to confront Mrs Southern with her terrible secret, and Mr Southern had to look into himself to see that perhaps he had become far too concerned with his own interests and just accepted his wife as an uncomplaining housekeeper.

Happily, in their case, the matter resolved itself. Mrs Southern was able to kick the habit, and from then on she and her husband knew each other better and enjoyed each other more.

Unfortunately this was not always the case. Sometimes the first I knew about a secret sherry drinker was when a patient (usually a lady patient) appeared with a liver damage that was almost beyond repair.

3

All Things to All Men

Our practice was run from a central surgery near the centre of the town. There was another branch surgery to cope with the few miners who lived in the terraced cottages.near Thudrock Colliery. We all, in turn, paid it one visit each week.

The branch surgery was very primitive: a disused garage with a row of coloured medicine bottles with a simple dispensing formula upon each bottle: 'One part of medicine to ten parts of water'. I never knew what was in the bottles but most of the patients knew whether they wanted the green or the red or the yellow medicine. They all seemed.fit and healthy, so who was I to argue?

As the only practice in Tadchester we not only coped with all the ills of the local populace, but also ran the cottage hospital. There we became surgeons, surgical assistants or anaesthetists, and sometimes perming any two from three.

I had worked for a couple of years in a large London hospital where there was a constant battle. The general practitioners tried to get rid of their patients by sending them into hospital. The hospital doctors tried to get rid of their patients by sending them back to their general practitioners. At Tadchester I found myself totally committed. After I had sent a patient into hospital, I had to look after him when he got there. If I did kick anybody out of the hospital, I had to look after him when he got home.

I still found my patients difficult to treat. One day I was called to see Granny Branch who lived in a tenement Up the Hill. I made an instantaneous and confident diagnosis, even though I was becoming more wary of doing this.

Granny Branch was lying in a stinking bed. She was covered in sores on her lower abdomen, was desperately thirsty, and a bit confused – clearly a case of diabetes. I had been taught as a medical student never to initiate treatment until I had confirmed the diagnosis, so I asked her daughter to bring a specimen of Granny's urine down to the surgery as soon as she could.

To my surprise the specimen was clear and inoffensive. To my greater surprise it didn't contain any sugar, and sugar was needed to confirm the diagnosis.

I went to bed troubled, calling round early the next day to find Granny Branch deeply unconscious; the family had not bothered to tell me because they knew I was coming. I rushed her into hospital and found that she was in severe diabetic coma – my original diagnosis. I received a tongue lashing from the house surgeon who asked why I hadn't tested her urine, which was loaded with sugar.

This didn't make sense. I called in on Martha, her daughter, and asked her had it been difficult getting a specimen from Granny.

'Well, doctor,' said Martha, hesitantly, 'you did say you must have a specimen of water or Gran might become very ill. I couldn't wake her up properly to get one, so I brought you some of mine.'

This was awful. Not only had I failed my patient, but now I'd got a bad name at the hospital. Was I going to be wrong with every diagnosis I made? Could even Mrs Jenkins be fooling me in some obscure way?

Mrs Jenkins was a patient who lived in an isolated cottage with a large vegetable garden in the flat pastureland of Down the Hill. I was called to see her because she was yellow. There were two possible diagnoses – she could only have either an infection of her liver, or gall bladder trouble. She seemed surprisingly well and untroubled by her colour, and the blood tests I had taken should have given a clear diagnosis of either gall bladder or liver trouble.

She was surprisingly active, carrying on with her housework and looking like a vigorous Chinese coolie. Doubts were beginning to cross my mind, so I rang the Path. Lab. All the blood tests were clear. Her blood was perfectly normal with no evidence of jaundice. Surely I couldn't have sent the wrong blood by mistake? In this case, I was certain her daughter hadn't slipped me hers because I had actually stuck the needle in myself.

I went back to the yellow Mrs Jenkins.

'How are you?' I asked.

'Fine, doctor,' she said.

'What is your appetite like?'

'Fine, doctor,' she said.

'Is there any food that you usually like that you don't like now?' (This was a leading question as people with gall bladder and liver upsets usually develop an aversion to fatty foods.)

'No, doctor.'

'Well, what did you have for lunch today?'

'I had a few carrots,' said Mrs Jenkins.

This was harmless enough and certainly healthy enough, even if a little strange.

'And what are you going to have for dinner tonight?'

'I think I might have a few more carrots.'

Slowly something began to dawn.

'Did you have carrots yesterday Mrs Jenkins?' I asked.

'Oh, yes, doctor.'

'And I expect you will have a few tomorrow?'

'Yes,' said the smiling patient.

I looked out on the large garden. If I had only taken notice of the whole of the patient's environment. The garden was planted with what seemed endless rows of carrots. Mrs Jenkins had carrotaemia – a pigment developed from eating too many carrots.

'How many carrots do you eat a day, Mrs Jenkins?' I enquired.

'Oh, usually about seven pound, doctor.'

'And what happens when they run out in the garden?' I asked.

'I keep a few in stock,' said Mrs Jenkins, opening a tallboy that was crammed from top to bottom with tins of carrots.

During the war, she told me, everybody had been encouraged to eat carrots and she had got a taste for them, tinned carrots being one of the few things in plentiful supply. Yes, she had noticed that she was getting a bit yellow but it had not bothered her; she thought it must be sunburn.

Another failure!

'I see awfully well in the dark,' she said as I trudged wearily to my car.

After Mrs Jenkins I resigned myself to the fact that if I considered every case to be abnormal, occasionally something straightforward would come up to confuse me. I didn't have to wait long.

To finish off a recovering tonsillitis I gave the patient some Mendells paint to paint his throat with. This was a sticky substance which cut down the soreness of swallowing. It is little used nowadays and has been replaced by sophisticated lozenges.

On my enquiring about the throat a week later, the patient said, 'Fine, but I find my shirt keeps sticking to my neck.'

He had painted the *outside* of his neck, and had so gummed up his clothing that he was thinking of sending me his laundry bill.

A child who had an allergic runny nose I treated with antihistamine nasal drops. There was a good response, so I said to the parents, 'I think we should now try and treat the condition with antihistamine tablets.' Two days later I was met by a furious mother and father who said, 'We want to see Dr Maxwell and have some proper treatment. Since we have been putting these tablets up Jenny's nose she can't breathe!'

My final call one Saturday afternoon was to a hunt accident. A very superior young lady in an immaculate white Land Rover and with an accent that matched her white teeth and breeches said, 'Come with me quickly, doctor! One of the hunt's come off his 'orse!'

Grabbing my bag, I jumped into the Land Rover. We bumped

across rutty fields into some woods to where two horses were tethered.

'We ride from here, doctor,' she said.

I hate horses. I once rode a camel quite successfully, but horses terrify me. And horses are like dogs – if they know you are terrified, they do their best to make the condition worse.

That horse was at least thirty feet high – I certainly seemed miles off the ground. I clung round his neck, forgetting my dignity, gripping as best I could with my knees. We covered the first stubble field successfully, but as my mount soared over the first hedge I became detached and crashed down into the ditch.

I had an awful pain in my back. My legs were not broken – I could move them – but apart from them I felt that every other bone in my body must have gone at least twice. I was covered in mud. At least it felt like mud, but smelt very much like an old farmyard.

By now the whole of the hunt had assembled around me. The man I had been called to see had recovered and helped to lift me back into the Land Rover. They drove me back to the surgery and with the aid of the grinning Jack Hart they laid me gently on the examination couch. The expression of the buck-toothed young lady who had originally picked me up had not changed

during the whole of our afternoon's companionship. As she left to go, she turned at the door and said, 'Thank you for coming so promptly, doctor. I don't think we appreciate our doctors enough.'

I was three days off with my back. My surgical partner, Henry, just couldn't understand it. If he had hurt his back he would have slapped a quick plaster jacket on himself and carried on. I wasn't made of such stern stuff.

My prompt attendance at the hunt became my introduction to the Upper Crust. I had made an impression on them; they had certainly made an impression on me, or at least my back. My guide with the teeth and tight-fitting breeches turned out to be Marjorie de Wyrebock, daughter of Commander de Wyrebock, R.N. Retd, a local gentleman farmer and a prominent patron of many local events. I was not at ease dealing with these sort of people.

As Mrs de Wyrebock informed me on one of my visits, when she was younger, the doctor was always admitted through the tradesmen's entrance. How democratic everyone had become nowadays.

Commander de Wyrebock was a fine, tall, rather deaf old man. Eight years previously he had been operated on for abdominal pain and at the operation was found to have a cancer of the pancreas gland. It was considered inoperable, his abdomen closed, since when he had had no more trouble and lived, apart from his deafness, a perfectly full, normal life. Just one more example to show that the people in this practice were quite different from those anywhere else.

I was once summoned to see Mrs de Wyrebock when she had a severe headache and fever. Her eyes were a bit puffy. She also claimed that her nose was a bit blocked. I had a good look at her and thought, again unguardedly, this was going to be simple: obviously sinusitis. Because of my uneasiness with the Upper Crust, I over-doctored. As well as giving her antibiotics, antihistamines and nose drops, I arranged to have her sinuses X-rayed, took some blood for a blood film, and asked for a specimen of urine to be sent to the surgery. I speculated on what the specimen would arrive in – probably a jewelled snuff box, at the very least a sterilised whisky decanter. It was sometimes difficult to believe that these people had to follow the calls of nature like us ordinary mortals.

I was asked – commanded – to see two other people on the farm while I was there – Janice, the wife of Kevin Bird, the farm manager, and one of the herdsmen, Bill Foulkes. Janice and Kevin were great friends of mine and I often went round there for meals. They were determined to marry me off and produced a series of possible mates, dragging me off to parties and dances with the usual, 'We think we have found someone you will really like to make up the party.'

I found that Janice had very much the same symptoms as Mrs de Wyrebock. She looked awful, trying to put a brave face on things, but had puffy eyes and a terrible headache and was running a temperature.

To my great surprise I found Bill Foulkes was complaining of exactly the same things as my two previous patients. I was always wary of Bill. He was such an old lead-swinger that he had everything that was going. However, like the other two, he had a temperature and swelling round the eyes, so I could not ignore the symptoms. There had been a high pollen count for the last two days and it did not seem unreasonable that three people associated with the farm should have high fever and sinusitis.

I now regretted having been so over-meticulous with Mrs de Wyrebock. I always considered myself a sort of working-class doctor with the same treatments for everybody, so Janice and Bill Foulkes got the same treatment as their employer's wife. They had antibiotics, antihistamines, nose drops, X-rays arranged, and blood samples taken. All three were National Health Service patients so I had to see everything was even.

The de Wyrebocks, although obviously wealthy, looked for everything that was given for nothing. Being a National Health patient was democratic, like letting your doctor in through the front door. They still of course expected private treatment as National Health Service patients. You felt that they thought they were doing you a favour by asking you to call.

This was a battle I was going to have to fight in future, but I resolved to have Mrs De Wyrebock queueing in the surgery one day for the repeat prescription for sleeping pills she always demanded should be sent round.

I called back to see my patients three days later, rather smugly looking forward to the welcome I would receive for having worked magic cures. Sinusitis is a miserable condition and I had found if you hit it hard at the beginning with nose drops, anti-histamines and antibiotics, the cure was often dramatic.

My first call was, of course, at the de Wyrebocks'. I was met by the Commander, with an anxious look on his face. 'The wife's not at all well, doctor,' he said.

This worried me. He was a nice, sensible old boy who did not take his wife's illnesses too seriously. But he was right. Mrs de Wyrebock looked ghastly. She was sweating profusely, eyes still swollen, and was obviously quite poorly. She was too ill even to put me in my place. They had motored the day before, in a private ambulance, to have her sinuses X-rayed, so the results could be ready for my visit. It was only their general practitioner they didn't pay, though I did have a sneaking suspicion that they had a private one of these somewhere in London.

I opened the X-ray envelope with trembling hands – it didn't look as if it was going to be my day. The radiologist's report slipped out of the envelope as I was opening it, and before I had time to examine the film. The report was brief – 'X-ray sinuses N.A.D.' Translated, this means 'Nothing abnormal diagnosed.' The clear X-ray plates which I held nervously up to the light confirmed this.

'Well,' said Commander de Wyrebock, 'what is the news, doctor?' I had to play for time. 'Happily the X-rays are clear, Commander,' I said. 'Antibiotics do take a few days to really establish themselves. We'll just carry on with the same treatment. I'll pop in tomorrow. Do give her aspirin if her head is bothering her, and I am sure things will improve in the next twenty-four hours.'

I fled the house, making my way to Janice, wondering what I was going to find, but it was very much the same picture. Her symptoms were worse – temperature, puffy eyes, looking poorly. She, of course, had not had her sinuses X-rayed, but there was obviously no need. There was something going on here that my medical training had not covered. Bill Foulkes looked at death's door; he was complicating the issue by vomiting. I just couldn't think what the hell was wrong with these three, but it certainly wasn't sinusitis.

4

Pork and Means

I was crestfallen when I left my patients and went wearily back to the surgery. What was I going to do? I would have to ask advice from one of my senior partners.

Fortunately Steve was in, sitting smiling behind his desk, with his half-moon gold spectacles. 'Well, Bob, what can we do for you?'

I poured out my story. Whatever could be going on? Steve pointed to a pile of pathology lab. forms on his desk. 'You might be interested to see these blood reports,' he said. I looked, and there were the blood counts of all my three as yet undiagnosed patients – Mrs de Wyrebock, Janice, and Bill Foulkes.

The blood counts all showed one thing: they had more of the type of white blood cells called eosinophils than they should have. Counting the different types of white blood cells in the body can often give a clue to the basic cause of some particular condition. But how did this help? It was getting worse and worse. The only conditions that I knew where you had a raised eosinophil count were in some types of asthmatic chest disease and in parasitic infections like worms.

'What does this mean, Steve?' I asked.

'Well,' said Steve, 'I saw something like this twenty years ago, and I have had five patients probably with the same symptoms as yours, one a nurse sent home from Dilchester Hospital with sinusitis. They all had the same type of blood count.'

Steve was obviously very pleased with himself.

'I also sent some plain blood from my patients and here is the report.'

At last it began to make sense.

The report read, 'Tricinosis larvae seen in the specimen.' This is the parasitic condition you get from eating under-cooked, diseased pork, the pig being the intermediate host for this unpleasant condition.

'But the de Wyrebocks!' I said, 'I can't ever imagine them eating diseased, under-cooked pork. Surely everything they have will be roasted to a turn, and served on a silver platter. Why didn't they all have it? Why just one in each family?'

'In the last epidemic we had like this I carefully questioned everybody. I couldn't understand why a family eating the same meal were not all affected,' said Steve. 'When I looked into it, I found that every patient who contracted the disease finally admitted that at some stage he or she had eaten raw sausage meat.'

'Do they get better?' I asked.

'They are pretty poorly for a few days,' said Steve, 'but they get over it.'

I laughed with relief; the clouds had lifted. I was going to enjoy my visit to Mrs de Wyrebock.

I couldn't get there quickly enough the following day. I walked in, looking serious and thoughtful. Mrs de Wyrebock was looking better than she had been the day before, still not well, but well enough to attack me.

'I don't think you know what is wrong with me, doctor. We would like a second opinion.'

'By all means,' I agreed. 'Who would you like?'

'There is a very good chap in Harley Street we know; we did take the liberty of phoning him and he can come down this evening if needs be.'

'By all means,' I said again. 'I am sure he will be interested in your case. I feel it is quite unique.'

39

Mrs de Wyrebock perked herself up. She obviously had something rather special.

'I have to ask you one or two more questions,' I said.

'Oh! Couldn't you leave them until the specialist arrives?'

'No, I must establish one or two things before he comes. Have you had any pork recently?'

'Yes, but I can't see what that has got to do with it. Bill Foulkes killed a pig last week. We have had roast pork on two occasions, and I made some sausage meat.'

'Did you have a pinch of the raw sausage meat as you walked through the kitchen?'

Mrs de Wyrebock sat up sharply in bed, blushing, as if she suddenly realised this rather shabby practitioner had either second sight or X-ray eyes.

'Yes, doctor, I did have a pinch when Cook was preparing it – only to see if the seasoning was right.'

'There is the cause of your trouble,' I said. 'You have the parasitic infection that you get from eating uncooked, diseased pork. Your symptoms will disappear in the next few days, and I am sure the specialist will be most interested to see this condition.'

'Err-r-r, I think we are quite satisfied with you, doctor,' rumbled the old Commander. I saw the suspicion of a grin on his face. 'I can't understand our pigs being diseased. We only have the best pedigree stock and they are meticulously looked after. I will look into it.'

'I am afraid the Medical Officer of Health will look into it for you, Commander,' I said. 'These things have to be followed up.'

Janice, who was also a bit better, confessed that she always had a pinch when frying sausage meat as she liked the salty taste. Bill Foulkes took raw sausage meat sandwiches to work. 'They've got a salty bite in the taste,' he explained.

(Bill was the culprit. He was allowed to keep a few pigs on the smallholding he attended himself. When one of his own pigs became a bit sickly he thought it reasonably economic to slaughter his pig and replace it with one from the pedigree herd.)

At the end of my interview with Mrs de Wyrebock, for the first time ever she didn't have very much to say. I packed my bag, and as I left I said, 'I shall need to see you at the surgery next week, Mrs de Wyrebock, to do some further tests.'

'Yes, doctor,' she answered demurely, 'I'll make an appointment.'

I was beginning to win.

Gradually I was settling into the practice. Although I made some mistakes, my partners always backed me up and were a great support and help.

One of the things I found most irritating when out on a home visit, was to be asked if I would pop in next door as they wanted to see me as well. It is not an unreasonable request, but I find that this particular situation irritates doctors out of all proportion. One probably had seven or eight visits still to make, on a tight schedule, to be followed by a surgery. One would go in, seething and reluctant, and with the worst grace treat the extra patient.

After I had blown off steam at coffee one morning about this particular hate of mine, Jack told me how he had come to terms with it. He had been called out to see a child with measles, miles out in the country. Having examined the child he was asked if he would pop in and see the next-door neighbour.

His extra patient was an old man standing by the garden gate, waiting for him. 'I knew you wouldn't mind looking in, doctor,' he said.

Jack, with his hackles at their highest, berated the old man as they walked up to the cottage together, swearing (or so he said) and being generally irritable – he was behind, he had lots of calls, why hadn't the man rung in? The old man walked implacably on, opened the door of the cottage, reached behind the ramshackle settee and pulled out a huge ear trumpet which he screwed into his ear.

'What were you saying, doctor?'

At this point Jack realised that he – and any doctor – had

41

to be philosophical. The only person he would wear out by a tantrum would be himself.

I asked Jack how he coped with the Burgesses, a family whose hygiene was the poorest of any on our practice list. Not only that, but they kept twenty-two cats and seven dogs, none of which was house-trained or showed any inclination to develop the habit. A few days earlier I had visited the place; the smell almost knocked me over, and it was all I could do not to vomit.

Simple, said Jack. His technique was to walk straight up to the house, open the door, and then walk back to the car to pick up his case. That gave a few minutes for the air to circulate inside the house. He once presented himself in his old A.R.P. gas mask, but the Burgesses thought he was a man from Mars, screamed, and wouldn't let him in.

I still enjoyed my coffee breaks. Steve had a fund of stories about his patients; I never quite believed half of them, but they were part of our morning coffee ritual.

He had one patient, he claimed, who had faithfully produced a new child every year for twelve years, and then suddenly stopped. Steve enquired the reason.

'It's all the fault of Dr Redditch, the local E.N.T. surgeon,' said Mrs Brown. 'You sent me to him, and he fixed me up with a deaf aid. Before I got it, every night when we went to bed my husband used to say "Shall we go to sleep, or what?" And I used to say, "What?"'

Our main surgery was in a converted house about a quarter of a mile from the middle of the town. It had been the home of the town's doctor back in the days when the practice had been a single-handed one. As the town grew, the practice grew, the number of partners increasing over the years to four.

The ground floor of the surgery was taken up with four consulting rooms, four examination rooms, a waiting room from which a reception hatch opened on to the room where the patients' records were kept and the telephone switchboard was situated. We had a small office-cum-laboratory where simple tests could be done, and where a typewriter and tape recorder were kept.

The top two floors were made into flats, one of which was occupied by a retired coal miner and his wife who acted as caretakers. The very top flat, where I lived, was kept by the practice for itinerant locums, assistants and partners such as myself, until such time as they had found their own establishments. It had the chief advantage that Jack and Ivy Bridges, the caretakers, could always take messages at nights and weekends when I was on duty on my own.

We had a full-time reception staff of three. Gladys, a middle-aged spinster and the head of the local Red Cross, went under the title of the Practice Manager. Second-in-command was Mary, who was the wife of the Under Manager at the Colliery. She was quiet and reserved, did all the typing and dealt with the administrative side of the practice. She was a complete contrast to Gladys, who was the least reserved of anyone I have ever met.

Gladys's booming voice dominated the surgery, terrified the patients, and kept us all in step. Far from thinking that she was employed by us, it was Gladys who felt she had four doctors working for her. She spent a great deal of time talking on the telephone to her many friends and colleagues in the Red Cross. One snippet of telephone conversation overheard was Gladys saying she wouldn't have to take on too many commitments over the next couple of months as she had to train a new chap. In spite of her booming, extrovert nature, she had a heart of gold. She got terribly worried if she upset people (which she invariably did), but could always be relied on not to flap in a crisis, and had excellent judgment as to what was urgent and what was not. If Gladys called you for an urgent call, you went.

The final member of the team was Jill, a lovelorn eighteen-year-old who always wore laddered stockings and seemed to be in a perpetual state of distress with yet one more love affair coming to an end. She ran my evening surgeries, usually with tears running down her cheeks. If I asked could I help her, she used

43

to answer, 'No, thank you, doctor. I have just been rather badly let down.'

There was a transient period when she obviously thought I would make a reliable companion, so for two weeks we had immaculate stockings, caked mascara and a plunging neckline that revealed a great deal of her charms. It had a disturbing effect on her work: no lady patient could get past the queue of young men lingering at the hatch asking if she could look up their National Health record number, check their appointments, etc.

Eventually she wilted under pressure. She blushed from ankles to nose when Bill Foulkes, with a loud voice in a packed surgery, said, 'I think I just saw your lungs move, Miss.' Steve, looking whimsically at her cleavage through his gold half-moons asked dryly, didn't she think she might catch a chill?

Although she made no progress with me, she did enrol a fresh batch of unfaithful admirers, and so was soon back to the ladders and the sniffles. The iced gateau that for two weeks had been coming in with my coffee was replaced by digestive biscuits.

I was soon to come under Gladys's command in her capacity as Commandant of the Red Cross. With the added support of Betty, the electrician's wife, who is a trained nurse, she either persuaded or commanded me to become the medical officer to the local Forward Medical·Aid Unit. This is a unit which, in the event of an atomic explosion, is supposed to set up outside the affected town as a sort of casualty clearing station.

We used to rush about with a van and unload ambulances, treat casualties, put on bandages and plaster and give general emergency treatment.

Their enthusiasm at this particular time was due to the fact that the Minister of Health was having a competition to see which was the best Forward Medical Aid Unit in the country. The four first teams were going to have a week-end in London with a grand finale at the Albert Hall, where all would be shaking hands with the great man himself.

The team consisted of a medical officer, a trained nurse and ten auxiliaries. I must say our ten looked a bit long in the tooth, and I was pretty confident that, after our first round, we wouldn't have to bother any more.

We went to our first away competition and to my surprise we won. It was the first time that I had come across a worthy body of people called the Casualties Union. These people spend every Saturday afternoon going round various competitions with bits of Plasticine intestine stuck on their abdominal walls, their faces whitened and plastic blisters stuck to their arms. They are known as Mr Third Degree Burns, Mrs Ruptured Viscer, and Miss Hole in the Chest. They all take it very seriously and most of them were so well drilled and made up that, by the middle of the competition, I got carried away and thought I was treating real casualties.

Having won our first round, the team became even more enthusiastic. Already they could see the lights of London looming.

I was never quite sure what we were supposed to do, but it had become obvious to me that, whatever it was, we seemed to be better àt doing it than anybody else. To my great surprise, we won round after round, and the competition final grew nearer and nearer.

We won the regional final, we won the national semi-final, and we were all booked for a trip to London.

Three of our team had never left Tadchester before. Two of them, who had been married over thirty years, had never spent a night away from their husbands. The thought of a night in London – we assumed we would be put up at the best hotel – caused tremendous excitement.

Eventually details of the final came. Far from being put up at Claridges or the Ritz, we were told that accommodation had been found for us at a mental hospital (which I knew only too well from my student days) about twelve miles out of London. This was a big disappointment, but we knew we were going to London, and we were going to the Albert Hall, and the cup was already stuck up in the town hall with our name inscribed on it!

The team got so keen that I wasn't sure whether I was a general practitioner or a full-time F.M.A.U. officer.

We set off for London on a Friday evening. When we arrived at this vast mental hospital (it had 3,500 patients) the girls were put up in the nurses' home, and the hospital secretary and I had to be put up in the side ward of an observation ward. (The following morning I had to rescue him from a self-locking toilet!)

The next day, with aprons and white coats starched, we set off in our bus for the Albert Hall. We were the first of the four teams in. We represented by far the smallest area, and we were competing against big teams like West London, Rugby and Manchester.

Something ought to have rung a warning bell when they told us the Army was going to assist us.

We were given our instructions by a very brisk military-looking man, who told us that we had to march into the arena as soon as the whistle blew. In the arena I had to report to the Army medical officer in charge. Then we were to take up our action stations.

At this stage, two of the ladies in our team asked if they could spend a penny. Our military man tut-tutted (they were obviously better trained in the Army). He was completely thrown off balance. He was under instructions that we must not be split up as a group, and must be kept under observation until we entered the arena. So, in the charge of an embarrassed corporal, we all marched off to the ladies' toilet. The two ladies' request was obviously infectious as the whole team took this opportunity of relieving their nerves. By the time they had reassembled, with me patiently waiting outside, I was busting to go myself. Whether it was mind over matter or matter over mind, I had to make my own request. There was obviously no sex discrimination here as we were all now marched to the gentlemen's convenience and my team, all trying to look the other way, had to wait until I had finished my ablutions.

At last we were ready. My girls were very nervous. If you

have lived in a small town all your life, to march into the Albert Hall suddenly and make an exhibition of yourself takes some doing. The whistle blew, and we marched into the arena.

There seemed to be scores of Army people and scores of stretchers. I looked round to find the medical officer in charge, and started to do a slow circuit of the floor of the Hall with my team of eleven girls following obediently behind me.

I went round the Hall once, and I could see nobody who seemed to be in charge. Casualties were streaming in, crying, limping, there was blood all over, and I still had nowhere to start work.

I knew I had been round once, because I remembered passing a battle-dressed officer peering into a terrible-looking wound. We circled the Hall again. My girls were getting more and more nervous and the casualties were piling up and bleeding all over the place. We were obviously doing very badly. I passed the officer for a third time.

I could still see nobody who looked remotely as if he were in charge, and seven minutes had gone of the twenty which we were given to treat people.

I eventually came round to the officer again.

'For God's sake,' I exclaimed, 'who is the medical officer in charge?'

'I am,' he said. 'Have you been looking for me?'

I should have expected that the man in charge had even less idea of what to do than I had. By then it was too late. My girls waded into the stacks of casualties that had accumulated, but had hardly coped with any before the whistle went and we all trooped out feeling miserable.

We watched the three other teams come in. The Army medical officer, now alerted, was waiting to greet them and direct them as soon as they came in – except for the third team when again he forgot himself by getting too interested in a case. I knew just how my opposite number felt leading his troop of girls round the floor, but he was stopped after one-and-a-half circuits.

The last team finished. We were all lined up and the results

47

were announced. We were last: our hopes of taking the cup back to Tadchester were crushed.

The winning team from Rugby consisted of a lady doctor, a male staff nurse and ten very fat auxiliaries. They went up to the platform to meet the Minister. They were presented with the cup to tremendous applause. This proved too much for the male staff nurse, who fainted, and had to be supported on either side by two of his stoutest auxiliaries through the whole of the National Anthem.

We trooped off to our bus disconsolately.

'Even if we didn't win,' said Gladys as she mounted the steps, 'we did at least finish on our feet.'

5

Ways of Life and Death

I soon found that routine visiting to the chronic sick and elderly infirm was a very important part of general practice. At first, as a young man itching to try my new medicine, I found it rather tedious, but as time passed I began to realise how important it was: so often the treatment for many conditions was simply to call and see the patient.

The day I qualified, I celebrated in a pub near home. One of the regulars (well into his cups, but still lucid) said, 'So, now you are a doctor! Well, don't forget a doctor's main job is to buck us all up.'

He was dead right. Bucking people up *is* one of the most important things a general practitioner does.

At Tadchester I found I was learning all the time. What seemed insignificant for one person could be a tragedy for another.

One of my regular visits was to an old couple, the Parkers, and the husband's brother. They lived in adjoining farm cottages seven miles out from Tadchester. Brother Jack from next door joined the couple for his meals, but returned to his own cottage to sleep.

Minnie Parker had nursed her diabetic husband for years. He had lost one leg through gangrene, and when I took them over they were battling to save the other – gangrene having appeared in his toe. Normally I would take this as a sign that the other leg was in danger of amputation, but the devoted nursing of Minnie kept the toe gangrene in check for two years. The district nurse used to call twice a day to give him his insulin, but it was Minnie who looked after his toe.

Eventually, when he came to operation, he managed to get away with having just half his foot amputated, enabling him to hobble still with his artificial leg.

They had a most meticulously kept garden and, although all well into their eighties, managed to tend it and more than keep themselves in vegetables and fruit.

The tragedy that struck them was not a medical one. Some sheep broke in through the fence of an adjoining field and ate all the tops off their cabbage and sprout plants. I arrived for my routine call unaware of their disaster, and found them weeping. Heartbroken, they showed me the remaining chewed stumps.

All that was involved, from my point of view, was that there would be three or four dozen cabbages less. Their view of the situation was completely different. This was a tragedy. They couldn't grow their greens for the winter, and travelling to town to buy them was quite out of the question. They could see half a year stretching before them without any vegetables, and there was no way of consoling them.

I had come across this attitude before in elderly people who managed marvellously until some small factor upset their rhythm.

One dear old lady used to give me tea from a beautiful china pot, using her best teaset of delightful china cups. Her house was spotless. She was bright, cheerful, perfectly self-contained and happy.

One day she burnt her finger on the stove, which meant she couldn't lift the teapot, couldn't lift pans off the stove, and couldn't carry on with the same rhythm that she had established.

She died a fortnight later. Although I put 'broncho pneumonia' as the cause of death on her certificate, what she really died of was a burnt finger and an upset life.

I used to put aside every second Tuesday of each month for visiting the elderly ladies who lived on the extremities of the practice. The qualification to be included on this round was that they had to be getting on in years and not be fit enough to travel to the surgery to see me. Although none of the ladies that I visited would consider themselves fit enough to come to the surgery, occasionally when I called I found a note saying, 'Out till five o'clock – gone to the chiropodist.' This seemed to be a standard finding – you have to be much fitter to go to see your doctor than to have your toe nails cut.

I liked my old ladies. Two of my favourites were a couple who had lived together since the beginning of World War I – Miss Gill and her companion Miss Booth.

Miss Gill, the elder member of the partnership, had been put to bed in 1916 for some mysterious chest complaint and had never been fit enough to leave it since then. She had spent forty-seven years in bed. Miss Booth had been brought in as her companion in the first year of her illness, and they had lived together since in a small cottage on the main sea road. They had suffered ill health and discomfort with fortitude and dignity for a full forty years before I met them.

Miss Gill used to lie in a bed near the window on a big lace pillow, surrounded by books, and newspaper cuttings from her friends in Canada; she had a mirror arranged so that she could look out of the window and see people passing by.

One would have thought that two ladies who lived at least two-thirds of their lives together in a small cottage, one of them never leaving her bed, would have led a small insular life and gained little from it. On the contrary: they led as successful and contented a life as anyone I ever met. Both these ladies were now in the evening of their lives. Miss Gill had recently celebrated her eightieth birthday. They had a wide circle of friends and a much wider circle with whom they corresponded. My main difficulty was seeing that they did not get overtired with too many visitors.

Miss Gill and Miss Booth were good people by any standards.

They were kind; they were what one calls 'practising Christians'. When I came in sometimes and they said, 'We pray every night for you, doctor', somehow I felt ashamed and so very much aware of my own shortcomings.

I eventually realised what pleasures they got from their lives when they showed me some photos of a robin feeding from a tray on Miss Gill's bed. They told me the story of how this robin used to come and perch on the sill outside the window through which Miss Gill looked, waiting for crumbs, how a friendship grew until he was a bold and constant visitor to her room, and how they named him Bobby.

They told me of a particular day when they had a Minister to tea. He put some sponge cake down for Bobby. Bobby, answering the summons of the tapped tray, came in and knocked the sponge cake off the plate – he didn't like cake with no fat in it.

They told me how Bobby brought his mate in and how one day, when he and Mrs Robin were chirping around the room, one of them whistled and a smaller robin, which they thought

must have been one of the children, came in to join them.

Bobby was their constant visitor for two years. He used to come whenever the tray was banged, and fly around the room. In the winter they put a saucer with food in it by the fire and I imagined them talking to him as they talked to me when I went to see them. They said, 'Do you know, doctor, he even came to say goodbye.'

One day when Bobby came in, it appeared that he had had some blow or injury because he fell four or five times in trying to climb over the window sill. He couldn't stand up, but he managed to eat his crumbs, struggled out of the window, and they never saw him again.

But they still had Bobby's plate to remind them of him.

Miss Gill's and Miss Booth's success story was that their enjoyment had been the company of other people – other people who sought them out in such numbers that they had to be limited on medical grounds – and small incidents like the robin, from which they got such pleasure.

Miss Gill summed it all up one day when she said, 'My difficulty is I see so many people, doctor, because they think I have time to listen.'

Round about Miss Gill's eighty-third birthday the Tadchester Round Table asked if they would like a television set. I wasn't too happy about this; these two ladies had become successfully adjusted to their environment, and now the world, and a very different world from the one they remembered, was going to be brought to their bedside. This could easily upset the whole pattern.

I wondered what their reaction would be if the first programme they saw was a modern play or a cowboy film.

My first visit after delivery of the set dispelled all my fears. I was met by two beaming faces. Miss Gill said, 'Doctor, do you know that for the first time since before the First World War, I have actually taken part in a church service.'

Television was a tremendous success. Sunday with its church services and community hymn singing was their best day. Miss

Gill was quite certain that one Sunday the Bishop had nodded to her during the service. Any programme about the Royal Family and people of title came next on their list. Their television took them round castles and cathedrals, introduced them to people of every creed and colour, and showed them some countries and continents as if they were seasoned world travellers. The world they had read and heard about for five decades was suddenly brought into their own little world of four walls and a window.

It never disappointed them, and by some sort of natural selection they never appeared to have tuned into a programme that was objectionable to them.

Miss Gill, whose health had for many years been about as poor as anybody's health could be yet still sustain life, died five months after she received her television set.

I last saw her two days before her death. She lay in bed, her eyes shining and bright, and said, 'We have just seen a most exciting finish to the Lords Test Match, and now I am sitting in the front row of Wimbledon watching the tennis.' Life had never been fuller for her.

It made a deep impression on me and I formed a new respect for television. This wonderful invention had made the last chapter of an eighty-three-year-long life the fullest; it allowed a fine old lady who had been confined to bed for forty-seven years to get up from it, and join in with us for the last few months before she finally left us.

Every other Tuesday I made certain that my last visit of the day was to Reg Dawkins who suffered from a complicated condition called pseudo-muscular hypertrophy of the limb girdle type. Reg was a fit-looking man in his forties who, until he complicated his long-named condition by breaking his hip, used to drive a bus for one of the Tadchester garages. What his condition meant was that there was some lack of nervous connection at waist level so he was left with his legs more or less disconnected from his trunk. Once he was upright, he could walk; once he was sitting, he could drive because he could use his legs; but bending and sitting up unsupported he was no good. Breaking his hip (which had to be operated on) stopped him taking any gainful employment, and he used to sit at home doing odd jobs and cooking from his wheelchair, while his wife, Mary, went out to work.

He was a great wit and I called on them every other Tuesday to be bucked up rather than to buck them up. I never really gave them any treatment other than an off-work certificate once every three months. Most of their spare time was spent on their hobby of making wine, and every visit I had to sample at least one of the bottles. I used to make it my last call, for a tumbler full of Reg's and Mary's brew laid me out for the evening. My favourite was one called 'Bullous', which was made from wild plums (which I had never seen) – or perhaps it was Reg pulling my leg! It was probably made of old washing-up water.

Mary had three sisters, and I could never fit the right name to the right sister. 'Now Annie is the fat one,' I said. 'No, she isn't,' said Reg, roaring with laughter. 'She's so thin she daren't eat aniseed balls in case she looks pregnant.'

The longer I stayed in general practice, the more patients I began to know, the more I realised how little I knew. I was learning all the time. I had my own views of what courage and bravery were, but had never examined them closely before.

The first time I was able to recognise sheer courage was when we found that Ben Fellowes had an inoperable growth.

As far as I knew, Ben had led an unobtrusive life. He was an upholsterer. I don't think he had ever been an easy man to work with, but I don't think he had been a terribly difficult one. He lived with his son in a little terraced house Up the Hill.

We had to send him to hospital to be diagnosed.

He accepted hospital life with the aplomb of a countryman, soon settling down to the routine of the ward. He had left things very late before seeking medical advice, and after some investigations it was found that he was far too advanced to be given any help.

Ben somehow got someone to tell him that, not only could

nothing be done, but that he had at the most six months to live. He must have wheedled it out of someone on the pretext of putting his affairs in order, as it was certainly not general policy to tell patients the worst.

When people ask if they are going to die, they ask only to be told they are not. I also didn't accept – and still don't – that a point of hopelessness is ever reached in modern-day medicine, as new cures are found every day and outlooks for certain diseases change overnight.

Past experience had shown me that to be certain of the cause of a disease is to be sometimes wrong. I knew also that, if you take away a man's hope completely, you immediately cut down the amount of time he has left with us.

With this in mind I sent Ben to a deep-ray specialist with a covering note saying that here was a man without any hope, could they possibly do something for him? But again Ben must have done or said something, as back he came with a note saying nothing could in fact be done. This time he even managed to get somebody to tell him that he couldn't live more than three months.

Throughout all this Ben had shown no obvious sign of emotion. He went about in a businesslike manner, putting his affairs in order. He would discuss, openly and unaffectedly, his coming death. He fixed up about his shop, settled his outstanding accounts, and gave me two coronation five-shilling pieces for all the trouble I had taken.

In the first month of the three, Ben went off by train to see and say goodbye to friends, explaining that perhaps he wouldn't be able to get around too well later. He then came back to stay with his son, travelling around with the firm's van or sitting in it quietly by himself behind the row of houses where his son lived, enjoying the last fine days of the summer. From the house Up the Hill there was a fine view of the town, the bridge and the estuary.

I never remember him complaining, and as far as I know he had no faith, creed or philosophy to sustain him. He was always pleased and grateful when I went to see him and never requested anything more than Codeine tablets to relieve whatever anguish he was suffering. He got progressively weaker, and died quietly on the exact day, the end of the three months, predicted as the longest he could live.

I only knew him in this last phase of his life, but I have always felt that he was one of those few men who, spurning hope, had the rare courage to stand up squarely to things as they are. That when he knew the problem without adornments, he said to himself, 'The only thing I have left to do is die. I shall make the best job of it I can.'

Ben was one of many who showed the kind of stoicism and courage I had not met before. Although I thought my patients in Tadchester were different from any elsewhere, I expect that people are much the same everywhere. The life that I had led before I qualified was the unreal one; strange people doing strange things are really the normal people. I looked at everybody that I knew in the area, my partners included, and realised that all of us were a bit offbeat somewhere. I felt (unless I was the odd man out) there must be many things that I did myself that looked strange to other people.

I had done just enough general practice to realise that one had to be aware that there were many things that one didn't understand, and for which there was no real explanation; that patience and observation were the two most important medicines and, although my very specialised knowledge was useful, the most important part of my work was the relationship with my patients and our understanding of each other.

6

Miraculous Draughts

I had been in the practice about six months when, one night, Kevin and Janice Bird rang to say, 'Tonight we are going to initiate you into Seine net fishing. You can bring Eric along if you like. Frank's taking his net out and is looking for a new crew.'

Frank Squires was the land surveyor for the County Council and lived with his wife way out on the estuary. It was like a small zoo, with goats, chickens, geese, ducks, cats, dogs, rabbits, and strange species of birds I was never able to identify. He depended on his salary for his living, but his life was the open air, the country, and the sea.

He had one-and-a-half acres of land which he ran like a small-holding. He sailed, fished, and was the leader of this mysterious clique that I had heard of, called 'Seine Fishers' who, at low tide, trailed their nets along the two beaches of Sanford-on-Sea. There were tales of huge catches and stormy seas. It all sounded a bit improbable.

'Bring your rugger shorts,' said Kevin, 'as many old jumpers and shirts as you have got, and something to wear on your feet.'

It seemed to me, if we were going to be wading about in the sea, a pair of bathing trunks would have been enough, but I took his advice and took a whole pile of old clothes with me.

We assembled on the beach that night at about ten o'clock.

When the tide is out at Sanford there is plenty of beach – it goes out for over a mile.

There was Frank, obviously in command, in a pair of shorts, with a short oilskin jacket, a piece of rope tied firmly round his middle, and an old felt hat jammed on his head.

'Come on, Dr Bob. Get your gear.'

'Won't bathing trunks be enough?' I asked.

'No,' said Frank, 'you will freeze to death if you don't keep yourself covered.'

There were eight of us in all – Janice and Kevin, Eric and myself, Frank and his wife Primrose, Joe Church – a bearded schoolmaster – and his wife Lee.

We marched out towards the sea, with Joe and Frank carrying a couple of poles on their shoulders, around which was wound a length of nylon net. Walking behind, the ladies pulled a little sledge which was really a box on two runners. The sledge was there, hopefully, to carry the fish.

We arrived at the water's edge and separated the two poles to which the net was attached. The net was sixty yards of nylon net, about six feet in depth, and each of the poles had two rope traces. These were attached to the middle of the pole. The pole was held upright in the water by the pole carrier. One or two people in front tugged and pulled the lengths of rope traces and helped the pole tow the net along during the trawling.

'You can come on the outer staff with me,' said Frank, 'and Eric can go on the inner with Joe.'

Frank then slipped the pole diagonally across his chest, Kevin and I took a trace rope each and walked off into the sea in front of him. Although the sea struck cold at first, our protective clothing kept the wind out and we soon warmed up.

The beach shelved gradually and we must have walked out two hundred yards before the water had reached chest height. There was a little bit of surf and as we walked we were continually jumping up to ride the waves, or ducking and letting them splash over us.

It was exhilarating, and great fun.

59

'Right,' shouted Frank when the water was up to our armpits, 'now we start work.'

Kevin and I tightened the trace ropes round our shoulders and started to tug at the staff that Frank was holding, walking along parallel to the beach, every few minutes either being lifted or covered by waves, pulling ourselves up on the ropes, laughing and spluttering.

The waves were fluorescent in the partial moonlight, and as I looked back I could see that Joe, with Eric tugging in front of him, had joined us in a parallel course to the beach. They were about twenty yards behind us and forty yards in, and the net was travelling along parallel to the beach like a letter 'J', the long arm of the 'J' being the outer one.

Frank's face glowed like an isolated skull with the fluorescent sheen from the water, the rest of his silhouette of black clothes being lost in the darkness.

We tugged and pulled for about twenty-five minutes. By now I certainly wasn't cold. I could have even been sweating under my wet clothes.

'Right,' said Frank. 'Let's have a draught.'

We swung round, going directly up the beach. Kevin's pole kept moving towards us until they were about ten yards away, then with the whole net taut, we marched side by side towards the beach, the net in a long thin 'U' streaming behind us.

I couldn't see that we had caught anything. I could make out the floats on the top of the net, bobbing behind us, but no sign of splashing fish, or signs of the huge hauls that I had heard about.

We steadily got nearer the beach, until the water came down to our mid-calves, but still nothing to see in the back of the net. Then we were on the sand, marching slowly up the beach, the net getting heavier all the time. Looking back, I saw a flash of white at the base of the 'U' of the net, and as we got into shallower water – to my excitement – I could see several splashes.

I dropped my rope to rush back to see the haul. I picked it up again when Frank bellowed, 'Keep pulling you stupid bugger! You will lose the catch! Keep pulling!'

We pulled on until the net was on dry sand, and then rushed back. I could see thrashing bodies of white in the base of the 'U' that now came almost to a point on the dry sand.

'Lights!' shouted Frank, and the girls came rushing up with torches, tugging their box behind them.

The bottom and top ropes of the net were together encasing the fish. When these were opened, I could see four flat fish and three round fish.

'Quick! Give me the trout!' shouted Frank, snatching up one of the round fish and shoving it under his jumper. 'We don't want to be caught with this.'

Frank identified the rest of the catch – two bass, three dabs and one sole.

The fish he had shoved under his jumper was a sea trout. Although we were fishing off a sandy beach that is packed with holiday makers in the summer, it still came under the River Authority, which did not allow game fish (which included sea trout) to be taken from the sea. Frank had twice been caught by water bailiffs and was due to lose his net if caught again.

I thought we had finished for the night, but I was wrong. This was just the beginning.

We made six more draughts, covering at least two miles of beach, and caught about thirty fish. On only two of the draughts did the net come out of the sea empty. The catch included slimy skate, whose little eyes appeared to be looking up straight at you; a chad, a sort of king herring that I had never heard of before; some more bass, which the locals prized more than salmon or sea trout; some mullet, which the rest turned their noses up at as they reckoned these were the scavengers of the sea; and two more small sea trout which were immediately hidden in the pockets of Joe's oilskin.

The rest of the catch was dumped into the box, now full to the brim with fish. We trudged back to the cars parked in the sandhills, now two miles away, where the road goes down to the beach.

The journey seemed endless. We had to carry the heavy, sodden net, which seemed to weigh a ton. My legs were getting cold as the wind swept along the beach. It had been much warmer in the water.

At last we got back to the cars, had a brisk rub down, and put on dry clothes.

I felt like a king.

Frank got a primus stove going, and we soon had hot coffee and sandwiches. I had not felt so fit in years.

The catch was divided evenly in what I understood was the traditional Seine-netting way of doing it. Frank stood with his back to the five piles of fish, and (unseen) Joe, behind him, would point to one and ask, 'Whose is this?' Frank would shout 'Eric' or 'Joe' till we all had a name to a pile and rushed up to see what our particular share was.

My share was a bass, one of the small sea trout, two dabs and a mullet. I had never had so much fish on my hands before and wondered what I was going to do with it.

'Now,' said Frank, 'don't forget you must clean your fish before you go to bed, otherwise it will be no use to anyone.'

Eric dropped me off at the surgery and I heaved my parcel of fish into the sink behind the dispensary, got an old scalpel from the cupboard, and tried to remember my days as a first-year medical student when the nearest I got to being a surgeon was operating on a dogfish. They say you really have to start at the beginning to practise medicine.

Cleaning the fish gave me some surprises. They were all quite different. The sea trout was almost spotless and aristocratic, and cleaned easily; the mullet was like a dirty old tramp, and filthy intestines came from it. I did not fancy it. The bass was halfway between both worlds – middle class – and the flat fish took very little cleaning.

I gutted them, washed them, put them in a polythene bag and put them in the fridge.

I was desperately tired by now and looked up at the surgery clock. My God! It was a quarter to four.

I shovelled all the offal from the fish into the dispensary pedal bin, washed up as best I could, then crept up to my flat, threw myself on the bed and went to sleep. I had a free morning the following day, thank goodness.

I woke up about ten and made myself a cup of tea. I was out of condition, not having taken much exercise since I had come to Tadchester, and was feeling a few muscles that I had not felt before.

I must have dozed off. There was Gladys banging on the door, and it was a quarter to two.

'Come on, Dr Bob, you have a surgery in ten minutes! It is a wonder there is a surgery here at all today – the whole place stinks like a fish shop. Wait till Dr Maxwell gets hold of you! He went to the refrigerator to get some penicillin and was almost buried by an avalanche of fish. You have a big surgery this afternoon and a medical afterwards, so look lively.'

I hurriedly dressed and shaved and went down. Gladys was right; it was a big surgery. It seemed to go on for ever. I could hardly keep my eyes open, and my muscles felt like knots. But at last I finished.

Gladys bustled in, with a cup of tea. She had a peculiar grin on her face when she said, 'I thought you might like a bit of refreshment before your medical, doctor. I think it is going to be a long and difficult one.'

I was a little puzzled but, in my exhausted state, did not take too much notice. I rang the bell for the medical examination, and in walked Gwendoline Jacobs, our beauty queen. Oh, God! This was all I needed. She was certainly not a girl to be deterred.

She was wearing a black plastic raincoat, fishnet stockings, and long black boots. As she took off her coat I noticed that if her skirt had been any shorter it would have started just under her arms. The plunge of her neckline started somewhere near her knees.

'Shall I get undressed, doctor?' she said.

63

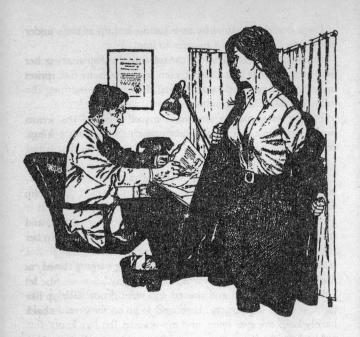

'No. Hang on, Gwendoline,' I said. 'I have a lot of questions to ask you first.'

I sat down and went laboriously through all the medical questions – date of mother's death, age of father if living, brothers, sisters, previous medical history, regularity of periods, etc., with Gwendoline looking straight into my eyes, leaning over the desk as if she were trying to eat me. She signed my record of questions and answers as being correct, then, with her eyes lit up – 'Now, doctor?'

'Yes,' I said, resignedly. 'Pop behind the screen and get undressed. You will find a sheet on the couch.'

She was off in a flash.

I couldn't help liking Gwendoline. There was something quite charming about her open sexuality.

She lay on the couch with the white sheet tucked firmly under her chin.

I took her pulse and blood pressure without disturbing her enveloping shroud. I was putting off the time when the surprises underneath it would be revealed to me.

'Now, I would like to have a look at your chest.'

She smiled in anticipation and sat bolt upright. Her breasts were supported in the same sort of material as her stockings. I must say it enhanced their silhouette.

'You will have to take your brassière off, Gwendoline,' I said.

'Oh! If you could just help me, doctor. It has a difficult clip at the back.'

She sat up, breasts bulging out of their restraining nets, and shoulders arched. I did a retreating battle, trying to unclip her bra as she tried to lean back on me.

She lay back, naked from the waist up, eyes half closed, as if in a dream. I put my hand on her upper abdomen. She let out a contented 'Ah!' and two deep purple nipples shot up like fountain pen caps with such speed that it made me jump back on my heels.

I hastily withdrew my hand, then listened to her chest, making sure it was only my stethoscope that touched her. I looked down her throat and into her ears while Gwendoline purred and writhed gently with delight or passion, but she still kept a twinkle in her eye.

'I have finished with the top half now,' I said. 'You can dress up there and we will tackle the other half.'

She struggled into her bra and blouse disappointedly, then slowly slid the sheet down to expose a sun-tanned stomach and the smallest pair of bikini pants that I have ever seen. Boldly printed on the front of them were the words, 'COULDN'T WE TALK THIS OVER?'

I had the greatest difficulty in stopping myself laughing.

Gwendoline looked up. 'Oh! I do apologise, doctor, I had forgotten I'd got these silly old things on.'

To Gwendoline's squirms of delight I palpated her stomach, tested her reflexes, and eventually finished my examination.

'That's all, Gwendoline,' I said. 'Thank you. You can get dressed now.'

'Is there nothing else, doctor? How do you know I am all right internally? Shouldn't that be checked?'

By now I was having great difficulty in preventing myself bursting out laughing. It was painful holding my sides in. I took up the examination form, pretending to study it closely, and said, 'No, thank you Gwendoline, I have carried out all the tests that they asked me to.'

Gwendoline ruefully started putting her clothes on as I retired back to my desk. I was determined to win this battle.

She came round from behind the screen, adjusting her skimpy clothing.

'Oh! There is just one more thing, Gwendoline,' I said. Her eyes lit up. 'Could you leave a specimen of urine with Gladys on your way out.'

She gave me a withering look, but she was not beaten yet. She put her hand in her handbag, shoved a ticket on my desk and said, 'There is a spare ticket for the Carnival Ball, doctor. I said that I knew you would come and present the prizes.'

She shot out of the door before I had time to give it back to her.

Gladys came in disdainfully. 'It must have been a complicated medical, doctor, for you to take so long, but I expect you can't skimp anything on someone so young. I think it's about time you found yourself a Mrs Clifford, or one of these bright young things is going to nab you.'

With Gladys and Gwendoline gone I checked through the notes of the people I had seen in the afternoon surgery. One or two of them would need follow-up visits, and three had to go for back X-rays of one sort or another.

Backache, I found, was an extremely common condition in general practice. It has replaced grandmother's funeral as a reason for a day off, and more of the most miraculous cures I saw were achieved by the settlement of compensation claims for injuries received at work. I would see a patient bent double, going round the tribunals and being assessed for his degree of disability. The next day I would see the same man again, upright, pitching hay or carrying hundredweight sacks of potatoes. It was not that he had had some miracle drug or miracle cure – it just meant his compensation claim for backache had been settled.

Backache cases were always springing surprises on me. Sometime previously, when Jack Dawson came complaining, I thought it must be in some way connected with his work at Thudrock Colliery.

He was a huge man, six foot three, eighteen stone, and famous for his boxing ability. He had, some years back, been a full-time pro, but now only came into his own the autumn week that the travelling fair visited Tadchester. He would appear on the first day, knock out all the new professionals in the boxing booth, then be employed by the booth, taking on all-comers for the remainder of the week. Any prize money he won would have gone on beer before the end of the night, but he was a good-tempered, amiable giant, slow to anger, and just the man to have on your side if there was trouble brewing. His presence alone was enough to dispel any thought of aggression by opponents.

Jack had a severe pain in the lower back, with pain going down the leg – obviously sciatica with a spinal nerve being trapped. He could hardly move.

I thought, with his strength and size, he must be at least a full-blown collier, thrashing away at the coal face with a pick all day, but not so. He actually worked in the pit-bottom office as a time-keeper's clerk, supplementing his income by taking betting slips for the local bookies.

I sent him home to bed with some pain killers, and visited him on his smallholding the next day. He lived with his wife, mother and daughter in a delightful thatched cottage in about four acres where he kept a few pigs and poultry. Sitting by the steps of the cottage when I arrived was an old lady (presumably his mother) who was just finishing off peeling a whole bucket of potatoes.

'Are you having a party, Mrs Dawson?' I asked.

'Oh! No,' she replied. 'We do a bucketful of these every day. This is my job.'

Jack was not in bed as directed – perhaps he had just come for a ticket after all. Eventually I found him in one of the poultry houses, where he greeted me with a, 'Good morning, doctor. I thought I'd work off a bit of the stiffness.'

As he was speaking to me, he continued to wring the neck of a poor chicken which was obviously going to accompany the waiting half hundredweight of peeled potatoes.

He wrung the bird's neck with no more qualms than he would have swatted a fly. There were obviously no emotional ties between him and this chicken.

'Well, what about this back, Jack?' I asked. 'Is it better, or what?'

'It is much better, doctor,' he said, 'but not quite right for work. I think it is my part-time job that's the cause of it. I think I'll have to give it up.'

I knew Jack worked down the pit. I knew he was a bookies' runner. I knew he farmed his smallholding. His appearances at the fair were famous, and I felt sure that he did a bit of poaching with salmon nets. What else could he be doing as a part-time job?

'I keep rather quiet about it,' said Jack. 'They say at the place we shouldn't talk too much about it. I am sometimes a relief hangman.'

Now I understood about the chicken.

I was then treated to a half-hour lecture on the art of hanging, of how the weights put an extra strain on your back. Apparently the ropes have to be tested with the equivalent weight of the intended victim. This means a whole lot of lifting of sandbags, up to a hundredweight, with the chance that if you had got your calculations wrong they could fall on top of you. I couldn't take it in. I was completely bemused by it all.

'If you could give me a certificate, doctor,' he said, 'I could send it to the Home Office. I really don't think I should do hanging any more. I can't let this back interfere with my normal work. I have a lot of people depending on me. I don't do hangings very often, but if they are going to interfere with my real livelihood, I'll call it a day.'

My certificate to excuse Jack his hanging duties apparently cured his back. He never came complaining of it again. I don't know whether they compensated him for his loss of earnings, but I did get a couple of badly plucked chickens left at the surgery by him soon after he had hung up his rope.

All in the Mind

The psychiatric services available in Tadchester were very limited. Once a week a consultant from the mental hospital outside Winchcombe used to hold an outpatients' clinic in this hospital: half of his time he would spend interviewing patients and the other half giving courses of E.C.T. (electro convulsive therapy) to patients under treatment.

I have never got on terribly well with psychiatrists: I often find it difficult to distinguish them from their patients. No man should spend all his time doing psychiatry.

Most of general practice is psychiatry of one sort or another, but you are seeing other patients with organic illnesses who help to maintain a balance. I was never sure how helpful psychiatric referral was to my patients and sometimes tossed up whether I should send a patient in trouble for a psychiatric consultation or for a course of physiotherapy. There seemed little to choose between the results.

Whatever treatment patients with psychiatric illnesses were having and whatever the psychiatrist thought he was doing, there was no doubt that we in general practice carried the brunt of most cases.

Mr Shannon, the local chief inspector of taxes, died suddenly and unexpectedly of a coronary in his office. He and his wife had been very happily married. She was completely overwhelmed by her tragedy and just could not cope. She became disorientated and I had to visit her daily, giving what support I could, together with various medications, to help take the edge off her fears and anxieties. She was an intelligent, well-balanced woman who just could not manage the situation she found herself in.

I seemed to be making little progress with her so I asked for a psychiatric opinion. I had a very long letter back from the psychiatrist telling me what I already knew, suggesting similar medication to that which I was giving, and saying he would see Mrs Shannon again in a month's time.

Mrs Shannon tried the psychiatrist's medication but preferred mine. She showed some small improvement in that, instead of my making daily visits to her house, she made daily visits to the surgery. This, initially, was a tremendous effort for her but a sign of a real step forward.

After a month she was seen again by the psychiatrist who, in a ten-minute interview, managed to upset her on several counts. He was impressed that she was improving and decided that she could wait two months until her next interview with him.

Mrs Shannon still visited me nearly every day. My main treatment was constantly to reassure and encourage her, repeatedly telling her that time to some extent would heal and that things would improve. Slowly she began to adjust and get back into a normal pattern of life. I encouraged her to find some sort of work and eventually she found a part-time job in Mr Southern's solicitor's office.

As arranged, she saw the psychiatrist after a two-month interval. He wrote me a short note saying that 'his' treatment had seemed effective in this case and he had discharged Mrs Shannon from his outpatients' clinic. 'Bully for him,' I thought.

I continued to see Mrs Shannon at decreasing intervals – three times a week, twice a week, then once a week, till we arrived at a situation where she popped in for a chat once a month to report that all was going well. It was a full two years before she felt there was no need to come and be consoled about her grief any more.

Assisting the psychiatrist was a marvellous breed of men called Mental Welfare Officers. They were men usually in or around their forties who had been trained as nurses and mental nurses, and were the people to call on when you were in real trouble with psychiatric emergencies. I valued their services at least as much as the psychiatrist's.

Jack Turner had a long history of psychiatric disturbances. When he became ill, he became very violent and aggressive and, as he weighed eighteen stone, he was very difficult to cope with. It was usually the police who rang us when Jack went on one of his destructive campaigns. We would arrive at the house to find the police prudently waiting outside, listening to the sounds of smashing glass and furniture from within. Then we would all charge in as a body and try to overpower him long enough for me to get a sedative injection into him. Once he was reasonably quiet he was put into a strait-jacket and taken off to hospital.

One of the most bizarre psychiatric emergencies I was called to was on a country farm just beyond the edge of our practice area A woman patient of mine was on leave from Winchcombe Mental Hospital and had come out to impose herself on two ladies who lived as man and wife in this isolated farmstead. They had met while having psychiatric treatment, and this was one of those love triangles between three ladies that I could never quite understand.

My patient, on arriving at the farmhouse and finding that neither of the residents would respond to her amours, tried to form a close relationship with a boxer dog. The two resident ladies, at their wits' end, managed to get her out of the house and lock her in a shed with one of the cows, leaving her to get on with it. It was all very sad. They were all young, attractive women. I wondered what paths had led them to this present situation.

Here again the Mental Welfare Officer and I had a fighting

scramble to slam in the sedative injection and put a strait-jacket on and get the poor disturbed girl off to hospital.

I found that as well as having to be at least a half-time amateur psychiatrist, I was keeping open a twenty-four-hour consultation service. It appeared I was even more reassuring on the phone than I was in the flesh. People used to ring at all hours with the most unusual worries. A common complaint was that, while bathing, they had found a little hard lump just at the bottom of their breastbone. Was it cancer? Of course it wasn't. We all have a little hard lump there. It is made of cartilage and it is called our xiphisternum. It was surprising the number of people who spent sleepless nights after finding it.

The bath was a great place for the discovery of moles, warts, lumps, and – just very occasionally – something of significance like a lump in the breast.

The medical problems I could cope with: it was the non-medical ones that took up most of my time. I was asked advice on house purchase, car purchase, the best time of the year to get married, and several times consulted about the health of various animals – dogs, cats, and once even a cow that was in labour.

Only once do I remember not coming up with some sort of answer. At ten o'clock one night I was rung by an anxious mother. Her son had won a talent contest for singing at the holiday camp from which they had just returned. Did I think he ought to cut a record? I had been up the whole of the previous night and had risked having a bath and getting into bed at eight o'clock. I couldn't give an answer – but nearly suggested that she cut his throat.

I had to explain to some people that running out of the Pill at eleven o'clock at night was not an emergency, and that you should ring up for advice before 10.45 p.m. to ask whether you are likely to get sunburnt in Majorca or not. Also, even more gently, I had to persuade people that one o'clock in the morning was not the time to seek advice about a fortnight's constipation.

The best treatment for so many conditions is reassurance: the negative result of an investigation often gives relief from actual pain as well as worry. I have seen intelligent, well-balanced people genuinely short of breath with crippling chest pains and in a mental torment waiting for their chest X-ray results. As soon as they knew their chest X-ray was clear, they lost all their symptoms and became one hundred per cent fit again.

Steve helped greatly in managing this sort of problem. He was kind, wise, and philosophical.

'Bob,' he said, 'one of our most important jobs is saving people's faces with themselves. You have to try and judge when you think a patient is about to break down and, by anticipating it, stop it happening. You will have patients coming to you, men and women, over-tired, over-anxious, exhausted and worried, wanting to be told what to do. Somehow you have to give them direction, and make them think that they have chosen this direction themselves.

'As a doctor you carry a certain authority. The patient believes this, and the people they are in contact with believe it too. If they go out armed with the message "the doctor says I must do this" or "the doctor says I mustn't do that", people will take notice.

'You will have to use your judgment about when you intervene in people's lives. If you find someone at the end of their tether, you may have to step in and direct them for a time, such as insisting that they go off work with a sick note for a spell, giving a specific reason, such as nervous exhaustion or a viral infection, for their spell off work. Whatever reason you give must save their pride, or they will otherwise take it as confirmation of their inadequacy.

'You may have to be firm with your direction, threatening them that if they don't take your advice, then they are in danger of cracking up. So often you will find they are hardly able to hide their relief on being directed. It is a bit like playing God, but providing you are not presumptuous or conceited about it, then it is a responsibility you have to take. This is general practice.

'There is a story,' he said with a smile, 'of an Archbishop

74

who died and went to heaven. He found he had to join a queue at the pearly gates, to be let in by St Peter. The Archbishop got irritated standing in this long queue, walked up to St Peter and said, "I am the Archbishop. Surely I don't have to wait in the queue like other men?" St Peter replied, "All men are equal here. I am afraid you will have to wait your turn." Standing disgruntled in the queue, the Archbishop noticed an old whiskered man on a bicycle, with a case strapped on the back, cycle the full length of the queue, knock on the gates, and go straight in. The Archbishop rushed up indignantly to St Peter and said, "I thought all men were equal here. How was it that old man could jump to the head of the queue and get in? Why should he be favoured?" "Oh," said St Peter, "that's God Himself; occasionally he likes to go back down to earth and play doctor."'

In spite of all the available medical services, psychiatric and general, many people continue to lead offbeat lives of their own. It is impossible to collect statistics of people who hide behind doors, because normally you never see them. As a general practitioner, with access to most homes, you find situations that normally never see the light of day.

One bank clerk, who to all outward appearances led a fairly normal life, I found spent most of his off-duty hours in a sort of blanket tent underneath the dining-room table. It was the only place he felt really safe in. As he managed most of his life pretty well, one couldn't interfere. I learnt later that several of his family had been killed in an air raid during the war: he had survived, protected by an old billiard table that he had been sleeping under.

Quite a number of people felt that other people were shining rays at them, or that there were men hiding in the television set, watching them. They would listen patiently to all your reassurances and then slip straight back into their little fantasy world.

Tadchester had its share of people with phobias. The most common were the agoraphobics – people who were terrified of wide open spaces. But there are phobias – i.e. irrational, illogical fears – about everything. I found, for example, that one girl's insomnia and bad school report were due to a bus phobia. She was literally terrified of being in or anywhere near a bus. She didn't know why, and there was no obvious reason for her fear.

I found these patients (particularly the children) most difficult to treat. It took a tremendous time of patient reassurance and encouragement to help them find the reserves of courage to face up to, and conquer, their fears.

There is so much that we don't know about mental illness and mental breakdown and I feel we are just at the beginning of our knowledge and could well not be pursuing the right lines of investigation. It is possible that there could be as much mental and psychiatric background to an acute appendicitis case as there is in some other poor disturbed patient whom we write off as being queer.

There are a few disturbed people who literally suffer the agonies of the damned, and who can be helped very little. Ron Towle was one.

Ron's was the most time-consuming psychiatric disorder that I ever had to cope with. More than most patients, he made me feel that psychiatric illness is just as real, and probably as organic, as pneumonia, pleurisy and even heart disease.

I saw him more than I saw any other patient over a period of five or six years. Sometimes he would make an appointment to see me: more often he would hang about in the surgery trying to catch me after the last patient, when he knew that I would have no excuse to cut short my time with him.

He was a short, prematurely grey man in his late forties, dressed shabbily in an old raincoat. His general appearance was unkempt, with frayed collars and cuffs and scruffy shoes. He had come from a good family, been away to boarding school, and was not without money. He was a sort of general dealer, buying and selling cattle, land, and turning his hand to sell anything that might make a profit. He drove round Tadchester in an old Austin Seven which he kept meticulously.

76

His main worries he related to his business deals. I would see him through one deal, supporting him through the traumas, and he would collect his money (most often he made a profit). Ten days later he would be walking up and down inside my consulting room, beating his chest and saying what a fool he had been, how he had got involved in another deal, he would lose all his money, people were taking advantage of him ... and so we would go on.

He was always in a terrible torment with himself, coming up with new symptoms. He had been many times admitted to the mental hospital, he had had every sort of psychiatric treatment, but it never seemed to lessen the torment. He would say, 'There is something terrible happening in my head, and you just don't understand. Why doesn't someone do something about it?'

I grew quite fond of him and sympathised with his turmoils. Some days he was better and would come in and chat. He was well educated, widely read, and was conversant with all the main topics of the day. He would talk for hours, given a chance. He had quite an infectious grin, but most days he would be beating his chest in despair, despairing about his attire, about his accommodation, about how far he had come down in life. He would eat up as much listening time as I was prepared to give him.

He lived in a small house in Park Lane, outside the park, four doors away from the prim Sophie and Elsie Emmerson. Somehow he was unable to join in society and make friends and communicate with people normally. He shaped his life in isolation around his business deals. In the same way that they destroyed him, they were also the things that kept him going. Our standing joke, when he came in, was, 'Well, Ron, have you bought the Eiffel Tower yet?'

Sometimes his business deals were out of town, and he would go off in his little car and come back chest beating, again moaning about some new venture he had got involved in: it was going to be his ruin, he was going to lose all the little money he had.

At his worst he became very disturbed. If I wasn't at hand

77

to settle him down, most often he would have to be forcibly admitted to the mental hospital.

Once, I went away for a weekend, after having seen Ron nearly every day for three months. He had a breakdown, was admitted to hospital for three days, then came storming in to the surgery accusing me of not being there when he needed me. I had let him down.

For one short period of a few weeks he seemed fine and well-balanced. He had been off to London to see some offbeat medical therapist whose consulting room was the back parlour of a council house in Clapham. Ron was cured. For those few weeks, whatever magic this young man from Clapham had performed on him seemed to work.

Ron's great desire was to be normal, to be accepted, to be married, but he never ever made it. He was on various medications, some of which seemed to help him, some of which obviously upset him. There seemed to be no area that we had not explored where he could be given special help for his torment. Ron really knew that nobody could help his particular case, and he was incapable of helping himself.

One day, as was always likely, he was found dead in his house. He had taken an overdose of tablets, whether by accident or design we will never know. I think it was by accident because he had always clung tenaciously to life, hoping that things would improve.

I feel that, as research progresses, help one day for the small group like Ron will be found, that their disturbance will have some chemical or physiological background. There was a time when you knew that if you had sugar diabetes or pernicious anaemia, there was no known cure. Nowadays people with these complaints can look forward to a normal and full life-span with small inconveniences of injections and diet. I think the time will come when poor unfortunates like Ron will be able to share these same expectations.

When I was a medical student and we were visiting mental hospitals, we had a patient pointed out to us who always claimed that he was tuned in to the BBC Light Programme. It was a great joke, but years later, I have often wondered whether in fact he was right. I found in general practice that so many problems had no answer – it was a matter of continual support and keeping people going, with not always a happy ending.

8

Curious Cures

Not long after I had given Gwendoline Jacobs her medical examination I found that things started to happen to me for which I couldn't find an explanation.

One night I had to swap surgery because Janice and Kevin Bird had asked me to a dinner party. I hadn't told anybody except Jill, my evening receptionist, about my change of plan, but at least half the patients who came on the wrong night knew about the change already.

On one or two calls in the country I would be flagged down by patients who would say, 'I heard you were coming this way, doctor, could you call in on me on your way back?' Something really strange was happening.

It was when I was taking complicated directions from a patient at Sanford-on-Sea about how to get there that my problem was solved – or that my problem really began. In the middle of our conversation a voice chipped in: 'You would be much better turning right by the gasworks, doctor, and going along the sea road.'

The voice was unmistakable. It was Gwendoline. I had forgotten that she worked on the telephone exchange. God, how many other of my conversations had she listened in to?

From then on Gwendoline haunted me. I was almost terrified

to pick up the phone. If she were taking my call I had a terrible time getting through her chit chat to actually get a number. She was always pressing me to go to parties, picnics or barbecues, and whenever I was asking for directions to outlandish places it always became a three-part conversation.

The trouble was she was sometimes useful – almost too useful. She would hang on to calls, knowing I was out, and save them till I got back. She became an unofficial receptionist, and in fact asked during one of our many conversations whether I would consider her for a job at the surgery if one ever became vacant, as she was very good on the phone.

I noticed that whenever Marjorie de Wyrebock phoned me (and her phone calls had begun to increase in number) that we were always getting cut off. Sometimes a very high-pitched, falsetto voice which was obviously Gwendoline's in disguise, would say 'So sawry. There seems to be a fault on the line.'

I could think of no answer to this particular problem. I daren't mention it to my partners – they would have laughed at me. If the phone rang when we were all having coffee together, I froze and never volunteered to pick it up. I couldn't really complain to the Post Office that one of their telephonists was being too helpful.

My haunting by Gwendoline went on for about two months. I was getting to a point of near despair when, in the middle of one evening surgery, I saw that one of the names on the patients' appointments list was Mrs Daphne Jennings, the telephone supervisor. I wondered could I use her to frighten Gwendoline off?

When Mrs Jennings came through the door, I saw to it that I was on the phone to Kevin. When Kevin answered the phone I started to ask him the most complicated directions to a place fifteen miles along the coast. I knew this was a bait that Gwendoline couldn't refuse. Once I had asked Kevin the question, I looked down at my watch and said, 'Help! I have an appointment to see Dr Maxwell. I wonder, Mrs Jennings, if you would mind taking these directions from Mr Bird?'

I gave Mrs Jennings the phone, dashed out of the room, and waited. Would my dastardly plot work?

I stayed out for ten minutes and then came back into the room. Mrs Jennings was like a beetroot, and hardly able to contain herself.

'How often does that girl interrupt telephone conversations?' she asked.

'Oh, I think she only tries to be helpful,' I said.

'We'll see about her being helpful tomorrow morning,' said Mrs Jennings.

That was the last I heard on the telephone from Gwendoline Jacobs.

I gathered she couldn't be sacked from the Post Office: as well as being the Carnival Queen, she was Miss Post Office for that year. However, she was demoted from the switchboard and sent to sort letters in the corrugated-iron shed that served for this purpose behind the main Post Office.

With Gwendoline off the phone, Marjorie de Wyrebock had no difficulty in getting through to me. She seemed to be able to find an excuse to ring me most days. It was either an invitation to a hunt ball or to ask why didn't I take riding lessons? She apologised for being the initial cause of my riding accident, and as she ran the local livery stables and was quite a good horsewoman (to judge by the size of her buttocks and thighs, she had been at it for many years) she would be my obvious instructor. I sometimes almost wished that Gwendoline was back jamming the calls again.

About this time I started to build up a regular eccentric clientele that was offbeat even for Tadchester. For some reason, they all turned up at my Wednesday evening surgery, over which Jill presided, surrounded by her usual ring of admirers asking for acne tablets.

There was Miss Bessie Oldthorpe from the sweetshop – she weighed 18 stone 3 pounds. I might have been forgiven for thinking she wanted to lose weight, but no! If her weight ever fell below 18 stone 1 pound, she thought she had a cancer, and I had great difficulty in reassuring her. She went about in mortal fear until she had regained the missing two pounds.

The only time she did lose weight was when – on very shaky grounds – she thought she might be pregnant. She lost two stones in three weeks, worrying, until Nature reassured her. Then she lost almost another two in trying to regain the weight she'd lost, to prove she hadn't got a cancer.

Next came Harry Jones. One must admit that Harry was a little simple. He always came in with the same symptom – he thought people knocked him out when he wasn't looking. He never had any bruises or marks, neither did he remember it happening; but as he logically argued, 'If someone knocks me out from behind when I'm not looking, how would I know?' And, of course, he was right.

Wendy Peebles had fits, proved by the psychiatrist to be completely hysterical. If there was no Wednesday night hop on in Tadchester, she came and had a fit in the middle of the surgery for a change. The rest of the Wednesday-nighters loved her performance. I must admit that, in my early days, she did worry me. It took me some time to realise that I was able to get her to come round quickly if I threatened her with a hypodermic needle or a bowl of cold water.

Mr Terence, the butcher's assistant, came regularly for stomach medicine and to talk about fly fishing. I had a feeling that it was damp river banks that gave him his indigestion, as it was quite clear he only took his medication at weekends.

Mrs Price, who worked in the supermarket, had anaemia. This was somehow related to the heavy floods of some years earlier. She used to love to describe the floods in such detail that I thought of saving up and buying her an ark. I daren't suggest that she had her womb taken away: it would have left her with one thing less – or perhaps one thing more – to talk about. She really would have liked a blood test each week as some kind of blanket insurance against anaemia, floods and hysterectomies. ('There can't be a drop of blood left in me, doctor.') As a sort of optional extra she would bring in her young son to show off his football bruises.

Jack Fingleton was a regular once-a-fortnight Wednesday-nighter. His wants were simple – some back tablets, a pound of cotton wool, and the largest bottle of liquid paraffin. He had been getting the cotton wool and oil before I came and he was such a regular that I didn't like to ask him what he used them for.

I got to know this group of patients so well that I began to remember them not by their names but by their conditions. On one embarrassing occasion at a cocktail party, I called George Ramsdale, my regular piles attender, 'Mr Bottom'.

The others were, variously, 'Mrs Varicose Ulcer', 'It's Me 'Art, You Know, Doctor', and 'Mrs It Keeps Dropping Down And I Can't Hold Me Water'.

At the time I was trying to adjust to this bizarre collection of patients and conditions, as if they weren't enough, I had two brushes with the Army. Retired Army officers, like private patients, I found difficult to get on with.

The first was Colonel Lotus. He came to see me in the surgery instead of consulting my senior partner, Steve Maxwell, who was his usual doctor. This was always a bad start. He came in, sat down and, in his clipped military manner, said, 'I'm afraid Maxwell's not up to it. I want you to look after me from now on.'

I should be able to have some trite and ready answer to squash retired military people, but I usually find that I am ill at ease with them. They bring out some hidden complex in me, and I am never able to deliver any prepared squelch. For a patient to say that Dr Maxwell was not up to it could only mean that there was something disagreeable about the patient himself.

I enquired about Colonel Lotus's trouble. He clipped out that he had had this damned neuritis for some years and that Maxwell had done nothing about it – what was I going to do?

I looked through his record card and saw the various investigations he had undergone. There was obviously nothing very seriously wrong, so I gave him a well-known brand of vitamin tablets and told him to come back and see me in a fortnight's time.

When he returned in two weeks, in spite of his fierce look, he was almost pleasant – I didn't realise he had it in him.

'Damned good pills, those, doctor,' he said. 'Feel better than I've done for years. Wish I'd come to see you years ago. Let's have some more.'

I was pleased that he was going to be satisfied with vitamin tablets and gave him another prescription.

An hour later he rang up, irate.

'You've given me the wrong pills, doctor,' he bellowed. 'Damned inefficiency. Let me have some more of the ones you gave me last time. Did me the world of good.'

I consulted his card (I often have a horrible feeling that

when I allow my mind to wander with a verbose patient, I will write down the wrong thing). I once wrote '3 The Elms' as the diagnosis part of a Health Certificate.

The other area in prescribing and writing certificates where I often lapsed was on the prescription form itself. In the top left-hand corner it says 'Mr/Mrs/Miss', two of which titles have to be struck out, depending on the sex and marital status of the patient concerned. In my speed of writing I often just took a wild slash at this group of prefixes, and my slashing was not always accurate. One day I was rung up by a mother who said that the elastic stockings I had prescribed for her baby's nappy rash didn't make sense, and the zinc and castor oil ointment I had given her for her varicose veins didn't help at all.

All it had on the Colonel's card was the vitamin tablets I was sure I had prescribed. I had to ring him back, and ask if he still had a tablet that he could let me see.

'Disgusting,' he said, under his breath. 'Damned records – I'll drop one in.'

At lunch time Gladys brought me a greyish-looking tablet that I was sure I had never seen in my life before. This is it, I thought – I must have prescribed the mental equivalent of '3 The Elms' in tablet form.

Even though this pill was apparently doing good, I didn't know what hidden harm it might be doing. I said to Gladys, 'We must find out what this is.'

We looked through his notes, without success, to see if it was something we had prescribed before. We checked it with every capsule and tablet we had in the surgery, and with every one of the coloured pill charts we kept.

I was in despair. I couldn't name this tablet, and the complex I have about treating retired colonels was very much to the fore. I didn't know what to do.

Eventually I rang Neville Jackson, the chemist, and explained my problem. 'Pop it round, old man,' he said. 'We'll soon find out what it is.'

I popped it round and went through all his stock – to no avail.

There didn't seem to be anything anywhere like it. We checked again, and still no identification. This really seemed like the end. The colonel was coming in to collect his pills in another half hour. We sat, and Neville said, 'Just a second – it couldn't possibly be ... you would never prescribe those ...' With my face getting redder, I said 'What?'

He went off to the veterinary counter and came back with a box of cats' worming tablets, opened it and showed me about fifty of the same tablets I was supposed to have prescribed. I hurried back to the surgery.

When the Colonel burst in, I was sitting with quiet dignity in my chair.

'Have you found out what those pills were? Disgusting – sheer inefficiency, bad book work, muddling things up. Never happened in the Army.'

'Sit down, Colonel,' I said, 'I've one or two questions to ask you.' He sat down, snorting.

'When you visited me last,' I said, 'were you alone?'

'What do you mean, alone?' he snorted. 'Of course I was.'

'No, no,' I said. 'Did you have any of your animals – the dogs, or cats – in the car?'

'Yes, yes,' he replied. 'I was taking the cat to the vet's – needed de-worming. Dashed good job he made of it, too.'

'I'm afraid, Colonel,' I said, 'the administrative mix-up has been on your part. The tablets that have done you so much good were the cat's worming tablets, and the tablets that have done the cat so much good were the ones I gave you!'

Colonel Lotus sat up sharply, as if he had been bayoneted in a tender spot. 'Ugh!' he exclaimed, then sat there silently, looking into space.

I left him in his trance for a few minutes, then enquired, 'Are you all right, Colonel?'

He replied with another 'Ugh', got up, and walked rather than stamped out of the surgery. I think for the first time in his whole life he simply had nothing he could say.

... General Branton did not attend the surgery, but was Army to the core, He fought his battles on his home ground.

To visit him was sheer hard work. The General, who had been famous for his exploits on the North West Frontier, campaigned just as vigorously against his bowels as he did against the Frontier tribesmen.

When I arrived he always had detailed communiqués of his actions of the last fourteen days. We then set out a working plan for the next fourteen days.

'What if I don't go tomorrow, and say I haven't been by Tuesday, and what happens if nothing really comes by Thursday?'

We waged an unremitting war against his bowels. It was important that we should never either win or lose completely, as he would have little else to live for. It was considered a reverse if we had to bring in the District Nurse to give an enema, whereas in the soft fruit season we sometimes had ten days of triumph.

I found, as time passed, that it had become less tedious. Like everything else, after a certain time you begin to get involved, start talking the same language. I began to get launched into his bowel manoeuvres just as intently as the General did, using suppositories and every conceivable laxative as my support troops.

Next door to the General lived Miss Wells, aged seventy-eight, who looked after her mother of 102. Her mother nagged her and chided her about not keeping the house clean, and not cooking as she used to. Although she was seventy-eight, Miss Wells behaved as if she were a young daughter and tried to improve her cooking and her scrubbing.

They lived very nearly at the top of Up the Hill. I used to see Miss Wells trudging with her shopping basket down the hill, across the bridge to the Pannier Market where she bought their weekly groceries and vegetables. Mother had always bought her stuff from the market, so poor Miss Wells had to follow suit.

She did confess to me one day in a moment of great weakness

that if the good Lord did take her mother away, perhaps she would at last have a little bit of life of her own.

Whereas General Branton's digestive tract represented the bottom end of the scale, the eating habits of the Tadchester patients (which are again quite unique) could probably be called the top end of the scale.

I had been called to *The Goat*, one of the larger pubs in Tadchester, to see the son of the landlord who was suffering from earache. I examined him, found that one of his ears was inflamed, and prescribed some antibiotics.

The landlord's wife asked, as I was there, whether I would mind having a look at the landlord himself, who had been complaining of indigestion.

The family had been in Tadchester for a few months only and I did not know the landlord very well. He was about twenty-nine but was already beginning to put on weight and would soon be able to make a matching pair with Bessie Oldthorpe.

I asked him about his symptoms, which seemed little more than some flatulence and a bit of epigastric discomfort.

'How much do you drink?' I asked.

'I really don't drink at all, doctor,' he replied, 'and if I do it's only light ale.'

This puzzled me: his symptoms sounded like an overdose of alcohol.

'On a market day,' he told me, 'I probably have about thirty short ales, but there are some days when I don't have more than about a dozen.'

He was obviously going to fit in well in Tadchester. For sheer peculiarity I would back the eating and drinking habits of Tadchesterians against those of any other town.

In my early days I treated two ladies for some peculiar disease for months without any effect, eventually calling in a specialist. I discovered they were eating a patent diet that they had read about in a national newspaper. It was completely devoid of Vitamin C and they were actually suffering from scurvy.

Mrs de Wyrebock's illness had shown me that raw sausage meat was a popular local delicacy and there were few Tadchester households which did not include a handful of seaweed with their morning bacon and egg. Eating too much was the general order of the day and I was plagued with overweight patients, none of whom, of course, ever ate a thing. One offender not only complained that I did nothing about reducing her weight, but loudly asserted that she vomited back every morsel of food she had taken for the last six months, and what was I going to do about it?

I tried every known slimming tablet and reducing diet on my gang of heavyweights but nothing happened. I asked Steve, 'Whatever do I do with all these fatties? Have you any favourite pill that works wonders?'

'I don't use pills,' said Steve. 'Just get them to write down every single thing they eat and drink each day for two weeks, then bring the list of their menus in to you.'

I followed Steve's instructions to the letter. My patients who never ate anything and were always putting on weight were instructed to make a complete diary of their food and drink intake and report back in a fortnight.

I weighed them all before they set out on this venture and again when they reported back with the mealtime records. It was amazing. There was an average weight loss of seven pounds per patient.

I was beginning to learn the art of general practice.

9

Formulae for Survival

I learned from my patients that only a few rare people have such a zest for life that they can cope unaided with all situations and seemingly survive them. Most people have to find some formula or philosophy of survival.

Often the formula was the discipline of a job. Just as often it was a hobby such as pigeon fancying, fishing or gardening. Life was the hobby: the daily grind of a job was endured merely to provide the means by which the hobby could be pursued. Other people were so weighed down with commitments that the commitments themselves were a formula. Ties of elderly sick relatives or young children decided for them how they were going to spend most of their lives – they had no option.

It was how people behaved when released from their commitments that amazed me. Far from entering a much wider and fuller life, more often they fell to pieces. The Harris family were typical of this group.

Granny Harris was the bane of her family's life. She had had a stroke and could not communicate properly, was intermittently incontinent, and had to be fed and washed. It was an unrewarding chore the family had shared strictly between them for ten years. They had promised her at some stage before her stroke that if she was ever ill they would never put her into hospital. They stuck to their word.

Eventually winter bronchitis took her off. She had led a cabbage-like uncommunicative existence for so long I felt I could not give her antibiotics to see this particular phase through. She died peacefully in her sleep, to what must, I felt, have been a great joy to her family.

The Harris's were one of the large local Tadchester families, so there was a splendid funeral. Although there were some outward signs of grief, it must have been a tremendous relief to all of them. They were close-knit and had shared, uncomplainingly, the task of nursing Granny between four of the households, each taking a three-month stint. Other members of the family saw to it that they were adequately relieved to go out and join in normal communal life as far as they possibly could. They were a great example of people looking after their own.

Within three months of Granny dying the family had more or less split up. They did not bother with each other any more; there were quarrels, gossip, and some sections of the family were not on speaking terms with others. I found it difficult to believe that Granny Harris, this immobile invalid, must have been the cornerstone of the family structure. Once she had gone the whole building had tumbled down.

Even more surprising was Charlie Leggo. He was in his seventies when I came to the practice and had been nursing his elderly parents at home for some years. His mother was in her very late eighties and his father ninety-two.

He washed them, powdered them, fed and clothed them. They were still just mobile when I first came to Tadchester but gradually deteriorated and were both confined to bed.

I never enquired too closely into how their toilet was managed, but they were both impeccably looked after, without a blemish on them. Charlie, who was an odd-fish bachelor, never grumbled about how much he had to do for them. He had spent most of his life with his parents. They had had a family butcher's shop in the town. Apart from a brief interlude in the Army in the First World War, Charlie had worked in, and later managed, the shop. He finally shut it when he was about sixty-three, only because the demands of his parents took up all his time.

His father, the weaker of the two ancients, eventually died. Charlie took it in his stride because his main love was his mother, and he was now able to devote all his time to her.

There was never a better nurse. He attended to her every whim, washed her, powdered her, rubbed her hands when they were cold, and would buy any tempting morsel of food that she might fancy, irrespective of cost.

Although Charlie wandered about all day in a brown overall and looked as poor as a church mouse, it was rumoured that he had tens of thousands of pounds in a case under his bed. I could quite believe this as he never appeared to spend anything on himself and it wouldn't have surprised me if he had pinched his brown overalls when he was discharged from the Army in 1919.

Six months later, in spite of Charlie's ministrations, his mother died. I wondered how he would adjust to living on his own.

He spent the first few months weeping, not leaving the house, castigating himself – and me – for not having taken greater care of his parents. Couldn't I have given her some different medicine? Was the medicine I had given them the right medicine? I, meanwhile, tried to urge him to get out and actually accused him of going nowhere and suggested I would have to get a psychiatrist in to see him.

'I do go out,' said Charlie. 'I go to all the funerals of the regular customers we used to have at the shop.'

Slowly Charlie began to take some interest in life. By 'interest in life' I mean 'interest in himself'. Now, relieved of his domestic duties, he had little to do other than prowl around his body looking for untreatable or incurable illnesses.

The only time he was away from his parents, during the First World War, he received a leg injury on the Somme which left him with a varicose ulcer that had withstood every medical treatment for several decades. His ulcer was really his pride and joy. Once, trying out some new technique, I did almost cure it.

From then on Charlie kept it tightly bandaged and wouldn't let me look at it.

One of his explorations brought to light a previously un-discovered cyst on his posterior, approximately the size of a garden pea. It was a nuisance, and would have to be removed. This was out of my province and would require his going to the outpatients' department at the hospital, where Henry Johnson would attend to it.

To my surprise Charlie accepted the idea of going to hospital with enthusiasm; he was living the life of a recluse now and rarely left the house. He was a martinet in his own home and vented most of his spleen on his home help who always did more than her duty, hoping that one day she might be remembered in his will.

I wondered how Charlie would get on at the hospital. He had always been so used to getting his own way. He had no great experience of hospital staff to help him dominate them but, to his eternal credit, he triumphed. The fierce theatre sister was handled more firmly than she had ever been in her life before, and Charlie went down in history as the only man to mount the hospital theatre table without first removing his boots.

When he was actually installed on the table, plus boots, it was with great difficulty that he was persuaded to lift his shirt so that the offending lesion could be admired.

As the operation was under local anaesthetic, Charlie was able to talk all the way through, dropping titbits of medical information, and refusing to come back and have his stitches out in seven days as he knew they should stay in for nine. Henry said afterwards he nearly put a stitch in his tongue.

When they were putting on his dressing, Charlie finally won the day. With a triumphant look in his eye he said, 'I shall need some physiotherapy for this.' How, why and from whatever angle I was never to know: three days after the operation he suddenly packed up and went south to live with a niece no one had heard of, and he never appeared again.

In complete contrast to the Harris's and Charlie Leggo,

Mrs Saunders was one of the happy few who seemed to survive without any particular formula. She was the respected, gentle wife of one of the Methodist lay preachers who lived Up the Hill. In addition to looking after her aged mother-in-law for ten years, she kept a spotless house and took meals in to the poverty-stricken lady who lived next door. The poverty-stricken lady next door, Miss Rudd, accepted any charity that was going (including the Christmas dinner at a local hotel that I arranged one year). She surprised us all when she died by leaving her dirty, untidy house almost crammed to the roof with share certificates, £1 notes, and Savings Certificates, to a total value of £37,000. This was not including the value of the house she lived in, which was her own.

Miss Rudd had died intestate, and a tentative enquiry was put out for any possible living beneficiaries.

Far from having no family, she appeared to have a vast one: relatives started to appear from all over England, to put a claim in for dear Auntie Gertie's fortune.

There were two devoted nephews and one niece actually living in Tadchester. They had apparently not managed to bring themselves to visit her for ten or fifteen years, but underneath really loved her dearly, and each one of the Tadchester three were quite sure that it was them in particular who Auntie would have loved to leave her money to.

I was happy that it was the solicitors who would have to sort this lot out.

Eventually Mrs Saunders' mother-in-law died and Mrs Saunders was left free to devote more of her time to the running and organising of the church that her husband was associated with. She had always somehow kept herself intact and not bowed down by her commitments. She had very rarely attended the surgery, so when she did come to see me one day, complaining of stomach pain, I knew there must be something really upsetting her.

I always took extra notice of patients who, like Mrs Saunders, only rarely appeared at the surgery. If they had made a special effort to come, it must have been for a good reason. Their medical record cards gave a great deal of information.

One man whose record card showed me he had not seen a doctor for twelve years came in for a bottle of medicine for his irritating cough. 'No need to examine me, doctor,' he said.

I did examine him, heard a few suspicious squeaks, and sent him for an X-ray of his chest. He had a cancer of the lung. Within six weeks of his seeing me, his lung had been removed.

It was the same situation with Mrs Saunders. She had obviously been having womb trouble for some time and, on my examination, I found that she had some internal growth.

I made an urgent appointment for her to be seen by the specialist. He admitted her to hospital within a week and carried out a major operation. In his letter to me afterwards he explained that, although he had removed most of the growth, the patient had really come to him too late, and there were signs that the growth was already beginning to spread.

Mrs Saunders, as expected, made a good recovery from her operation and for six months was out and about, brighter than ever.

Then came signs that her disease was beginning to catch up with her. She complained of increasing pain in her right leg – obviously the growth must have infiltrated the sciatic nerve of the affected side. She was requiring increasing quantities of drugs to relieve her pain, she wasn't eating, she was losing weight. Her pain was slowly killing her.

I hoped that we might be able to make her last weeks (or months) more comfortable and asked the consultant anaesthetist from Winchcombe Hospital if he would come over and see her. I felt that if he could kill the nerves in her leg (this could sometimes be done by injecting alcohol into it) it would make life more bearable for her, although it would not halt the progress of her disease.

The consultant anaesthetist came over and skilfully injected her leg. Twenty-four hours later, Mrs Saunders was completely pain-free, and eating properly again. Within two weeks, she was up and about, busying herself with town and church matters.

This was a marvellous response to treatment. I wondered how long it would be before her disease finally caught up with her.

Once she was free of pain, Mrs Saunders stopped attending me. There was no point in my reminding her that she had a very unpleasant medical condition.

Months and years slipped by and the details of her particular case became submerged in the mass of other problems I had to deal with.

Seven years later I was called to her house again. She had fallen down the stairs and broken her hip. She went into hospital, had her hip pinned, was home and walking again after two weeks, and never looked back.

The surgeon who pinned her hip said there were still signs of the growth but for some reason (I have no explanation for it) it hadn't advanced. Apart from some numbness in her leg where the nerves had been killed, she had no complaints.

I am sure that if her pain had not been relieved she would have died. I became aware that people do die of pain; that people in bad accidents have a much better chance of surviving if their pain is relieved. I also came to realise that if I predicted too closely the course a certain disease would take, I would be proved wrong as often as I was proved right.

Mrs Saunders' story was one of the happy rewards that I occasionally came across in general practice. Unfortunately, too often, there were events of great sadness.

Silas Lister was a recluse who lived in a flat over some garages near the quay on the Down the Hill side of the river. He kept himself to himself, rarely communicated with anyone, was reputed to have money but lived in a miserly fashion. He refused to accept things like electricity and gas, and would be found bundled in several layers of dirty old coats picking up driftwood from the side of the river when the tide was out. At night, through his curtainless windows, his flickering candle could be seen moving as he passed from room to room.

The Social Services made several offers to help him but he refused, was belligerent to anybody who approached him, and kept himself behind the locked door of his flat.

He did not appear for days sometimes, and the only evidence that there was still life in the flat was that the pint of milk delivered each day at some time disappeared inside. He had behaved in this way for as long as anyone could remember, and was of indeterminate age.

One day the milkman reported that no bottles had been taken in for three days: he could not get any reply when he knocked on the door, and felt that either Silas had gone away or was ill in his flat.

I went down but couldn't get any reply either, and there was no way of looking into the rooms as they were one storey up.

I called the police, who broke into the flat for me, and we were met by a scene of absolute carnage.

In one corner of a bare, untidy room lay the shrivelled and obviously dead body of Silas, but it looked as if there had been some terrible and bloody struggle. Blood literally covered the floor of virtually every room of the flat, with Silas's bare feet occasionally showing their imprint on the dark stains on the floorboards.

On closer examination there seemed to be no evidence of a struggle after all and, what was stranger still, in my brief examination of Silas I could find no evidence of where he had been bleeding from. He was thin – almost emaciated – and obviously undernourished, with spindly legs and huge varicose veins running down both ankles.

It was a complete mystery.

I went to the post mortem and the mystery was solved.

The pathologist showed me the cause of Silas's downfall. There was a small hole in one varicose vein on one of Silas's ankles. He must have caught his ankle while wandering about in the dark, or semi-dark, of his flat, and pottered about, slowly letting his life blood drain away. You would have thought that he would have been conscious that the floor was wet and sticky, but we were never quite sure how much Silas was conscious of anything, and in some strange way this is probably the way Silas would have chosen to go – a slow ebbing out of his life force, painlessly, and followed by a long and lasting sleep.

In any other circumstance, one small dressing or a finger pressed on this tiny wound would have stopped the bleeding.

10

Down the Mine

It became my lot to take over the surgeries at Thudrock Colliery.

I liked coal miners and looked forward to my excursions to the primitive surgery that we had there.

Coal mining was in my blood. My grandfather had been a collier, my father had been a coal mining engineer, until his untimely death, and at the end of the war I had had two years down a mine as a Bevin Boy.

One of the factors that made me choose the Winchcombe area was that it was one of the very few parts of Britain which had the benefits of the south of England and its better weather, the sea coast, and a coal mine not too far away.

The Thudrock miners loved having a doctor who was a qualified collier, who could talk the same language and knew all about the perils of the coal face and underground roadways. The few I was unpopular with were the lead swingers who failed to put it across me because I knew it all – even a bit more than some of them.

I was taken on trips underground, up to the coal face, and felt a strange nostalgia for the time when my daily task was with a pick and shovel in a 3 foot 6 inch seam.

*　*　*

As a medical student, I had volunteered to go down the mines. In December 1944, six of us were sitting in the Biology Lab. in Epsom College. We were a sub-section of the Medical Six who had been sitting the first M.B. and the Conjoint Board Premedical Examination. These were our last few days as schoolboys. The war was pressing on to its conclusion; we were too young and isolated to appreciate its horrors, and indulged in schoolboy fugues of heroism and daring acts. None of us wanted to go straight away to Medical School. We had opted as one man for the Fleet Air Arm where, with pride, we'd learnt that the average life of a pilot in the air was thirty-six hours. What would they think at the Youth Club when we came in in our uniforms?

I discussed the situation with my mother, who always kept me on a loose rein. She thought some experience before Medical School would be valuable, that the Fleet Air Arm certainly sounded glamorous, but the way things were going the war would soon be over, and that the chances of reaching air crew would be virtually nil: I would be wasting my time for a few years doing some mundane job. If I really wanted to do something valuable which would widen my experience and make a contribution to society, why not go down the mines for a year? The Bevin Scheme was under way at the time and men were being conscripted for the mines as they were the Armed Forces.

I have a streak in me, that has persisted, of doing the out-of-the-ordinary. The mines caught my imagination. So I went to the Labour Exchange and asked if I could go down the pit for a year. They said they would be delighted to have me – as a medical student I could come out when I liked – and so I signed on there and then. My mother's wisdom prevailed: my five friends went into the Fleet Air Arm, spent five months making paths across airfields with clinker and coke, and were then given an early discharge. Thus, on 1st February 1945, I set out for Doncaster with a bright Ministry of Labour label on my case.

Proudly flashing the label as if it were a D.S.C. or at least a Captain's pips, I reached Askern Main Colliery, one of the main initial training establishments for Bevin Boys in the Yorkshire coalfields.

I was at Askern for a month, part of a very mixed bunch. With my Boy Scout's enthusiasm, I could not understand why my colleagues were not delighted to be able to go down pits and dig out coal. Most of them were either from industry where, with the reduction in arms production, they had become redundant and had been conscripted for the mines, or were air crew, many of whom had been training in Canada where there was a reduction in personnel with the war drawing to a close. When I look back and think of the adjustment that these Officer Cadets had to make, one minute being feted in Canada in smart uniforms and with reasonable pay, then almost overnight being transformed into coal miners, I realise it must have been almost too much to bear.

There were one or two straight conscripts who were neither redundant factory workers nor ex-Air Force. These included a concert pianist and one poor lad who had never strayed from his father's estates, where he had a private tutor, his only glimpse of the public being when he was supervising hop-picking on the family estate. In one of our many political discussions – and this was at the time of the Socialist revolutions – poor 'Lord Tom' as he was called, in a very hostile environment put forward the suggestion that the only possible government was that of genuine aristocracy. On reflection, after thirty years, I think he was probably right.

In addition to the change of circumstances, for most of my fellow Bevin Boys there was a marked reduction in the amount of money they had. Many had been making very good money working long hours as bench hands in Midlands factories.

We were good company. There were various dances and social engagements, and one of the local farmers asked a group of us round for ham and eggs in quantities that I had not seen since before the war.

We had our delightful eccentrics, two brothers who were the

sons of, and bore the name of, a famous cough-medicine manufacturer. They had a row with their father, and volunteered for the mines that day. They distinguished themselves when being posted to their pit near Nottingham by living at the most fashionable hotel in the town and crossing the lounge in the evening in their pit boots and helmets on their way to their rooms for a wash.

We were housed at Askern in the proverbial Army Nissen hut, with stoves, bunk beds and lockers. We ate at the pit canteen for lunch but came back to the hostel for our evening meal. Our day was split up between lectures, physical training and visits down the pit. The lectures were very simple, about life underground, and I still have the books that I won for being top in the examination. Physical training was the routine stuff with a regular ex-Guards sergeant.

Visits underground were quite different. This was a new experience for all of us. Half of the colliery was in production and the other half was used for the training of Bevin Boys. I never liked, and know of nobody who does like, going down in a pit cage. You hurtle down into the darkness to the accompaniment of the hissing of compressed air pipes and, usually, dripping water. With the slowing down of the cage at the bottom you feel you are shooting back up to the top again.

Only once had I been in a pit cage when anything unusual happened. On this occasion there was some technical fault. We had neared the bottom and then were lifted back up half-way, a quarter of a mile from daylight and quarter of a mile from the bottom. Tension mounted steadily. We were hopeless, helpless, and did not know what was going on. I could feel the tension rising. One cannot contemplate shinning up a quarter of a mile of rope, neither sliding down one. Happily, after ten minutes, we went down and were got off on to safe ground.

The training shaft at Askern Colliery had an added refinement in that there was a two-tier cage, of which only the top tier was used. The reason for this was apparent on our first trip. We huddled together as the cage sped down, thinking we were almost certainly plunging to our deaths. The end of the journey finished in a loud splash which confirmed our worst fears. What in fact was happening was that the sump (which is the space below where the cage stops to unload in the pit bottom) was full of water into which the bottom tier of the cage used to splash to unload the top tier. It was all too much for our pianist who was claustrophobic and quite hysterical. He made two or three more attempts to go down the pit, but was eventually discharged as being unfit to serve underground.

We climbed along tunnels, through coal faces, spent half a day working in a place called Garsides, which was extremely hot. After four weeks, in which we had just got to know each other, we were split up and posted to various collieries in the South Yorkshire field. A few of us managed to stick together and were posted to Dinnington Main Colliery, near Sheffield. We had been living in hostels till now, and were transferred to another hostel (Nissen huts, bunk beds again) but were expected to find accommodation in Dinnington Village once we had settled in.

During our first month at Dinnington we were put through a hardening-up process, which meant that at six o'clock every morning we had to report at the pit top and unload a twenty-ton railway wagon full of stones or clinker. This was our day's work. Here we acquired our blisters and developed our shovelling muscles. As the old miner in charge of us said, 'If you shovel at an elephant's feet, it will fall over.'

One of the few things that has remained with me from my mining days is skill with a shovel. You aim always for a flat surface, and you start shovelling at the bottom.

I managed to find lodgings in Dinnington with a collier and his wife with whom I stayed happily for two years. We still keep in touch – Auntie and Ike Bradley, who gave me full board, lodging, laundry, love and care for twenty-five shillings (£1.25p) a week.

Toughened up, I was ready to work underground. I hated my first job down below. It was working in the pit bottom, assisting in putting tubs on and off the cage. It was cold, noisy and relentless. There seemed to be streams of tubs loaded with coal coming at you all the time. You stopped a tub by pushing what was known as a 'locker' between the spokes of the running wheel, which acted as an instant brake. You had to be careful not to put your hand in or under the wheel, and if you missed with your locker a stream of tubs could come pouring down, smashing the cage and halting the drawing of coal. As far as I remember the drawing rate was sixty times an hour: one only had a few seconds to unload a tub, push the empty tubs off the cage with the full tubs, shut the gates and leap back. There were horrific tales told of men catching their sleeves in the up-going cage, and I hated it.

There are two shafts in a coal mine: one the down shaft in which the air is drawn into the mine, and the other the up shaft where the stale, but now warm, air is drawn out. I was at the bottom of the down shaft. In mid-winter it was very cold.

I had come to be a coal miner and would settle for nothing less than a pick and shovel. I was only going to be down a year, and I wanted to do the whole lot. Colliers were the fighter pilots of the industry. They were the real men who had a confident swagger, knowing that whatever anybody else did, they were the men that mattered and the rest were just supporting troops. When eventually I was a collier myself, I likened the experience very much to that of the small amount of rock climbing that I had done; there is the same physical effort, some hazard, and the sense of achievement and accomplishment at the end of the day.

After four weeks on the pit bottom I was moved to a job further in the pit which was reckoned to be one of the softest jobs going. In a little airless side passage we had a compressed-air prop-straightening machine. Nearly all the pit props and roof supports – bars – were iron. The bent and twisted ones were brought off the coal faces to be straightened in this machine.

I was Ben Burgess's assistant. He was an old collier, past retiring age, a great character, who was delighted to have a medical student as his sidekick. The job was tedious to the extreme. It was so hot and airless that it was very difficult to keep awake: the job had no incentive. Sometimes we would run out of props and bars and would sit, fighting to keep awake. The worst sin you can commit underground is to fall asleep. It is a bit like falling asleep in the snow – you may never wake up.

We had visits from the deputies (foremen) and the overman (foreman in charge of underground shift) who would pass the time of day with us. The few remaining pit ponies – underworked, overfed, savage beasts – used to come with their terrified drivers to carry our props away in small trucks. The pit ponies that I saw didn't need anybody to feel sorry for them. They did little work, were extremely well fed and looked after, were extremely difficult to control, and were, proverbially, as strong as a horse.

My friend Albert, who is now a successful Birmingham jeweller, came flying past one day, hanging on to the bit of his aggressive pony, not being able to stop him for a further half mile, with always the danger that the pony would pull the tub off the rails and bring down the roof of the narrow underground passages – 'supply gates' – through which they travelled. They were only about five feet in height – tall enough for the pony but not the driver.

My days with Ben seemed to go on for ever. If you have been half asleep in a boring lecture you know the agony of being nine hours a day in this situation. Ben warned me of the perils of the coal face. I had a safe job with him, but I wanted the coal face – the complete experience. So, after only two months underground, I was offered the job of coal face borer.

A coal face borer was by far the worst job – at least for me – on the coal face. It hadn't the sheer strain and exhaustion of actually getting coal, but the frustrations and the difficult positions one had to get into more than made up for this.

In 1945, face drills were driven by compressed air and there was a compressed-air pipe the whole length of the face. This was covered with lumps of loose coal, coal dust, and had coupling valves every fifteen to twenty yards. The face borer had first to blow out any dust from the pipes without getting his head blown off, then with a six-foot drill and thirty yards of rubber tubing, had to scramble up and down the coal face as the colliers requested holes for blowing their coal. He had to find the valves hidden in the dust, make sure his machine did not jam, make sure that he had sharp bits for his drill – and all this while carrying a hand lamp.

It was the nearest to Dante's inferno that I have been. There was the noise of falling coal, dust, shouts and screams of the colliers who wanted 'the bloody borer', and acrid smoke following the face as shots were fired further along it. If the shot had not been placed in deeply enough (a flanker) the whole face became thick with blinding smoke.

On some faces the conveyor belt was put right up to the coal face and the collier had to dig a hole in for himself to get working. The poor borer had to travel up and down this three-hundred-yard length, hopping in and out of the waste behind the coal face that might come down at any minute, clamber over the conveyor belt with huge lumps of coal trying to knock him off all the time, and perch sometimes across the belt with coal whizzing between his legs as he fought to drill a six-foot hole into the coal. His other duties were to put props, clay for shot firing, and wooden nogs (which were used to stop props slipping) on the end of the face belts so the colliers could pull supplies off for themselves as the material passed them. It was an absolute nightmare. You were nobody's friend.

On my first day as a borer I was sent to Five's Face where the coal was thicker than anywhere else in the pit, being about five feet from roof to floor, and getting about was rather easier. Half way through my first shift I saw everyone down tools and get off the face very quickly. I thought 'Ah! snap (lunch) time,' and wandered slowly off the face, surprised at the noise of the creaking and grinding of the roof. I was even more surprised when the coal face behind me started to burst, shooting lumps of coal right across the belt. Only when I got off the face and somebody grabbed me, not too politely, did I realise there was what was known as a dreaded 'top weight' on: a major rock subsidence which can squash a coal face flat – in spite of props, timbers and bars – in a matter of minutes. This was the only top weight I experienced in more than two years underground, and I was too naive to know its implications.

I was a coal face borer for three months, itching to have a go with pick and shovel. I would be paid more, and there was always something degrading about being a borer; how much you were at people's beck and call, how the whole face could be at a standstill if you did not get your pipes blown out.

At last the great day came.

'No borers needed on Fives. You can have a go at a stint, Bob lad,' said the Deputy. Pleased as Punch, I swaggered off with my pick and heart-shaped shovel. I was going to be a collier at last.

My first stint was on Three's face, which had a certain notoriety. It had bad roof faults which made timbering and propping difficult and had slips where the coal cut narrowed out, and rock and coal had to be taken together. It was also the furthest face out – one had to walk one and a half miles uphill along a narrow low supply road to the face – it was also the hottest.

We used to walk to the face in our pit clothes. Trousers, jacket and, for some reason, waistcoat were always fashionable underground. But working gear comprised solely a pair of short cotton pants, heavy pit safety boots with metal toecaps, and fibre pit helmets. Although head lamps with the battery attached to the waist were becoming the fashion, we had only heavy, electric hand lamps, like miniature lighthouses. One man in six also carried an oil lamp for gas testing.

Working at the coal face on a stint was by far the hardest work I have ever experienced. We arrived at the coal face at six o'clock and I eventually cleared my stint with the help of a collier in the next stint by two o'clock. There was no stopping for lunchtime breaks – just an occasional swig at the water bottle and a terrible race of flashing shovels, flying coal, back-breaking putting up of metal bars with metal props which, if not put in properly, could fly out like catapults and maim you.

I was completely exhausted after my first shift. My friend, Albert, helped me on to the Paddy train and up in the lift cage. 'Stupid bugger,' he said. And this became my daily task. For sheer physical graft and endeavour I have never known its equal. It was hot, noisy, dusty, with smoke coming from shots being fired.

The work was always just a bit more than I could manage and Bill Whitely, in the next stint, very often had to help me out. It can't have pleased him because each stint was enough for any one man. At its easiest you got twelve tons of coal to shovel, push and lever on to the conveyor belt, but threequarters of your shift could be spent getting your coal down and into workable-sized lumps. Occasionally I would arrive and things were just as they should be – the coal had blown through to the back; this meant that all the loose coal (gumming) had been cleared out before the shot had fired. Some of my Bevin Boy friends on the previous shift knew my stint number and looked after me as best they could.

I was on a stint continually from June 1945 till December 1946. It was completely exhausting work, but had a particular satisfaction that I have never met elsewhere. Once you were finished, you were finished: the next day brought a fresh battle but each day brought a fresh achievement, and you left the battlefield and went to a world outside.

Some time in 1945 I had a letter from the Ministry of Labour giving me a number, inferring that I would be doing a full stint of National Service. I made no protest about our original agreement. It seemed only fair. Anticipating a discharge towards the end of 1947, I applied for admission to a teaching hospital in London.

I went down to London for an interview – the only professional collier they had considered. To my surprise, not long after I got back, I received a letter from the Dean saying that they were creating a number of places for ex-service men in January 1947; they had applied to the Ministry of Labour for my release, but had been turned down.

At the last Mineworkers' Union meeting I had been to, and knowing that I was applying for a hospital, the officials said, 'Don't you worry, Bob lad. As soon as they offer you a place in the hospital, we'll see you get your release.' I took my Dean's letter to the N.U.M. and on the 28th December 1946 I received a letter from the Ministry of Labour saying that I could go.

I did my last shift, and forty-eight hours later had started at the hospital as a medical student. But this was not to be the end of mining for me. It was in my blood.

In the long vacation of the summer of 1947, the Coal Board fixed me up with a pit in Nottingham – Rufford Colliery, near Mansfield. I stayed in a theatrical boarding house, missing Caroll Levis's Discoveries by one week. I was on the haulage for a week to acclimatise myself to underground conditions and then spent the next six weeks working on the coal face. I worked with a collier in the corner of the face where the coal was some distance from the belt and had to be thrown in two moves – the collier to me, and then me to the belt. I soon rediscovered a few muscles that I had forgotten, and collected a fine set of blisters.

After six weeks I came back fit and strong for the beginning of the rugby season. It was the most rigorous training I had ever done.

In 1949 I again went back to the pits in the long summer vacation, this time to Bolsover Colliery in Derbyshire.

At Bolsover I had a week in an eighteen-inch seam where they were heading out a new face. The face was so low that you either shovelled on your stomach or came off from the face and returned on your back. There was no room for your pelvis between the roof and the floor.

A week of this was plenty for me, but some men, particularly in the Durham coalfields, spent their lives working in these conditions.

I had thought at one time of doing industrial medicine, but found that I would have to spend most of my time checking first-aid boxes in pit canteens and doing routine medical inspections. General practice was the thing I was destined for.

One morning in my surgery at Thudrock a miner came in and asked if he could sign on as a temporary resident. There was something slightly familiar about his face, but his cap was pulled well down over his eyes. He didn't begin to fill in the temporary resident's form, but just stood, staring at the table.

'How can I help you?' I asked.

He pulled up his right trouser leg, and there was a round blue scar, plumb in the middle of his calf.

'Is it hurting?' I asked.

'No,' grunted the collier. 'I just wondered if I should sue the man who did it.'

He looked up, grinning. It was Albert Catts, one of the deputies at Dinnington Colliery, where I had spent my two years. I had given him that scar.

One day on the coal face, swinging away with my lightweight pick, I had not heard Albert come up behind me and had swung my pick straight into his leg. His language had finally completed my education.

It was marvellous to see him again, and we had a very beery evening at the Miners' Institute – a place I found difficult to get away from without drinking my weight in beer.

I was to be the medical officer at Thudrock Colliery for many years, and made many friends there. The good times I had with the colliers were balanced with the accidents that I had to deal with, but down the pit – that's life.

I I

The Nightmare

I was at Winchcombe on my half day off, doing some shopping, when the fire took place.

I arrived back in Tadchester to find the town stunned, and a pall of smoke still hanging over the school. People were walking about, stern faced, not talking, not smiling.

Three ten-year-olds at the large secondary school had broken into the senior laboratory during the lunch hour to make some stink bombs – or so their friends said. Whatever they had done, they had started some conflagration which had trapped them, and all three had been burnt to death.

It was just frightful, and nobody could bear to think about it. All three families were patients of Steve Maxwell's so, thank God, I wasn't the one to have to go round and do the comforting.

I could think of no one better than Steve, with his kindly presence and gentle ways, to be with them and help them cope with this awful situation.

These were the times when Steve was at his best. There was a saintliness about him. He was painstaking, unselfish in what he did. A bachelor, his life was medicine and his patients were his children.

I slept badly that night, thinking of this terrible tragedy, and worrying about how the families would have to cope and live with it.

There was a very small surgery the next morning. For once people were not thinking much about themselves – they were more concerned with the tragedy that had fallen on the community.

I was surprised to get a call from the police midway through the morning, asking me if I would go down to the mortuary. They thought they would need me there, they said.

I was led into the mortuary by a red-eyed constable, who was nervous, apprehensive, and ill at ease.

'The mothers have to identify the bodies,' he said. 'We thought that they ought to have a doctor with them.'

Normally the police would have sufficed, but it was just all too much for this particular constable. Oh God, I thought. Am I going to be able to bear all this?

I looked through the glass into the waiting room and could see the three mothers waiting patiently to undergo this ghastly ordeal. Two of them I knew slightly, the other I hadn't seen before. All three sat with their heads bowed, not talking; perhaps unaware of, or not having come to terms with, this horrific situation.

'Would you like to go in on your own for a bit first?' said the constable.

He opened the door, and then shut it behind me. He certainly didn't want to go in there again.

In the room were four trestle tables, over three of which were stretched white sheets, silhouetting the small bodies that they covered. I lifted each sheet and looked at the charred remains of what were, yesterday, happy, playing children. It was awful. The tears were running down my cheeks. How was I going to face this?

I dried my eyes, composed myself, went back to the door and said, 'Perhaps the first mother would like to come in.'

Fortunately there had been some reasonable degree of identification from the clothes, and I was not, I hoped, going to have to expose these mothers to the sight of three destroyed children.

The first woman came in. She was the one I didn't know. It

was ghastly. I just couldn't relate to being there. She was ashen, trembling and nervous, clasping her hands tightly round the strap of her handbag.

I shut the door behind her. I said, 'My dear, there's only you and me here. There is no need for you to see your child if you don't want to. I am quite prepared to vouch that you have seen her.'

'No,' said the woman. 'I must see my little Emma. It would have been her eleventh birthday tomorrow.' As she said this the tears started to course down her face.

I walked over to the table on which we thought were the remains of her daughter, and lifted back the sheet.

'Oh God! No!' she cried.

I caught her just before she fell to the floor.

I covered the remains of her child with a sheet. I put my arms round her, and she clasped me, then after a few minutes, composed herself.

She stood up, wiped her eyes, said, 'Thank you, doctor,' and let herself out of the room.

I just had to sit down. I called the policeman and said, 'Have you a cigarette?' He didn't come through the door but handed me a packet, and I smoked a cigarette before I could face the ordeal of the second mother.

Both the other two mothers in turn, as they came through the door, clung to me – I knew them slightly. Both were frightened to look at these terrible white mounds that confronted them. In each case I again said, as I had with the first, that I would swear that they had identified their child. There was no need for them to look if they didn't want to. But both insisted they should have a last look at what once had been their happy child. I had to support both of them in turn with my arm.

It seemed to go on for ever.

The last mother, having had to wait for the first two to finish their inspection, collapsed completely and we had to call an ambulance to take her home.

For some reason it was the mothers who had come to do this

worst of all jobs, not the fathers. Perhaps children are closer to their mothers, or mothers closer to their children. I knew two of the fathers and they were fine men, neither of whom would shirk their responsibilities.

God, how do people stand these situations? How could I advise them what to do in this sort of catastrophe? I would not have been able to cope if it had been a child of mine. What right had I to advise and tell them what to do, or try and give them some trite word of comfort?

Perhaps the situation makes the man. I don't know. I only hoped that I would never ever have to be tested in circumstances like these myself.

The morning had been a nightmare. I somehow managed, tight lipped, to get myself out of the building after I had seen the mothers away. I got into my car in a daze and drove a couple of miles out of the town.

I parked in a lay-by, put my head on my knees, and wept.

12

Miracles and Malingerers

In my early days in practice I became very much aware of how much people's personalities affected both their chance of recovery and speed of recovery. Patients who were determined to die, most often did. I had read of primitive tribesmen turning their faces to the wall and dying. I hadn't believed before that it could happen in what we call our civilised society, but it undoubtedly did.

I had Tadchester patients who made up their minds to die and then died, for no other reason than that they did not want to live.

I saw some miracles for which I had no explanation. Joyce Taylor, the wife of Jack Taylor, one of the local outfitters, developed an abdominal pain and a lump in her stomach. Henry opened her up and found she was riddled with cancer. It was quite inoperable. He stitched her up again, not having interfered at all, and after a stormy passage she got over her operation.

She was an intelligent woman who demanded to know the score. Had she got a cancer? Was it operable, and how long had she to live? She had plans to make.

When people asked me whether they were going to die I nearly always said no: this was the answer they were looking for. I found by experience that if you told patients that they had not long to live or that they had some incurable disease, this shortened the time they would have had with us. There were some people like Joyce Taylor who defied all the odds.

She planned out her six months and carried on quite normally. The six months spread into seven, then to eight, then it was a year since her operation. Henry used to see her from time to time and found the lump in her stomach was gradually disappearing. For no accountable reason, Joyce Taylor was still going on quite happily sixteen years after she had been told she had six months to live.

Morry Loudson was a rough diamond who kept a scrap yard down at the back of the railway station. Although he ostensibly made his money from collecting old metal, he was into every fiddle that was going. I am sure a few stolen cars went his way, as did a few rustled cattle and any deer that were unwise enough to stray within ten miles of Tadchester.

He came to the surgery to see Jack Hart with swollen legs and a swelling of the lower abdomen. He was investigated at the hospital and eventually had an exploratory operation, when it was found that he had a rare tumour of the inner muscles of the back. This type of cancer was inoperable, would not respond to drugs, and was insensitive to X-rays. He, again, was told the full score. He sold his scrap yard and decided that he would end his days in the happy oblivion of alcohol.

He became grossly swollen from the waist down and could hardly walk. It was difficult to say if it were just his swollen legs that were limiting his walking as he always had a shipload of booze on board. One day he was found drunk and unconscious at the side of the road and had to be brought into hospital, have his head stitched, and be kept under observation for a few days.

He was given some drugs to get rid of the excess fluid in his legs, was deprived of alcohol for a week and, with a reduction of his swelling, he began to look more like a human being. He cheerfully discharged himself after seven days and then, like Mrs Taylor, suddenly began to get better. After two years, with no money left from the sale of his scrap yard, he took on a job as a brickie's mate with one of the local builders and, as far as

I know, never looked back – except to make absolutely sure that the pub doors were firmly shut.

'Blessed are the meek for they shall inherit the earth' was certainly sometimes true about patients. If a patient in the hospital was a pleasant, likeable person who got on well with the nursing staff and caused as little trouble as possible, then the nursing staff were all over him and would go much more out of their way to help him than they would a loud, demanding patient who always knew his rights.

Sister Doherty, the sister in charge of the men's ward at the hospital, was like the angel of death. If she saw a patient and did not think much of him, his number was up. He would rarely last more than two or three weeks. I was never sure whether she was a discerning diagnostician, unaware of the powerful primitive instinct that she had in her or whether she was such a grim, forbidding person that if she decided somebody was going to die, nobody dared contradict her.

One of the most unforgettable cases that I saw in my early days was that of a young, soft-spoken farm labourer who came in with extensive gas gangrene of his leg. He had cut his knee a couple of weeks before while pitching manure and then came into hospital, desperately ill, with this bloated, smelly leg that crackled when you touched it, and with swelling ominously going up into the lower abdomen.

He didn't complain. He stoically received any treatment that was given him. The whole hospital loved him and willed him to get better. The chances were that, at best, he would lose his leg, and at worst, he would die, with the second of the two much more likely.

I never remember the hospital so geared into action. Jack and I shared the giving of the anaesthetic as we were having to pump blood and various other substances into his veins. Henry operated, with Steve assisting him.

'If I take the leg off,' said Henry, 'it is still not going to help. It has extended to the abdomen. We will just have to keep cutting.'

The enemies of gas gangrene are fresh air and blood. The organism that causes it lives only in dead tissue where there is no oxygen. It spreads by poisoning and killing the surrounding tissues and extends progressively as it creates the surroundings which it likes best.

We had eight hours in the theatre the first night, with Henry patiently cutting each pocket of dead tissue; cutting it away, encouraging bleeding, with the ever patient Steve swabbing and pulling retractors. The four of us, with the theatre staff, worked right on through the night. The theatre porters (who could well have gone home) stayed on just in case they could be of any use and proved invaluable, rushing further supplies of transfusion fluids and making themselves generally useful.

I had never experienced such a will to fight for a man's life being shared by a whole hospital. Every patient and nurse in the place knew about him. They all enquired how he was getting on. People forgot their own troubles and their own illnesses. This man's life suddenly became the focal point of the hospital. Nobody was going to spare himself or herself.

Eventually, at six in the morning, Henry said, 'This is all we can do for now. If I have cut the abdomen clear we will have the leg off later, and he will stand a chance.'

We took over Henry's practice duties that day so he could remain with the boy all the time but by two o'clock in the afternoon we were all back in the theatre again. The leg had improved but the gangrene was beginning to spread further across the abdominal wall. Henry continued to cut dead tissue, to explore, to clean, to swab. Steve held the fort in the practice on his own while Jack and I fought to keep this young man alive, not only from this deadly organism that was attacking him but from the terrible mutilation that Henry was having to inflict in order to try and stop the disease taking him over.

Four times more in the next three days we went to theatre with the boy semi-conscious all the time and his life hanging on a thread. But on the fourth day he began to improve, and he continued to improve. The whole hospital lit up – he was going to make it.

He had another three or four troublesome weeks in hospital and had twice to go back to the theatre. But he survived.

He kept his leg – a terribly scarred leg – but, what was much more important, he kept his life.

Six months later I saw him hobble into Outpatients, still with his gentle, pleasant smile, with no other scars from this terrible ordeal other than the knife marks on his leg. He would not be able to work on a farm any more but there were other jobs he would be able to do, and I felt that he owed his life to himself. It was his own gentle, unassuming personality which created this tremendous spirit in the hospital to get him better.

I had not appreciated before what a powerful effect the real concern of people for each other could have on their chance of survival. Stoicism was a different quality. There were some tough old men in Tadchester – hard as nails. You would see them walking about in winter without jackets – just a shirt, boots, no socks – particularly the miners from Thudrock Colliery. While I was shivering in my overcoat they seemed oblivious to the elements.

The National Health Service, whose advantages I feel always outweigh its disadvantages, offers what is called the Domiciliary Consultation Scheme. This enables me to call a specialist from the hospital (provided I can get him to come) to see patients in their own homes. This saves the patients having to trek up to the hospital feeling unwell, or sometimes from having to be admitted to hospital.

One of the physicians from Winchcombe Hospital, my old friend John Bowler, was always happy to come. John was a delightful man in his early forties. He pretended he was a frustrated general practitioner, and enjoyed entering people's homes and seeing patients in their own surroundings rather than giving brief impersonal examinations in Outpatients.

If I was worried, John would come. He got a small fee from the Health Service for his visit, but the fee was small enough to discourage many of his colleagues from rendering the same service.

The difficult people to get out on domiciliary consultations were the surgeons. Surgeons are always wealthier than physicians because they make most of their money from private operations.

There was a private nursing home in Winchcombe and two of the surgeons spent more time operating there than they did at the hospital where they were supposed to spend at least nine-elevenths of their time.

They were able to remove an appendix for £50 or do a hernia for £100, but they were reluctant to travel fifteen miles to Tadchester to see someone in their own home for a fee of £7 which could not be paid in cash and would be taxable.

With Henry away on holiday one summer, I had to call in one of the Winchcombe surgeons. It was a real battle to get him over.

It was for old Tom Barnsley who lived Up the Hill. A retired collier, Tom had intense abdominal pain. He had had it for two or three weeks before I saw him, and adamantly refused to go to hospital. It was only when he had been vomiting for forty-eight hours and had obviously become obstructed that he agreed, reluctantly, for me to get a surgeon out to see him.

The senior surgeon from Winchcombe, who was also the duty

surgeon, eventually and with poor grace agreed to come. He arrived late, and parked his Bentley outside Tom's terraced house. He examined Tom without talking to him and without even removing his overcoat.

'Yes,' he said to me, in a high nasal voice, 'we will have to operate on this man. If I do an incision here' – pointing to Tom's abdomen – 'and cut across here' – drawing with his finger tip a line from Tom's ribs to his navel – 'I should be able to resect this blockage. It sounds like an appendix adhesion to me, but I must get cutting as soon as I can. Get him over straight away.'

Tom, who had a dignity of his own, did not blanch while the dismemberment of his body was under discussion. As the surgeon turned to go, Tom, quite seriously and meaning every word, said, 'Could I make a request, sir?'

'What is it, my man?' said the surgeon, turning impatiently to him.

'I realise you are going to do all this cutting up of my stomach,' said Tom. 'Would it be possible for me to have some sort of anaesthetic?'

The surgeon stamped out of the room without answering him. Only I had realised the genuineness of the question.

'Don't you worry, Tom,' I said. 'We will see that it doesn't hurt. I will make sure that you're fast asleep before he starts.'

'Thank you, sir,' said Tom. 'Maybe in my young days I could perhaps have put up with it, but I am getting on a bit now and it might be more than I could manage without something to deaden the pain.'

I loved Tom at that moment. I knew who I'd take with me on a tiger hunt if I had to choose between Tom and the surgeon.

Alas, all my patients were not stoical. They were outnumbered by at least ten to one by the non-stoical or even minus-stoical.

A great non-stoical was George Barrow. For some time I had been suspicious of him and felt he was getting the better of me.

He used to come periodically to the surgery with, 'It's my chest again, Doc.' He produced a most convincing cough which, he said, prevented him sleeping nights. Work, he said, was quite impossible.

I would say, 'Is there anything else?' and wait for his stock reply which was, 'Yes, my stomach's bad too, Doc. I think it's the phlegm that gets on it.'

I would listen to his chest, but could find nothing. I had him X-rayed a couple of times, and the films were always clear. In spite of this he was still able to convince me of the sincerity of his story. He would be off work for three or four weeks, and then come back with a martyred expression on his face and say, 'I've still got the cough a bit, Doc, but I have to get back to work.'

I found him out eventually, one day after he had reported sick. I happened to call out into the country, at a cottage where

Jack Tomlinson – a schoolmaster – had a smallholding. Jack was repairing a shed roof to make it waterproof for the winter. And there was George Barrow working away in his overalls.

'What's the matter, George?' I said. 'I thought you were off sick.'

'I thought I would give Mr Tomlinson a hand,' he said. 'You know – until I find my feet again.'

'I'll give you a hand, George – back to work,' I said, and signed him off on the spot.

Jack then told me the story. There were a lot of run-down cottages about. Whenever one needed doing up, George – who was a man of many parts – would have a few days off sick to help restore it. He was an expert cottage restorer and was in great demand.

I was never sure whether the people whom he helped with their restorations knew that he was off sick or not. Jack obviously knew. He said that at one time George was even going to suggest to me that I came in on a percentage; that if I put him off sick while he was repairing somebody's cottage, I could have a percentage of his National Health Service money.

This time he had said to Jack, 'That friend of yours, Doc Clifford, he's a fine doctor. I went into the surgery and sat down, he took one look at me and said, "Mr Barrow, you have got the broncho-bloody-itis. You are not fit to work." So if I can't go to work, while I've time on my hands, I had better give you a hand with the cottage.'

I thought I had stopped George's tricks until one day he came into the surgery smiling, and said, 'I wonder if I could have a sick note, doctor.'

'What's the trouble, George? Chest again?'

'No, it's my hernia, doctor – it's giving me trouble.'

I looked back through George's records and found that he had had his hernia for fourteen years.

I said, 'It's a bit late in the day to come.'

'It's giving me pain, doctor, I can't work with it.'

'Very well then,' I said. 'We will fix you up to have it

operated on at the hospital. Dr Johnson is in the surgery – we'll make arrangements now.'

George's face fell a mile.

I visited him on my hospital rounds, but then I lost track of him until, about four months later, I saw him whitewashing another dilapidated cottage out in the country.

'How long have you been back at work, George?' I said.

'I'm not really back,' he said. 'This hernia, you know, never really settled down after the operation and Dr Hart said he didn't think I was quite fit to return yet, so I thought I would fill in a bit of the time painting.'

George grinned, and I tried not to. But I couldn't help smiling. We both knew he had won.

Little Miss Shepherd walked briskly into the surgery. She was a bright, twinkling seventy-five-year-old whom I saw very little of in the surgery. She lived about five miles out from Tadchester, away from the coast, in a woody area called Hart's Woodlands. She was one of those uncomplaining patients who were over-grateful for any small service you did for them. My one visit to her home to treat a very severe bronchitis was rewarded by a bottle of her specially made sloe gin being sent to the surgery for me.

Her complaint this particular morning was that she had slipped and bruised her hip. Could she have something to rub on it?

I examined her hip carefully, and tried its full range of movements. My pulling her about caused her very little pain so I prescribed some anti-inflammatory tablets and gave her some oil of wintergreen to rub in. I had learnt that Tadchester patients loved warm and smelly ointments. It was all part of the cure.

I saw her a couple of times more in the town on market day. She got a lift in with a neighbour and sat in the Pannier Market with assorted vegetables, dressed chickens, home-made chutneys and jams for sale.

I was surprised, two months after her first visit, to have her limp into the surgery, not so brisk this time, and obviously in a lot of pain.

'I am afraid my hip is getting worse, doctor,' she said. 'Do you think I've got arthritis?'

Her hip was painful on movement and I noticed that the foot of the affected side was turned out, as opposed to her good leg where the toe pointed firmly forward.

'We'd better have it X-rayed, Miss Shepherd,' I said. 'We will see just what is going on in this hip of yours.'

I got her X-rayed that morning and went to see the wet X-ray plates with the radiographer. I was appalled at what I saw. The whole of the head of the left femur had crumbled. I had missed an impacted fracture of the neck of the femur. I had heard that people could crack their hip bones and walk about on them for months, but had never seen it happen before.

Poor Miss Shepherd.

We sent her across to Winchcombe Hospital where her hip was pinned. Happily, two weeks later I saw her in Pannier Market. There was a little bit of a limp when she walked over to me, but she was as cheerful and bright as ever.

'Thank you so much for all your help, doctor. They have stuck me together again and I am fine. There are one or two little things I am sending round for you. I am so grateful.'

I cringed. This was all for a misdiagnosis on my part.

Back at the surgery were two bottles of sloe gin, a couple of chickens and a basket of assorted, scrubbed, and neatly tied vegetables.

From then on anybody who had hip pain was going to be X-rayed.

A woman holidaymaker of forty-two had slipped on a rug at home and had been given aspirin by her own doctor. When she came to me her hip was aching more because she had been swimming. She also had the foot of the affected side pointing out a bit, so I had her X-rayed: again, I found an impacted fractured neck of the femur.

She had to be sent to Winchcombe and on my half day I

went over, very pleased with myself and my brilliant diagnosis, looking forward to thanks and gratitude, especially as I was making an effort on my half day to visit this person who was far from home. Instead of gratitude I got blistering abuse for having spoilt her holiday. I was dumbfounded.

When I told my tale of woe to Steve, he smiled.

'In general practice, Bob,' he said, 'you will find that you get a lot of praise where you don't deserve it, you will get a lot of abuse when you don't deserve it. But on balance we get far more praise than we do deserve. You just have to take the rough with the smooth.'

13

Birth of a Doctor

One of the reasons I had been invited to join the Tadchester
practice was that I had an additional qualification in midwifery
– D.R.C.O.G. (Diploma of the Royal College of Obstetrics and
Gynaecology).

Steve Maxwell was wanting to give up midwifery: he felt he
had done his share. Henry, who somehow combined surgery and
general practice, was making grunting noises about cutting down
a bit in the area because his operating sessions were going to be
increased.

I had done a year's residence in midwifery and gynaecology
in London. I had also had a long-lasting and serious affair with
Brenda Collins, one of the midwives there. The affair didn't
increase my medical knowledge vastly, but it did teach me a lot
in other directions.

I had got as far as taking Brenda home to meet my mother
when she decided that one of my colleagues, who was going to
specialise and was better breeched than I, was better husband
material than just a potential general practitioner.

It was after the end of our affair that I took the position
of Senior House Officer at Winchcombe General Hospital. From
there I had gone to Tadchester armed with all the latest
midwifery knowledge and techniques. I had been used to
working with a back-up team of nurses, house surgeons,

anaesthetists, and hospital theatre facilities. I had actually done three Caesareans on my own. When I say 'on my own', the obstetrical registrar assisted me throughout and held my hand.

I felt equal to any childbirth emergency that Tadchester might provide and preened myself on the fact that my three partners were looking to me as the specialist.

We were very badly off for midwifery facilities at Tadchester. There were no maternity beds at the hospital. A couple of miles down the road, however, was an old nursing home where the National Health Service allowed us to confine twelve patients a month. St Mary's, the nursing home, did have running water, electricity, and a resident nursing staff, but when I looked round for anaesthetic machines and the instruments and apparatus I had been used to working with, the others just laughed at me.

'You are on your own here, Bob,' said Henry. 'You pack everything in your bag: needles, stitching material, forceps – the lot.'

'What about anaesthetics?' I asked.

'Oh,' said Henry, 'one of us will come and put a drop of chloroform on for you. You will notice there is a bottle in your bag.'

My heart sank. There were no transfusion sets, no blood, no oxygen, and none of the special apparatus for reviving the newborn.

The only hospital midwifery beds were at Winchcombe, and totalled just fifteen. They had to serve an area covering a fifty-mile radius. All my partners considered it a failure to send a pregnant mother into hospital. They filled me with horrific stories of swinging on forceps and removing afterbirths from patients lying in feather beds. It all sounded terrible.

During my first delivery at St Mary's, which I was doing myself with the aid of a part-time nursing auxiliary, the Matron's spaniel wandered into the labour room, lifted his leg against the table on which I was conducting the confinement, then made a dignified exit.

This was country midwifery?

Somehow we never had any real trouble at the nursing home although we had several scares. Winchcombe Hospital, with all its sterile, aseptic wards and nurseries, was always getting infections and cross-infections. At St Mary's, in spite of the primitive conditions, we never ever had an infection.

Once a fortnight we ran an ante-natal clinic at the surgery. Nurse Plank, our district midwife, helped us with the documentation and assessment of each case. Nurse Plank was one of the pillars of the community. She was in her late fifties when I first met her. I expounded on the latest techniques and what we should be doing now rather than the old-fashioned ways they were using. She just nodded as if she had seen this all before. She was, in fact, an absolute gem. The mothers loved her.

In her thirty years in midwifery she had delivered some thousands of babies, most often on her own. She was calm and unruffled during deliveries, and never turned a hair when there were great haemorrhages or when things were not going right. I found to my chagrin that, in spite of my up-to-date knowledge, she knew a great deal more midwifery than I did. I came to rely on her so much that if I knew she wasn't going to be at a confinement, I used to get cold feet, hoping that she would be back before the baby arrived.

The vast majority of women in the town had their babies at home. To get into the nursing home you either had to have something wrong with you or be without some of the basic necessities, such as toilet facilities, electricity, and running water.

I did conduct confinements in front of open, blazing fires, with only a few small glimmering candles to supplement the firelight. On average I had three home confinements a fortnight. They could last for anything from ten minutes to two or three days, with me nipping backwards and forwards, wondering whether I should interfere and whether I was just giving up if I sent a mother into Winchcombe.

It was one of the most satisfying aspects of general practice. Pregnant mothers are one of the few groups of patients with whom a doctor can look forward to a happy ending.

Confinements I enjoyed most took place in the outlying farms that surrounded Tadchester Down the Hill. It was so much part of natural farm life – just like lambing time. Nobody would look for complications, and they very rarely occurred.

We would be sitting in the bedroom during the confinement – Nurse Plank, usually the farmer himself, and the mother in labour. There was a relaxed air about it all. The deliveries always seemed to be relatively straightforward. After delivery, they were all delighted to get some new healthy stock. There would then be a cup of tea and scones all round, or sometimes cider or sloe gin, the local speciality.

One farm confinement I didn't enjoy was when the mother began to haemorrhage profusely after the delivery of her baby. I pumped in the maximum dose of every drug I had that might have reduced the haemorrhage, blocked the bed, reassured her as best I could, sent for an ambulance and sat with her, watching her get paler and paler as the flow kept on.

At that time there were no midwifery flying squads. The ambulance always took at least an hour to arrive, and if it were summer with holiday traffic about, it might take one and a half hours to get the patient into Winchcombe Hospital.

In those days we didn't carry transfusion sets or plasma, and I had to sit there watching this young mother slowly fade away in front of me. There was nothing more I could do.

The mother must have caught some of my concern. She asked anxiously, 'Can't you do anything, doctor? I'm not going to die, am I?'

But it had gone past the time when I could reassure her. And she sensed my anxiety.

After what seemed years, the ambulance arrived with two hearty, cheery ambulance men. I have never been so pleased to see anyone. They had transfusion equipment aboard, and I was able to get a plasma transfusion going. Slowly her pulse, which had dropped to a flicker, began to pick up and was easier to detect. She had lost so much blood that the bleeding had stopped. I thought she couldn't have had any left.

I rode with her in the ambulance to Winchcombe, checking her pulse every few minutes. She just held her own till she got there. She was whisked to the theatre and in twenty-four hours she was sitting up, bright as a button, feeding her baby as if nothing had happened.

I felt at least fifty years older.

* * *

I still had not taken part in any real heroics, the sort my partners bragged about, where they had had to put their feet on the bed to help them pull out babies with forceps. But my turn was to come ...

I had one young expectant mother at home who obviously had a huge baby, and who was not making progress. Although I had helped babies out with the small forceps we used for low forceps deliveries, I had never put on the great big ones or had to use any degree of force to help with the extraction.

I had to ring Jack and Henry to come and give me a hand – we were obviously in for a picnic!

Jack anaesthetised her by dropping a mixture of chloroform and ether on to the gauze mask over her face. Henry prowled round, grunting and unconcerned, while I, the specialist in midwifery, sweated. I was going to have to prove my worth.

'Hurry up,' said Henry, taking his ear from the woman's stomach. 'The little one in here is beginning to get fed up with it all.'

I managed with great difficulty to get the forceps applied to the baby's head. This was a huge one.

Then I started to pull.

'Hang on!' cried Henry. 'I'll hold her arms.'

So, with Henry pulling one end and me pulling the other, the poor woman was almost being dragged in two. Nothing was moving. I just didn't know what to do.

'Come on, lad,' said Henry. 'If you don't do something we're going to lose the baby.'

I put my foot on the end of the bed for leverage, and pulled. The baby's head came through, tearing the tissues round it. The bed, which was raised off the ground by four wooden blocks, came off its blocks and crashed down on the floor, making a terrible din.

The poor girl's husband, who was sitting below, came running up the stairs at the noise, wondering what could have possibly happened to his precious one, and was just in time to see the rest of the baby appear.

It was a bit blue in the face but after a few slaps by Nurse Plank it breathed and cried lustily.

I had joined the club!

'Well done, lad,' said Henry. 'She would have lost this baby if it hadn't been for you.'

This particular mother and father actually lived some miles away and were not our patients. They had come to Tadchester to have the baby in the home of the girl's parents. So, after the delivery, I lost sight of them.

Some years later I saw them again, walking through the town. The little boy must have been about seven years old. I noticed that he had a walking iron on one leg. It looked as if he had had polio.

'What has happened to the young man?' I asked. 'Did he have an accident?'

'No,' said his mother, blushing. 'They say it was the result of a birth injury.'

I remembered how proud I had been, leg levered against the bed, tugging for all I was worth to get this baby out. But, of course, if I hadn't he would never have seen the light of day.

Happily, as obstetric care has improved and more hospital beds have become available at Winchcombe, we don't nowadays have to deal with this heroic type of midwifery.

My next forceps birth was quite different.

I had been called by Jack to give him a hand at a gypsy encampment. They had sent for him after labour had started – she had never been seen by a doctor during her pregnancy.

She was obviously in obstructed labour. Jack said he would rather give the anaesthetic and let me try and pull the baby out.

It was a tiny caravan with a bunk bed. There was only just room for me to work at the foot of the bunk. Applying the forceps was not too difficult, and after just a moderate traction pull the baby came out quite easily and all was well.

I cut and tied the cord. We had not been able to locate Nurse Plank for this one. I picked up the baby to put it in its cot before I tackled the afterbirth. Forgetting the confining strictures of this particular labour room, I took one step backwards and fell through the half-door of the caravan down the steps, clutching the newly born baby to my chest. I had never felt so foolish, and the baby didn't like it at all.

There were six or seven Romany men sitting round the camp fire watching all this with interest. As I tried to get up from the grass, at the same time trying with one hand to keep the baby clear of the ground, one of them strolled over.

'You a bit new to this game then, doctor?' he said, grinning. I could have kicked him.

People seemed to have babies in all sorts of places. Although the vast majority did have them at home or in the nursing home, I was called to deliver in buses, taxis, garden sheds, fields, and once in the back row of the cinema.

But I wasn't always there in time.

One morning I had a call at two o'clock. I heard a gruff voice say, 'Is that you, doctor?'

'Yes,' I said.

'This is George Hobbs here, of ...' went on the gruff voice, and he named a hamlet ten miles from our surgery.

'Would you come and see the wife straight away?' he asked.

'What's the matter?' I enquired.

'I think it's a maternity case,' said George.

'What do you mean?' I said. 'You *think* it's a maternity case. Has your wife seen a doctor recently?'

'No,' he said. 'I think it's a maternity case.'

'Is your wife in labour?'

'I think it's a maternity case,' said the gruff voice, and George rang off.

I got out of bed, grumbling, and set out to find the cottage of Mr Hobbs. This was a new type of call. I had never had anybody before call me in any doubt about whether the case was a maternity one or not. They were usually sure it was – or, like Mrs Richards whom we shall meet later, certain it wasn't.

I eventually found the isolated cottage, and a six-foot, thickset, unshaven farm labourer let me in. He was completely unconcerned. We walked through a downstairs room where there was one chair, one table, and no other furniture.

'Come upstairs, doctor,' he said.

I followed him upstairs. In one of the filthiest rooms imaginable was a bed in which a woman was lying with a baby between her knees, with the cord still attached to the afterbirth, and the afterbirth still firmly in the mother.

On one side of the room were four children lying asleep on the floor with a pile of blankets on top of them. Through another door I saw a further room with three more children sleeping, covered with a similar pile, either lying directly on the boards or with a thin mattress beneath them. Even at this time I occasionally found conditions like these.

I immediately set to and completed the delivery of this now lustily bellowing child. It was completely hopeless to try and nurse it at home, so I sent the husband off for Nurse Plank. Ringing up from the nearest farm I fixed up to get the wife into St Mary's for a few days. There was not even a towel, a sheet or anything to dry your hands on in the house. I had to tie off the umbilical cord with a piece of string I found on the floor.

I also rang the Welfare Officer, who said she would come and give a hand with the other children. I then came back to the house, where the children were beginning to stir. There seemed to be no food in the place but nobody seemed terribly bothered.

Nurse Plank followed me in and started to bustle around. By this time it was seven o'clock in the morning. I refused the tea proffered in a dirty cup, and wearily packed my bag and made for the car.

George leant over the gate watching me go. He seemed dirtier and more unshaven than ever. He grinned, or rather leered, knowingly at me. 'Well, doctor, I were right – it were a maternity case, weren't it?'

Every doctor I meet thinks that his patients, and particularly his midwifery patients, are stranger and more complicated than any other doctor's patients, and can hardly wait for someone to finish telling him of their own particular hazard or mishap before he is telling them his own. Though I would not claim that the complications, sites of delivery and excitement of my own cases are second to none, I feel that I could hold my own in most company.

I have had patients who have sworn they did not know they were pregnant or in actual fact didn't know they were.

Mrs Richards, a woman aged about fifty, who lived near the cemetery, sent for me one night with 'ramping' abdominal pain. On examining her stomach I noticed how large her abdomen was and that she was having regular rhythmic contractions.

'When did you last see a doctor?' I asked.

'Oh,' she said, 'I saw Dr Hart when I started the change of life eight months ago. I was putting on weight and he gave me some slimming tablets, but now I've got this terrible "ramping" abdominal pain.'

I said, 'I hate to break this news to you so suddenly, but you are going to have a baby in a few minutes.'

'Oh, good God!' she said. 'It can't be true. My daughter expects a baby any time now. I could be a grandmother by the end of the week!'

... Nellie Block could have been described as the young man's comforter in the village. Poor Nellie was a bit simple, and quite unable to refuse the approaches of any man. Over a few years I delivered her of five children of mixed fatherhood.

Her last pregnancy was a bit different. Usually she turned up at about six months with a swollen tummy and an ashamed look. This time she came in with the right statistics but looking triumphant. As she entered I said, 'Well, Nellie, where do you want to have the baby this time?'

'Oh, there's no baby,' said Nellie with a superior air.

'Are you sure?' I said.

'Oh, yes,' she answered, and fished out a dirty piece of paper from her pocket. 'The young man that I'm going with has given me a certificate to say that he's only got one kidney, so I know I'm not pregnant.'

Events were to prove her wrong.

By far my most enjoyable confinement ever was when Lily Biggs, the wife of Jack Biggs, the local scoutmaster, had her baby at home.

Jack was a great handyman and had rigged up every conceivable aid to make the whole process easier. This included a television set at the foot of the bed.

The climax of her labour came just as Freddy Trueman was beginning to get through the Australian wickets in the England versus Australia Test on the television. I couldn't see the screen properly from the side of the bed so Lily said, 'You could hop up next to me, doctor, until the pains come.' So, between pains, I lay on the bed with Lily admiring the batting. During pains, I crouched at the bedside, encouraging her.

'Come on, Lily,' I said. 'Let's see if you can push this new young wolf cub out before the end of the next over.'

Young Freddy Statham Biggs grew up to be a great credit to his parents.

14

Come Quickly, Doctor

I was called out of my morning surgery by Henry Johnson, my surgical partner, to come and give a patient a whiff for a difficult obstetric case. This was a typical unruffle-able Henry. A 'whiff' meant anaesthetising patients with chloroform, which had hazards of its own and meant something had really gone wrong.

I leapt into my car with the anaesthetic bag and shot up to the council houses that covered the top of Up the Hill. I was some time finding number 47, which was the number Henry had given me, as it lay back from the main row of houses in a cul-de-sac.

Obstetric emergencies in the home were always nightmares to me. I had been so used to all the comforts of a maternity hospital. I shuddered at the primitive way things were carried out in the country.

I entered a rather dimly lit room to find a pale, thin woman with an absolutely huge abdomen lying on a bed in obstructed labour, with Nurse Plank fussing round, and Henry, in a detached way, looking out of the window.

Henry was one of the tallest, thinnest men one could wish to meet. When clothed and gowned, with his rubber gloves on, he looked like some willowy ghost.

'Got a breech here, Bob lad,' said Henry. (This meant that the baby was arriving feet first instead of head first.)

This would have worried me to death, but not Henry: nothing seemed to perturb him.

'If you could put her to sleep, I will bring the legs out.'

Henry was marvellous practically, but I was never quite too sure about his ante-natalling. Normally one would have expected to have found that the baby was in a breech position before this stage.

I got out my cotton mask and chloroform bottle, added some ether to the chloroform and started to pour drops on to the mask over the patient's face. I hated giving anaesthetics like this. One had so little control. There were no aspirators to suck out mucus from the patient's mouth, or proper airways. The patient often went into spasm trying to breathe these noxious vapours and there was no preparation for anaesthesia. For all I knew this patient had a stomach full of plum pudding and might vomit any minute. But there was no alternative other than to get on with it.

As soon as she was well under, Henry, who was so capable with his hands, delivered the legs of the baby which were holding things up, and in a couple of minutes the baby, who looked about six pounds in weight, emerged.

'Well done, Bob,' said Henry, 'you can bring her round now.'

I looked at the huge stomach that I had noticed when I first came in; its shape did not seem to have altered at all.

'Are you sure we have finished, Henry?' I asked.

'Oh, the afterbirth will come all right,' said Henry. 'Get her round.'

'I am not thinking about the afterbirth,' I replied. 'She still looks as if she is loaded.'

Henry reluctantly put his hand to her abdomen.

'Oh my God, lad,' he exclaimed, 'you are right. There is another one here.'

In a short while, after a few more efforts, a second baby appeared head first this time. The patient had had five previous pregnancies and once this baby's head had seen the light of day, it shot out to join its five-minute-old brother.

'Bless my soul,' said Henry. 'Twins! That is a surprise.'

I looked down at the abdomen. It had decreased in size, but not as much as I expected.

'You wouldn't like to check once more would you, Henry?' I said. 'It still looks a bit big to me.'

'Rubbish, lad,' he said. 'She is bound to have a big placenta to feed these two. Give her some ergometrine.'

He casually palpated the stomach and started to take his gown and gloves off.

As ordered, I gave the injection of ergometrine. This is a drug that makes the womb contract. It reduces the chances of bleeding after childbirth, and although it can trap the placenta in the womb, it is often expeditious in helping it come early.

A minute after I had given the injection, the woman gave a cry, and I looked down just in time to see a third baby being literally shot out of her. The ergometrine was certainly working.

'I thought there might be three,' said Henry. 'Tip him up a bit, he looks a bit blue.'

I wondered what effect the catapulting into the world of this little fellow would have on his future psyche. Nurse Plank, who was almost as unruffled as Henry usually, lost her cool. She now had three babies to bathe, and had to find somewhere to put them, as well as enough linen, nappies, nightdresses, etc., for this treble chance. She scurried about, muttering under her breath.

'Thank you, Dr Johnson,' said the patient as soon as she came round from the anaesthetic, 'you were marvellous.'

'Don't think about it,' said Henry. 'The place to have your baby is at home, no need to go into hospital.'

It was all so incredible, I thought I might have a nervous breakdown. Somehow all the catastrophes that might have happened had not; we had three healthy babies where we thought there was only going to be one, and we had a healthy mum. It always seemed to be this way with Henry; he did not appear to worry that things might go wrong, and somehow things never did go wrong.

The mother of the new three was a Mrs Sarah Wilkins – she now had eight children to contend with. She was a thin, emaciated woman, who seemed to carry all the cares of the world. As she explained to me, when some time later I had to visit one of the triplets, 'It's when my husband gets his gym shoes on, we always click.' She went on eventually to finish up with eleven children.

Mrs Wilkins was not the only one of my patients who was given bizarre signs that her cohabital duties were about to start. Mrs Merchant (married for the second time at the age of sixty, having been widowed in her mid-fifties) married a retired farmer from Canada who had returned to his mother country to spend his last days in Tadchester. When she married him she believed him to be sixty-five – in actual fact, he was eighty-seven. His physical prowess, however, was in no way related to his age. Mrs Merchant said that she had had to put up with more physical demands for her services from her new octogenarian husband than she had had from her first husband (a sailor) some forty years previously. 'Doctor,' she said, 'he is just wearing me down. If he starts drumming his fingers on the table after supper, it is always a sign that I am for it. Couldn't you put something in his medicine?'

Returning my anaesthetic bag to the surgery after the triplets, I was pounced on by Gladys. 'An urgent call, Doctor Bob. There is a child in a caravan at Sanford-on-Sea who has difficulty in breathing.'

I grabbed my case and made what speed I could to the permanent caravan park at Sanford-on-Sea.

All the caravans had different names. There was no system of numbers and 'Kosicot', the name I had been given, could have been any of the one hundred or so scattered round the field. It was winter and only a handful were occupied at this time of the year.

I drove round for a while, trying to pick up the name, then got out of the car to ask more specific directions from a caravan that looked as if it might be occupied.

As soon as I had turned my engine off and climbed out of my car, I got my directions. From three caravans down from the one I stopped at I could hear what sounded like the barking of a seal.

I rushed to the caravan. There were two young, anguished parents walking up and down, wringing their hands, and a baby girl of about eighteen months lying on her back in a bunk, blue in the face, fighting for her breath, and with each intake of breath making this harsh barking sound that I had heard when I got out of my car.

'Doctor,' said the mother, 'she was well until an hour ago. Do something. Please do something. She can't breathe. I think she is dying.'

The baby looked awful. I hated croup. It is caused by swelling usually due to infection of the lining of the main breathing tube (trachea). Sometimes the only remedy is a tracheotomy, which means opening a hole in the throat and inserting a tube. I had never had to do one and hoped that this wasn't going to be my first.

I picked up the baby, cleaned the mucus from her mouth with my handkerchief, and cradled her in my arms, with her head down.

'Put the kettle on!' I snapped. 'I want some steam.'

The mother, all thumbs, seemed to take an age to fill the kettle and put it on the gas. I waited impatiently for the kettle to boil, cradling the baby. Her breathing had become a little easier since I had been holding her. I think babies do pick up their parents' apprehension and someone from outside, appearing to be in control of the situation (although I am sure I felt as nervous as the parents), somehow gets through and reassures them.

When the kettle had boiled I told the mother to pour the water into a bowl. Then, arranging a towel round the baby's head with the bottom end encompassing the edges of the bowl, I held the baby's face over the rising steam.

In minutes the noisy breathing had stopped. In ten minutes the baby was happily sucking a bottle as if nothing had happened. Mother, father and I sat drinking a cup of tea made with the remnants of the water from the boiling kettle.

'It's wonderful,' said the mother. 'I thought we were going to lose her.'

I went over the baby's chest with my stethoscope and prescribed an antibiotic. I instructed the parents on how to give steam if the baby's breathing became difficult again, and suggested that they keep the atmosphere in the caravan steamy for a while by keeping the kettle on the boil.

I hated dealing with croup. This time steam had worked like magic, but it wasn't always so effective, and I had had nightmare ambulance journeys to hospitals with gasping babies, wondering whether we would get there in time. Somehow we always had.

After my second emergency I returned to the surgery a bit weary. I knew there was bound to be a third before the day was finished ... and I did not have long to wait. I had just seen one patient, a very smartly dressed Swedish lady visitor who came in as a temporary resident. The style and cut of her clothes gave the impression that money was not a problem, but she had filled in a card to have free treatment on the National Health Service, and had waited her turn with the other patients. She sat down in my surgery and in the most delightful broken English said, 'Doctorh, I passed zis snake zis morning; do you sink zere iz zomething in ze food?'

She opened her handbag and pulled out a Kleenex tissue which contained one of the largest roundworms I had ever seen. It certainly did not match her coat and gloves, and was certainly not her style.

I explained to her that this sort of infestation could be picked up from unwashed vegetables and prescribed some pills and medicine that would rid her of any possible relatives of this offending beast. I wondered which snake in the grass had managed to infect her thus.

She was followed in by Gladys with the inevitable third

143

emergency. 'Sorry about this, Doctor Bob, but someone has collapsed in the barber's shop Up the Hill. There are not any more details.'

I shot across the bridge to the barber's shop, to find the 'emergency' fully recovered and having the other half of his shave. He had been nicked on his left cheek and fainted when he saw some of the blood on the barber's towel. He had been tipped back in the chair until he came round, then the operation had continued. Everybody was apologetic, but I was happier when an emergency turned out to be a false alarm rather than a terrible medical drama.

Charlie Lang ran the barber's shop Up the Hill with his son Nigel. Charlie was one of the old school – a tough lad, taciturn, a real Tadchesterian, with about five hundred relatives in the town. He knew exactly what he wanted and what he was going to do. He liked his pint, and had obviously been a bit of a lad because, in his history, there was a report from his Merchant Navy discharge record that he had had venereal disease. This left some scarring in his waterworks which held up the flow of urine from the body. This meant that, to have a clear flow of water, every so often Charlie would have to go up to the hospital and Henry would have to dilate his water passage with some probes.

When you are dealing with waterworks in men you have to be very careful that you do not introduce infection when you are dilating the urethra (tube) in the penis, or passing a catheter (drainage tube). Any slackness in technique could result in the introduction of infection, causing cystitis and inflammation of the kidneys.

Charlie had to attend regularly every three months for dilatation. He did this for many years and then, suddenly, stopped. We thought he had gone away as neither of my partners nor I were called on for our professional services. Reluctantly, however, one day he did have to come to the surgery. He had a tooth abscess, didn't want to go to the dentist, and wanted something to clear it up. One of his characteristics of dress was that he wore an old, battered, brown bowler. I felt sure that he even wore it in bed because he had it on every time that I saw him; he wore it when he was cutting hair, and he was wearing it as he showed me a mouthful of dirty, septic fangs in the surgery.

'How are the waterworks, Charlie?' I asked. 'I see you haven't been up for some time.'

'Oh, I manage it myself now,' said Charlie. 'I couldn't be bothered to keep on going to the hospital.'

This puzzled me. I could see no way that Charlie could manage it himself.

'How do you mean,' I said, 'you manage it yourself?'

'Well,' he said, 'I went to an auction sale at a doctor's house in Winchcombe and bought myself a catheter. Whenever I want to pass water, I just slip it in my Jimmy Riddler.'

'And,' I said, 'what happens if you want to go now?'

'Well, I would just pop into the toilet and slip it in,' said Charlie. As he said this, he removed his hat and there, inside the hat, wrapped in a dirty piece of newspaper, was an old gum elastic male catheter.

Charlie had obviously watched Henry Johnson carefully when he was passing his probes. He must have been catheterising himself several times a day with a dirty, infected catheter and somehow the Good Lord (and it could only have been Him) was keeping the germs away.

'Does your water ever burn, or do you feel unwell?' I asked Charlie.

'I did a bit at first,' said Charlie, 'but I have no bother now.'

With that he picked up his prescription and made a hurried exit.

I talked to Henry and Steve about it the next morning at coffee. I could not believe that anybody could defy all our careful aseptic techniques and get away with it. But Steve said Charlie wasn't the only person administering his own therapy; there were one or two other elderly patients who catheterised themselves and there existed, in fact, fancy silver catheters that one could carry in one's breast pocket like a fountain pen and slip in and turn on the tap as required.

Henry said he thought these old boys must initially have had infections but were too tough to worry about them, eventually building up a resistance to the germs they pushed in several times a day, becoming immune to them.

I never thought much of Charlie's hair-dressing salon – it was dirty, scruffy and very unhygienic. I resolved that under no circumstances would I ever go there for a haircut, for who knows, I might not be as resistant to Charlie's germs as he was.

15

Thick Ears in the Sunset

One of the things that I had not taken into account in coming into general practice was the extra-medical or para-medical duties that would be thrust upon me.

The Forward Medical Aid Unit was the first group to obtain my services. Being flattered that people should approach me for my extra-medical skills, I foolishly took on virtually everything I was asked to do. I became Hon. Medical Officer to the Tadchester Boxing Club. This meant attending all their boxing tournaments, listening to small boys' chests and pronouncing them fit to go into the ring and half batter each other to death.

I had boxed as a medical student and shared the apprehension of these white-faced little boys as they kept running off to spend pennies before climbing into the ring to do damage to their friends.

My own boxing career was a very chequered one. I had, in all, about a dozen fights for the hospital, and at one stage was awarded the name of 'One-Round Clifford'. I was usually in the ring for just one round – but this did not mean that I destroyed all my opponents. In actual fact it worked out at exactly 50–50. Half the time I destroyed them. The other half, they destroyed *me*.

When I first went to the hospital, having come straight out

of the coal mines, I thought that with long and hard practice I might eventually make the hospital boxing team. Two weeks later, I was boxing against a dentist from Guy's Hospital at the Coldstream Hall before a crowd of several thousand.

It was a painful experience. My opponent was almost as unskilled as I was, and although we could attack, our defences were terrible and we solidly battered each other over three rounds before he was given the verdict on points.

My opponent later achieved fame in the Press at the time of his society marriage. The day before his wedding he had had to have an anti-typhoid injection, and he arrived at the church feeling very poorly. When he joined his bride at the altar steps he was visibly swaying on his feet. The vicar, a teetotaller and a leading man in the Temperance Society, immediately assumed he was drunk, and refused to marry them.

I found that the only qualification you had to have to get into a university or hospital boxing team was to be foolish enough to be willing to take part. So few people take up the sport that even Oxford and Cambridge Universities sometimes are unable to turn out a full team. It is the quickest way of achieving notoriety in sport and the easiest way of winning a Blue.

We had in our hospital the undefeated flyweight champion of London University for five years. He achieved this without a scar as, in fact, he didn't have a single fight. There was nobody of his weight who would volunteer to fight. Only once was he in danger of losing his title. This occurred when we found he was two pounds above his weight limit. We forcibly administered castor oil and in a matter of three hours had him back on the scale below the limit and earning two points for our team.

My second fight was against Oxford University at Oxford. There was some sort of matching of people of equal ability and I was to fight their secretary who was, according to them, about my standard. When I got there I found that (a) he was a welterweight – I was a lightweight – and (b) I had had one, unsuccessful, fight and he was in the Ceylon Olympic Games Team.

I lasted just under a minute in the ring before they carried me out.

My friend George Potts, who had come along for the ride, agreed to fight – only because his opponent in the match was a young man who had never fought for the university before. What they had not mentioned was that he was the Royal Navy's middleweight champion, George lasted either three seconds more or three seconds less than I did. We both claimed the longer distance.

Against Cambridge University I somehow got my thumb in the eye of my opponent in the first round. I watched the eye swelling during the round and prayed that it would close completely in the interval.

My prayers were answered. The referee came over and stopped the fight. I had my first victory. It was thumbs up for me!

On one occasion I found myself in Dublin fighting against Trinity College for Guy's Hospital, who had borrowed me for the occasion. It was Trinity Week and I had a glimpse of what university life used to be like before the war. The sports meetings, rowing, beautifully dressed ladies, and men in frock coats and top hats. There was even a picture of me in the Irish *Tatler* being rubbed down by Mat Wells before my excursion in the ring.

I climbed into the ring with some trepidation but after a few seconds realised my opponent was even worse than I was. I got him into a corner to finish him off, then suddenly I found myself in a dark room, with water pouring down from above on top of me. I couldn't understand it. Was I dead? What had happened?

This is a gap in my life that I have never remembered. My friends told me afterwards that, as I pinned my opponent in the corner, he shut his eyes and swung in despair with his right, nearly knocking my head off. I vomited for two days after this brief encounter and my closest friends say I have never been the same since. The saddest part was that the great steaks that I brought back from Ireland (the meat ration in England was then about a shilling's worth a week) I was too ill to eat.

It was at this same match that the Guy's heavyweight lost his unbeaten record. He was a huge brute of a man, and the small Irishman who had been put up as a sacrifice stood trembling in his corner before the bell rang for the first round. As his elephantine opponent approached him, he ducked to miss the oncoming blow. The Guy's champion caught his arm in the ropes, dislocated his shoulder, and the Irishman was declared the winner.

Of my twelve fights I won six and lost six. I have a prize possession – a cutting from the *Evening Standard* describing one match against Cambridge University where it said the most punishing bout of the evening was when R. D. Clifford fought G. D. Lockhurst. It went on, 'R. D. Clifford, after surviving severe punishment, rallied in the last round, to beat his opponent on points.'

This just about sums up my boxing career.

Giving a helping hand to sports I did not mind. I did enjoy them and felt that I had to put something back into the games I had taken part in. The activities that I found most tedious were lecturing to groups like the Women's Institute, Church-women's Guild, and Mothers' Union. Tadchester seemed to have at least one of these organisations on every street corner. I became an expert at judging fancy egg and comical potato competitions and had to make judgments on flower arrangements, needlework, cake baking and a dozen other such competitive indoor sports.

One disastrous day I foolishly agreed to judge a baby show. I started the day thinking that my decision would have to be made between the six babies that were presented to me, and spent over an hour deliberating. It was then that I discovered there were another eighty-three to see.

My judging went on for hours, past feeding times, resulting in expeditions being sent out for powdered milk and an exhibition of mass breast feeding in the reserved tent. This resulted in the curate having a nervous breakdown – hearing so many babies crying, he walked into the tent to see if he could help and, for the first time, really found himself in the bosom of his parish.

My final judgment caused joy only to the parents of the baby who was awarded the prize. Three of our patients with babies transferred to another practice and I made several mortal enemies. How could anybody possibly think any baby was better than their Jane or Susie?

My main love as a student was for rugby and I soon became a Vice-President of the Tadchester Club. If I had not played rugby there was little doubt that I would have qualified a year earlier. Rugby was an extremely important part of medical school life: in fact, when I first went to my hospital they unashamedly offered rugby scholarships to boys who had the necessary academic qualifications. This meant that when we played against other hospitals in the Hospital Rugby Cup Competition we were always greeted with cries of 'Come on the Professionals!'

I tried one or two games when I first got to Tadchester but general practice was very demanding and I could never train or get properly fit. When I came out of one game with a painful knee, Steve pointed out very gently that a one-legged G.P couldn't climb the stairs of country cottages as well as a two-legged one. I got the message and, reluctantly, hung up my boots.

I became an ardent supporter of Tadchester and was conscientious in my duties as Vice-President, helping behind the bar, attending committee meetings, and acting as Hon. Medical Officer.

Tadchester were a good little team, with ambitions to break into the big time. The only really first-class side they played were Winchcombe, the local giants. Winchcombe really played a different league. They had everything to lose in this particular match, whereas Tadchester had everything to gain.

Eric and I watched a lot of rugby together, and we muffled up on a cold, wet day to watch this annual battle.

The Winchcombe men seemed twice the size of the Tadchester players. Two threequarters with foreign-sounding names I had never seen play before. It was a good spirited game but Tadchester were completely overwhelmed, losing by thirty points to three. The main architects of the victory were these two foreign threequarter backs who turned out to be French and were working for a year with a Winchcombe electronics firm. They ran and handled so much better than their British counterparts. Drinking in the bar afterwards with them took me back to my own rugby-playing days as a student and my first French rugby tour.

*　　*　　*

I shall never forget the first French tour. And I shall never know how I survived it.

We had assembled at Victoria Station the day after a very hectic Cornish tour. I had played three games in three days, the third game being abandoned in the middle of a torrential downpour.

We were to go by boat and train to Paris, stay the night, then by train to three games in the Rhône Valley area, train back, a further night in Paris, and then back to London. It sounded marvellous.

We were going to play some of the best French rugby sides. I had some doubts when I looked at the motley collection of people who were arriving to make up our party. For some years the hospital side, with half a dozen current Internationals in their strength, had been one of the best in the country. By some means these stars had just qualified, making the Cornish tour their rugby swan song. From now on the hospital was going to have to rely on lesser mortals like myself.

Combined with the withdrawal of these experts, the French tour itself coincided with the hospital inter-medical examinations. It had been impossible to raise the invited twenty-eight players from the first three hospital sides, so the vacant places had been offered to people who either deserved to go, like the jovial captain of the 'B' XV and the rugby club social secretary, who never really played rugger but arranged the rugby dance on which the finances of the club depended, or some who didn't deserve to go, like the beer-drinking layabouts from the extra 'B' and 'C' XVs.

There was one character I couldn't place. I assumed he must be somebody's relative. He claimed to be a trainee manager from the Savoy Hotel. How he came to be included in the party I never knew.

We had a calm crossing but one or two of us, still feeling the effects of the Cornish tour and the rained-off game, felt sick.

We arrived in Paris with a night to spend before we went on to Lyons. We had been told that tea, coffee and old suits fetched good money on the black market in Paris, and we came well supplied.

We had a hectic night in Paris, first selling our tea, coffee and suits on the black market, then on to pubs, night clubs and, eventually, the Bal Tabarin, from which we were finally evicted at four in the morning. There was little money left when we staggered to the train at 8.00 a.m. the next day.

We had an interminable journey to Lyons, where we entertained the French by wandering down the corridors, singing the filthiest English rugby songs.

From Lyons we got another train to Tarrare which was the venue of our first match. Arriving in the middle of the afternoon we were whisked straight from the station to a champagne reception at the hotel, and then to a dance that went on until three in the morning.

I had learnt two French expressions before I came away – *Tu a des yeux bleu*, and *Voulez-vous me donner le plaisir de cette danse?* Both served me well during the evening.

We were the first English side to play in this town since the war and they really did their utmost with their hospitality.

We were playing a local representative side the next day, and everyone assured us how easy the game would be. This was the equivalent of a first division soccer team playing one of the southern league teams.

The morning following the dance we had a Civic Reception. This was followed by a tour round a silk factory where we were wined and given champagne until an hour before we played.

We played on a sun-baked pitch in the evening against this local enthusiastic side. We had not put our strongest team out, although I am not sure what our strongest side was. If we had played all twenty-eight of the party I doubt if we would have been as good as the normal team.

There was an impressive start. The French kicked off a high, long kick for their forwards to follow up. Our full-back from the 'B' XV, the most sociable chap, stood there like a rock waiting for the ball to be caught and safely disposed of. If he had been able to wear his glasses there is no doubt he would have been a first-class rugby player, but without them he was as blind as a bat. As he stood there, arms open, firmly fixed to the spot, the ball bounced about twenty yards behind him for a French forward to pick up and score a try.

The French, realising then that we had a blind full-back, exploited this for the rest of the game, and we lost 12–11. They all nudged each other, and said, 'These English, they keep their cards up their sleeves, wait till they play the big game tomorrow.'

Again that night they treated us to another dance and champagne party. The captain of the 'B' XV, celebrating his success, sat at a table quietly on his own with thirteen empty champagne bottles in front of him.

The next day we played Lyons at the Lyons Olympic Stadium. Before we started, a band of white-gauntleted gendarmes paraded round the pitch playing martial music. An immaculately turned-out French team trotted on to the pitch to the cheers of the crowd, and then we trotted on. It was the first time

I had really taken a look at us as a group from, shall I say, an aesthetic point of view.

These were the days of clothes rationing and rugby clothes were the last thing for which coupons could be spared. We had played in Cornwall, our kit was still wet and filthy from the mud bath of the rained-off game. Nobody had cleaned his boots, we were caked with mud and really looked scruffy.

I was better dressed than most. As a spare shirt, I had taken an old green one (we were playing in blue) that my grandfather used to wear for playing soccer; it had a lace-up neck, to which I had laboriously sewn a semi-stiff white collar. ·

We lost to Lyons 25–3, but we weren't disgraced. They were pleased to win, and it was quite a good game. It was always best on a French tour to just lose each game; you then can be assured that the social side of the tour will be marvellous.

We had a dinner in Lyons with the Lyons Club, which ended by our captain doing a naked Zulu dance on the table during which he accidentally poured a glass of wine over the head of Madame la France who had been the head of the Resistance for that area and was the guest of honour at the dinner. She must have wondered what she had achieved with all her heroic efforts.

She had helped to oust the Germans from her country only to have them replaced by a naked South African pouring wine over her.

We had a scrum down in the hall against Lyons, during which all the glasses were broken – then, drunken and singing, we were led to the bus that was to take us to our next destination.

The bus journey was a nightmare. We had been playing rugby and drinking and travelling now for as long as I could remember. People were being sick, people were fighting, people were being obstreperous.

We arrived at our next destination where we were being boarded out with families, instead of being put up at an hotel. There were rows of cars and pleasantly smiling French people to welcome their allies and liberators. The only way to describe our leaving the bus was to say that we spewed forth from it. Immediately the waiting hosts saw us, half the cars disappeared without taking anybody. Several of the boys lay down in the Square, quite unconscious, and half of us, instead of sleeping the night in comfortable French beds, eventually finished up roughing it in a barn.

The next day, after one more Civic Reception, we were to play this town which had a very good side. The previous year the hospital side, with all stars present, had come back from 17–10 at half time to win 20–17.

We were in pretty desperate straits by now and agreed to play the substitutes. This was about as un-British as one could be in rugby, but our substitutes served us manfully. Every one of the whole twenty-eight of the party came on to the pitch at least once. Our waiter, and I am quite certain he wasn't the trainee manager from the Savoy Hotel, came on five different times in five different positions. The captain of the 'B' XV played in the forwards, where he didn't have to see the ball and played much better. The social secretary came on as wing forward in the first half. After tripping everybody up and getting in everybody's way, he committed his worst crime at half time: throwing his orange peel off the field, he hit our only mobile threequarters in the eye with it and disabled him for the rest of the game.

We had all taken Dexadrine tablets to help liven our performance but at half-time we were down 30–0. The French, remembering the come-back of the year before, waited hopefully. After half-time our Dexadrine began to work. We were up. We stormed the French and we got seven points in as many minutes – a dropped goal and a try. This was the stuff they wanted.

The crowd was on its feet, but in a few minutes our Dexadrine had worn off and we were eventually beaten 45–7. We played so badly that this town didn't invite another English team for five years. There was the inevitable Ball and Banquet after the game. By some booking mistake we had no seats back to Paris the next day, and we had to stand, crammed between the toilets of the two coaches. Another night in Paris and then home.

I was flat out in bed for four days when I got back. When I did finally emerge and ring round my fellow players to see how many were still alive, I found that I was the first to surface.

I went on several French tours after this, but never again to the Rhône Valley – they wouldn't look at us.

I never forgot my first French rugby tour – and obviously the French never forgot the English.

16

Swings and Roundabouts

My duties in the general practice at Tadchester were to be split
up between the ordinary general practice duties such as surgery,
visits, midwifery, etc., and my work at the hospital. There I
doubled with Jack Hart for emergency anaesthetics, and kept a
day to day check on patients of mine in the wards, some of
whom might be under the overall care of one of the consultant
physicians from Winchcombe.

Most of the Winchcombe consultants held outpatients' clinics
at Tadchester Hospital and would come over and see cases that
we were worried about or felt needed extra special care.

In addition to this I had to take a rota share of doing
casualty duty at the hospital.

The casualty sister at Tadchester Hospital was a short, plump,
fierce Welsh lady called, strangely, Sister Jones. What she lacked
in height, she made up for in ferocity: many a Saturday night
drunk was completely sobered by the sharpness of her tongue.
She was a hard, unsympathetic, efficient woman who kept herself
very much as a private person, someone you could work with for
a hundred years without ever knowing. She was very uncommunicative, but completely reliable. If she called you
for an emergency, you went. There was no argument. Her
assessment of priorities was always exact, and while a doctor
was treating patients she would stand over him, fussing, trying to

tell him what to do as if she knew much better – which, of course, she probably did.

I was terrified of her, would ask her nodded approval before I would start any procedure, and never had the strength or courage to contradict her. She had a succession of staff and pupil nurses to work for her, whose lives were made a complete misery. They were nagged from dawn till dusk and were never given a word of praise when they did something well or efficiently.

When Sister Jones was not on duty the atmosphere in Casualty was quite different. The nurses smiled, got on with the jobs capably and did not seem to need this all-seeing dragon to keep them up to the mark.

The main casualty duties were in the summer when Tadchester was jammed with holidaymakers. There were two holiday camps at Sanford-on-Sea, numerous caravan sites tucked away Down the Hill, one or two small hotels in the town and larger ones dotted in a radius of five or six miles around, some with their own beaches reached by pathways through the cliffs.

Holiday visitors had special categories of ailments of their own. There would be a whole string of patients suffering from jellyfish stings when the tide had thrown up more than its usual collection of these transparent menaces.

Food poisoning was always rife in the summer and on one occasion both the two holiday camps were stricken, with everybody wanting to sue the management, holidays ruined, and terrified chefs fleeing the area for their lives.

The fairground that came in late August, as well as producing numerous cuts and scrapes from people falling on and off the roundabouts or sticking legs outside dodgem cars, usually produced a crop of venereal diseases, and a couple of weeks after it had gone one or two shamefaced young men and ladies of the town would come and present themselves with pain in a very embarrassing area.

Occasionally some of the fairground attendants would come for treatment for this same condition. It was obviously a hazard of their trade, and there was no doubt that the young ladies of Tadchester were fascinated by these romantic men of the road and could easily be induced to give their all.

The Casualty Department seemed to be filled from the beginning of the summer to its end: the slackening of casualties was an indication that winter would soon be upon us.

We were unable to persuade holidaymakers to visit the surgery for their wasp stings, sun burns, and small cuts and grazes – hospital was the place for them.

This was unfortunate for us, as one of the strange anomalies of the National Health Service was that we did our casualty work as a charity. We reaped the vast sum of £10 per year for all our hours of sweated labour, whereas if these hordes of patients had visited us at the surgery they would have been signed up as temporary residents under our G.P. umbrella and we would have received £1 for every one we saw.

We had a continual battle with the Authorities to make it financially right for our service, but there was no loophole by which they could pay us, even if they had been willing. Rather than give up this service, we soldiered on for next to nothing.

Henry philosophised: 'It's swings and roundabouts; we must keep on with it;' whereas Jack said, 'Swings have always made me sick; I would much rather stick to roundabouts.' Swings or roundabouts, casualty duty gave a division of work which for me was invaluable, for I was able to continue to practise many of the skills that I had learnt as a house surgeon.

There were tedious procedures like getting beads out of noses, foreign bodies out of eyes and ears, but there were rewards like splinting broken arms and legs and a great deal of stitching up of wounds. Stitching practice was very important: one's skill as a seamstress determined whether a badly cut face would be scarred or not.

The summer holiday traffic brought innumerable road accidents. During the season we had to battle to save the lives of dozens of horribly maimed and mutilated victims, in situations where all our skill and resources had to be used just to keep life flickering until more sophisticated equipment could be brought into play. Having to keep on our toes for these emergencies made better doctors of us all.

Sometimes we were called from Casualty to attend to accidents themselves. One I never forget was on the main road leading to Sanford-on-Sea where a family car, packed with mother, father and two children, with all the paraphernalia of food, blankets and stoves, had crashed head on with a young couple driving an MG sports car. The MG was a complete write-off, with the young couple both dead, with broken necks.

The scene in the family car was chaotic. Its older vintage had made it more robust than the sports car and it had not disintegrated in the same way on impact. When I arrived the father was struggling out of the front seat with blood pouring down his face, the two children screaming on the back seat, and the mother unconscious, with both legs trapped and bleeding under the compressed dashboard.

We managed to get both children out, one of whom had a broken leg. Borrowing a sledge hammer, I got into the back of the car and smashed open the door by the mother, applied tourniquets round both her legs and then, with the help of a crowbar, levered up the dashboard, dragged her out and into the waiting ambulance.

It was a night's lost sleep for all of us.

The mother had broken both legs and had suffered severe lacerations. Henry, Jack and I were in the theatre for two hours with her.

The husband and children had to wait for their treatment until we had patched up the mother. The husband had lacerations to the scalp and a broken arm. One child had a broken leg and the other a broken arm.

I imagined them setting off happily for their holiday, to have it destroyed in one blinding, flashing moment, the same moment that took the lives of the young couple, out for an evening's drive. Instead of a summer by the sea this family spent some weeks in Tadchester Hospital, the mother being transferred to

Winchcombe after a few days for more specialised orthopaedic treatment.

* * *

Like other branches of medicine in Tadchester, Casualty had its collection of curios.

One day I was called urgently because a holidaymaker had gone into labour in the Casualty Ward. When I got to the hospital she was stretched out on the small operating table in the casualty theatre with the baby's head just beginning to emerge.

The staff nurse – Sister was off duty – said this was a girl from Bristol who wasn't due for a month and had suddenly gone into labour. There was a fifteen-year-old youth standing nervously beside the screen in a corner of the room whom I assumed was her brother.

Looking at the emerging baby, I thought the girl must have been wrong about her dates: this baby certainly was not premature. It was a good eight-and-a-half pounder, and she had a fair old push to get it out.

There was something familiar about the girl's face but it did not register at the time. When the baby had been safely delivered and the umbilical cord tied, the staff nurse took the baby to be bathed while a student nurse and I waited for the afterbirth to come.

At this moment the girl on the table said, 'Can I go now, please?' and tried to get up. If we had not restrained her, she would have been up and out of the Casualty Department in a flash, with the cord trailing and the afterbirth still inside her.

We tried various manoeuvres to get the afterbirth, but after an hour it was firmly stuck. As she wasn't bleeding, I decided to send her to the obstetric unit at Winchcombe Hospital to have it dealt with.

We rang for an ambulance and packed her off. Just as she was about to leave, the fifteen-year-old-boy asked if he could go with her. I still assumed that he was her brother, so reluctantly gave my permission, and they were whisked away.

Next day I learnt the full story from the girl's mother, whom I knew quite well.

The girl's face *had* been familiar after all, and the fifteen-year-old boy was no brother: he was the baby's father. And this wasn't the first child they had had between them – it was the second. I remembered clearly an account of their first mating when, apparently, he was thirteen-and-a-half and she was fifteen-and-a-half, and he had got his way with her by offering her a bottle of ginger beer. Their union was blessed and subsequently adopted.

I asked the mother had she noticed that her daughter was pregnant, and she said no. Her daughter had worn a wide flared skirt with a high belt, and she had had no idea about the increased pounds and swelling tummy underneath, and in fact the girl had been working as a cleaner at the hospital a few weeks previously.

She decided to keep this baby rather than give it away like the first. The parents of both sides got together and decided, as there was strong or even duplicated evidence of a long and lasting relationship between these two young people, they should be given the opportunity to marry when the boy became sixteen.

'Not on your life,' said the girl. 'I wouldn't marry him for anything. We're only friends.'

* * *

I enjoyed my hospital work and got to know most of the staff well. Whenever some bright-eyed nurse took my fancy and I tried for a cuddle in the dark room of the X-ray department I was always put off with, 'You will have to wait for Christmas.'

Preparations for Christmas in the medical fraternity in Tadchester started in early November. There were draw tickets to be bought from the Sister of each ward of the hospital. They all vied with each other to have the best show and I had, as

163

early as October, been invited to carve the turkey on the children's ward on Christmas Day.

The hospital was only one of several medical institutions that were competing for our services over the festive season. St Mary's Maternity Home put their claim in. Steve looked after a home for mentally defective children. It was called a 'home'; in fact it was more like a hospital, with 150 patients, and although it was called 'for children' some of the inhabitants were in their seventies and eighties, having spent all their lives in institutional care. I enjoyed the odd occasions I had to visit the home. They were mostly mongols, who were friendly and affectionate and led happy, trouble-free lives, with other people doing all their worrying for them. They had an extremely high standard of care there and, whatever age, all remained children. It was like a house full of Peter Pans, with excitement when anything interrupted the routine, like trips to the seaside or holidays away.

High up Up the Hill was a small isolation hospital which, since the virtual disappearance of tuberculosis, was hardly ever used but had to keep a staff in case there was an outbreak of some virulent infectious disease. The staff there had more time than any to prepare for Christmas.

Last, but not least, there was the Old People's Home or Hospital. This was the old workhouse that had been converted into a home for the care of the aged and although a couple of wards there were full with people whose bodies were still alive but whose minds had died some time ago, most of the patients or residents were ambulant and Christmas was the highlight of their year. It was a time when relatives who tended to neglect them most often turned up and when relatives living away, coming home for Christmas, had their only opportunity of visiting Gran or Grandad.

As Christmas approached, my mantelpiece became filled with invitations to all these various hospital or near-hospital functions, and by mid-November I saw that I had every night booked from 21st December till 2nd January. They must have had a very good medical fixture secretary somewhere as none of the dates clashed.

It looked as if I was in for the most hectic Christmas ever. I had had a few hospital Christmases as a hospital resident, which had been hilarious, and all very drunken. I was obviously going to have to pace myself over this fortnight as there would no doubt be people requiring my medical services during this time, particularly if they had to follow the same party schedule as I did.

My first four pre-hospital parties were similar, in fact almost identical, as exactly the same people were at each party. They all wore exactly the same clothes at each function and apart from slight variations of drinks and eats, it would have been difficult to distinguish one party from another.

Eventually Christmas Eve arrived, with the traditional carol singing round the hospital. It looked most moving. The nurses wore their capes turned inside out so that the scarlet lining showed, and carried candles. An assembly of friends and hospital staff joined to swell the volume of carols as we did a circuit round the wards. This was the highlight of the year for the hospital pharmacist, as he walked round accompanying the singers on his piano accordion.

We must have totalled about seventy in number and, when in full voice, made all the hospital timbers rattle as we limbered up with our First Noel in the courtyard. It was all for the patients' benefit. However, because we tried to get as many patients home for Christmas as possible, there were only about a dozen patients left in the whole 150 beds. Most of these were pretty poorly, one or two in oxygen tents.

We set off trooping round the wards. It was a delightful and moving sight, with the lights turned down, illuminated Christmas trees in each ward, and the flickering of the nurses' candles silhouetting their white headgear. In the women's ward the two ladies in oxygen tents must have been very apprehensive of all the naked candle flames slipping past them. The two remaining ladies fit enough to breathe without artificial aid were so overcome by this moving scene that they sat up in bed with tears streaming down their faces.

We toured all the wards – women's medical, women's surgical, men's medical, men's surgical – and there was no doubt that the patients who were well enough to appreciate it absolutely loved it.

I was happy that they had managed to clear all patients out of the children's ward, which was up a flight of stairs. I thought that they might have been a bit overwhelmed by the noise because, as we got more confident with our carols, so our volume tended to increase. But tradition was tradition, and although there was nobody in the children's ward we solemnly, all seventy of us, walked up the stairs, circled the ward in full voice, and then walked down to be received by Matron with coffee, mince pies and Christmas cake.

Christmas had begun.

Christmas Day proved to be an absolute nightmare. Every department of the hospital vied for one's attention. Steve had warned me: 'You miss having a drink in one department of one hospital and you will be blacked for the whole of the year.'

The nurses in each ward dressed up the doctor who was to be their particular carver. I was to be Batman and had to struggle into some black tights, a red jersey and face mask. This was to be my costume for the day. A glance in the mirror showed me that since I had stopped playing rugby my waistline would have shamed Batman. The tightness of my tights showed to the world at large that I was fairly well endowed in one part of my muscular anatomy that they probably had not had a glimpse of before. I now knew how ballet dancers felt.

I started off on my pre-lunch tour of the hospital. Not only did it mean a drink in each department, but it meant embracing every nurse in every department. By the way some of them clung on I felt they were all trying to get rid of a year's inhibitions in a day.

I had a sherry on women's medical, a sherry on women's surgical, a sherry on men's medical, a sherry on men's surgical.

By now my mask was half covered with lipstick and my tights had begun to sag.

I had a sherry in dispensary, a sherry with the operating theatre staff, a sherry in Outpatients, and a sherry in Casualty.

I then staggered up to the children's ward and did my carving for the staff there. Two children had been admitted in the early morning, both with moderate burns, and were not at all interested in the riotous goings on.

I had finished my carving by one o'clock and then set out, with sherry coming out of my ears, to do my rounds of the other medical and semi-medical places. My tights were no protection from the bitterly cold weather and I received derisive cheers as I drove round the town in my Batman's outfit.

I had a sherry and a mince pie at St Mary's Maternity Home, I had a sherry at the Children's Home, I had a sherry at the Old People's Home and then, finally, my last duty sherry at the Isolation Hospital, who were offended that I wouldn't stay and have a second glass with them. 'Nobody spends any time here,' they grumbled.

By now it was half-past three in the afternoon, and I could hardly see to drive. I eventually made it to the Harts', where I was having Christmas dinner, got out of my Batman outfit into warm, respectable clothing, and set to work to remove the lipstick from my face.

I staggered downstairs. 'What will you have to drink?' said Jean Hart, smiling. 'I know you need something to pick you up.'

I groaned, sat in a chair, and fell fast asleep.

Fortunately the Harts had become adjusted to hospital Christmases and Christmas dinner was not until eight, by which time I had begun to come round from my over-indulgence.

The post-Christmas week was slightly different. This was the dancing week. There was the Tadchester Hospital Dance, the St Mary's Nursing Home Dance, the Old People's Home Dance, the Isolation Hospital Dance, and the Children's Home Dance. Most of them were related to raising some funds for one charity or another but, again, apart from a few guests who had come over from Winchcombe, the assembled company was exactly the same as it had been at the four cocktail parties the previous week.

During my first Christmas in Tadchester I came to realise that I had a strange facial characteristic that made me look as if I were a man who preferred whisky to any other drink. Even in the hospital wards where sherry was the proffered refreshment, there was always a wink from whoever was in charge and a, 'Don't worry, doctor, I saved a bit of the hard stuff for you.'

I had to fight to stick to the same type of beverage, as I actually preferred sherry to whisky, which I don't really like at all. The impression that I gave in the hospital was reflected in the gifts from my grateful patients. They had all been generous when I first came into practice. Christmas gave them a great opportunity to redouble their efforts. Although I was given a turkey, Christmas pudding, Christmas cake, sweets, and a couple of pheasants, the main bulk of my gifts were bottles of whisky, ranging from quarter, half and pint bottles to what must have been two-litre bottles. There was enough whisky in my flat to have happily bathed in it.

At every visit I made over the Christmas holiday there was usually a glass of whisky thrust into my hand, and to have refused it would have caused great offence. I would down it as quickly as I could, and be off, but of course I would go on to my next visit smelling of whisky. So, whatever drink there was about to be offered would be hastily exchanged for half a tumblerful of this terrible amber fluid.

This routine went on day after day and I had begun to lose track of time and place and found it terribly difficult to concentrate on my work.

It is indeed, a terrible physical affliction – to have the face of a whisky drinker!

The last engagement on the calendar was the Grand Ball on New Year's Eve. This was the Tadchester Hospital Ball, held in Tadchester Town Hall, and was different from the other hospital functions in that all the local civic dignitaries had been invited as well as most of the consultants and hospital management staff from Winchcombe Hospital.

It was a very good Ball, so I'm told. I was in such an alcoholic blur that I couldn't really remember what happened. Somehow I got through it without disgracing myself too much.

For some time afterwards, one or two ladies complimented me on excelling myself at the Ball. I had no idea what they were talking about, but as each finished her conversation with a knowing wink I had obviously been close to a few fates worse than death.

New Year's Eve was on Friday evening and, thank God, I was able to get to bed at three o'clock on the Saturday morning.

I knew I could not take much of this.

I fell sound asleep and woke up to find myself in the dark. I was puzzled because my watch showed it was six o'clock. I had to turn on the radio to discover that I had slept through till six p.m. Sunday.

I resolved, of course, never to take alcohol again.

By Monday morning I had begun to feel better, and went off to work with a good heart. The surgery was light, people were not yet well enough to come and see their doctors.

I set off to have a look at my patients in hospital, wondering what scenes of destruction would greet me there, but it was as if somebody had waved a magic wand. All the Christmas decorations had gone, the wards were full.

There was hustle and bustle. The familiarity of Christmas had disappeared. We were back at work again.

Christmas was over.

17

Friends and Neighbours

Among the inhabitants of Tadchester I found some great characters and made some very good friends. There were the young group that I went around with – Kevin and Janice, Frank and Primrose, Joe and Lee, and the ever-faithful Eric.

We fished, swam and supported the rugby club together, and spent some of our most delightful evenings Seine-net fishing. Our mishaps were perhaps the greatest part of the fun. Once, I remember, we fished all night and caught nothing. Only when we got back did we realise that there was a hole in the back of the net through which a medium-sized shark could have swum.

On one occasion we joined with another net and swept from both ends of the beach. It was a big tide and there seemed to be miles of sand to cross. Janice and Primrose were pulling our box of fish, which got heavier and heavier. We could see them occasionally in the darkness as we came out of the sea.

When we were walking back to the car Janice said, 'This sled is running easily now. You wouldn't think we had all that fish in it.'

A quick flash of the torch showed that they had been pulling the box on its side for the last half mile. We had to trek back looking for sledge marks, trying to pick out the fish that were beginning to blend into the beach. Frank, to whom fishing was almost a religion, said some unprintable words which certainly weren't religious..

My favourite Tadchester character was Old Bob Barker, who had the secondhand bookshop by the slipway at Sanford-on-Sea. He was in his eighties when I first met him, and was the gentlest and wisest man I ever remember.

For many years Old Bob had had a large bookshop in Tadchester, which became a meeting place for writers. He had a room at the back where he held small literary lunches, and he helped several famous authors take their first steps into the pages of public literature. When it all became a bit too much, he sold his big shop and had this small secondhand bookshop at the water's edge. He and his daughter would always take time and trouble in finding or searching through catalogues for books for customers. They charged very little for these services. Their enjoyment was in doing things for people, and they were happy just to make a reasonable living from their work. Book orders came from all over the world, and this rather shabby little shop and its gentle proprietor were quite famous.

I used to spend hours poring over the old books on the shelves. After some time I was invited to have tea with the great man himself and eventually a great friendship grew up between us. Although Old Bob was a non-smoker, he saw to it that in his desk there was always a box of my favourite cigars, with one ready for me when I joined him for our cup of tea. It became a ritual that I would sneak away for an hour a week with Old Bob. I would listen to his tales of the people of the area, the lords and ladies, the tradesmen, the craftsmen and other types of people who went to make up the community.

Between us we used to set the world aright and we both looked forward to this hour of stolen time each week. He used to be desperately disappointed if, for some reason, I failed to make it.

He was very conscious of his growing years and his frailty.

'All I want to do now, Bob,' he said, 'is to slip quietly away. I am tired and old and I have done my share of living. It would be nice just to float away one night.'

I wasn't Old Bob's doctor; he preferred me as a friend. Jack

Hart looked after him for many years and always coped with his medical requirements.

Jack found that Old Bob had some waterworks trouble and would need a prostatectomy. It was a great blow. Old Bob hated the thought of it – hospitals, operations, pain, strangers, and away from his beloved bookshop.

I went to see him for our tea and cigar a week before he went into hospital.

'You know,' he said, with a twinkle in his eye, 'I have kept on saying for so long how much I would like to slip peacefully away. Now there is a chance of it happening, I have suddenly remembered an awful lot of things I still want to do.'

He survived his operation and lived on for several more years. He had been the parish church organist for many years, had a great love of music and many friends in the music world. In his eighty-fifth year the BBC recorded him and presented him as a portrait character of the Somerset coast.

When he died, he left a gap that has never been filled. He was a wise counsellor, the gentlest of men, and the greatest of friends. Since he died, whenever something nice happens to me, I think that somehow, somewhere, Old Bob Barker has had a hand in it.

He inspired in me some yearnings to do some writing myself, and in his will left me a beautiful old bound volume of *Chamber's Book of Words*.

Two other elderly people I looked upon as friends were the two Miss Emmersons – Sophie and Elsie. They lived in a semi-detached house in Park Lane, separated from the river by the park, where they could watch the children playing on the swings and slides and keep a close eye on the Council gardener, as they more or less regarded the flower beds in the park as their property. They would say, 'Our dahlias are doing well,' or 'What do you think of our chrysanthemums?' and I would be meant to look, not round their tiny garden but across to the huge flower beds in the park.

Both had been brought up as ladies, but were now in reduced

circumstances. They lived in this little house on what must have been a small income compared with their earlier days. They described some of the houses they had lived and stayed in, the balls and banquets they had attended, and the young toffs who had sought their hand.

The contents of the house bore witness to their former glories. They had the most beautiful china and silver and some lovely old furniture. Although they did not now have the income to live in the style they had been used to, they kept their gentility and manners. We became, I thought, firm friends.

They were both frail and needed check-ups from time to time and were particularly plagued by winter coughs and colds. Sophie, the elder sister, was the more dominant one and twice the size of the bird-like Elsie.

This was a visit that I couldn't get away from without having a cup of tea, and a cup of tea was not just a cup sitting on your lap. If the doctor called it was served at a table from a silver teapot, with the best bone china, scones and home-made cake. I could rarely get away in an hour and they just wouldn't have understood it if I had tried to explain how many other people I had to see that day.

They preserved their standards and I admired them and looked forward to my visits. They didn't gossip, were not malicious, and they gave me an understanding of a gracious world that I knew nothing about.

One day Elsie complained that she had begun to get pain in her lower leg if she walked any distance. If she stopped walking, the pain would go, but as soon as she had walked a further distance it would come again. It meant that if she was out in Tadchester she had to stop after every few shops and pretend to be looking in the window.

I examined her leg and found it a bit cold. The pulses were difficult to feel. She obviously had poor arterial circulation of that limb.

'Well, doctor,' said Sophie, 'what is the matter with Elsie?'

'Miss Emmerson,' I said, 'she is suffering from a condition

called intermittent claudication. I will have to get her something to help her circulation.'

This was a day on which I was in a hurry, and didn't have time to explain it more carefully.

The next time they were ill they sent for my senior partner, Steve Maxwell. They had become such regulars of mine that I thought it was a mistake, but Gladys confirmed that they definitely wanted Dr Maxwell. I assumed that they must have thought I was on holiday, and when Steve came back I asked him how the leg was.

He said that there had been no mention of the leg. Miss Sophie had bronchitis. They had made no comment about my treatment or my visits to them.

I racked my brains to try and think of some way I might have offended or upset them. It always hurt me when patients changed from me to one of my partners. (I always seemed to understand it if one of my partners' patients came to me.) And the Emmersons changing really upset me – we had been such good friends.

The same pattern went on for several months. Steve was summoned whenever the sisters were ill; my services were never mentioned and I was never asked for.

One day Steve called me into his surgery, pretending to look grim but hardly able to stop himself laughing.

'I have had to see Miss Elsie Emmerson today,' he said. 'She is complaining of a pain in her leg on walking. I believe that is what you treated her for. What did you tell them was wrong?'

'I told them she obviously had poor arterial circulation and was suffering from intermittent claudication.'

Steve rocked back in his chair.

'Do you know what they *think* you said?'

'No,' I replied, puzzled.

'Intermittent fornication. Get out of that one!'

I realised that things between myself and the Emmersons would never be the same again. Steve tried to explain to them this medical term, but I was not to be forgiven for quite a while.

I think that my misheard diagnosis struck home deeply. Perhaps between the grand balls and banquets they had attended, escorted by the gentry, the toffs and Army officers – perhaps on some occasions, with the blinds drawn or in some secluded hotel – there had been a few moments of intermittent fornication. Perhaps poor Miss Elsie thought I had read her mind. She thought her past was catching up with her.

It was far too delicate a subject to try to explain the misunderstanding. So many people think that doctors are like God and that, simply by looking at their patients, they can tell exactly what they are thinking and what they have been doing. But if Miss Elsie only knew. To see her there in her flat-heeled shoes, her long black dress, sparse grey hair and row of pearls, barely making the journey round the room, the last thing I would ever accuse her of would be fornication, intermittent or otherwise.

But eventually I was forgiven. In Miss Sophie's will two years later – and it was a very meagre will – she had left me £50 for my services to herself and her sister. She had left Steve Maxwell nothing. I did wonder whether she thought this was hush money for me to keep this guilty secret safe.

One of the penalties of helping people recover from their illnesses was that, as a reward, I would be asked to dine with them. I would be asked in such a way that there was no possible chance of escape. Like, 'Can you name a night in the next two months that you will come and have a meal?'

Though I had sweated blood to get them better, the probability was that I did not like them very much (it always seemed to be so in this type of case). I now had to face giving up a precious evening and sharing their company while they wined and dined me.

On their part it was a type of inverted snobbery. Once I had agreed to eat with them, I was on social terms and it was as if they had evened the score. I had saved their lives, they had accepted me into their house as an equal and forced an unwanted meal on me. From then on they would assume that our doctor/patient relationship was different. They would start calling me by my first name. It was a great social fillip, for example, to ring the surgery and ask for Bob Clifford as opposed to Dr Clifford.

This was the case with the de Wyrebocks. Mrs de Wyrebock was certainly anxious to level the score. A gold-embossed invitation card was sent to me, inviting me to dine with them. Pencilled on the back was, 'A dinner jacket, please.' This was to put me in my place, to show that everybody else would obviously know what to wear, but an ignorant peasant like myself would most likely turn up in a tweed jacket with leather elbow patches.

I dreaded the thought of this dinner, but it was impossible to refuse it.

I arrived at the house, to be shown in by the butler. Apart from Marjorie de Wyrebock, who was my own age, the other ten who were assembled looked as if they had all been dusted and brought out of museums.

To my great surprise the company was quite delightful. They were all old men and women who had led adventurous and full lives. These were the fit, or should I say once-fit, who feature as the survival of the fittest. I heard reminiscences of places that I had read and dreamt about. Afghan frontier expeditions. Malaya. The Boxer rebellion in China. The slaughter of the Great War when they had lost most of their friends. I did not have to speak: I just sat back and listened to these delightful old gallants and the stories they had to tell.

Even Mrs de Wyrebock was gracious and pleasant to me. The ladies did not leave us when the port was passed round. I think they were all too old and stiff to get up from their chairs, or were limited in the number of up and down movements they could make in a day.

When the port had gone round for the last time, a few of the poor old codgers were dozing in their chairs. Mrs de Wyrebock said, 'I am sure you two young people would like some fresh air. Marjorie, why don't you show Dr Clifford round the vinery?'

It was only when I got up from my chair that I realised how good an evening I had had. I was full to the brim with sherry, port and wine. I had been entranced by the tales that I had heard. I was full of love for my fellow men. Even Marjorie

de Wyrebock, who was advancing towards me, looked quite attractive. Seen through an alcoholic haze, her teeth seemed to have shortened, and the bosom that was peeping out of her dress was certainly not unattractive. Her riding calves, which were one of her most prominent features, were hidden from view by her long dress.

She took my arm, probably to steady me, and we wove our way towards the vinery.

When we entered this large glass-walled room I nearly passed out. It was hot and humid; I was back in one of the Malayan jungle stories I had just heard.

There were double basket chairs round the room. Scattered on tables were copies of *The Tatler*, *Vogue*, and *Country Life*.

I had to sit down quickly because the room was reeling. I made for the nearest double basket chair, with Marjorie still on my arm, and dropped into it. Marjorie came down on top of me.

'Oh, doctor,' she breathed. 'I knew you felt the same as I did!'

Two horsey lips, stoutly reinforced by supporting teeth, were clamped firmly on my mouth. With her free hand she started to stroke my hair. I think 'groom' would be a better word to describe her action, and I began to sympathise with her ponies.

I must say that she didn't taste too bad and, as somehow her lips covered her incisors, I was in no fear of laceration.

With the wine and good spirits of the evening I got a bit carried away. I responded to her grooming by what I suppose in horsey circles would be called 'stroking her withers'.

Just as I had begun to raise my sights and explore her plunging neckline, the vinery door crashed open. In stormed Commander de Wyrebock.

'Gad, sir!' he shouted. 'Is this the way you repay my hospitality? I should be grateful if you would leave!'

Marjorie began to adjust her dress as if I had tried to rape her. I had to walk my unsteady way past the still occupied dining table (nobody had had the strength to move yet), collect my shabby raincoat from among the twill jackets on the hallstand under the disdainful glare of the butler, creep out of the front door, and drive myself home.

I must say my recollection of Marjorie wasn't too bad, but after getting back to my flat and having a few sobering cups of coffee, I realised how fortunate I had been to escape. Another half hour of Marjorie's uninhibitedness and it could have been a shotgun wedding. Mrs de Wyrebock had won after all. She could now send for one of my partners as, with reason, she wouldn't have that 'damned new young doctor' in her house.

I did think of putting an empty sausage skin in my thank-you letter for the dinner, but thought better of it. You can't win them all — and this had been really nearer to a draw than a dead loss.

179

18

After the Ball

Janice and Kevin Bird had invited Eric and myself to make up a party with two potential brides to go to the Tadchester Carnival Ball. The two ladies were New Zealanders, distant cousins of Janice. Janice was always trying to marry me off, but her idea of a desirable catch never quite tallied with mine, and I had only just got over pining for my London midwife, Brenda Collins.

When I first met Brenda she had been a young probationer, coming from a home of poor circumstances in the north. I was one of the first boys that she had been out with, and when I first met her she was untidy, badly dressed, and shy, but underneath her untidiness she had a rare beauty. She had long, shoulder length, blonde hair which she twisted into plaits and piled on top of her head when she was working. She had the most beautiful aquiline face, and perfect white teeth. I was happy to take her to her first dance, help her buy her first ball gown, and watch her grow in confidence and stature under the shelter of my company.

We were inseparable and went boating on the Thames at weekends. I took her home to meet mother. Strangely, mother and she never quite got on. Brenda always carried a chip on her shoulder and, having spent so much of her life as a Have-not, she had determined that she was going to be one of the Haves.

As her confidence grew, so did her choice of clothes. She paid much more attention to her hair, and she changed from being a frightened little probationer until she was without a doubt the best looking nurse of her year.

These were days when I was in my first year of clinical studies as a student. We were both penniless but our joy was in each other's company.

Until the time I qualified we spent our holidays together, most often camping. In our third year of camping Brenda, who had now become quite a sophisticated city girl, looked wistfully at the large hotels near the camp site and asked, 'How long before you take me to those?'

We could only see each other intermittently during the first year after I had qualified, and she went off to do her midwifery. We wrote practically every day and, by writing often enough, never seemed apart. I accepted, when we met, that she would be a bit different. She had to find to some extent her own way in life, and she did go to parties and dances without me. I only had one night a week off and I couldn't expect her to sit in every evening.

We met up together in the same hospital again where she was now a midwife and I was the obstetric house officer. She urged me to specialise, as most of my friends were doing, but I was set on going into general practice, which I felt I was best equipped for.

Brenda hated the idea of being a general practitioner's wife, tied to telephones, part of a small community. She grew more and more attracted to the bright lights, and she was increasingly being squired by Roger de Silva, one of the obstetric registrars, who was destined for Harley Street and was already partly equipped with a Bentley and a great deal of family money behind him.

It all came to a head when he asked Brenda to join a party hiring a yacht in the Mediterranean. We had bitter arguments about it, but she was determined to go.

I gave her an ultimatum, that if she did go it was all over between us.

Brenda did go, and she was engaged to Roger when she came back.

I kept out of her way as much as I could, heartbroken, to the end of my year's obstetrics. Then I applied for a mixed house job at Winchcombe Hospital which was in the area that I hoped to practise. I had at last got her out of my system – I hoped – and I wondered what the evening would bring.

* * *

Eric and I fortified ourselves a bit too long and too late before going to Kevin's. We had dulled our inhibitions sufficiently to cope with both the exotic and the just plain awful.

We arrived at Kevin's late, apologising that we had had trouble with the car. Kevin smelt my breath and said, 'Yes, I can see that. It is something to do with your fuel injection system.'

The girls were twins and could only be distinguished by the small scar that Jennifer (the older twin by half an hour) had on her right cheek. Jennifer was to be mine for the evening, and Eric had to settle for her sister, Laura.

It was obviously another bad match. I didn't fancy either of them. They were both tall, full-busted girls and, by the way they grabbed our hands on introduction, eager for the fray.

We had a drink with Kevin and Janice and then the six of us set off for the Ball.

It was packed. Everybody who was anybody was there.

We fought our way through the crowd to the bar, waving and shouting good cheer to our friends. I could see Frank and Primrose, Joe and Lee, but the noise was so great I couldn't hear what they were shouting across the room to us.

We got ourselves settled by the bar and Jennifer (who must have been over-filled with gin by Kevin before the Ball) started becoming amorous, pressing one of her great bosoms into my shoulder and stroking the back of my neck with the hand that wasn't holding her, yet one more, gin. She insisted on dragging me on to the floor for a dance and almost raped me in front of my patients.

'Bob,' she said, 'we are hitch-hiking round Europe next month. If you have got any holiday due, why don't you join us? You can share my hike tent – there is plenty of room for both of us and Laura likes sleeping out in the open anyway.'

This was going to be a frightful evening.

I fought my way back to the bar. There was only one thing to do – blot out the evening with alcohol.

My third pint was almost knocked out of my hand by the clashing of cymbals and the smash of a drum. I turned, to see the spotlights fixed on the stage and there, emerging from what used to be the old orchestra pit, in all her glory – skin-fitting deep purple dress, presumably to match her nipples, and plunging neckline that was no encumbrance to her physical charms was – Oh! my God – Gwendoline Jacobs, the Carnival Queen. I had forgotten all about it.

The M.C., Mike Thomas, Secretary of the Rugby Club, came on to present Gwendoline, who played her part, gently undulating from side to side on the stage. The Coltz XV who were sipping their shandies at the back of the stage nearly flipped their minds.

After Gwendoline had been suitably crowned and presented with a large bouquet of flowers, Mike Thomas then announced that the Carnival Queen would now start the Ball rolling with a ladies' invitation/excuse-me dance; the first man to dance with her would be her King for the night.

Gwendoline stood on the stage, sniffing the air like a foxhound. I ducked my head, trying to hide behind Jennifer's left bosom. Surely to God it wasn't going to be me. I remembered that Gwendoline was fairly determined when I examined her for her medical. I didn't look round. The bosom was soft and if I leant against it with my right ear there was room between it and its right counterpart for me to sip my pint of beer.

183

The room became silent. I suddenly became conscious of an overpowering smell of cheap scent. Then Gwendoline's voice.

'Doctor, will you give me the pleasure of this dance?'

There was no escape.

We had to do an exhibition dance round the floor with Gwendoline stuck to me like a limpet. Her nipples pierced my rib cage like two steel spikes. I prayed for somebody to come and excuse me.

Jennifer's embrace was like a pygmy's compared with that of Gwendoline's.

All the time we danced Gwendoline was muttering in my ear.

'Give way to your impulses, doctor. Live. We may all be dead tomorrow. I have got a caravan in Skegness for a weekend in a fortnight's time. Why not come and join me? I promise I won't tell anyone.'

I suddenly heard a horsey voice say, 'Excuse me', and a hand clutched my shoulder like a vice. I was literally torn from Gwendoline, with Gwendoline falling back looking as if she could commit murder.

I turned to face my saviour and nearly scalped myself on a row of flashing buck teeth. It was Marjorie de Wyrebock!

Whereas Gwendoline had clung to me like a limpet, Marjorie rode me as if she were a stallion. She had one hand firmly pressed to the lower part of my back, somehow pushing me up under her saddle area, and half carried me round the room.

'Doctor,' she said, 'we are going on a cruise in a few weeks' time. Mothah finds she has booked an extra cabin by mistake. What about joining us, eh? Needn't cost you a penny. At one or two places we are stopping there is some damned good riding.'

By now the floor had filled with other dancers and was so packed that I was pushed even further into Marjorie's embrace. I could have sworn that she was gripping me with her knees and managing to walk me round at the same time.

I became conscious of a small, sweet voice, persistently saying, 'Excuse me. Excuse me.'

Deliverance at last!

I brought my head up quickly and accidentally hit Marjorie's bottom jaw, causing her to drop me as both rows of her flashing teeth stuck firmly into her tongue.

I turned round to greet my rescuer and there, looking as lovely as I have ever seen her, was my faithless midwife, Brenda Collins.

She twined round me, cheek against mine, and we were moving smoothly round the floor as we used to a year ago. It seemed we had never stopped.

'Oh, darling Bob,' she said, 'at last I have come to my senses. It just didn't work without you. I am starting at Winchcombe next week. I had to be near you. Couldn't we start again?'

At this moment it all became too much. The after-game booze, the gins at Kevin's, and the pints since, ganged up together and decided to leave me, and with an 'Oh, I am so sorry dear,' I was sick all over Brenda's sequin dress.

I don't remember any more of the dance. Kevin and Eric somehow got me home. They said, when they had got me sufficiently conscious with coffee, that they had to fight off Jennifer, Gwendoline, Marjorie and Brenda all at once. Each of them claimed me as her own.

What the hell was I to do?

I woke next morning with a terrible hangover and staggered down to the surgery to be met by Gladys, scowling and looking really grumpy.

'There have been four personal calls for you already this morning, Doctor Bob,' she said, handing me a list.

I didn't need to look. It was Jennifer, Gwendoline, Marjorie and Brenda.

What was I to do?

I had a week's holiday due, but where could I go to escape this lot?

Suddenly I thought of my mother. I really was being driven back to the womb. My mother had been widowed when I was three, was young and active, and led her own independent life.

We were good friends and she was always a good counsellor. She spent a great deal of her time as an active member of the Liberal Party. We wrote to each other frequently and always kept in close touch.

I rang her and explained my problem. I could hear her laughing at the other end of the phone. 'Well, Bob,' she said, 'you had better come away with your old Mum. I am off to a quiet hotel near Bournemouth for a week. Just throw a few things in your case, and come.'

I spent the remainder of the week avoiding my four admirers. Gladys was a marvel on the phone. From her answers I was out on emergencies for forty-eight hours on the trot.

Eventually I made my escape. On the Friday I sneaked out of the house and got into my car at two o'clock in the morning. I daren't travel by daylight – I was sure there would have been road blocks.

I arrived at my mother's hotel at Boscombe at eight in the morning having spent some time at an all-night cafe en route, anxiously looking out of the window to see if I had any pursuers.

I slept the whole day and made my first appearance at dinner.

My mother was young and attractive and had already made several friends in the hotel. Most were much older than I, but I had noticed a couple of girls sitting at a nearby table who were round about my age.

But did I really want ever to have anything to do with girls again?

Both these two looked very pleasant – I particularly liked the blonde one. Neither of them looked like the pack of man-eaters I had just escaped from.

We all sat round having coffee after dinner and I found the two girls were called Pam and Joan. Pam worked for an advertising magazine and Joan was a secretary in London.

Pam and I got on like a house on fire. She talked to me as if I were her Father Confessor. I had been introduced to her as a 'Doctor', so perhaps that was why it was. She told me all about her broken engagement and how she had come away with a friend to try and sort herself out and forget the upsets of the last few months.

Eventually the older people went to bed. Pam looked a little bit puzzled when my mother went, and eventually Joan slipped away, leaving us sitting on the settee together.

We found we had an awful lot in common. She thought I was terribly funny and laughed at all my jokes; but there was something hesitant in her manner and if I moved a bit too close to her on the settee she would spring away as if she would have been electrocuted if I touched her.

She agreed, reluctantly, to have a game of squash with me next day. I assumed that she still was grieving over her lost fiancé. She warned me that she had never played squash before. But she was nice, easy to be with, and for once it looked as if I would have to make the move towards the opposite sex rather than the other way round.

Pam looked lovely in her squash clothes – small red shorts and a tight-fitting singlet. She really was super.

I instructed her in the rudiments of the game and then began to show off atrociously. Not to be outdone, Pam chased round after every ball I hit. I ran her almost to the point of exhaustion, but she still kept on going.

She somehow managed to return one of my smashes to the bottom left-hand corner. I leapt across the court to make yet one more impossible retrieve. As I flashed my racket back it hit something soft, and there was Pam doubled up on the floor of the squash court, not breathing, completely winded by my blow to her solar plexus.

I rushed over to her, alarmed. She really had stopped breathing. I pressed on her chest and nothing happened. Only one thing for it, I thought – mouth-to-mouth resuscitation. As my lips met hers I found her chest beginning to move. Thank God she was all right.

At this moment I looked up to see that there were at least

a dozen people in the spectators' gallery, all completely transfixed by this drama taking place in front of them. It is not often you see a prone couple in a squash court, lips and bodies locked.

I got up and helped Pam to her feet. She was sweating from her exhaustive running and shaken from my winding blow. She looked terribly worried. 'Oh, Bob,' she said. 'Whatever will your wife think?'

'My wife?' I said. 'I'm not married.'

'Well who is the lady you are with? She is Mrs Clifford, isn't she?'

I burst out laughing.

'That's my mother, you nut.'

'Oh,' said Pam, 'I thought she looked so young and smart – just a bit older than you – and you were man and wife.'

The rest of our holiday passed in a happy blur. We were marvellous, humorous companions. Pam looked even better in a two-piece bathing suit than she had done on the squash court. This was for real – and mother liked her too.

All too soon the holiday was over and I knew this was something I was going to follow up. Pam, unfortunately, lived in Surrey which was many miles from our practice. I found that my partners were tolerant about me getting away for long weekends. When it was my turn to have a weekend off, I used either to motor down to Leatherhead where Pam's parents lived – when I would watch her in the amateur dramatic society where she always seemed to play the maid – or we would go up to my mother's and spend the weekend with her in London.

The months soon passed.

I was to have a week's holiday over Christmas and the New Year and Pam had promised to come to the hospital New Year's Ball with me. She was going to meet all my hospital friends and it was going to be the first time that we had ever dressed up to go out together.

She emerged from my mother's bedroom looking radiant in

a red taffeta dress which highlighted her bare, slightly freckled arms.

The ball was a great success and my friends loved her. This was the girl for me.

We were dancing together as midnight struck and the New Year of 1950 was chimed in. As the old year went out I stood back, took her face in my hands, and said, 'Pam, darling, will you marry me?'

'Of course I will,' she said. 'Your mother has been dinning the duties of a G.P.'s wife into me for the last two months.'

We were soon surrounded by smiling, congratulating friends. All my old rugby mates, some of them married already, some just about to take the plunge, and some who were determined that no event such as this was ever going to interfere with their beer drinking.

Suddenly a loud voice came over the Tannoy. The music stopped and the voice of the Admiral, the lodge porter who had been at the hospital for at least thirty years, who had been a father and uncle and just about everything to all of us at some time or another, brought the proceedings to a halt.

'Ladies and Gentlemen,' he began, 'I would like two minutes' silence. Bob Clifford has just got engaged – one more rugby player has bitten the dust.'

Pam hugged me.

Life was going to be different from now on.

Postscript

There is the fable of the old man sitting outside a town, being approached by a stranger.

'What are they like in this town?' asked the stranger.

'What were they like in your last town?' replied the old man.

'They were delightful people. I was very happy there. They were kind, generous and would always help you in trouble.'

'You will find them very much like that in this town.'

The old man was approached by another stranger.

'What are the people like in this town?' asked the second stranger.

'What were they like in your last town?' replied the old man.

'It was an awful place. They were mean, unkind and nobody would ever help anybody.'

'I am afraid you will find it very much the same here,' said the old man.

If it should be your lot to ever visit Tadchester, this is how you will find us.

Not There, Doctor

Illustrated by Nick Baker

CHAPTER 1

The voice on the telephone left no doubt about the urgency of the call.

'Come straight away, doctor. It's our Mary. She's bleeding to death.'

The phone was abruptly replaced. It was eleven o'clock at night. Mary? Mary who?

There was one clue: I thought I recognised the voice as that of Mrs Prentice. She had an eighteen-year-old daughter Mary, and I knew where they lived – 5 Salterns Terrace, Up-the-Hill. But the message had given no clue to where 'our Mary' was bleeding from, or why.

I grabbed my medical case, jumped in my car, and

headed off as fast as I could for Salterns Terrace, hoping at least that my diagnosis of the name and address was correct.

It was. Number 5 Salterns Terrace was ablaze with lights. The voice of a young girl, presumably Mary, could be heard screaming right down the street. I rushed in the open front door, pushed my way through a group of peering neighbours, and found Mary – very much alive and screaming at the top of her voice. Her mother and father stood at either side of her with blood-soaked towels pressed to her ears.

I saw immediately what the trouble was, and knew that Mary was going to be all right . . .

When I was a hospital resident, each particular post I took became after a few weeks the one I was definitely going to specialise in. When I was a house surgeon, I was going to become a surgeon; when I was a house physician, I was going to be a physician; when I was doing midwifery and obstetrics, gynaecology was going to be my speciality. There was only one exception. I did a four-week locum in psychiatry, and resolved soon and firmly never to be a psychiatrist.

Later, in general practice, I was still able to pursue some of my skills in medicine and obstetrics but through sheer lack of practice my surgical skills slowly dwindled. I clung on obstinately as long as I could to the few surgical procedures I was still allowed to do. One of these was the removal of sebaceous cysts – lumps, mainly on the scalp, which could be surgically removed under local anaesthetic.

My operating sessions were conducted after-hours in the surgery. Sebaceous cyst surgery tended to be rather messy, with lots of blood, and Gladys, our senior receptionist, scowled her disapproval whenever I took time out to do some. Eventually one of my partners – Henry Johnson, FRCS, who was the surgeon at the local hospital – with support from Gladys, persuaded me that it was much better if *he* did this minor surgery in the Casualty Department of the hospital.

'It's much cleaner if I do it there,' said Henry, 'it doesn't keep our surgery staff late, and,' he added, with a twinkle in his eye, 'I *am* rather better at it than you are.'

Reluctantly I succumbed to the pressure. It left me with only one outlet for my surgical skills – ear piercing.

I became very proficient at this art, was even thought to be better than the Tadchester jeweller. I attracted more customers than he did, not just for my skill but because I was a National Health Service doctor and could not charge my patients for this service, whereas the Tadchester jeweller charged them £1.

Mary Prentice, a sweet eighteen-year-old, came timidly to have her ears pierced. She was nervous and apprehensive. Happily, everything went like clockwork. Sometimes one fumbles trying to get the gold sleepers into the pierced holes. My technique was old-fashioned but reliable. A dot with my pen on the earlobe as a target, a cork behind the ear, a quick spray of freezing solution and a large hollow hypodermic needle plunged straight through the lobe into the cork. The end of the sleeper was stuck into the open end of the hypodermic needle when I had disengaged it from the cork. The operation was then completed by pulling the needle back through the earlobe, bringing the sleeper end with it.

Mary had rather fancy sleepers, each with a little star on it, which I admired. They gave her a gypsy-like look, and certainly suited her.

. . . so when I arrived at 5 Salterns Terrace, diagnosis was instant and easy; removing the towels from Mary's ears confirmed it.

Mary had rushed home to change a jumper. As she pulled the jumper over her head, it had caught in the little star shapes on her sleepers – and torn the sleepers right through both earlobes. Poor Mary!

I dressed her wounds and drove her to the hospital

3

where Henry carefully stitched up her torn lobes.

It was a great lesson to me. From then on I warned everyone whose ears I pierced of how easily this could happen. But it was not a lesson to Mary. One year later she turned up again in my surgery, earlobes completely healed and with not a sign of a scar. 'Would you mind piercing my ears again, doctor?' she said, blushing.

'Certainly, Mary,' I said, 'providing, in future, you keep any stars in your eyes and not on your earrings.'

I was the junior partner in a group of four in a little Somerset town called Tadchester. Tadchester (population 6500) stands on the estuary of the River Tad, in one of the most beautiful parts of the Somerset coast. It is a market town, with some fishing, some light industry, and a great deal of farming. Six miles north is Thudrock Colliery, half of whose work force lives in Tadchester.

The town is split in two by the River Tad, and further split by the large hill which dominates one side of the river. The other side of the river is flat pastureland, stretching off to marshes and the sea coast. You are not just a Tadchester resident – you are strictly Up-the-Hill or Down-the-Hill. It has important social distinctions as whereas the population Down-the-Hill tend to be made up of Haves, the population Up-the-Hill tend to be the Have-nots.

We were the only general practice in the town, and in addition to our general practice duties we took care of the local hospital. The four partners each had a special interest at the hospital: Steve Maxwell, the senior partner, had a special interest in medicine; Henry Johnson, the second senior and sebaceous cyst poacher, was the surgeon; Jack Hart, the third partner, was the anaesthetist; and I, as the junior dogsbody, did most of the running around and was reckoned to be the expert in midwifery.

We practised from a central surgery Down-the-Hill, above which I had a bachelor flat and fended mostly for myself, scrambled eggs and baked beans playing the main role in most of my menus.

I had been in Tadchester for two years and had recently become engaged: in fact, I had been back home from London for only five hours when I was called to Mary's bleeding ears. I had got engaged in London on New Year's Eve, two days before I returned, so had yet to announce my news in Tadchester, and I wondered what sort of reaction it might bring.

I had reached a horrific situation the previous summer when three of the local availables – Marjorie de Wyrebock of the riding school; Gwendoline Jacobs, the local beauty queen; and Brenda Collins, an old flame – had all tried to stake their claims on me in the same evening at the Tadchester Carnival Ball. I escaped by fleeing on holiday, with my mother as chaperone and bodyguard. While on holiday, I met Pamela, to whom I became engaged at my old London hospital's New Year Ball.

My first surgery to be held in the New Year was the morning after the torn earlobes episode. I wondered when would be the best time to announce my engagement. I would tell my partners when we met for morning coffee, but how and when to tell the surgery staff – not least the town – I still had not decided.

I didn't have to make a decision. I was embraced by Gladys, our senior receptionist, as soon as I came through the surgery door. 'Congratulations, Dr Bob,' she said, 'and not before time.'

Mary and Jill, our dispenser and junior receptionist, came up and kissed me, and offered their congratulations.

Tadchester had not let me down.

Somehow, as happens in most small communities, everyone seemed to know what you were going to do before you knew it yourself. As one of the local councillors once told me – 'It is not we councillors who break the secrets of

5

the confidential meetings – it's those we tell in confidence afterwards who let us down.'

I had been eased out of the difficulty of announcing my engagement, but still had the problem of my three original lady suitors. Pam, my wife-to-be, lived in Surrey, well away from the practice. My courting had all taken place out of Tadchester; Pam had visited the town only twice, briefly, and had therefore not registered on the community's sense of proprietorship as my possible future wife.

I started to go through the pile of mail that had accumulated on my desk while I had been away. One scented envelope. Help! I opened it anxiously. It was from Gwendoline Jacobs. Dear Gwendoline. Childlike, direct, tantalisingly over-developed and hopelessly over-sexed.

'Dear Dr Bob,' it read. 'Just a note to say I have been given a job in the Piccadilly Strip Bar. Do look me up if you are in London. I can always give you a bed for the night.'

It was written in a large, childish hand, and the bottom of the page was covered in large kisses. Gwendoline's openness always made me smile. I felt that in a strip bar she would at last come into her own.

Amongst the pile of hospital reports and letters there was a note from Brenda Collins. Brenda was a London midwife with whom, in our student days, I had had a long and idyllic affair. Things had changed after I qualified and Brenda went off to do her midwifery. She developed a taste for bright lights and monied specialists and became engaged to an obstetrician bound for Harley Street, but the engagement didn't work out. That was why Brenda turned up on that disastrous Carnival evening to press her claim on me. My last vision was of her standing there, horrified, after I had been sick all down the front of her sequinned dress.

The note was brief. 'Dear Bob,' she wrote. 'In the time we have been apart you seem to have turned into a

6

drunken degenerate. I do not wish to have anything more to do with you.'

There was one letter – or rather, card – that made my heart sink. It was brief and to the point. 'Commander and Mrs de Wyrebock request your company for cocktails on Sunday, 12th January, at 12 noon.'

I felt the card should have read, 'Mrs and Commander de Wyrebock command your company for cocktails . . .' There was no doubt that Mrs de Wyrebock was much more the commander than her husband. She never requested anybody to do anything: she just ordered them to report.

On my last visit to the de Wyrebocks, because of a small misunderstanding in the vinery I had virtually been chased from the house. The Commander seemed to have thought that my intentions towards his daughter were not entirely honourable. But my last meeting with horse-mad Marjorie at the fated Carnival Ball had left me in no doubt that she had picked me out as a desirable mount.

Two down, and one to go.

I couldn't believe that Marjorie would be as easily got rid of as my other two suitors. She was older, had begun to reach the desperate stage, and was severely handicapped in the marital stakes by two rows of teeth which would have looked good on a horse but which didn't do much for her.

There was no way that I could cross this bridge before I came to it, so I got down to my first surgery after the winter break.

It was packed. The news of my engagement apparently was not just confined to my surgery staff; the whole of the town appeared to know. Nearly half of the patients had come not for medical advice, but to congratulate me and wish me well. The medical consultations were mostly routine – winter coughs and colds – and regulars who came for monthly blood pressure or weight checks.

After surgery, I went for coffee with my partners. It was all back slapping, rude jokes about my engagement, and

7

advice from the three of them. They were delighted I was to be married, apart from the fact that, by and large, patients preferred married doctors.

Ron Towle was waiting to catch me when I came out from my coffee break. Ron was one of my poor disturbed patients, a loner who made his living with vague land and cattle deals. He took up more of my time than any other single patient.

Could he please see me just for a minute?

I mentally wrote off half an hour.

As soon as he came into my surgery he started to walk up and down, beating his chest. I had let him down. Where had I been? I was never there when he needed me.

Apparently, while I was away he had become more disturbed than usual. He had started to become abusive to his neighbours, and my partner, Jack Hart, had to have him forcibly admitted to Winchcombe Mental Hospital for three days to cool him off.

As usual with Ron's crises, this one was related to some business deal with which he was involved. He had bought some agricultural land that had a fair chance of being converted to building plots. Planning permission had been refused, and he now couldn't get the price he had paid for the land in the first place.

He was ruined. People took advantage. It was a plot. Those buggers on the Council had it in for him.

I let him go on for about ten minutes, then started to cool him down. It was another ten minutes before we achieved a normal rational conversation. I even managed to get him to laugh and, for a while, was able to persuade him that his business deal wasn't such a disaster after all.

I knew he would be back on the same tack the next day, or the day after, but I had learned to live with it.

'Now, Ron,' I said, 'I have some news for you. I have just got engaged.'

Ron was silent. He sat there, thoughtfully nodding his

head. Then he said 'You are a lucky, lucky man. It means you will get married and have children, and people will care about you.' He sat numb, more aware of his isolation than usual. 'You are a lucky, lucky man,' he repeated.

He got up slowly. His shabby old raincoat and frayed cuffs looked even shabbier than usual. He seemed small and crushed by all the indignities the world had heaped upon him. He turned when he reached the door. 'I hope you will be very happy, doctor,' he said, 'you deserve it.'

I sat thinking when Ron had left. Yes, I was very, very lucky. Did I deserve my good fortune? Perhaps not, and Ron certainly didn't deserve whatever mentality, chemistry, physiology, upbringing or environment which had created the situation he was trapped in.

The morning seemed to fly. I just had time for a quick sandwich before I started on the move again. There was a steady stream of visits all the afternoon, mostly to influenza victims.

Several patients were very ill. One man said his heart had been out of control in the morning. He was better now, he said, and all seemed well, with pulse normal and blood pressure normal – but on listening to his chest I couldn't hear his heart at all. It *did* seem that something could be wrong.

I discussed the case on the telephone with a very nice lady registrar at Winchcombe Hospital. I said I couldn't believe that my patient could have a pericardial effusion and seem so well. She said, 'Send him in and we will do a chest X-ray and electro-cardiogram and make sure.'

I was always pleased when it was a lady doctor 'on take' at the hospital. They are much easier to talk to. Or perhaps I just prefer talking to ladies anyway.

All turned out well in the end. I made a note to buy a new stethoscope.

My evening surgery started at five. A great number of children seem to come to evening surgery, it often being

9

the only time one parent is able to bring them. There they were – with the usual infected ears, tonsils, colds and coughs.

Then all the myriad adult problems – indigestion, athlete's foot, shortness of breath. They wanted advice on family planning, on how to lose weight, how to put on weight. There were people who were worried about their children, and children who were worried about their parents; people who were worried about their jobs, and people who were worried that they hadn't got jobs; people who were just out of hospital and people who were just going into hospital; people who needed X-raying, and people who needed fairly complex investigation.

Surgery finished at 7.15 p.m. Home for a meal of bacon, eggs and beans again, and then, eight o'clock, my last Red Cross lecture of the series to the local detachment. It was finished. I went through a rough resumé of all we had covered during the course and to my surprise was given a box of cigars. A nice lot of people.

There were two night calls. 2.30 a.m. – a car crash. The driver had fallen asleep at the wheel – multiple bruises, no obvious fractures. Both occupants felt they were lucky to be alive – the car was a total write-off. Fortunately the only other casualty was a tree at the edge of the country road.

Four a.m. – the second call. Just when I was getting off to sleep. This time a twenty-five-year-old girl whose baby was delivered two-and-half months ago. She was now acutely depressed and had been weeping for twenty-four hours. There was no medical emergency here, but I read the anxiety of the family and had to swop my sleep for theirs.

The girl was sobbing, not talking, the house was alight and alive, and nobody was sleeping. Two boys were play-ing cards downstairs, baby was crying, sisters and brothers walking about. However many people lived here? I couldn't sort out all this girl's problems at that hour, but got her to swallow two sleeping tablets (I watched her to make sure she did), then sent everybody off to bed. I would see her tomorrow, when I knew she would have had at least a good night's sleep behind her. No, not tomorrow, it's already today. My main function had been to go along as an authoritative outsider and accept the responsibility for the situation. Now everybody could rest – someone else had taken over.

The weather had brightened the next day but after my nocturnal interruptions I came down rather bleary-eyed. There was more mail on my desk – investigation results, letters from specialists. All the partners saw all of the mail, thus keeping in touch with the developments of each other's patients. Gladys brought a cup of coffee, and slowly I felt like a human being again.

There were some surprises in the mail. One patient whom I thought was anaemic had such a high blood count that I suggested he became a blood donor. Another, who was just having some routine investigations, complaining of nothing really, turned out to be grossly anaemic and would have to be investigated further.

The surgery started at 9 a.m. The partners had an efficient appointments system and we avoided massive roomfuls of people waiting for hours. Not many appointments had been taken when I started, but by 11 a.m. I had seen twenty people: the usual coughs and colds and several being signed off to resume work.

Then came my biggest problems: depressed people and people under stress. This was – and is – the commonest single condition I had to deal with. It presented itself in many different ways. Sometimes a person was just feeling depressed, but more often feeling tired, run down and uninterested. It could take some time to ferret out that what was being presented as backache was really the cover for acute depression.

I once had a girl who attended surgery for weeks, complaining only of a painful thumb. Eventually I was able to find that her real reason for visiting was her fear of the physical side of her forthcoming marriage. She was to be wed in a few months' time, but was quite ignorant of what really happened – or was expected to happen – during the sex act.

I arranged for an interview with her and her fiancé together. We discussed the problem openly and, by facing it and exploring it, made it disappear. Her fiancé was a kind and considerate lad and the answer to their problem was for them both to be kind, considerate and patient with each other in the early days of their marriage.

The greatest problem in the treatment of depressive and anxiety states was my feeling of inadequacy. So often I could only treat the symptom. I couldn't change people's economic circumstances, couldn't find houses, new jobs or new marital partners. All I could do was support, listen, advise where it was appropriate, and sometimes prescribe anti-depressants or tranquillisers. These didn't help the fundamental problems but did lessen the anxiety, made it a little easier to cope and, by coping, to come to terms with, or solve, the problem. Sometimes the bereaved needed a tremendous amount of support and patience until they found their feet again. All I could offer was my compassion and a transfusion of my own energy. And this was not taught in medical schools. I wondered just how I would cope with the situations many of my patients had to contend with.

Other cases during the morning – a man of fifty-one complained of indigestion. As far as I could tell, on examination, his trouble was gastric, but there was a seed of doubt so I fixed up an appointment for him to have an electro-cardiogram. Mary, our dispenser, had been trained to use this machine and did her tracing by appointment in the surgery, or in the patients' homes if they weren't well enough to travel.

A few of the run-downs and feeling-tireds merited some investigation, and blood and urine samples were taken and put out to be sent to the Pathology Laboratory.

Then the usual light relief. Patients were always finding odd lumps they hadn't seen before when they were bathing or taking a shower. They were usually boils or simple cysts or fatty lumps, all innocuous. It meant, usually, sleepless nights thinking they had cancer, until they saw the doctor. They came in generally worried to death, and went out rejoicing. If I were asked what was the single most important thing a general practitioner did, I would have said it was to reassure, and he reassures with the weight of his knowledge of illness and its associations behind him.

I had got to know several people fairly well in my two years in Tadchester and knew, roughly, their behaviour patterns. It was helpful because I was able to notice if they started to behave differently. So, when Vera Vanston. the Chairman of the Women's Institute, arrived in my morning surgery saying she felt like a gramophone that was running down, I thought there must be something wrong. Mrs Vanston rarely came to the surgery and was one of those seemingly inexhaustible women who had time for everything and everybody and, if she were not running every local organisation, would at least be a committee member.

She told me she was tired all the time, felt cold, was putting on weight, her hair and skin felt funny, and she just hadn't the energy or enthusiasm to tackle half the jobs that she normally got through without any trouble. She had tried slimming and all sorts of patent tonics, but was getting worse.

I had already made my diagnosis before she had finished giving me her history. When I examined her I found that she had put on weight since the last time I had seen her; her skin was coarse, the outer third of her eyebrows were missing, and her hair was thin and wiry.

'Well,' I said, 'your problem is a simple one. What is happening to you is that your thyroid gland is not as

13

active as it should be.'

The thyroid gland is very much like the air intake into a kitchen boiler. If it is left fully open it will roar away and burn up so much body fuel that you lose weight and become thin. This is what happens when the thyroid gland is over-active. When it is under-active (and this most commonly occurs in late middle age) it is similar to closing the air intake to the boiler, when the stove doesn't heat up enough and you don't burn up the body fuel, feel cold, and put on weight.

I sent a sample of Mrs Vanston's blood to the Pathology Laboratory, whose tests confirmed my suspicion that she had an under-active thyroid – myxcedema. Once having my diagnosis confirmed, I started her on thyroid tablets which she had to take every day to replace her deficiency. In three months Mrs Vanston was back to her old weight and figure, and leading all her organisations with the same zest as she had done before.

She called to see me at the surgery when she had been on the treatment for six months. I had never seen her looking better.

'Vera,' I said (we were old friends), 'you are looking marvellous, I only wish I were ten years younger.'

'Dr Bob,' she replied, 'you should try taking your own medicine – I *am* ten years younger.'

I had a second coffee at the end of what had been a very routine surgery, and was then off to do my visits.

Three calls for children with stomach pains. One for a sore throat. It *was* a sore throat, but closer examination showed it had been going on for some days. There was a mass of exudate on both tonsils and generalised glands all over. This was probably glandular fever, so I started the patient off on an antibiotic and took blood samples to clarify the diagnosis. It wouldn't make any difference to the condition; it would get better anyway. But I would then know whether there was glandular fever about in the district and on the patients' records they knew quite firmly that they did have glandular fever.

Of the three tummy pains, the two that might have been appendicitis turned out to be nothing, and the one who had diarrhoea (or who reported that he had diarrhoea) had had one small loose stool and presented as an acute appendicitis, so I had to send him off to hospital.

Two elderly patients. Both had a flare-up in their bronchitis and needed an antibiotic and some watching for a day or two. One of them was not too mobile and would need the district nurse to help her with her toilet and bathing.

Check calls on the two emergencies of the night before. The wife in the car crash had a badly bruised leg and a fracture had to be discounted, so I rang Winchcombe Hospital and fixed up an X-ray. Both husband and wife had found new bruises and were stiff and sore, but were thankful to have got off so lightly.

The sobbing young mother had slept well, but was still depressed and weeping. Her child was illegitimate and there was no supporting man in the background. A nice girl, and a lovely baby. She would get better and would survive, as people do get better and do survive. Nothing would improve at once, but the bad times would get less frequent. I could help her through the bad times with support and medication. I couldn't make them disappear, but I could blunt the sharp edges.

And so to lunch.

After lunch, just two ante-natals to be seen in the afternoon, then odds and ends – a medical representative, a cervical smear, and an examination for life insurance.

Ante-natal clinics are always pleasant things. Instead of people who are ill, there are healthy young mothers with something to look forward to. It is nice for a change to have medical conditions where there is a positive, happy end product.

Nurse Plank, the District Midwife, had both ante-natals all prepared for me; urine tested, blood pressures taken, and a reminder to me that another patient needed a further blood test.

Nurse Plank was one of the finest women I had known, a completely dedicated, caring midwife. She had never married, but nevertheless had thousands of babies she almost called her own. It was due to her skill alone that many of them were able to arrive in the world at all, and her caring did not just stop with the safe delivery of the baby; she was always scouting around for clothes, prams, etc. for the less well off. She gave advice and counsel to young mothers far beyond that required by her job. As I was beginning to find for myself, she had to give advice on house purchase, marriage, schools, and even such things as whether to buy a car. She never, to my knowledge, beat the request I had late one night when a mother rang to say her son had won a talent competition at Butlin's, did I think he should cut a record?

After seeing the ante-natals, a cervical smear. Again, everything was to hand. Nurse Plank had the forms filled in; instruments, slides and swabs were laid out for me, ready for use.

Next was my insurance examination. The patient grumbled at the fee of £4. I didn't really blame him for I knew just how he felt. We had just had a bill for £190 from our solicitors for drawing up a new partnership agreement.

I always felt rather sorry for medical travellers (pharmaceutical representatives). They used to have to sit about waiting for us to give them some of our time, then bring forth their latest wonder drug that was better than any other drug had ever been. I repeated my corny joke each time I had to interview a representative. I would examine his product, look intent, and then say, 'It must be good – the advertisements speak so well of it.' It never raised a flicker and I am sure none of them understood what I was getting at.

The medical representative would give us drug samples.

We would use them, then the patients who were given them would ask for more, so without meaning to, we had launched one more drug into circulation and the medical representative had achieved the object of his visit.

As I was about to leave the surgery a small boy was brought in. He had fallen off his pushcart and cut his head. With the help of Gladys, who stood by to pass instruments and cut stitches, I put three sutures in his head. He was terribly good, making no noise, and went on his way smiling after being rewarded with a sugar lump, very proudly wearing a bandage on his head.

Normally, on this day, I would have done a surgery at the boys' boarding school I looked after, but it was a half-term holiday and I had this extra spare time. I used that afternoon to catch up on some of my routine visiting of the elderly.

This was a most enjoyable area of medicine. Often the main treatment that you give elderly people, and the main medical treatment they require, is a visit. They just want to see a reassuring face come through the door, a reassuring face which has time to chat not only about medical conditions but about what is going on or, more often, about how things used to be. Most of the elderly people seem to miss the discipline of the old days. It is fine nowadays to do as you please, with no one looking over your shoulder, but in the old days there was always the Squire to go to if you had any major problems, and the Squire could, and did, give treats. Yes, they were better off than they used to be, but they did miss those treats when everything was arranged for them.

Young men and women in their early twenties, with spanking new sociology degrees, somehow were no substitute for the Squire, and I found it was primarily the doctor, the vicar, the health visitors and district nurses who had to bridge that gap.

Sometimes minor adjustments had to be made to patients' treatments, sometimes I would have to impose some new restriction.

It was very difficult to convince Mr Smith, aged ninety-three, that it was just not my lack of medical skill that was causing him more effort on his daily ten-mile walk. Bully for him! In all weathers I used to see him trailing round the country lanes with his stick.

There were some delightful old people of great age who had fought their lives' battles and, having survived that long, were gentle, philosophical people. I only wished I could spend more time over cups of tea, chatting over the cares and delights of the day.

The afternoon went all too quickly. A cup of tea, then back to the evening surgery, every appointment taken. There was never an easy surgery, and this one was delayed because, in the midst of it, a baby was brought in with a bad chest infection. I had to rush the child straight off to Winchcombe Hospital by ambulance from the surgery for immediate treatment. My surgery went on until eight o'clock, and I still had three calls to do.

Half past nine, home at last. I sat smack bang in front of my television set, my pipe firmly clenched between my teeth. Jack Hart was on for night duty, and unless someone came bleeding to the door I had an undisturbed night ahead of me. Woe betide anybody who should try and shift me from the box, regardless of whatever programmes might be showing.

My busy week had stopped me thinking too much about my impending visit to the de Wyrebocks' cocktail party. Sunday, the 12th, was in two days' time. They passed all too quickly. After a hearty breakfast I set off for the big house, prepared for the worst.

I rang the doorbell, and waited apprehensively. The door was opened by Commander de Wyrebock himself instead of the usual stone-faced butler.

'Come in, Dr Clifford,' he boomed, slapping me on the shoulder. 'I am damned glad to see you.'

The Commander was always pleasant, but this was a bit enthusiastic even for him, especially as on my last visit he had all but thrown me out. I was sure Mrs de Wyrebock wouldn't greet me with the same warmth.

I was led into a room where there were about a dozen of the County Set, all elegantly dressed and just as elegantly sipping sherry. I knew only a few of them by sight; the rest looked like relatives.

Mrs de Wyrebock detached herself from the group she was talking to, and came towards me. 'Now for it,' I thought.

She walked straight up to me, smiling, and kissed me on the cheek. 'Delighted to see you, doctor,' she said, 'though I hope we may call you Bob from now on – or do you prefer Robert? I thought we would just keep it family this morning. Don't you agree?'

A sudden terrible unease began to creep over me. What in God's name was happening?

The various males in the party one by one detached themselves from their various partners and came over and growled 'Congratulations' or 'Every happiness', always in rich, fruity, blue-blooded voices.

I was no longer uneasy about what was going to happen next – I was scared to death.

'Bob dear,' said Mrs de Wyrebock, 'Marjorie won't keep you a minute. She does feel she wants to look her best, and she is so excited.'

This couldn't really be happening. I was in the middle of a nightmare. Why wouldn't the alarm clock go off?

Marjorie didn't keep us waiting long. She came bursting in, and I had to admit she didn't look too bad. The Tadchester beauty salons must have been better than I thought. Her hair was done nicely, she was skilfully and tastefully made up so that the outline of those teeth was a little less horse-of-the-year than usual.

To my horror, Marjorie walked straight over to me, as her mother had done, and kissed me on the cheek.

'Isn't this all absolutely spiffing?' she said. She gripped my hand then, turning to the assembled company, said in the loud voice that she used to rally the Pony Club at gymkhanas, 'Ladies and gentlemen, I have an announcement to make. Dr Bob, this dark horse here, and I have become engaged.'

I felt the world beginning to collapse around me.

CHAPTER 2

I couldn't remember proposing to Marjorie even in my most drunken moments. And anyway, I hadn't seen her for weeks. Feebly, I began to protest. She cut me short and went on, 'Dr Bob is an old and dear friend, and we all depend on him. I hope you will all treat him as one of the family. The great coincidence is that he became engaged on New Year's Eve, the same night that Paul and I became engaged. It was such a coincidence that I wanted to share my engagement announcement with him. Now I would like you all to meet my fiancé, Paul Charteris.'

Through the door stepped a huge ape of a man of about forty-five, smartly dressed, obviously County and belonging, and with one particular physical characteristic – he had teeth that were even bigger than Marjorie's!

I nearly fainted. I knew then how relieved they felt at Ladysmith.

The rest of the party passed in a haze of champagne and the whinny of horsy voices. Eventually I got away and drove home, completely exhausted. I felt as if my whole life had just flashed before me. The sooner Pam and I were married, the better. I couldn't stand too many shocks like this.

My shirt was soaked through with perspiration. I was having lunch with some farmer friends – Janice and Kevin Bird – and had to go home and change before I went on to them. I arrived late and exhausted. They collapsed with laughter when I told them my story.

'Come on, Bluebeard,' said Kevin, 'get stuck into some prime rib of beef. It will settle your nerves.'

After lunch we drove to Sanford-on-Sea, and walked along the beach. It had been raining in the morning, but a watery sun broke through in the afternoon, and the walk along the beach, well wrapped up against the cold, blew the fears and the remnants of the morning champagne away.

Kevin and Janice were great friends of mine and had put Pam up on her two brief visits to Tadchester. Eric, my other close friend and companion on most bachelor expeditions, was keenly courting a girl called Zara. The bachelor days for both of us were numbered.

Zara was a tall, artistic-looking blonde who drove round in a Morris Estate car with a pet owl on the top of the back seat. I would defy anyone to guess her occupation. She dressed beautifully and at parties looked as if she had stepped straight out of the pages of *Vogue*.

Zara was employed by the county council – as a rat-catcher. She must have been the most beautiful and exotic local Pest Control Officer any council had the good fortune to employ. Jeremy, her owl, was never short of a supply of fresh meat.

I bumped into her once when we were both visiting the same farm.

'Look at my haul for the day,' said Zara. In the back of her estate car she showed me a sack containing some one hundred and fifty dead rats.

'None of these for Jeremy, poor old thing. I've poisoned this lot.'

Zara once disgraced herself at a farm when she was attacked by a prize rooster. To fend it off, she took a swipe at it with her heavy metal poison spoon, and neatly decapitated it.

There was litigation between the farmer and the county council for weeks, and we teased poor old Zara unmercifully.

'Look out, Eric,' I would say, 'she might easily decapitate *your* cock.'

Every week I would make some time to have a cup of tea with my old friend Bob Barker at the second-hand bookshop at Sanford-on-Sea, near the slipway. He was one of the nicest, wisest old men I have ever met and always kept a box of small cigars in his desk drawer so that he was able to offer me one on my visits.

I could sit and listen to him talk for hours about old local families and the landed gentry; how there was always one of each generation of these families who carried the inherited spark of success. They would become prosperous businessmen, politicians, or military men. However unlikely a particular litter looked, there was always one who carried the vital gene that kept him in the uppermost group of men of distinction and property.

He would point out other successful men as being the bastards of various members of the aristocracy where perhaps some parlour or dairy maid had spirited the winning line away from a family.

He was delighted to hear of my engagement.

'Women, Bob,' he said, 'I have never understood. I have had what is called as successful a marriage as anyone has had. We have brought up a happy, healthy family, and have grandchildren and great-grandchildren. Then, one day,' he said, with a chuckle, 'a few weeks after our golden wedding three years ago, I was watching my wife bustling round the house. She has been a marvellous wife, mother and grandmother. The house is meticulously clean, she never forgets a birthday, and she's a wonderful cook. As I watched her, I realised that I had never known her. She was a stranger I had lived happily with for fifty years. I never ever knew what real thoughts went through her head.

'I realised, looking back (and it was only when looking back that I saw it), how badly and inconsiderately I must have treated her at times. I was so concerned with myself and my music, my books, my importance, my relationships with other people, I just don't know whether she ever noticed or minded.

'I often think about it. Once or twice I have tried really to get to know her, to know how she ticks, but I have never got anywhere near. After fifty years, she still surprises me sometimes.

'That could be the secret of a successful relationship – marry someone who never ceases to surprise you . . .'

He took out another cigar and pushed the box across the desk towards me.

'I think,' he said, 'that there is a group of people who would make a successful marriage with whomever they happened to settle with, and another group of people who could only make a marriage with one specific person, a twin soul.

'I have never known which group I belong to, but whichever it is, I have been lucky. As well as that,' he said, 'I have enjoyed and loved my music.' (Bob had been the organist at Tadchester Parish Church for forty years.)

'I have learnt some things, but somehow, the older I grow, the less I seem to know. One of the things I have learnt, and knowing your agnostic views you must excuse me for using the Church as an analogy, but,' he said, with a twinkle in his eye, 'the successful church is the one whose organ fund has never closed.'

I would have to work that one out.

'That's enough of an old man pontificating. Today is a special occasion; whether you are on duty later on or not, you are going to have a glass of Madeira wine with your cigar.'

Old Bob was a gem. I wish I could have recorded all his anecdotes and our conversations. I was always encouraging him to write his memoirs but he said he was not a writer, although his whole life had been spent among writers.

Before moving with his wife and daughter to the semi-retirement of his second-hand bookshop at Sanford-on-Sea, he had for many years had a flourishing bookshop in Tadchester itself. It had been a focal point for Somerset and West Country writers. He had had a small dining-room at the rear of the shop where he held literary luncheons and introduced writers to publishers. Many a struggling author had been advised and encouraged by Old Bob if, indeed, not supported by him.

He talked without bitterness of a most successful author, now a household name, who for years came to him for free meals, loans of manuscript paper, money, advice and support. 'I even once,' Old Bob said, 'gave him three of my shirts.' As soon as this author had become successful, he left Old Bob's little circle, never bothered to keep in touch, and did not even pop in and see him when he was visiting Tadchester.

Duty called, and reluctantly I tore myself away: I could have stayed all day with Old Bob and his twinkling advice.

'The successful church is the one whose organ fund has never closed.'

I just couldn't get it.

There were many things I couldn't get. I could never get over the fact that I was not always my patients' first choice as their doctor. I would work extremely hard over a patient to get him through some particular illness only to find that, as soon as he was better, he would attend one of my partners. It was no consolation to me that he had been attending this particular partner for years before I had treated him. I couldn't understand why anyone who had been cured by me should ever have another doctor. I must have been one of the most supreme egotists in my early days.

Miss Harmer and Miss Chesterman helped to cut me down to size. They lived a few houses down the road from Miss Gill and Miss Booth at Sanford-on-Sea. Miss Gill and Miss Booth were great friends of mine and were remarkable for the fact that although Miss Gill had been bedridden for nearly fifty years, looked after by Miss Booth, she had led one of the most full and successful lives that I have ever known. They were inundated with visitors and Miss Gill said 'The thing is, doctor, people come to see me because I have time to listen.' We were good friends and I knew that they prayed for me, which always gave me a twinge of conscience.

I never reached quite the same closeness with Miss Harmer and Miss Chesterman, although they were sweet old ladies and never had a bad word for anyone. The set-up was both similar and different. Miss Chesterman was obviously a lady of means and Miss Harmer was a paid companion/help, though at the time of their life that I met them it was impossible to tell who helped whom.

Some time before I came to the practice in Tadchester, Miss Chesterman had been very ill. She had been looked after by my predecessor, Dr Cookes, who had resigned from the practice before my arrival because he could not keep up with his self-inflicted pace of work.

There was no doubt that Dr Cookes was a fine doctor. His patients adored him. He was selfless in his time and devotion to them and he was a good clinician, but he was probably the first man to admit, in truth, that he couldn't see the wood for the trees.

Miss Chesterman and Miss Harmer could do nothing but sing his praises.

'Do you know, doctor,' they would say, 'sometimes on his Sunday off, Dr Cookes would spend more than two hours here and we used to say to him, "Shouldn't you be back at home with your wife?"'

Nobody could live up to this sort of devotion, including Dr Cookes, who just couldn't meet the demands on his loving care that he himself had created and encouraged. He retired and went off to Canada where, I expect, being the man he was, he would re-create the situation he had just left.

If he had been able to make a proper charge for his services, then his time ratio per patient would not have mattered quite so much. But from what I heard of him he would find it very difficult to ever present anyone with a bill. A lovely man and, as is the nature of lovely men, in hard, crude, commercial terms his own worst enemy.

I looked after Miss Chesterman and Miss Harmer for many years. They both had rather poorly hearts. Miss Chesterman had repeated chest infections and I was a constant visitor, but never on my Sundays off. And never did I – could I – spend two hours with them, even when they were ill. Eventually one of Miss Chesterman's chest attacks was too much for her and she died, cared for to the last by her devoted companion.

After a few months I managed to get Minnie Harmer into an Old People's Home where she soon settled down and was loved as the gracious, selfless person she was. Some years later, when I was married with a family and

Minnie was well into her nineties, she came to spend Christmas Day with us. She was marvellous, telling us all her life history. The gold locket hanging round her neck was given to her by her previous master and mistress for devoted service, which only ill health had caused her to give up. She worked for them for twenty-five years and she had retired in 1911.

It was 1961 when she came to have Christmas lunch with us. She loved the Christmas tree, my mother, Pam my wife, and the children. She was gracious and amusing. I drove her back to the Old People's Home at Sanford-on-Sea. She had had a lovely day and sought to pay me the greatest compliment that she could. 'Well, doctor,' she said as she got out of the car and I helped her into the Old People's Home, 'Miss Chesterman and I were right about our first impression of you. We both said that you would be the nearest we would ever get to Dr Cookes.'

I smiled to myself. This was accolade.

Fifty years ago Tadchester was one of the most important fishing ports on the Somerset coast. A feature of the town was the fishing boats unloading on the quay, with the locals queueing up to buy fresh fish straight from the boats. As in many other coastal areas, the fishing industry had dwindled and Tadchester was left with one fishing trawler going out regularly, one fishing trawler going out intermittently, and the salmon fishermen, who fished for salmon in the estuary with their nets.

There were two fresh-fish shops in Tadchester. One was owned and supplied by the Hadcock Brothers, who owned the only full-time fishing trawler. Les, the eldest brother, ran the shop, and Jack and Charlie did the fishing. The other fish shop received its supplies from Billingsgate, one hundred and fifty miles away in London.

The Hadcocks were all patients of mine; fine men, whose family had fished the waters of the Somerset coast for many years. They were steady men, devout Methodists, but not without a sense of humour. Jack, the middle brother, was the cleverest of this generation of Hadcocks. I liked them all, the two fishermen especially.

'When are you coming out on the boat with us, Doc?' said Jack. The thought of twelve hours out at sea, trawling, appealed to me.

Eventually we fixed a day which suited both my medical timetable and their fishing programme, and I set off with Jack and Charlie in their trawler, the *Lady Alice*. We chugged down the Tad to cross the bar three miles out of Tadchester, by Sanford-on-Sea, then into the open sea.

I felt very manly and nautical standing by Jack in the wheelhouse, but didn't like too much the smell of diesel oil drifting up from the engine-room.

I had not taken anything against sea sickness; although I am not very good about moving over the water I felt confident travelling in local waters. Going down the Tad, where there was not a ripple, confirmed that this was the right decision.

Once over the sand bar that protects the mouth of the estuary from the ravages of the sea, the boat started to pitch slowly up and down in the swell, but still this didn't appear to bother me.

'Well, you have got a good day for it, Doc,' said Jack. 'We won't get a much calmer day than this.'

I began to feel a little bit queasy when we had been out in the open sea for about an hour. The boat began to roll more as Jack and Charlie commenced to pay out their net. Half an hour later, with a further slight increase in swell, I was definitely much more than queasy – I was green.

'You had better lie down in the cabin for a bit, Doc,' said Jack.

The two brothers were fully engaged with their fishing. I went and lay down in the small stuffy cabin. It smelt of fish and diesel oil and I felt awful. I stuck it for quarter of an hour, then came back on deck. I had just reached the side when I started to be as sick as I had ever been in my life.

In between the bouts of sickness, I lay down by the side of the boat wishing I could die. Jack and Charlie were far too busy with the winches, running the boat and getting their net out, to be bothered about me.

'You will be all right, Doc,' they said. 'Sorry we can't help you.'

I looked at my watch. I realised with dismay that, with the tides as they were, there would be another eight hours before we could turn round and head for home.

The day seemed endless. Jack and Charlie did three long trawls and seemed to collect mountains of fish. While they were trawling, they got to work on gutting and cleaning the fish of the previous haul. This didn't help me one bit and their offers of soup and coffee only encouraged me to make more visits to the side. I could quite happily have jumped into the sea and finished it all, even with the knowledge that I had only a few more hours to stick it out. Thank God there were no press gangs any more. It would have meant an early and untimely end for me.

I tried to sleep in the shelter between the boatside and the cabin, and did eventually doze off. When I woke up, I felt somewhat better and the boat had lost its undulating movement. I raised my head above the side, to see that we had crossed the sand bar and were chugging up the Tad. Half an hour and we would be home.

Strange: I felt better as suddenly as I had felt ill earlier.

Both Jack and Charlie were concerned about the bad day I had had, but coming up the river I even felt well enough to tackle my sandwiches and Thermos of soup before we finally docked.

'Thank you for the day out,' I said to Charlie and Jack. 'It has helped me to lose a few pounds if nothing else.'

'Oh, don't let this beat you, Doc,' said Jack, 'you must try it again.'

The defeat and shame of my day with Jack and Charlie hung over me. I felt people were smiling at me behind my back, as even strangers began to come up to me and ask how I had enjoyed my day's fishing.

I resolved to go again, but this time I kept clear of diesel fumes, filled myself with anti-sickness pills, and had a most glorious day out, with the sun shining and hardly a ripple on the water. I helped with the net, even gutted some of the fish between hauls, was ravenous for my Thermos and sandwiches halfway through the day, and was allowed, with Jack's guidance, to steer the boat home over the bar and set it chugging up the river.

They grinned good-naturedly as I got off this time, with a bag of fish to split between my partners.

'I knew we would make a fisherman of you,' said Jack, 'we might even sign you on as a regular hand.'

I thought that, having regained my ground, I would probably leave it at that, particularly as the next day there was a Force 8 gale and the weather was so bad that Jack and Charlie had to ditch one of their nets and head for home.

With our Seine net fishing on the beaches, I did at least always have one foot almost on the ground.

The River Tad was well known for its salmon, and the Tad salmon industry was a very profitable one. However, through over-fishing, particularly by the estuary nets, the number of salmon caught gradually diminished. The salmon rods, which were extremely expensive further up the non-tidal part of the Tad, were not only costly but unrewarding. But the idea of a spell of salmon fishing was so attractive to the people in the bigger towns that they would spend a lot of money on a fruitless fortnight talking about the ones that got away. It did give them the kudos of being able to talk about the salmon stretch they had hired that spring.

One could while away a very pleasant hour in the afternoon standing on Tadchester Bridge; watching the commercial salmon fishermen shooting their nets in the bridge pool at low tide was fascinating. With one end of the net on the shore, the rest piled up in the stern of the boat, the boat would be rowed out in a huge circle, the piled net being paid out as they rowed. When the boat touched shore again, a circle of floats a quarter of a mile in circumference marked where the net lay. Then, with two men on either end of the net, one on the top rope and one on the leaded bottom rope, the net would be slowly and systematically drawn in. Watching from the bridge, one peered down into the dark water, trying to see if there was anything in this haul (*draught* was the proper word).

As the last corks reached the side of the river, activity could be seen in the bunt (end of the net) and the last portion of the net was quickly and carefully hauled up the bank. Long silver shapes could be seen thrashing about, entrapped in the bunt. The netsmen clambered over them, hitting the heads of the fish with short lead pipes, killing them instantly.

There was usually something in each haul. I have seen as many as twenty salmon brought out; beautiful fish, weighing between five and fifteen pounds, lying on the bank. The catch usually included a few sea trout, some small flat fish, and the occasional mullet.

Net fishing in the estuary had a long tradition. Someone was making a lot of money out of it. The general public saw only what was taken out during the day; just as many fish were obviously taken out at night. Occasionally I would be left one of these great beauties in the surgery by a grateful patient or by a patient who hoped to get a sick note that he was not fit enough for work – which meant he had a licence to go net fishing.

One more aspect of the fishing scene was unfolded to me when Gladys popped in at the end of one spring evening surgery and said 'Sorry, Doctor Bob, there is an extra patient who insists on being seen. I have tried to get him to go up to the hospital but he won't go, and his language is appalling.'

Gladys blushed and for Gladys to blush the language must be really rough. The Thudrock colliers never drew a line between what they called 'pit talk' and how they asked for prescriptions and appointments in the surgery. Gladys coped with them all right, so I waited for my 'extra' patient with some interest and a little trepidation . . .

CHAPTER 3

There was a knock at the surgery door. Before I'd time
to say 'Come in', in walked a big man, wearing a tweed
hat, anorak, and tweed trousers tucked into a pair of
wellington boots. He walked stiffly, with his right hand
clutched to the corresponding buttock.

'I'll have to shake hands with me left, doctor,' he said as
I greeted him.

'Fine by me,' I said. 'Won't you sit down?'

'If it's all the same to you,' he said, wincing slightly, 'I'd
rather stand.'

It was John Denton, River Authority head bailiff on the
Tadchester end of the River Tad. Born and raised in the
industrial North, his love of fishing and the outdoors

had taken him away from the smoke, out into the country, and eventually to what he termed, 'T'last bloody 'ole God ever made' – Tadchester.

Though he had been away from the North for nearly twenty years, he had not lost his accent; in fact the longer he had been away, the thicker it had become. His favourite words were *bloody*, *bugger*, followed closely by *sod*. These words, in richest Mancunian, could be heard nightly in the Tadchester Arms and contrasted strongly with the fruity accents and public school vocabulary of the pukka salmon and trout fishermen, and with the West Country burr of his local cronies.

John, in other words, was a character. Big, bluff, boozy, but a dedicated bailiff and angler; as ready to take a youngster patiently through his first attempts with a rod as to put the toe of his large right wellie into the pants of a poacher.

And now he had a problem.

'I've had 'em in some bloody funny places before now, doctor,' he said. 'But this bugger beats all.'

He turned around and lifted his anorak. There, dangling from the seat of his pants, was a large piece of pink metal. 'It's a Devon minnow,' said John – a salmon lure. It was dangling from a vicious triangular hook which had obviously gone in much further than the tweed.

'Eh, don't *you* soddin' laff,' he said. 'I've had enough o' that from them daft buggers down at the river. Especially the one who put it in me with his cack-handed castin'. He soon stopped laffin' when I threatened to put a gaff up his jacksi . . .'

I gathered from this information that the lure was being used by an inexpert angler whose skills John had been attempting to improve, and whose first cast had been made before the coaching had taken effect. I was relieved that John had not put a gaff up his jacksi, or I really would have had a busy morning. (A gaff is a butcher's-

35

sized hook on a handle, used for lifting out beaten salmon, and jacksi is a non-medical term for that part of the human anatomy which is roughly bull's eye when viewed from a posterial elevation in a subject who is touching his toes.)

'All right, John,' I said. 'I promise not to laugh. Now take your anorak off, and bend over with your hands on the seat of that chair.'

John did so, and I felt gingerly around the point at which the hook had penetrated. His thick trousers and some thicker undergarment defied accurate diagnosis.

'I'm afraid I'm going to have to spoil your trousers, John,' I said.

'Feel free, Doc. Supposed to be thornproof tweed, these bloody things. Pity the buggers weren't hookproof as well.'

With a small pair of scissors I cut a circle of cloth from the trousers, and a corresponding one from the thermal long johns I discovered underneath. I then shredded both circles to clear the hook – or rather, hooks.

A treble hook is just that: three hooks mounted back to back at angles of a hundred and twenty degrees to each other. Two of the hooks had penetrated John's buttock beyond the barbs. Once a hook has penetrated beyond the barb, it can't come out the way it went in. The only thing for it is to cut off the end of the shank, and then push the hook through the flesh, point first. John manoeuvred his trousers and long johns down over his gigantic rump so that I could operate unhindered.

'Want an injection, John?'

'Nay, lad. Yer'll no doubt be givin' me some anti-tetanus or anti-fowlpest or some such when yer've done. Just dab a bit of freezer on it an' I'll grit me teeth.'

John gritted his teeth, and apart from a smothered 'Jee-sus Christ!' as the second hook came out, he uttered not a word.

It was quite a neat job, though I do say it myself. Just

two pinholes where the hooks went in, and two more where they came out. I cleaned and dressed the spot, gave John his anticipated anti-tetanus jab, and stuck a large plaster over the inside of the hole in his trousers so that he could face the world without embarrassment.

'Thanks, doctor,' he said. 'I'll get back to t'river now and see who else that daft bugger has maimed. If he's crippled any of his mates, I'll send 'em on to you. Tek 'em on as private patients – and charge 'em plenty . . .'

. . . At evening surgery, John was back again.

'Trouble?' I asked, trying desperately to think of any complications which might have set in. Surely lightning could not have struck twice in the same place.

'No, Doc,' he said. 'I just brought you summat, that's all. Didn't want to leave it outside for everybody to see.'

From under his anorak he pulled out a long, newspaper-wrapped parcel and plonked it on my desk.

'Good 'un, that,' he said. 'Fifteen pounds, fresh-run. Until this afternoon she were still in th'watter.'

It was a salmon: a beautiful, silver, spring salmon. On its flanks were half a dozen sea lice, the hallmark of a fish fresh-run from the sea.

'John,' I said, 'I'm overwhelmed. I really don't deserve this just for treating a . . . a – '

'Pain in the arse?' said John. 'Nay, lad. Get it down yer. It'll do yer good!'

I bumped into John quite often after that. Sometimes, after evening surgery or a round of calls, I would call in at the Tadchester Arms for a quick pint before going back to the flat, only to have a large scotch plonked in front of me by the barman.

'That's on Big John,' he'd say. And there would be John, either further down the saloon bar giving the benefit of his wisdom to some tweed-clad game fishermen, or winking through the hatchway from the public bar, where he would be engaged in more earthly conversation with the Tadchester locals – some of whom I recognised as acknowledged poachers.

John was very friendly with Jack Dawson, the time-keeper at Thudrock Colliery. One day, in a moment of weakness, Jack confessed to me that his secondary job as a part-time hangman gave him back trouble and I had had to issue a sick note to the Home Office stating that I felt his hanging duties were bad for his back.

These two huge men were a formidable combination and most people went out of their way to keep on the right side of them. Jack had been a professional boxer. It was only strangers to Thudrock who ever risked getting into a punch-up with these mighty two, and they always found that they had chosen the wrong side.

'Get it down yer, Doc,' he'd say. 'It'll do yer good . . .'

I didn't have the heart until much later to tell John that I didn't really *like* whisky. I always seem to have been blessed, or cursed, with a whisky drinker's face – whatever that is – and John was only one of many patients who assumed that the Doc liked nothing more than a hefty scotch.

The bailiff-poacher relationship puzzled me until I realised that such a situation was often the case with men operating on opposite sides in the same field of activity. Certainly it was so with the local police and the local villains, and with the local ex-soldiers and their opposite numbers. One summer the Tadchester British Legion played host to a party of German ex-servicemen: ex-Desert Rats and ex-Afrika Korps men toasting each other and swapping stories in boozy evenings at the Legion Hall, and everybody having a whale of a time.

'It's like this, yer see,' said John, one evening when I'd asked about the company he kept. 'The local lads know me and I know them. If I catch them on my beat, they know they're in for a belting. But they're only doing what I would be doing in their place. And they give me the nod if we get any outsiders coming down after the fish –

sometimes they'll see 'em off for me, and that saves a lot of trouble.'

Organised gangs of poachers from outside Tadchester were one of John's big problems. They would come down from as far away as London or Birmingham in Land-Rovers with nets, poisons, gaffs, snares, snatching tackle and wicked three-pronged fish spears. Working at night they would operate by flashlight, or even small search-lights. Working quickly and moving from pool to pool they could strip almost every resting salmon from quite a long stretch of river.

John had had several brushes with them and had twice been badly beaten up – he now rarely went out at night without Jack in tow.

'There's not a lot you can do when you're on your own against half a dozen hard cases. Nowt except mebbee make a lot of noise and hope you've frightened them off. I've given up wading straight in and trying to nab 'em. My name's Cupid, not Stupid.'

Warned by local poachers of an impending raid by a gang from outside, however, John had been able to move in once or twice with a scratch posse of these same locals and a couple of constables, and bring a gang to court. John never knew, nor did the police, how word of a gang's impending arrival worked its way into the Tadchester local villains' grapevine, but he knew when not to ask questions.

Another of John's pet hates was the system of licensed netting at the mouth of the Tad. Local fishermen were permitted to operate with nets during the salmon runs and to take a specified and limited number of fish.

'Limited be buggered,' said John. 'One feller there entered twenty-one salmon on his catch record, and I was there when he brought his boat in. There were a hundred and fifty fish if there was one. That part of the river was outside my beat, so there was nothing I could do except bring in the police – and if you've tried waking the

39

buggers up in Tadchester after midnight, you'd know what a fat lot of good that would be. The bloke would have been off and gone with his fish before the local Flying Squad had got on his bike. Apart from which, the netsmen don't take kindly to interference, and I've grown quite fond of me front teeth.'

There was quite a bit of the poacher in John, as there is in most gamekeepers. One morning in March, I was taking the air by the banks of a brook which ran into the River Tad, before facing morning surgery. Walking the other way, a haversack slung over his shoulder, was John.

'Mornin', Doc,' he said. 'What are you after – a couple of trout fer yer dinner?'

'No, John, just taking a breather. Shouldn't think there'd be any trout in this brook anyway – it doesn't look wide enough for sticklebacks.'

'Don't you kid yerself, lad. Here, hold me bag.'

From the haversack John took a short-handled landing net, and cut a stick from a hedge nearby. He waded into the stream – never went anywhere without his wellies, didn't our John – and pushed the net into the water under the overhang of the far bank. With the stick in his other hand, he thrashed the water about four feet upstream of the net.

When he pulled out the net, it held two thrashing brown trout. After a quick smack on the head each with his priest – a small weighted club – he laid them on the bank and tried again further upstream. Just one trout this time. A little further up – another one.

'There y'are, Doc lad – two fer thee and two fer me. Nowt like a fresh trout unless it's two of 'em.'

'Thank you very much, John,' I stammered, amazed at the speed of the operation and even more amazed that there were any trout in the brook at all. 'But isn't this – er – sort of against the rules?'

'Aye . . . yer could say that,' said John, slipping his

brace of trout into his haversack and slinging it over his shoulder. 'But just you wait until you taste the buggers...'

Now and again I would be called in to do a post mortem on a case of drowning. There were always several in the holiday season and most of them were straightforward, but one puzzled me. The body was found in fresh water, beyond the tidal reach of the Tad, yet the water in the lungs was salt. No foul play was suspected – the person concerned was last seen alone walking the rocks on the beach just before an incoming tide – and it was put down to a freak of the currents: the drowning was in the sea, and yet somehow the body had found itself well upriver.

It puzzled me for months, and one day I mentioned it to John.

'Oh, aye,' said John. 'And was it found by a boatman?'

'Yes,' I said, and mentioned the name of a local fisherman.

'He were daft to use a sea drownin',' said John. 'But you'll get a few which finish up a long way from where they went in. It were an offcomer, that one.'

He explained that for bodies found in the water within the local authority area, a reward of £3 was paid to the finder. For bodies found on the beach, or for those up-river under county jurisdiction, nothing was paid – so enterprising boatmen who found a body would tow it to the stretch of the river where some cash was to be had. 'Offcomers' as such bodies were called by the locals, had contributed to the beer money of Tadchester boatmen ever since the statute granting the reward was enacted in 1887.

John was a great raconteur. One of his favourite stories was about The Brother Who Got Religion.

Two Scottish brothers came to fish the Tad for a week, both expert salmon fishermen. One of them had recently contracted a bad attack of religious mania. He wore rough

41

wool next to his skin, ate only the plainest food, drank only water, ignored the comfortable hotel bed and slept on the floor, and prayed every three hours on the dot through the day and night.

John had pointed out a decent salmon lie to the brothers and left them to it.

After a while, Jamie – the 'normal' brother – hooked a huge salmon, thirty pounds if it were an ounce. He played it for half an hour and eventually got it near enough to the bank to gaff it.*

'Angus!' he shouted. 'The gaff! Quick, man!'

There was no reply. The salmon bucked and streaked off back into midstream. Jamie used all his skill to play the fish back to the bank.

'Angus!' he screamed. 'The gaff! For God's sake, man!'

Again there was no reply.

Jamie turned his head to see Angus at the top of the bank, kneeling with eyes tightly closed and hands clasped upon his breast. It was the three-hourly prayer time. And, salmon or no salmon, Angus was praying.

The salmon bucked again on the tight line and leapt clear of the water. This time Jamie was not quick enough to release enough line to absorb its lunge. The line snapped like cotton – and the salmon was away.

'The last I saw of those two lads,' said John, 'was Jamie streaking across the field waving the gaff and screaming Scottish war cries – and Angus breaking the four-forty-yard record for holy men . . .'

The poacher in John certainly helped him to recognise the poacher in others, even the most unlikely looking.

One of the regular salmon fishermen on John's beat was a highly respected member of the Tadchester community:

---

* The gaff is now banned on many waters, especially early in the season. Many anglers today, anyway, prefer to use the tailer – a wire noose on a handle – to bring in the fish, by looping it round the 'wrist' of the tail. But in those days the gaff was generally used.

prosperous fishing-tackle dealer, Rotarian, JP, and author of countless articles in the angling press in which he extolled the virtues of the salmon and the vices of those who took them by unfair means. His name was Smeaton; he carried himself with a military bearing, spoke in the clipped tones of one born to command, and insisted on being addressed as *Major* Smeaton.

Sitting as a magistrate, he was given to lecturing offenders on decency, discipline and the British way of life. He obviously modelled his delivery on Field Marshal Montgomery and talked a lot about 'straight bats' and 'hitting you people for six' ('you people' being whichever miscreant happened to be before him).

He was especially hard on anybody accused of poaching or breaking the fishing bye-laws on the Tad. Too hard, in John's opinion, and for a while John took only the most serious cases to court.

John did not trust the Major. There was something shifty underneath that brisk manner, and something strange about the Major's bags of salmon. He could catch fish when nobody else on the river could – including John – and would wring the last ounce of publicity from his feats. After a particularly bad fortnight on the river, during which the Major had bagged half a dozen salmon and nobody else had had so much as a bite, John was pondering his success in the Tadchester Arms.

'Only one thing would make them buggers bite this week,' he said, 'and that's putty. I'd swear he was using . . . eh, by God, that's it – the bugger's using putty!'

The use of 'putty' – salmon roe – as bait was highly illegal, but difficult to prove. The putty was soft enough to come off the hook in the water as soon as the angler jerked the rod, so a putty user would strike – pretending he had a bite – as soon as he saw the bailiff . . . and all that would be left would be the lure around which the putty had been squeezed.

One afternoon in January – with still a week to go before

43

the salmon season began – John noticed the Major's car leaving the river bank and heading for the road. John was near enough to head it off while it was still on River Authority land.

('Might have been dodgy if he'd got on to t'road, lad,' said John later. 'I wouldn't have been within me rights then.')

'Mornin', Major,' said John.

'Ah, morning, Denton. Nice day, what?'

(The 'Denton' bit offended John's North-country sensibilities. He had a handle to his name.)

'Beautiful day, Major. And the river's running well. Plenty of fish moving already, I gather. Been spyin' out the land fer next week, have yer?'

'What? Er, yes, Denton. Spying out the land. Exactly. Looking out some promising lies. Nothing like a spot of reconnaissance, as we used to say. Patrolling in depth, what?'

This didn't impress John, who knew that the Major's finest hours during the war had been spent with the Pay Corps in darkest Manchester.

'You won't mind if I look in your boot, will you Major? Purely routine. Got to get into practice, like.'

'I certainly would mind!' snapped the Major. 'Now be a good fellow and get out of my way. I've an urgent Watch Committee meeting to attend!'

'Won't take a second, sir. And you can tell t'Watch Committee you've been setting a good example.'

'Now look here, my good man! . . .'

That did it. Big John was nobody's good man. His tone became quiet, which was always a bad sign.

'I've got the right ter force this boot, Major. And I'd rather not mek a mess of a gradely car like this. If yer wouldn't mind, I'll 'ave them keys . . .'

The Major handed over the keys, his mouth set in a tight line under his clipped moustache. Inside the boot was just a waterproof fishing cape.

44

('When I saw that,' said John, 'I thought I was for it. Mood 'e was in, me feet wouldn't have touched.')

John lifted the cape. Underneath were six salmon. All fresh run, none under twelve pounds and the biggest a handsome twenty-pounder. And the season was still a week away.

'Now look here, my man,' thundered the Major, exploding into one last bluster, 'you'll be in very serious trouble for this! There's a perfectly logical explanation!'

'I know,' said John. 'I know. You left the boot open, turned yer back for a second and the buggers jumped in and closed the boot after them . . .'

In spite of his contacts in the town and on the Bench, the Major was heavily fined and banned from the water for a season. Before the season was out, he had sold his tackle business and moved to Scotland to open another one.

'Think yerself lucky,' said John, as the Major raved at him outside the courtroom after the case. 'If I'd have had owt to do wi' it, yer'd have been banned for life – *and* got six months like any other poor bugger.'

When the Major finally left town, John was troubled by remorse. Under his bluff, tough exterior, he was really soft-hearted and didn't like doing anybody down – even though the Major had got far less than he deserved.

'Yer see, Bob lad,' John said over a pint in the Tadchester Arms, 'it wasn't so much that he was using putty – thought we couldn't touch him for that. It was that for years he'd been such a bloody hypocrite.'

I knew what he meant. John himself was no angel – but at least he had never pretended to be . . .

To some forms of poaching, John turned a blind eye. Another respected pillar of the Tadchester community, well into his fifties, had fished the river since he was a boy with only moderate success. He lived in the shadow of his long-dead father, whose skill with a rod was legendary and whose obsession with salmon was total. The son had inherited the obsession, but not the skill.

He used to tell a story of how, as a boy, he had seen his father play a salmon into shallow water over a gravel bank. The salmon had leapt from the bank about ten feet into a nettlebed higher up. His father had dropped his rod and dived into the nettlebed after the fish – but the salmon had leapt again, snapped the line and somersaulted back to the river and freedom.

I heard the sequel to this story, not from John – who never breathed a word of it – but from the Tadchester businessman himself, who came into the surgery with a streaming cold about a week after the incident.

He was walking along the bank one day, towards the spot where his father had had his famous encounter. Suddenly, right in front of him, a salmon leapt clear across from some way out and landed in the shallows over the gravel bank. Something snapped in the businessman's brain.

'It was like Moby Dick,' he said. 'I was convinced it was the same salmon – after forty-odd years, the *same fish* – and I owed it to my father's memory not to let it escape this time.'

Immediately he dived into the shallow water – clad in bowler, pin-stripe suit and clerical-grey raincoat – and grabbed the salmon. It flipped from his hands back into the water and then, with a mighty flick of its tail against the gravel bottom, shot straight up the bank into the same nettlebed.

The soaking-wet businessman followed, screaming, 'You got away from my father, you swine – but I'm damned if you'll get away from me!'

There was a titanic struggle among the nettles, the thump of a rock on bone, and eventually the businessman emerged, soaking wet, covered in mud and incipient nettle rash, and with a three-foot-long bulge under his raincoat.

John greeted him as he reached the road.

'Bit dampish today,' said John.

'Er . . . yes, John,' said the businessman. 'Silly me. I slipped and fell in.'

'Anything' movin' in the river?' asked John, as if the sight of a dripping and muddled pillar of society were the most normal thing in the world.

'Not a lot, no, In fact . . . er . . . not a thing as far as I could see.'

'Well you get yourself home,' said John. 'Before you catch your death.'

Next day, the businessman bumped into John again.

'Nice fish you had yesterday,' said John.

'What?' said the businessman. 'How did you – er – that is . . . blast it, why didn't you book me?'

'Any man who would go to that much trouble for a fish deserves all the salmon he can get,' said John. 'And besides – who'd have believed a bloody silly story like that . . .'

CHAPTER 4

Ante-natal clinics are happy, healthy places. Obstetrics is the one branch of medicine where there are truly happy endings, a positive end product rather than just a restoration of the status quo.

It is only very occasionally today that childbirth is marred by the death or disease of either mother or baby. It happens so rarely in fact that one tends to disregard it as a possible factor in a birth.

I made a mistake in one case, to some extent a justifiable one – and one which did not involve any real tragedy – but still a mistake.

Gertie Shaw was a big, fat, pleasant woman. She had a ten-year-old son and longed to have a second child. She was huge. Her starting weight was something in the area of twenty-five stone, and when she appeared at my antenatal clinic she had already increased this by another fourteen pounds.

Pregnancy tests of patients' urine in those days were unreliable and expensive and not undertaken very often, and apart from early diagnosis there did not seem much reason to do so: Nature, in time, always demonstrated quite clearly whether a woman was pregnant or not.

Gertie Shaw came in, beaming, saying she was four months pregnant. She certainly looked pregnant: on the other hand, I could never remember a time when she didn't. Her pregnancy was confirmed by the fact that she had ripe breasts, prominent veins round the nipples and was already beginning to secrete some milk. She had a huge abdomen that externally was just a huge abdomen; I was unable to palpate anything through the thick layers of fat. Attempting to perform a vaginal examination was impossible: her thighs met somewhere just above her knees and I had no idea what was really going on inside. I wondered how she had managed to even conceive at all.

Pregnant she was without doubt. She claimed she was four months gone, calculated from the time her periods stopped.

Gertie put on weight exactly as she should have done, even a bit more. Each month she showed an increase of six or seven pounds, her breasts increasingly produced milk (which is the case with some expectant mothers at an early stage). She had no sign of a period and although I could not – as I would normally do – hear the foetal heart through the thickly padded walls of her abdomen, she assured me that the baby kept her awake with its kicking and this was a real lively little one.

She continued to progress well until about four weeks before she was due to be confined. I had booked her into St Mary's Hospital as her home facilities were poor. Not having any idea of the size and shape of the baby nor, in particular, which direction it was pointing, I sent her for an X-ray.

She came gleefully to the next ante-natal clinic, asking 'Is it twins, doctor?' I had been teasing her for a long time, saying that it must be at least triplets, she was so huge. But I had some awful news for her: the X-ray was completely blank.

Gertie had what is called a phantom pregnancy. (She had some famous predecessors, including Mary Tudor and Marie Antoinette.) Her wish to become pregnant again had made her body follow the signs and symptoms of pregnancy. If she had been ten stone lighter, I could easily have excluded a real pregnancy, but her sheer weight and bulk prevented me from making any proper assessment. With the wonderful intruments that we have nowadays, such as ultra sound, it would have been no problem, but these were not available then.

There had been no doubt in either of our minds that she was soon going to have her second desired offspring. She had cashed her maternity grant; she had bought a pram. Everybody knew she was expecting. She had become one of the close family of mothers, the exclusive club that forms amongst pregnant women. It is a close and warm circle.

I had to explain the situation to her as gently as possible. Not only could she not believe it, but she was left with the problem of what to do. She was now nearly twenty-eight stone, with a giant belly and huge, sagging breasts. The whole family, the whole street – in fact almost the whole town – was looking forward to her delivery. She was beside herself with frustration, disappointment and wondering how she would be able to face the outside world. She swore me to secrecy and we formed a plan that she would go home to bed and stay there.

Gertie kept her maternity grant. It was rumoured (and the rumour was never denied) that she had lost the baby.

Somehow, behind her closed doors (she would not let even me in for the first weeks), she sat down and starved herself. In four weeks she had lost five stone, and everybody accepted that she had been through the tragedy of losing a baby.

She was able to sell her pram with some dignity, and we kept her secret: in fact she rather enjoyed the fuss and sympathy she of course deserved. Sympathy she got – she had lost a child, a much loved and cherished one too. It was such a pity, it *would* have been much loved and cherished.

Ante-natal clinics had other surprises to offer, mainly related to the appalling, and sometimes frightening, lack of knowledge that mothers-to-be had about reproduction and childbirth.

There was one patient who had put a piece of Elastoplast over her navel, convinced that she was suffocating the baby. Another was sure she was pregnant for the first time but would not allow me to examine her because she was in the middle of a period.

Mrs Yvonne Petranger was a tall, slim, smartly dressed woman who lived in a modern split-level house overlooking the estuary and was a member of Tadchester's small, hard-drinking, sophisticated set. Her husband was a car salesman or, rather, a garage owner, and had garages both at Winchcombe and Tadchester.

If I were awarding a prize for lack of maternal knowledge, there is little doubt but that Mrs Petranger would be a strong candidate for first prize. She had spent the first five months of her pregnancy in Winchcombe and had now come to Tadchester, where she wished to be confined. I did not know what the medical standards of her general practitioner in Winchcombe were, but there were no records of blood being taken for blood grouping and anaemia tests, or of the other usual routine investigations that one does in the early part of pregnancy. All that had been recorded were a few blood pressure levels and a pregnancy test on Mrs Petranger's urine, showing that she was actually pregnant.

I was obviously going to have to start at the beginning.

Nurse Plank, the midwife, snorted with disgust when she saw the notes of the Winchcombe doctor. She was meticulous about her midwifery; she lived for it, and was loved by what must have been thousands of mothers whom she had seen through childbirth. I knew that if I dared put a foot wrong she would be on me like a ton of bricks.

We had some difficulty getting blood samples from Mrs Petranger. 'Is it really necessary, doctor?' she asked. It took some fairly sophisticated chit-chat before we managed to persuade her that it *was* essential. The actual sticking of a needle into her arm and extracting the blood turned out to be a major operation.

'Now, let's have a look at you,' I said.

She went behind the screen and got undressed and lay on the couch. I came round to examine her.

'Doctor,' said Mrs Petranger, 'I wonder if you would mind checking. My mother is a bit small in her outlet and had some difficulty in being delivered. She thinks I might be the same. I would be very pleased if you could check that for me today. My husband would really like me to go to a private clinic in Winchcombe but I asked if I could see you first – they say you are so good with mothers and babies.'

'Certainly,' I said. I was going to do so anyway, it being part of my general examination.

She smiled. She had obviously chosen her doctor well.

I put on a rubber glove to do an internal examination, and lifted the sheet off her stomach. She was still wearing a pair of small black briefs. I said 'You will have to take those off, Mrs Petranger.'

She looked puzzled and, slowly and reluctantly, took

them off. She lay back, looking mistrustful, and watching me cautiously.

I put some antiseptic jelly on my gloves, then reached for the lower part of her abdomen in an attempt to do an internal examination to assess the size of her pelvis and whether she was likely to have any difficulty with the delivery of her baby. As my hand began to make contact with this rather vital area, Mrs Petranger shot up, screaming, pushing my hand away as if I were indecently assaulting her (which I expect I was in a way), shouted '*Not there, doctor!*', and collapsed in tears.

The hardbitten, sophisticated, well-dressed Mrs Petranger knew very little about the facts of life. She must have had what was almost an immaculate conception as her virginity had not been completely destroyed, and Mr Petranger must have completed his fertilisation at a fairly long range.

Somehow she had arrived at the age of twenty-eight thinking that when babies were born they were delivered through the umbilicus. It took an hour of patient explaining, tears, and a cup of tea, to tell her what the whole thing was about.

'You won't tell anybody, doctor, will you?' she said.

I had come across Mrs Petranger's situation before, as a medical student when we had a gynaecologist's daughter who had the same way of thinking.

In cases of infertility, where couples had been trying unsuccessfully to have a child, I learnt in time before I did any investigations to check exactly where, and how, they were trying to conceive. Somehow the navel, to a small minority of people, has a magic of its own, and I knew of at least three couples who had fruitlessly tried to pursue this as the route of conception.

Mrs Petranger gave up all thought of the Winchcombe private clinic after our first frank discussion on the route by which babies entered the world.

53

She had a normal pregnancy, but a fairly rough delivery; she could not co-ordinate her pushing very well and eventually I had to do a forceps delivery in St Mary's Maternity Home, with Jack Hart dropping chloroform and ether on the other end.

Before I put on the forceps I had to complete the small operation required to eliminate the remnants of her virginity.

I had a word with her husband after delivery about their marital life.

'I can never get near her, doctor,' he said. 'She is always running away from me. She doesn't like sex – she is frightened of it – and I understand that her mother was the same. Will it be all right now she has had a baby?'

'Yes,' I said, confidently, knowing full well that there was no longer any barrier to prevent her husband making headway.

I discussed Mrs Petranger's case with Steve, my senior partner. He told me that, in his experience, alas, this situation was not uncommon, but the birth of a baby too often may not be the end of a couple's physical difficulties. Somewhere along the line there may be some inbuilt psychiatric damage. To resolve it would require a lot of patient psychiatry which, frequently, the patients decline to have.

'But for some,' he said, 'the birth of a child resolves all their physical problems, and they go happily on from there. I hope that the Petrangers fall into this group.'

Pam and I fixed 9th September as the day we would get married. The wedding would be held in Leatherhead, and we had seven months to fix all arrangements and for me to find some accommodation for us. The flat above the surgery was far too small for two and we could not afford to buy a house, so I set about finding somewhere to rent.

Eventually I found a first-floor flat in a three-storey house Up-the-Hill. It stood on its own in about a quarter of an acre of garden; the large ground-floor flat was occupied by some Americans who were tenants of the owner of the house and we were to be sub-tenants of Herbert Barlow who rented the top two floors and lived alone in a room on the uppermost floor.

Herbert Barlow, as I came to know him over the years, was one of the most remarkable and memorable men I have ever met. He claimed to be a gentleman, a writer and a man of the theatre, and he was without doubt the most available man I have ever known.

He looked like a writer, sounded like an actor: a stern dignified face, carefully groomed silver hair, and a deep resonant voice that trotted out theatrical platitudes, punctuated with growling 'my dears'. He had a perfect set of teeth.

He looked, and was, a man acting a part. Through all the time I knew him I fluctuated from thinking that he was a complete sham to joining in with him and saying the right words and lines. He lived frugally, explaining that when his last marriage broke up he decided to dispense with possessions, leaving himself free to dash off to the south of France, New York or Italy if anybody required him.

He said, 'I don't have any dependants now and I don't intend to be dependent on anybody else.'

There was no doubt that he did write, for in his little room there were five fully prepared manuscripts of plays on his desk.

'Once I get a couple of these on in the West End I shall be made. Look at dear old Maugham [Herbert considered Maugham was an intimate and an equal], he had exactly the same trouble, and finally had five plays on at the same time.'

These plays were always *nearly* being produced. Herbert would say 'Dear old A is interested,' dropping some theatrical household name, and I would pretend to believe him. One day when I was with him in his room, the phone rang, and there *was* old A asking for Herbert and obviously knowing him, but somehow his plays still never got produced.

In all, I knew Herbert over ten years, during which time he wrote twelve plays. His manuscripts, beautifully prepared, could not be bettered; they included intricate stage directions, and for some of them he built elaborate model stage sets.

I read them all. For the very professional way they had been prepared they should have been produced. On picking up the manuscripts and folders one knew immediately, as when one first met Herbert, that these were professional plays, written by a professional and a man of the theatre. But on reading them they seemed to be all dialogue and manuscript, stage directions, lights, props; there was no story, no characters emerging, and I could never understand what he had been trying to say until he explained them himself.

Herbert used to talk of his days before the war, in the south of France. 'My natural home, old boy.' He was then a film script writer and living on half the income he was receiving. 'Went there to die, old boy. My dear friend Dr X, who is now a medical superintendent at The Great Y Hospital, said I had consumption, coughing up blood, thought I had only six months to live.'

This was the kind of hackneyed, classical melodrama around which all the episodes of Herbert's life seemed to revolve. 'One of the biggest disappointments of my life at that time,' he said, 'was Daisy, half of a famous dancing sisters act. We had been living together for eight years. As soon as she knew I was ill, she left me. Eventually she married Lord Z.' Anyone connected with Herbert couldn't possibly have married into anything less than the peerage.

'Do you see your friend the doctor at all now?' I asked.

'No, old boy, haven't seen him for years. He married again and I just couldn't get on with his wife. If I was ever ill though I would, of course, go straight to him.'

Any of the important people Herbert knew were at all times just out of reach. They were, without exception, intimates, but there was always some reason why they would never be in touch with him; either they brought back old memories, or there was some area of friction such as a new life, or he didn't want to get in touch with them until he was once more re-established in the theatre.

'Of course,' he said, 'the war finished my stay in the south of France. Had to come back to England.'

It would have been typical of Herbert to say that the Government had sent a battleship to rescue him in the teeth of enemy fire, or that he had at least swum from Dunkirk, but he never gave an account of the circumstances of his return.

What was certain was that, at the beginning of the war, he was the manager of a large London theatre. He talked about the royalty he had entertained there, about the private film shows for the prime minister, how he was on intimate terms with them all. Coupled with these stories of his association with such people, his theatre, and his writing achievements, were his stories of daily triumphs in the local market where he had got a penny off coffee, twopence off cheese, or found a remnant of material from which he could make a shirt.

He had bought an old sewing machine for £2, and could make any type of wearing apparel – he made a shirt for me, and an evening dress for Pam.

I am sure that sometimes he went hungry. He had no visible means of support, other than some occasional play 'doctoring' for ambiguous theatre companies. 'Plenty of money backing this, old boy,' he would say. 'They have asked me to make something of it.' I saw two of these plays.

Having his manuscripts typed cost money. Posting them cost money. He used to say, 'I have a couple of hundred pounds capital, old boy, but don't like to touch it.' I was never able to bring myself to believe this.

He claimed to have stage managed sometime or other every London theatre, starting after the first world war at the old Alhambra Theatre with 'Bing Boys on Broadway' and the Diaghilev Ballet.

Herbert tucked himself away in his top-floor room with his memories, his manuscripts and his great associations. Life was as simple as possible – in his room he had only a bed, a desk, two armchairs and a double gas ring. He used to come down to our flat for his weekly bath. A devoted daily called Elsie came and 'did' for him and took no payment for her services; she adored him and always thought of him as a great man.

He had so arranged the domestic pattern of his life that he was ready at a moment's notice if he should be required by a theatre or film company. 'I could pack and be off for six months tomorrow if they needed me, old boy,' he would say. He even didn't like being out of the district in case he missed a call that he knew one day would come – the call that would lead to the success which so far had eluded him.

Of the ten years I knew him, the last two he spent fighting a terminal illness that would have finished most people in six months. During those two years he wrote a spiritual play which was to be the climax of his life and work. He finished his play and sent it round, but it had the usual rejection slips. Nobody was interested. Obviously, although he had been a very good stage manager and could improve other people's manuscripts, he just couldn't write plays himself.

He was getting much weaker now, so I took it upon myself to get in touch with his great friend Dr X, super-intendent of The Great Y Hospital in London, and to my surprise Dr X was a great friend and offered to take him straight into his own hospital and give him full VIP treatment.

Herbert's health was failing so rapidly that I knew he

would never attend another first night. Unbeknown to him I contacted some of the great men of the theatre he had mentioned, explaining the position and the importance to Herbert of his last play. Again to my surprise, they knew him and all had a great affection for him. He had been a successful film script writer and a well-known stage manager.

The friends and I got together, and one of the more influential of them wrote to Herbert saying how much he liked this last play and that he hoped to produce it at some date in the future – a date, we all knew, when Herbert would no longer be there to help with the stage directions.

Herbert accepted this letter calmly. 'I knew, old boy,' he said, 'that there was a purpose in my struggling on these last two years. I know this play has a message,' and his eyes shone with triumph from his now gaunt face.

Herbert died with dignity as I knew he would. I contacted those relatives I could find and, having perhaps been closer to him than anyone else, offered to help pay the funeral expenses. But Herbert had left £200 in the bank – enough for all the expenses, and some left over for Elsie who had worked for him for nothing for so many years.

On the desk in my study I keep a pile of beautifully prepared play manuscripts in a cardboard folder, tied round with a piece of brown ribbon. Nobody will ever produce them, but they are my memorial to my great friend, Herbert Barlow, Gentleman, Writer and Man of the Theatre. A man who always kept himself available, never realising that he had spent so much of his life pretending to be the sort of person he actually was.

CHAPTER 5

Tadchester continued to surprise me with the unusual characters that kept bobbing up.

One morning, returning from a 6 a.m. call I came across Ivy Henshaw struggling across Tadchester Bridge with two large suitcases, off to catch the early morning bus from the terminus. I drew up and offered her a lift, which she gratefully accepted.

'I think I would have missed the bus without you, doctor,' she said.

Ivy had been the usherette at the Tadchester Picture Palace for as long as anyone could remember. She was the Queen of the Upper Circle and Balcony, and ruled her little empire with good nature and a loud West Country laugh. She was a big girl, with poor eyesight, but in the gloom of the cinema she could recognise and name nearly all her patrons.

Outside the cinema she led a very quiet life, living in a small house in Quay Street, a tiny street off Bridge Street in the centre of Tadchester. What she lacked in intelligence and education, she made up with good humour. She lived quite alone, but kept an eye on and did the shopping for the young crippled man who lived next door to her. Sometimes, on a Sunday, I would see her having her weekly treat – lunch in the quayside snack bar.

'Now, where are you off to, Ivy?' I asked.

'Poland, doctor,' she replied.

I thought she was joking. I would have put Ivy's maximum range as a package coach trip to Plymouth or Torquay or, at the most, a couple of nights in London.

'Are you really going to Poland, Ivy?' I asked.

'Oh, yes, doctor.'

'Is it a package holiday?'

'No.'

'Do you know anybody in Poland?'

'No.'

'Well, why are you going?'

'Oh doctor,' she said, 'I go somewhere different every year,' and she told me her story.

Ivy's local accent was so broad that it was very doubtful if anyone who lived more than ten miles away from Tadchester could understand what she was saying, but for two or three weeks every year she would go off to a new country and somehow find her way around it. She told me that she had gone to Russia the previous year, Spain the year before, and was going to Poland this year. She hoped, perhaps, that Bulgaria might have something different next year. 'I didn't like those Spanish trains,' she said.

As we drove to the bus station, I discovered that Ivy's method was just to book her flight or train to whatever

61

country she had an inclination to go to. Then, on a very limited budget, without any knowledge of any foreign language, and with her almost unintelligible English, she would manage to travel round and find accommodation in this new country.

She didn't seem at all concerned about this trip to Poland. I tried to imagine her talking to booking clerks in Spain, Russia, and Poland; at reception desks in foreign hotels and boarding-houses. I couldn't imagine how she did it – but I could have hugged her . . .

Two weeks after dropping her at the bus station, I received a card. It was a picture of some Polish square, with a cobbled road and tramlines running through it. It read:

Dear Doctor,
At the moment I have seen Wrzesnia, Konin, Lowicz and Poznan. Just left Zola, Zowa, Wola, birthplace of Frederick Chopin. The 18th-century country house stands in a beautiful park and is now a museum. Thanks for the lift to the bus depot. Ivy.

For the first time I thought about how people from this small crowded island that I lived on, at one time colonised and administered about half the world. It was people like Ivy going forth, oblivious to difficulties – language, financial or otherwise – who had founded that vast empire. A few Tadchesterians would have maintained it quite happily and would have thought nothing of it.

A month later Ivy came to my surgery, full of beans, sporting an engagement ring on her finger.

'Did you have a good holiday?' I asked.

'Marvellous,' she said, 'and look, doctor, I am engaged. It is a Polish count.' (I felt certain Ivy would settle for nothing less.) 'He was the porter at the hotel I stayed in in Warsaw. Do you think you could give me some tablets to lose weight? We hope to get married in six months' time, and I want to lose a stone or two before then.'

I talked to Ivy about her diet, and gave her some amphetamine tablets, which would not only restrict her appetite but would give her a bit of 'get-up-and-go' which would help in getting rid of some of her excess weight. Somehow I had an awful feeling at the back of my mind that the marriage would not come off. I don't know why: Ivy seemed so happy.

A month later Ivy returned. She had lost nearly a stone in weight but no longer wore her engagement ring.

'What has happened to the count?' I asked.

'Oh,' said Ivy, cheerfully, 'when I wrote to him it was his wife who replied. He was married all the time, and she said his ring was worthless. I think he must have got it from one of those little crane machines.'

She seemed quite unmoved by her emotional disaster.

'I would like some more of those tablets if I could, doctor. I've been roaring all over the place since I started them.'

I gave Ivy another month's supply and cautioned her not to exceed the prescribed dose.

When I first went to Tadchester, 'soft' drugs were unknown, anyway by name. We knew of – or at least had heard of – heroin and cocaine addicts in the big cities and were beginning to suspect that pethidine, which was pretty freely available, should not be prescribed too often.

Barbiturate sleeping tablets, and the stimulant amphetamines, were in everyday use. It was common practice to take an amphetamine stimulant if you had a night drive or you needed to keep awake for some specific purpose.

I was then Medical Officer to the Tadchester Forward Medical Aid Unit. This unit, which consisted of a doctor, a trained nurse and eight members of St John's or the Red Cross, composed a team which travelled round the country successfully competing against teams from the larger towns.

To both settle my team and give them a bit of 'gee-up' before entering competition arenas (we usually had forty or fifty made-up casualties to treat in the middle of a large hall) I would often give them a Drinamyl tablet. No one suffered any obvious ill effect, and we usually won.

Nowadays, such has been the abuse and misuse of drugs like the barbiturates and amphetamines, you would be breaking the law, and could actually be prosecuted, for just having some in your possession. In the good old, bad old, days of my early years in practice, barbiturate sleeping tablets and amphetamines were widely and usefully used. If you were overweight, you were given a long-acting amphetamine tablet to reduce your appetite. (I shudder when I think of how such treatment would be viewed now.) Sometimes, in addition to the appetite-depressing amphetamines, we prescribed thyroid tablets to help burn off surplus fat.

Widow Cox was one of my constantly overweight patients. She regularly came for amphetamine tablets to suppress her appetite, but each month (Gladys used to weigh her on each visit) she hardly ever varied. She might be a pound up one month, or a pound down the next, but she made no impression on her basic fourteen and a half stone.

I had almost given up the battle. She swore she didn't eat large meals, but on two occasions at least, I had seen chocolate wrappers sticking out of her handbag.

One Thursday she came to my surgery for her routine monthly check a completely changed woman; a change, unhappily, for the worse. She had obviously lost weight but, in doing so, looked ten years older. On checking the weight slip, I found that Widow Cox, whose weight had been stationary for at least ten months, had dropped by twenty-two pounds in just four weeks.

'Well done, Mrs Cox,' I said. 'This is marvellous. How did you manage to do it?'

'Oh, doctor,' she replied, 'whatever have you done to

me? Why did you make me take the tablets at night instead of in the morning? I haven't slept for a whole month. I feel a complete wreck.'

I knew perfectly well I had never prescribed slimming tablets to be taken at night, but Mrs Cox had been taking them just before she went to bed. On enquiry, the reason wasn't hard to find.

When I was writing prescriptions, if I wished a tablet to be taken in the morning I wrote 'OM' beside the number of tablets I was prescribing; if I wished tablets to be taken at night, I wrote 'ON'. In the turmoil of a busy day, my N's and M's were not always too distinguishable.

Mrs Cox had had her prescription made up at Neville's, the chemist's shop in the town; somehow it must have escaped his proper scrutiny. I had to explain to her how the mistake had been made and make sure her next prescription was clearly marked 'OM'.

The next month Mrs Cox reported back, bright and breezy, her old self again; in fact, exactly her old self again! She had put back the twenty-two pounds she had lost the previous month. As soon as she had stopped taking the Dexadrine tablets each night, she slept for three days and nights, then got up and bustled around.

We went through her diet together. No, she hardly ate a thing. No breakfast, hardly any lunch, and just a bit of supper. 'In fact,' she said, 'if I didn't take a couple of bars of chocolate each day for energy, I wouldn't be able to keep going. I think my glands must be wrong, that is what is making me overweight.'

I stopped Mrs Cox's tablets. We were obviously not making any headway, but I continued to keep an eye on her weight. To my surprise, the next time she came to the surgery, four weeks later, she had lost seven pounds. This weight loss continued each month without any help from me until she was down to a trim figure, with no weight problems at all. I wondered how she had done it.

The answer came to me one Sunday afternoon on Tadchester quay. There was Widow Cox walking along the quay, dressed in her Sunday best, on the arm of a tall, thin, angular man. Widow Cox was courting. It was obviously a much better cure than any of my tablets.

Poor, sweet Miss Jessie Braithwaite was the opposite to Mrs Cox. She had never had a weight problem but one afternoon when I was visiting her sister, whom she looked after, she did confess to me how badly she had been sleeping recently. (Her sister Ethel had a bad heart that we were able to keep under control providing she did not overdo things, but an attack of bronchitis had overstrained her heart and I had had to insist that she have a spell of bed rest.)

Jessie's problem had started at the beginning of Ethel's illness. She had been up for two or three nights, had her sleep pattern disturbed, and not been able to drop back into a regular sleeping habit since.

I explained to her that the commonest cause of insomnia was having formed a habit of staying awake. If she took a course of some sleeping tablets for a few nights, she would form a regular habit of sleeping again and all would be well.

I gave her half-a-dozen pills from my bag, assured her of a good night's sleep, and told her I would come and see her sister the next day.

The next day I found both sisters in bed. Miss Jessie, who was rarely ill, was completely incapacitated with a bad back.

'Now, Miss Jessie,' I said, 'have you been trying to lift your sister?'

'No, doctor,' said Jessie. 'My bad back is through your tablets.'

Apparently poor Miss Jessie had taken my advice and taken one of my sleeping capsules, a barbiturate, about an hour before she was due to go to bed. She slept soundly, and woke to find herself fully dressed, lying halfway up the

66

stairs. The action of the tablet had been far too swift for her – and her backache was caused from the hard edges of the stairs sticking into her back through the night!

Troubles arose with both amphetamines and barbiturates when patients started to mix them with alcohol. Alcohol made both more potent. Not only did it add to the effect of the barbiturate sleeping tablet; it resulted in its being absorbed much more quickly. A moderate dose of barbiturate plus a moderate tot of alcohol could combine together to form a lethal mixture, and a number of untimely deaths were recorded throughout the country where people had taken sleeping tablets after having had a few drinks.

Similarly, alcohol and amphetamines gave all sorts of bizarre results. People behaved strangely and out of character – there were accounts of people walking out of windows at parties, being aggressive and acting in all sorts of strange ways. With both barbiturates and amphetamines, users could reach a stage where they could not do without them and would beg, rob, or even kill, for their drugs. The dangers were recognised and thus, over a period of years, two valuable medical drugs were gradually withdrawn from use by the general public.

Pam and I had fixed our wedding day for 9th September at St Mary's Church, Leatherhead. There seemed to be a tremendous amount to do and Pam came to Tadchester as often as she could. I had arranged to take over the flat from Herbert Barlow in April; from then on Pam came down every other weekend and managed to spend a whole week in Tadchester at the beginning of June.

The Harts were always very kind and provided her with accommodation. We were closely chaperoned and although we tentatively suggested that I could sleep on the settee in my flatlet, or we could put up a camp bed in Herbert Barlow's flat, it was gently pointed out to me that this sort of thing was not approved of in Tadchester.

Tadchester was largely Methodist. There were in fact two Methodist churches, one in the High Street and one in Mill Street. This did not mean that the other churches did not have their adherents. There was one Congregational church, one Baptist, and about six others of various shapes and sizes, like the Unitarian, Christian Scientist, Free Gospel and Tabernacle, apart from a staunch Roman Catholic element and, last but not least – in fact, the biggest of them all – the Anglican church which was big enough to merit having a prebendary rather than a vicar as its minister.

I looked after at least a dozen ministers of religion of different sorts. The Church had a great influence on the community; it was said in Tadchester there was only one certain way of getting on the Council, and that was by being a Methodist.

Pam was awe-stricken at her first meeting with Herbert Barlow. His voice dropped a few octaves when he spoke to her, rumbling away in his most austere tones. Did she know the de Quinceys in Leatherhead? One of the richest families in England. Great friends of his. She must send them his regards when she got back.

As I started paying rent for the flat from April, Pam was free to come and measure for curtains and carpets; she had me putting up shelves, painting and wallpapering. It was a large first-floor flat – two huge reception rooms with Claygate fireplaces, a small guest bedroom, a large double room for ourselves, and a large kitchen/breakfast room. The bathroom was communal in the fact that we had to provide a bath once a week for Herbert and Miss Gulliver – not together: Miss Gulliver had the three rooms on the top floor not occupied by Herbert.

In addition to paying the rent, we had to buy some furniture which had been left there. At one time Herbert had lived in the whole flat with one of his wives (presumably his last). In the bedroom was a huge, ornate double bed with a padded headboard and attached wing cupboards. The bedroom suite had come from a film set, and Herbert told us that Marlene Dietrich had lain on the bed during some film whose title he could not remember. I could hardly wait to get to bed! There was a wing-back armchair in the lounge that Herbert had made himself, and in the dining-room a dining suite which matched well enough and, in fact, was very good furniture. There were Regency chairs, a sideboard that looked as if it were Sheraton but was in fact a very good one from Maples' store, and a polished dining table, all hallmarks of the dignity of Herbert's past.

Much of each weekend was taken up in introducing Pam to local people. She loved Bob Barker at the bookshop, and thoroughly enjoyed her formal tea with the de Wyrebocks. If I had been asked to name two ladies who had nothing in common, I would have said Pam and Marjorie, but in fact they got on extremely well. They both had their forthcoming marriages in common. Marjorie was getting married a week before us and Eric and Zara, who had become engaged, were getting married a month after. Pam and Zara became the best of friends and arranged a couple of shopping trips in London on weekends that Pam did not come to Tadchester.

Frank and Primrose Squires took us Seine net fishing, with Joe and Lee Church making up the party. It was to be Pam's initiation into the art. Frank had his own net with which we trawled the beach at Sanford-on-Sea at night, hoping to catch sea trout and various flat fish and bass. Frank was the land surveyor for the county council – a real outdoor man – always shooting, fishing or sailing; a born leader, with an infectious humour. Joe Church was the games master at the local grammar school.

Usually five or six of us took the net out. It was about sixty yards long, had a pole at either end, with traces like

69

those on a dog sled leading off from each pole. With one man on a pole at either end of the net, holding it upright, and as many volunteers as possible pulling on the traces from the pole we would trawl parallel to the beach in as deep water as possible with the outer pole (outer staff) ahead of the inner pole so the net trawled parallel to the beach like a letter 'J', the idea being that the men on the outer staff would drive the fish into the bulging bottom of the 'J'.

On Pam's first night just the three of us took it out, Frank and I on the outer staff, with Joe on the inner. It was really hard work. We could only slowly move the net along through the water, and the girls had to help us pull it up the beach once we got clear of the sea. We had one of our best catches ever, several sea trout, which were stuffed in jumpers and pockets in case the Water Bailiff saw us, four large bass, some mullet, about a dozen skate and various flat fish.

Every couple of hundred yards we would pull up the beach – these were called draughts – and any fish in the net were mercifully killed by a bang on the head with a piece of lead piping, then thrown into a little box on runners which it was the girls' job to tug along the beach.

The box filled rapidly and the girls complained how difficult it was to pull, offering to swop places with us in the water while we pulled the catch.

We decided to trudge back with the catch whilst the girls went for a midnight swim. They had no costumes with them and as we got some distance away, we could hear their giggles through the darkness. They were obviously going to swim in the suits that Mother Nature had provided.

The box was heavy and we were a good three quarters of an hour trudging back to the cars. We dried ourselves, changed, and sat waiting for the girls, periodically flashing our torches to show where we were. About a quarter of an hour later they came running up to us. We sat round, drinking coffee, eating sandwiches and talking.

Pam went to the car to fetch a rug and came back in tears.

'Oh, Bob darling,' she cried, 'I seem to have lost my engagement ring.'

This was awful. We had covered miles of beach so the chances of us finding the ring were very small. We set off back across the sand, following our footprints and sled marks, towards the sea's edge.

After walking for ages the marks in the sand suddenly took a right-angled turn, the point where we had left the girls. To our absolute delight, there, winking up from the sand in the torch beam, was the diamond in Pam's ring. Our chances of finding it like this must have been thousands to one.

Pam clung to me with relief.

'You've got a right one there,' said Frank. 'When she decides to bathe in the altogether, it is really in the altogether, she doesn't even wear a ring.'

Wearily, but happily, we turned round and trudged back to the cars.

CHAPTER 6

In winter, Tadchester was a rugby town. The local rugby club turned out five sides each Saturday and the main winter social events were associated with the splendid clubhouse and bar that the club had built for themselves.

To produce seventy-five young men each Saturday the club had to have a pool of one hundred and fifty players. Many of them worked on farms or had other occupations that meant they were not available every weekend. Added to that were the inevitable injuries, weddings, funerals and christenings that all took their toll.

In the rugby club the après-game was probably just as important as the match. The Saturday night sing-song was an event not to be missed. Tadchester boasted more than its share of pretty girls, many of whom were ready volunteers to help with the food and the bar at the clubhouse. This was an added attraction for the players to linger, and if after a game the clubhouse was actually cleared by midnight, it was unusual.

Although Tadchester was not a first-class rugby club, it was probably not too far off being one. As it was located in a seaside town and offered good hospitality, it attracted touring sides. Many of the best teams in the country, such as Cardiff and Bristol, would come down to play the local side, usually making a weekend of it, playing Tadchester on the Friday and Winchcombe on the Saturday.

Tadchester had its own soccer team, too, which played in the Western League. They had a magnificent stadium, owned by the Council, and each year had the excitement of the preliminary rounds of the FA Cup. They had no actual chance of reaching Wembley, but there was always the hope that they might get far enough to attract some famous side down to Tadchester.

This local team, however, was not composed of locals. They were professionals, some ex-League players. They played football as part of their livelihood, not as part of, or really representing, the town. Many came from as far as fifty or sixty miles away and the end of a game was followed by a quick cup of tea and everybody scurrying off. So unlike the home life of our own dear rugby team.

If rugby was the town's favourite winter sport, cricket was the important exercise for the summer. It had to compete with tennis, swimming, golf and surfing for the No. 1 position, but every hamlet for miles had its own cricket team. In the Tadchester area cricket was more than a game: it was an obsession. There were knockout cups, evening and Sunday leagues, and if you didn't play at least the occasional game of cricket – whatever else you did or didn't do – you didn't belong.

I sometimes kept wicket for the Thudrock Colliery team. Though one of the worst teams in the area, Thudrock probably enjoyed their game more than most. It could have been something to do with their working underground that made them unable to sight the ball properly in daylight on the surface, but they went on cheerfully playing for years without winning a match. As a substitute wicket-keeper, I was absolutely of their standard. The number of byes I let through would sometimes amount to more than the total score of runs made with the bat by our opponents.

Thudrock once put out an open challenge to play any team *underground* for a side stake of £50. They never ever found a challenger. Where they would have played if somebody had taken them up, I have no idea. The biggest open area was the pit bottom which, at its widest, was fifty feet. There would have been boundaries galore from the opposition. However, none of the other teams seemed keen on the idea.

Tadchester Cricket Club played on a pitch at Sanford-on-Sea, a few yards from the sea wall which prevented the low-lying land from being washed away. As it was situated close to the seashore, it could boast a cricket gate as big as many of the county sides. The holidaymakers who invaded the town in the summer would, after a few days, get fed up with making sand castles and waiting for the tide to come in. Looking for some distraction – and there were few others at Sanford-on-Sea – they would climb over the sea wall and watch the cricket matches.

There being nothing like a crowd to attract a crowd, the beach would soon become practically denuded of people. During a match the beach would be populated only by the odd grandma asleep in a deck chair and a few die-hard children, doggedly building intricate sand walls that they knew, definitely, this time would keep the tide at bay.

All would be well, with a couple of thousand people

watching, ball by ball, the fluctuations of the cricket match. Then there would be a scream from one of the abandoned grandmas, wakened by water lapping round her ankles. This would signal a mass exodus by the crowd, who shot off to rescue their towels, picnic baskets, deck chairs, transistors and any other possessions that had not already been swept away by the incoming tide.

The Tadchester Cricket Club worked in close harmony with the tide, and always passed the hat round whilst it was still ebbing, knowing that if they delayed their collection until the tide changed, a take of what might be easily as high as £200 could be as low as £2.

There were few more pleasant sights on a summer's afternoon than that of Kevin Bird, as Tadchester's opening bat. His broad-shouldered hits would send the ball flying over the sea wall time after time. If farming had not been his first love, he could certainly have made a living as a full-time cricket professional.

I watched the cricket as often as I could, but after my first year in Tadchester I never ventured on to the adjoining beach. Interspersed amongst the holiday makers were always a dozen or two of my patients. Seeing their doctor available and unencumbered, it seemed the ideal time to approach him with their latest medical problems. As they were mostly half undressed or in their bathing suits, it was much easier for them to show off their lumps, cuts, rashes, jelly-fish stings and bruises, and saved a long trip to the surgery.

The one thing about the beach was that my patients didn't get lost, as they sometimes did in my surgery.

I had, to some extent, acquired a reputation of being forgetful in the undressing situation. Across from my consulting room was an examination room. If I had someone who needed a full examination I would send him or her off to this room to disrobe while I was seeing the next patient. On a few occasions I became so engrossed in the next cases that I forgot all about my waiting customer. One very embarrassed gentleman whom I had sent to get undressed came back complaining, 'Doctor, there is already a naked lady in the room.'

Twice I had finished my surgery and was off to join my partners for coffee when I heard sobbing in the examination room. On both occasions I found an almost frozen young women who had been sitting in her nether garments for two hours since I had said, 'Go into the examination room, take your clothes off, I'll be with you in a minute.'

My final break with the beach came one sunny afternoon when I had dozed off there in my deck chair. I was wakened by someone surreptitiously coughing in my ear, to find there was a queue of eleven people of different shapes and sizes waiting to consult me . . .

I followed the Tadchester Cricket Club whenever possible and sometimes went on away fixtures with them. I was rewarded on one occasion by being asked to give the toast of 'The Cricket Club' at their annual dinner. I rather fancied myself as an after-dinner speaker and with a responsive audience in the palm of my hand encouraging me, was somewhat inclined to go on and on.

With my stories getting progressively more outrageous, I could have talked all night. I was brought back to earth by the Chairman kicking my ankle and pointing to his watch. Up to this point, having got into my full flow and being a bit full of wine, I had failed to mention the Cricket Club. I made the ultimate gaffe when, having been brought to a halt by the Chairman's kick, I stopped and said, 'Gentlemen, it is with great pleasure that I ask you now to raise your glasses and drink to the health of the Tadchester *Rugby Football Club*.'

They never asked me again.

A quarter of a mile along the coast from the cricket ground

was the famous South Somerset Golf Course. In its heyday it had been one of the main championship courses in the country, but the sea wall wasn't as good as it used to be and didn't protect the land as well as it should have done. During the winter gales the sea would make great inroads through the wall on to the course and the damage to greens and fairways was never quite made up.

There was another problem. Through some ancient bye-law, every householder within a radius of about twenty miles had grazing rights on the common, which included the golf course. As the local population grew, so did the number of people taking up grazing rights, and the common was packed with cattle, horses, goats, sheep and any other quadruped that was able to get some nutrition from the overgrazed grass.

Apart from the hazards of animal droppings on the green, you weren't always safe from the animals themselves: many of the horses were half-wild. Frank Squires once had half his golf bag eaten by a hungry horse as he concentrated on a difficult putt, and one stout lady patient was chased right across the common by two amorous stallions.

When the spring weather came, the golf course became the happy hunting ground of the local 'flashers', who lay behind the bunkers and leapt out, exposing their credentials to whoever might be unfortunate enough to be passing at the time.

Things deteriorated so much that, in time, a round of the South Somerset Golf Course became an endurance test rather than a game of golf. A returning golfer, emerging alive after the completion of a round and being asked how he got on, might well say, 'I was six over par, lost three balls, had two indecent exposures – one of whom I managed to catch with my niblick – one horse bite, one donkey kick, and my feet are covered in sheep droppings.'

The wiser golfers had someone armed with a club and a Polaroid camera riding shotgun for them. The club kept most of the animals away and the camera seemed to be the ideal deterrent for flashers. However great was the desire of these unfortunate and sick men to show their wares, to have them appear in full colour in the Rogues' Gallery at the clubhouse meant that they had entered an area quite outside their personal ambitions. This was one case where it didn't pay to advertise.

CHAPTER 7

Once a week I held a surgery in the branch surgery – a disused garage – for the miners of Thudrock Colliery. These premises were primitive in the extreme, the waiting room and surgery were poorly lit and heated, and the stock of medicines which I had to dispense from consisted mainly for four large bottles filled with different-coloured liquids. On each of the bottles was a printed notice 'Dilute one part of medicine to ten parts of water'.

Somehow these four bottles of medicine were enough to control the health of this small mining community. The medicines were coloured red, green, yellow and black. The black medicine was special and was seen to be special, as written on the outside of the bottle in large letters was 'Special Mixture – Poison'.

I was never quite sure what the medicines contained. I knew the special mixture had some ipecac and a small amount of one of the morphine derivatives in it, but what the others contained is still a mystery. One was reputed to be suitable for coughs, one helped indigestion and one was supposed to be for diarrhoea. However, patients certainly didn't stick to these areas of effectiveness. Often the diarrhoea medicine was demanded for a cough, and the cough medicine for diarrhoea, and so on.

These four bottles of medicine were a tradition, and the miners usually knew which one they required for their particular ailment. A patient would come in and say, 'I think a bit of the green would put me right, doctor.' I never questioned their judgement in these matters, and prescribed accordingly.

One of the more intelligent patients happened to stray into the small room that served as a dispensary and saw me mixing his potion, pouring water to dilute the medicine from one of the stock four bottles.

'Is that all you do, doctor?' he said, 'I could do that.'

'Come on then,' I said, 'mix what you think is right.'

He rejected my offer and grumbled under his breath, 'Yes, I expect you have to have some sort of training.'

The mystique of Medicine had triumphed again.

Always prominent in the medical lore of the hamlet of Thudrock was the black medicine, the Special Mixture. Whereas it could be said that the red, green and yellow bottles were tradition, the black special mix was definitely folklore. I feel sure that it cured as many people and solved as many crises as the mass of antibiotics we have available today.

When an anxious-looking collier called at the surgery and asked, 'Could you come and see my mother, doctor? She is very poorly; I think she'll need a bit of the special,' not only did I know that something was really the matter with Mother, but that I would find a very ill patient.

I also knew that when the patient was given the news that the doctor was on his way and was bringing some of the 'special', she would take heart. However bad she was, she would begin to counter-attack her disease, in much the same way that pioneer American settlers, surrounded by hostile Indians, would buck up when they saw the pennants of the Seventh Cavalry approaching in the distance.

I'd had two years down the mines under the Bevin Scheme at the end of the Second World War, a year and a half of which I had spent at the coal face in a 3 ft 6 in seam with pick and shovel. I learned that miners were marvellous people and that coal-face workers had the same sort of skill and courage as mountaineers.

Twice I was called to Thudrock to go down the mine to attend colliers who had been injured by roof falls. My own mining experiences came back to me as I scrambled along dusty pit roadways with the roof creaking and groaning, threatening to fall.

My first call was to Harry Gilroy, a nineteen-year-old boy whose back had been broken by a fall of rock on one of the pit roadways. In spite of all our care and excellent first aid by the miners on the spot, he finished up paralysed from the waist down. It had been almost impossible to assess his medical condition in the poor light and cramped conditions we had to work in.

About thirty yards of roadway had fallen in, and the boy had been caught at one end of the fall. If he had been in the middle, he would certainly have been killed. The fact that he was on his way to the pit bottom and the fall came up to him from behind rather than in front, meant we were able to get to him direct; otherwise we could have been hours fighting to get through the blocked tunnel.

Whilst I was attending to Harry some colliers had come up from the pit bottom and were adding timbers to protect us from the threatening roof. Each man, as he worked, knew that the roof might come in on us at any moment, but they stuck to their task, erecting metal props and overlapping metal bars, shoring up the roof.

Eventually we managed to get Harry on to a stretcher and start the journey back to the pit bottom. All the time we had been attending him he had been worrying, not about himself but about his pit pony stabled the other side of the fall.

Four of the colliers stayed behind to dig a way through the fall to get the pony out. It was ten hours later that a call was made to Harry in hospital – Black Ben was safe.

Harry Gilroy, now paralysed from the waist down, was engaged to be married. I wondered how this was going to work out.

My other call was to a man with a broken thigh. Working in a 2 ft 6 in seam, a metal prop supporting the roof had flown out and hit him. I had to crawl into the face on my stomach and give him an injection of morphia before we could move him, splint his leg and get him out of the pit. He had been lucky – with proper care he would make a complete recovery.

There was an excellent pithead bath and canteen at Thudrock. The miners could go to the pit in their clean clothes, leave them in their clean lockers, then move across to the other side of the shower room to their dirty lockers and put on their pit clothes.

After they had completed their shift down the mine, they would come back to the baths, put their dirty pit clothes in their dirty lockers, then bath and shower and change into their clean clothes from their clean lockers. After a slap-up subsidised meal in the canteen, they would go home – as clean and well dressed as if they were doing an office job.

There were, however, a few diehards who scorned these modern facilities. They went to the pit half dirty and came home completely dirty.

Not all of Thudrock was fully plumbed, and for some of

these few it still meant heating water in a boiler and bathing in a tin bath in front of the fire. There were still some old-timers who refused to wash their backs at all — they reckoned it would weaken them.

Sometimes a miner would attend the Thudrock surgery outpost in his pit dirt. I tried to discourage this, but the occasional patient slipped through.

One of these was George Marriott. He obviously had some worrying problem, and the coal dirt on his face hid only some of his embarrassment.

'It's like this, doctor,' he said. 'I'm getting married in a month's time, and I have this problem. It's my private parts. It happened in London when I went up for the Cup last year. I had a few too many drinks.'

I could think of no other diagnosis than that of a fairly long-standing venereal disease.

'Let's have a look at you, George,' I said.

George was black all over with coal dust; he could have been signed up for the Black and White Minstrel Show on the spot.

Though I say 'black all over', when he undid his trousers I saw this was not strictly true. Although the rest of him was black, he had scrubbed clean the most male part of his anatomy so that it stood out as a shining white pillar on a black background.

'Now, George,' I said, 'what is the trouble? Have you a discharge or a sore anywhere?'

'Oh, no,' said George, 'nothing like that. When I was five parts gone in London, me mates dragged me into a tattooist, and look what they did to me!'

I had great difficulty in stopping myself laughing.

There was the sheepish, embarrassed, coal-black George, with his spotless white member protruding. On it, in an almost copperplate hand, was tattooed *God Bless the Queen*. I thought I had seen tattoos on every part of the body, but this was a new one for me.

Trying to look and sound as serious as I could, I said

'Yes, George. I see you have a problem. I will send you to a skin specialist. Sometimes they can remove tattoos. If not, he may be able to change the writing into a blue line – and it will look like a coal scar.'

The tears of gratitude from George made white lines down his black face.

The four partners – Steve, Jack, Henry and I, always met for coffee each morning. It was the time to discuss problems, hand cases on, and to produce some funny story to lighten the day.

Steve, my senior partner, was a marvellous audience. He usually burst out laughing before I had completed my stories, and had a fund of improbable stories of his own which usually capped whatever tale I might produce – true or otherwise. I could hardly wait to tell them of my 'God Bless the Queen' experience.

The next morning, when I described my encounter with George, Henry and Jack roared with laughter. Steve smiled rather than laughed, and said 'Once I had a similar case. A young man came to the surgery with a boil in his groin. I noticed, during my examination, that he had the letters LDO tattooed on his penis. The boil needed poulticing, so I sent him out to the nurse to have the poultice applied, and arranged for him to come for dressings.

'We had a particularly attractive nurse at that time – Audrey Deryton. She came back to me at the end of the surgery, not knowing whether to laugh or die of embarrassment.

' "Oh, doctor," she said, "did you see where that man had LLANDUDNO tattooed?" '

We collapsed, laughing – Steve had won again.

I welcomed Albert Scotherm when he retired and came to live in Tadchester. He had been a coal miner in Yorkshire and was one of those wise old men like Bob Barker whom I could sit and listen to for hours.

He was an old scallywag, and had been a well-known south Yorkshire local councillor as well as a coal miner. He had not lost his broad Yorkshire dialect. He would say: 'It was like this Bob, lad. Council meetings were getting a bit dreary. They just droned on doing nowt. So one day I took a revolver in t'council chamber. When t'Town Clerk were in the middle of some speech about rehousing, I fired t'revolver under t'table. It were only a blank, but it gave out a reet good bang. It really shook 'em all up, but it were a bad joke. Town Clerk collapsed wi' a heart attack, had six weeks in hospital, and I was banned from all t'council meetings for a month.'

Albert had gone down the pit at the age of fourteen to work on the haulage. By going to night school and day-release courses at the university, he had reached the position of colliery manager by the time he retired. What was more important to me than Albert's anecdotes was that he had been a close friend of my father's. I had lost my father when I was very young, and my memories of him were blurred. Albert could fill in the gaps in my knowledge about him.

He and my father had attended Sheffield University on day-release courses from the pit when they were both working underground as electrical engineers. They stuck at their course and both eventually passed their degree papers in mining engineering.

'We were pleased as Punch,' said Albert, 'but then Sheffield University wrote to us saying that they could not award the degrees as neither of us had matriculated. As we'd both left school at fourteen this weren't surprising. If we wanted our degree, they said, we'd have to do us matriculation. That were enough for me,' said Albert. 'I gave it up, but not your Dad. He were like a terrier, he stuck at it.'

My father apparently, after a hard day's work down below, went back to his miner's cottage in the evening and started the tedious task of taking his matriculation by correspondence course. This included French – and if his Yorkshire accent was anything like Albert's, this must have been akin to climbing Everest. Amid all his studies he still took time off to work on his various inventions – my mother still draws a small royalty from some automatic coal-tub braking system he invented. Somehow he got through his matriculation only to be told by the university that they now required him to take his inter BSc examination before they would award his degree. Undeterred, he went back to his cottage kitchen, setting up his own apparatus for his physics and chemistry experiments.

I had found bits and pieces of this experimental apparatus in a drawer at home. There was a piece of glass from an old chandelier which he used as a prism, and a gold-leaf electroscope that he had manufactured himself. He passed his inter BSc with a credit in physics, only to be told by the university that all he was now required to do for his degree was – to sit the final papers again.

This was too much, even for my father. In the meantime he had been awarded his AMIEE, and he decided to call it a day with universities. There was some poetic justice for him in that some years later, when he was an internationally known engineer, Liverpool University honoured him with the degree of Master of Engineering, *honoris causa*.

Father's university setback seemed to spur him on. At the age of twenty-five he grew a moustache to make him look older and managed to get appointed as the chief electrical engineer to the Kent coalfield, and became in his spare time the Chairman of Deal Rowing Club. For many this would have been enough, but my father hated coal mines. After a few years he gave it all up and became the personal assistant to an eccentric American millionaire.

Giving up a safe job (he was married by then) must have been a tremendous risk. The idea was that he and the millionaire would work together on inventions. Either the inventions were not successful or the partnership didn't work out, for after a year my father found himself out of work. He eventually managed to get a job with the Central Electricity Board somewhere in the north.

From then on he never looked back. He rose steadily through the ranks of the electricity supply industry, finishing up as member for operations and personnel of the Central Electricity Generating Board which controlled the entire production of electricity in England and Wales. On the way up, he collected a CBE.

Outside his work he was involved in all sorts of activities. He founded a club of engineers called the Nasmyth Club, named after one of his heroes – James Nasmyth, the inventor of the steam hammer. This was a dining-club of engineers who would invite celebrities from outside the engineering field to dine with them and be interrogated about their work and way of life. Their guests included a poet, a medium, and Shipton the Arctic explorer. They invited H. G. Wells to be a guest but the great man reversed their invitation and acted as host to the club at a birthday dinner at his home.

In addition to all this, my father was collecting all sorts of awards for learned papers, including the John Hopkinson award and the Williams Medal as well as various American honours. He became the first English-speaking president of CIGRE, which is an international organisation for countries that have grid systems of electricity. He was host to three thousand delegates of that organisation at a conference reception at the Palace of Versailles.

He was a restless ambitious man and after a time felt he had explored the electricity industry, so he moved to private industry and even greater success. He was a talented writer and broadcaster; some of his short stories were broadcast in the intervals during celebrity concerts. He was a first-class black-and-white artist – I still have some of his drawings – as well as being an accomplished pianist.

But, above all, he was a kind and sensitive man who apparently valued his relationships with people more than he did any of his achievements.

Albert said that my father's office was like a psychiatrist's waiting room, with people going in for advice not about engineering and their jobs – but about their despairs, depressions, family and economic troubles. I realised that I would never be as brilliant as he was, nor as well remembered.

He didn't even waste a spell in hospital. In the next bed was a blind and deaf airman called Wally Thomas and my father, being my father, was frustrated at not being able to communicate with him. After his discharge from hospital he set to and invented a blind-deaf aid. It enabled people who did not know the hand language by which you can communicate with the blind-deaf, to tap out on a normal typewriter keyboard what they wanted to say. The blind-deaf would pick up the typed transcript message on Braille studs attached to the machine. The Carnegie Trust eventually paid for the final development and production of this aid.

'Well,' said Albert one day as he was recounting my father's achievements, 'you may bring lots of new babies into the world, Bob lad – but I'll bet you'll never give birth to new inventions like your Dad did.'

CHAPTER 8

I found in Tadchester that I had to compete with my medical skills against the local folk medicine and old wives' tales that were so dear to the hearts of the locals.

Women coming to my ante-natal clinic were asked routinely if they were having any trouble with their bowels. Most would say, 'No, doctor. I go about five or six times a day.'

What they meant was that this was quite the normal output for any woman pregnant in Tadchester. It was a firmly rooted tradition that if the pregnant young mum was dosed often enough with large quantities of liquid paraffin it would grease the baby and help towards a smooth and easy delivery. However much I protested against this procedure and enlarged on its dangers, I knew that as soon as the young woman got home grandma would say, 'Don't you take any notice of that young man; he's barely out of medical school. Here, have another spoonful. I've mixed in a bit of orange squash to make it taste better.'

Any skin blemish on a newborn baby, never mind a birth-mark proper, was immediately related to something that had happened in pregnancy. A mouse shape was supposed to mean that the mother had been frightened by a mouse. Any sort of semi-circle was identified as a horse-shoe and meant the mother had been frightened by a horse. I thought they would be caught out when I delivered a baby with a tuft of hair over its right buttock, but the mother, after much deliberation, came out with an answer. She remembered being bumped into by a Shet-land pony.

Signs in pregnancy, I was told, would predict charac-teristics of the coming baby. If the mother had indigestion it meant that the baby was going to be born with a lot of hair. If the baby kicked a lot then it was definitely going to be a boy. In Tadchester, however, if the expectant mother wanted definite sexing of her coming child, she would visit Granny Watson in her caravan, and for the sum of one shilling she would get her answer.

Granny would dangle the mother's wedding ring on a piece of cotton over the mother's navel. If it swung to and fro, it was going to be a boy; if it swung round and round, it was going to be a girl. Many amateurs tried to emulate Granny Watson, but she was accredited with having the true sensitivity. She must have had a high success rate because she was never short of customers.

The only infallible sexer I knew was Henry Johnson. When he was asked by a mother-to-be 'Is it going to be a boy or a girl, doctor?' he would put his hand on her stomach and then make an instant diagnosis, saying positively either, 'This is going to be a boy,' or, 'This is going to be a girl.' He would then make a show of taking out his diary to write down his prediction.

What the mother didn't know was that what he wrote in his diary was the exact opposite to the prediction he had made to her. When the baby was finally delivered, if what he had originally predicted was true, it was all congratulations. If, however, it was the exact opposite from his prediction, he would look puzzled, take out his diary, then with a smiling face would say, 'No, I *am* right – look, I wrote it down in my diary when you asked me.'

I am sure he did a lot of irreparable psychological harm to a lot of young mothers, leaving them confused and worried about their memory, but nobody ever doubted Henry and he always got away with it.

One of my biggest battles conducted in the ante-natal clinic was against the amount of weight that some of the young mothers put on. There was a Tadchester granny's theory – 'The bigger the mother, the bigger the baby.' Some of these poor young women must have had a sympathy with the poor Hungarian geese who are literally stuffed alive to make *pâté de foie gras*. I could not convince them that having a big mother didn't make a big baby, that all it did was to make labour and delivery more difficult and cumbersome.

Folklore even crept into breast-feeding. Hardly any Tadchester feeding mother would eat oranges: it was felt that they curdled the milk.

More than one person believed that if an expectant mother put sticking plaster over her navel it would kill the baby, and a cough during pregnancy was always attributed to the baby's foot tickling the mother's windpipe.

Unwanted pregnancies in Tadchester were about on a par with most other places. The standard abortifacients appeared to be mainly castor oil and gin – they were rarely successful.

I discovered a more original method when a young couple, girl and boy-friend, came in together. They both complained that they had trouble with their right feet. They both had a right foot-drop which meant they were unable to lift the top of their foot up towards the knee. This was a sign of some neurological trouble, and the fact that both should have absolutely identical symptoms seemed extremely strange. I had to send them off to be completely investigated by a neurologist. The results of the investigations were that they were both suffering from lead poisoning. Happily, said the specialist's report, once the source of lead was tracked down and stopped, the nerve debility in their legs should recover.

It took some probing and prying to find their lead source, but eventually the girl confessed that she was pregnant, and that she had bought some pills to try and get rid of the pregnancy. To make sure that they weren't harmful to her, she had insisted that her boy-friend take at least the same quantity as she did. Analysis showed that the pills had a fairly high lead content – and this was the cause of the trouble in both of them. Once the pills were stopped, their legs did recover. The baby was quite unaffected and arrived at the exact time and date predicted.

A local cure for mumps in Tadchester was to rub the swellings with a snail. Always the lumps went away afterwards. That they also always went away without rubbing them with a snail didn't seem to make any difference to the treatment. Tadchester people wore copper bracelets to ward off rheumatism, but the *Tadchester Guardian* of 1805 went one better when it announced that a new cure for the same condition had been found – to bury yourself up to the neck in the churchyard for two hours. I wish this treatment was prescribable on the National Health Service. I could think of several patients I could recommend it to – and not just to cure their rheumatism.

One of my old ladies kept a magnet at the side of her bed to keep rheumatism away, and another used to turn her slippers over at night to stop the cramps. Another practical cure for the cramps was two ounces of sulphur on a plate under the bed.

There were two schools of thought for the treatment of lumbago. One believed that a belt of leather next to the skin was the most effective treatment, whilst another preferred a violin string tied round the waist. I wondered if this latter remedy was the precursor of the G-string – perhaps some old-time stripper had seized up just before her performance and decided that the show must go on . . .

When examining patients in their beds at home, I was always coming across odd potatoes between the sheets and sometimes a pocket magnet or piece of camphor in the pyjama pocket. For warts there was a battery of recommended treatments, but most people waited until the fair came for the summer carnival, when the gypsy fortune-teller would charm the warts away. Spiders' webs were put on cuts: these did help the blood to clot, but were also likely to infect the wound with a hefty dose of bacteria.

I once went out to an isolated farm to find the farmer with an infected, almost gangrenous, leg covered with a dressing of mouldy bread.

'What on earth have you put that stuff on his leg for?' I asked.

'Oh doctor,' said the farmer's wife, 'we always keep a loaf of mouldy rye bread in the ceiling rafter for infected cuts.'

'These old-wives' tales will be the death of all of you,' I said. I was furious.

I had to admit the farmer to hospital, where he was found to be diabetic. He had a long spell on both insulin and penicillin before we were able to get his leg into good enough shape for him to go back to his farm.

Talking to Steve about this patient one morning at coffee, I said, 'When will these people ever learn? Fancy putting mouldy bread on infected cuts.'

Steve said, 'Don't you be too hasty with them, Bob. Mouldy bread has cured more infected cuts than it has let go bad. These people discovered penicillin long before Sir Alexander Fleming did. The mould on that bread is mainly penicillin mould: it's been used in this way for some hundreds of years. And it's not any old mouldy bread; it's good rye bread, hung up in the rafters where it's well ventilated.'

He laughed. 'I will agree with you, it's a bit out of date now, but belief in the treatment plus a bit of medication goes a long way towards a cure.'

Steve's words were only too well illustrated by Harry Bagshaw. Harry was a labourer at the brick works on the Up-the-Hill side of the river. He came to my surgery one evening straight from work and covered in brick dust.

'I think I've ruptured myself, doctor,' he said. 'Could you fix me up?'

His diagnosis was correct. He had a double rupture, a large round swelling in each groin.

'I'm afraid it's a hospital job for you, Harry,' I said. 'I'll get you an appointment to see Mr Johnson at the hospital. You need an operation to put this right.'

'No,' said Harry. 'I can't be off work. I've got eight kids to feed. I just want a truss like some of my mates have.'

He wouldn't be persuaded to come into hospital, so I reluctantly wrote out a prescription for him for a double inguinal truss. This is a strap-like arrangement that belts round the waist and pulls up pads in both groins to support the hernias.

I didn't see Harry for two years. One evening he turned up at the surgery, again in his brick dust.

'I'd like another truss please, doctor,' he said. 'What with all the dirt and sweat at work, this one has got a bit worn.'

I raised the question of an operation again, but once more Harry declined.

'I've had no trouble at all since I've had this truss, doctor.'

'Well, let's have a look at you.'

Harry reluctantly slid his trousers down. I found that he now had a *huge* swelling in each groin – much worse than when I had last seen him.

'That truss isn't doing much,' I said. 'These hernias are much worse. Bring your truss in to me tomorrow and let me have a look at it.'

'I'm *wearing* it,' said Harry. 'I never take it off.'

He took off his shirt and there, strapped round his chest, was his truss – with the pads that should have been supporting his groins firmly ensconced under each arm. I could hardly believe it, but I saw Harry's logic. They looked like braces, so he wore them as braces.

He still would not agree to go for operation, so I ordered him a new truss, made him bring it to the surgery and showed him how to put it on. He was to report back after wearing it for a fortnight. He duly reported after two weeks and I asked, 'How are you getting on now, Harry?'

'I expect things are better in one way,' said Harry, 'but it were much more comfortable when I wore 'em round my shoulders.'

I knew that with so many of my patients like Harry I would always be fighting an uphill battle.

I never minded my casualty duties at Tadchester Hospital. We worked a rota system, sharing the duties between five of us. The only time it became a bit onerous was in the summer. With the population swollen by some thousands, you tended to work very hard all the time you were on call for casualty.

There was no resident doctor at Tadchester Hospital, which had sixty beds and came under the loose category of a cottage hospital. Apart from the work done in the hospital by our practice, various consultants from Winchcombe Hospital held out-patient clinics there, and one of the Winchcombe surgeons had two major surgical operating sessions each week.

Although the occasional regular patient of mine would get up to casualty to buttonhole me about some particular worry, casualty was mainly casualty: instead of having to listen so much to people, I would be doing practical work with my hands.

Casualty work was extremely varied. I gave some anaesthetics for Henry when he had fractures to reduce or abscesses to open and explore. There was a great deal of stitching up of cuts to do, and I prided myself on my needlework, taking a great deal of time and trouble to produce a neat job. The time I took used to make the casualty sister very restless. She would look over my shoulder impatiently and say, 'Are you hoping that they are going to hang this in the Tate, doctor?'

One casualty seemed very familiar. She was – it was Gladys, our senior receptionist.

'What are you doing here?' I asked.

'I've been trying to attract somebody's attention in the surgery all week,' said Gladys (and I must say that I had been vaguely conscious of Gladys limping around a bit). 'If I walked in with an arrow sticking through my head, all I would be asked would be "How many patients are booked in today?" so I've come here for some attention.'

I had a look at Gladys's leg. She had an extensive burn down its whole length. I couldn't imagine how she had managed to keep going; it must have been very painful. I got the staff nurse to dress it and told Gladys she would have to have a week off from work.

'Rubbish!' said Gladys. 'It's much better. If one of you had had a look at it a week ago it would probably have been completely cured by now!'

There was no doubt that we neglected medically the people with whom we were in immediate contact. Patsy Johnson, Henry's wife, once got so fed up with trying to get him to take some notice of a rash she had on her arm, that in the end she made a surgery appointment to see her husband, and sat in the waiting-room with the rest of the patients, in her hat and coat. Even the phlegmatic Henry, after ringing for the next patient, was taken somewhat aback when his wife stormed in, saying, 'Now about this arm I've been asking you to look at for weeks . . .'

I was an expert at getting foreign bodies out of ears and noses, but not so expert about getting them out of other places. One afternoon I had a male patient arrive at casualty, limping and in obvious pain. He insisted that he saw me in a cubicle on my own, away from the nurse.

'It's very embarrassing, doctor,' he whispered. 'I slipped and sat on this glue pot and it stuck in my back passage.'

I thought how unfortunate the poor chap had been and was surprised that he wasn't more shocked. It didn't occur to me at the time that he couldn't have had his trousers on when this catastrophe happened. I made a painful and unsuccessful attempt to remove it, then called in Henry. With some difficulty he removed the pot while I gave the patient an anaesthetic.

'Have you ever seen anything like that before?' I asked Henry. 'The chances of its happening must be infinitesimal.'

Henry roared, 'Good God, lad, you didn't believe him, did you? That's the way he had his fun. He is, for want of a better term, a sexual deviant.'

With my innocence shattered I was at least in some way prepared a few months later when a smartly dressed young man appeared in casualty and asked to see me privately. I showed him into a cubicle. His dress was immaculate, he was relaxed and when I asked about his particular problem, he replied nonchalantly, 'I've got a cucumber stuck, doctor, I would be grateful if you would yank it out.'

Nonplussed and grasping for some words to answer his nonchalance, I asked, 'Is it peeled?'

The reply was scornful in the extreme. 'Of *course* it's peeled.'

I was able to manage this particular operation without calling for help and marvelled at the eccentricities and strange private pastimes of my fellow men.

One part of casualty duty I did not enjoy. This was dealing with people who had tried to take their lives as the answer to their problems, most commonly through an overdose of drugs. We had to put them through the degrading process of being held down while a tube was forced down the throat into the stomach and the stomach contents washed out. During my time in Tadchester, the number of attempted suicides steadily increased year by year until it became the commonest single cause for admission to the medical ward.

The casualty staff hated dealing with these overdoses as I did. 'These awful physical fights to get stomach tubes down really degrade us, doctor,' the staff nurse said.

We kept the would-be suicides in at least overnight. They were seen the next day by the psychiatrist who tried to explore the problem that had led to their attempting to take their lives. A few would agree to go into his hospital and have themselves sorted out, but most packed themselves off back home – and back to their problems – as soon as they could.

I talked to the psychiatrist, Dr Lester, who was based at a large hospital near Winchcombe. I asked if there was any answer to this increasing problem of attempted suicide, and what it was all about.

He said that of every hundred patients whom he saw who had attempted to take their lives (and he preferred the term 'self-poisoning' to 'attempted suicide') ten had some long-standing type of depressive illness, and fifteen had some sort of mental abnormality. Of the remaining seventy-five, the only common factor was that sixty-five per cent of them either knew someone closely who had tried the same thing, or had in fact attempted to do it themselves before. He thought that the whole problem was a social rather than a medical one.

'For example,' he said, 'if you have a large resident community such as a factory hostel or a nurses' home, and one girl attempts self-poisoning, in the next few months several more will have a go. It's almost as if it were infectious. It's the same with local communities. The highest attempted-self-poisoning rate is in a rural area of Wales.

'The answer lies to some extent in how we house people, where communities are situated, what access they have to recreation and distractions away from their particular problems. The break-up and present-day looseness of family ties isn't any help. There are no longer the great family structures that people could fall back on for support and help.'

I discussed the problem with Steve. He agreed with most of Dr Letter's views.

'If you notice, Bob, that of our young mothers in Tadchester who become depressed after childbirth, ninety per cent of them are not natives of the town. They haven't grans and mums and aunts to help them through this very important period of their lives.'

'Is there an answer?' I asked.

'I believe there is a very simple answer to everything,' said Steve. 'I believe there is a formula. If people could form the habit of making a conscious effort to do one unselfish act a day, most of the problems of everyday life would disappear. The simpler any remedy is, generally the more effective it is.'

Steve was the most unselfish and self-contained man I ever met. If most of us were ever able to reach his sort of standards, I would agree there would be few problems of any sort.

CHAPTER 9

There was an emergency call to Sanford-on-Sea holiday camp. By the time I arrived it was too late to do anything.

A child had been found drowning in the small paddling pool in the middle of the camp. She had been pulled out of the water and a holidaymaker, a first-aider, had taken over the situation and had given her mouth-to-mouth resuscitation. She was quite dead when I arrived.

It was only at the post-mortem that the full extent of the tragedy was revealed. The child had not died of drowning, but of suffocation from vomit in the back of her throat – blown into her lungs by the first-aider. If she had just been laid on her face, and nobody had tried to revive her, she might well have lived.

There were two lots of people to console: the grief-stricken parents and, possibly even more so, the poor first-aider. He had done what he had been trained to do, what he had been told always should be done, and had probably done it extremely efficiently within the limits of his training.

Subsequently I had a continuous running battle with the senior first-aid administrators. It was my view that mouth-to-mouth resuscitation was not always the best method of reviving people, particularly in cases of drowning.

The one procedure that all first-aiders know, or think they know, is mouth-to-mouth resuscitation. They are all dying to have a go at it. They have been trained on resuscitation Annies (lifelike rubber facsimiles of a young girl). They have to blow into rubber Annie's mouth and watch her chest expand. There are various other things to be done – look into her mouth, pinch her nose and position her head properly. Thousands of first-aiders all over the country become very proficient at using Annie. For many, alas, this is as far as the proficiency goes. There is a great deal of difference between a rubber dummy and a human being.

Before attempting to give mouth-to-mouth resuscitation, you have first to be skilled enough to be able to determine whether the patient has actually stopped breathing or not. A doctor, with his skill and his instruments, finds it difficult enough. Often only a slight change in the position of the patient's head is enough to restart breathing.

It has always been one of my private nightmares that one day I could be in a situation where I had some difficulty in breathing. Just when I was beginning to get my breath back, I would be pounced on by a great big first-aider and I would be too weak to prevent him from clamping his mouth on mine and trying to blow me up.

The biggest hazard in mouth-to-mouth resuscitation is something blocking the airways. However much you look into the mouth (and I am sure our first-aider *had* looked into the little girl's mouth) you cannot see round the back of the pharynx unless you have a special instrument (a laryngoscope). There doesn't have to be much material lurking round this corner. It could be some thick mucus, a bit of seaweed, or as in the little girl's case, some vomit. One steady blow into a debilitated patient could put this material straight into his lungs and possibly kill him. I am never sure when I read reports of people being saved by mouth-to-mouth resuscitation whether they recovered because of it or in spite of it.

For the average first-aider the chances are that perhaps only once in a lifetime will he be called on to give artificial respiration. I can never see how he can be expected to give it properly and effectively, including all the medical assessments that have to be made before starting the procedure. How much simpler to lay the patient on his face with the mouth clear and unobstructed and get air into the chest by pressing rhythmically on the back. A less efficient method, but so much safer.

I wonder if the people who outlined first-aid treatment had the same sort of practical experience as I had as a GP in a coastal holiday town where drowning and collapsing cases were only too frequent. Were their views based on their own experience or were they just sticking to their first-aid book? Every procedure must be under constant review.

For years the treatment of adder bite in this country was to rush the patient to hospital and give him some anti-venom. Apart from tying a ligature round bitten limbs, this was the standard treatment.

Then there came a time when the British Red Cross Society asked the School of Hygiene and Tropical Medicine to investigate the treatment of snake bite in Britain. Their findings were that the only available anti-venom at that time was (a) no use at all against adder bites; it was made in South America and it was therapeutic against one specific type of South American snake only; (b) because the anti-venom was made from horse serum, to which sensitive people can react fatally, the anti-venom injections were not only useless against the snake bite but more dangerous than the bite itself. It is only recently that an effective anti-venom has become available.

I fought a lone battle over my views on mouth-to-mouth resuscitation. I have the greatest respect for the first-aid organisations, and hope that perhaps one day they will have another look at all resuscitation procedures.

The girls in my Forward Medical Aid Unit were a mixture of Red Cross and St John's. They were a marvellous lot and all did stout work at the holiday camps and beaches at Tadchester during the summer. They all learnt mouth-to-mouth resuscitation, or anyway they learnt to blow up rubber Annie. But we discussed resuscitation as a whole: they would think before they tried any procedure; they would assess the whole situation of a collapsed, unconscious or drowning patient and look to the best way of revival. They did not, as so many appear to do, say to themselves, 'At last I've found somebody who's stopped breathing; here's my chance to see if I can blow him up.'

Alas, I had no control over visiting first-aiders and, although I managed to stop one giving mouth-to-mouth resuscitation to a boy who was having an epileptic fit, I was unable to stop another enthusiast who insisted on continuing to blow for more than two hours into someone who was dead from a broken neck.

One morning over coffee with my partners, I asked the phlegmatic Henry for his views on first-aiders giving mouth-to-mouth resuscitation.

'Lot of bloody rubbish,' said Henry. 'Just take their teeth out, lay them down on their stomachs, and give them a thump on the back.'

Henry, being Henry, was somehow always successful in any procedure he tried for whatever purpose. It always seemed to work for him, or anyway he got away with it. I thought his suggested resuscitation procedures were probably as good as any.

I think our lighter moments, when we shared our morning coffee, were of tremendous benefit to us. We could discuss our worries and laugh them off. Life can be so cruel, so tragic and so unfair. I believe it is only by trying to laugh at our troubles that we manage to survive them. However, some people seem to have a much greater share of misfortune than others – and some troubles are beyond laughter.

Amongst my patients there were many who complained of misfortune and the way life had treated them harshly, and how unfair it all was. Those, however, who really had had a raw deal from life – whose misfortunes were of a magnitude that one questioned whether there was any justice anywhere – did not seem to complain in the same way. They accepted their burdens as part of their lot and carried on with tremendous courage the task of living.

One such family were the Whites. They lived out in the country, Up-the-Hill, about two miles from the main residential area, in a tied cottage, Mr White working as a farm labourer. There were six normal, happy and healthy children. They were a self-contained family and did not ask for much from anybody, and were as successful at the level they lived as anybody could be. They rarely visited the surgery so I did not get to know them until the youngest son (Nigel) was brought to me. He 'wasn't himself': he was floppy and listless and obviously had something generally wrong with him which had been insidious in its onset. By the time I saw him he had difficulty getting about; he felt listless, lethargic, and was a bit withdrawn.

I sent him to the children's specialist at Winchcombe who, in turn, sent him to Great Ormond Street Children's Hospital in London.

He came back with a diagnosis of some strange disease that I had never heard of and which meant that his nervous system would gradually break down, that he would become progressively weaker, and would be unlikely to survive more than a couple of years.

Nigel looked fit and healthy apart from the fact that he couldn't hold his head up and his limbs drooped. He was a large eight-year-old and, as his condition got worse, his mother had to carry him around as if he were a baby. There were several attempts at treatment of his condition but he didn't respond. The poor lad barely survived the two years predicted as the maximum he could live.

The family took his death well – if any death can be taken well. It had been obvious that it was coming and they had prepared themselves for it, although this did not lessen the awful loss when it came.

I feel that people who are close to the land and are involved in the rearing of livestock are better equipped to deal with the life/death situation. The animals they rear have to be sent off to be killed; they see animals die, and thus accept that death is inseparable from living.

It was only six months after Nigel's death that I was called to see his ten-year-old sister, Dorothy. I made a confident diagnosis of appendicitis (she had had abdominal pain and sickness) and sent her to hospital. I gave her the anaesthetic while Henry operated, and expected that it would be a simple operation, and that she would be home in a matter of about a week.

When Henry opened her abdomen we found, to our horror, that her pain was not from the appendix but from a widespread cancer of one of her ovaries. I did not even know it was possible for children to have this condition.

Henry did his best, without offering any hope, and I broke the news to the parents as gently as I could. For eighteen months we lived in a nightmare, watching with the parents their second child fade and eventually die.

Towards the end of her illness Dorothy would see no one apart from her family and myself. She would scream filthy abuse at the vicar when he called, but would accept me because to some extent I could relieve her fears and pains.

For the second time the family had to face a terrible loss and, not least, heavy funeral expenses. The wage of a farm labourer at that time was little above subsistence level. All the family rallied round and helped out with the expenses. The fact that they were a large family helped them survive this second, awful ordeal. They *did* survive it, but for a time they were very bewildered, and for some months Mrs White was apprehensive about any of her children becoming ill. She would bring them to the surgery for the slightest cough, cold, ache or pain. The odds for either of those two conditions arising in any family were so small that you could almost eliminate the possibility. That the odds were defeated twice left me with an emptiness that I could not describe.

The Whites were a good-living family – solid, respectable, hard-working people. Why should they have had to bear all this? I could think of many people who merited ill fortune: I could see no reason why this particular family deserved any ill fortune at all.

A year later Mrs White, who was almost past child-bearing age, gave birth to a baby girl. The child became the spoiled darling of the whole family, demanded everybody's attention and managed to help erase some of the memories of the losses of the previous two years. Somehow it seemed that Nature – or whatever – had thought that they had suffered enough and did its best to balance their loss and sufferings.

Dealing with situations such as those in the White family made me take a long, hard look at myself as a general practitioner. It was too easy with so many people dependent on me to perhaps unconsciously develop inflated ideas about myself as a doctor – that I had to solve most people's problems, that I was important.

The Whites brought home to me the fact that there were whole areas of medicine where I just acted as a signpost to my more specialised colleagues, that any hope of cure lay with them alone; that all I could do was to pass patients on to them and be available to act as a comforter if necessary.

Daphne Wallcott was an attractive blonde-haired nineteen-year-old, and a keen tennis player. She worked in the bank where I had my account and always waved to me when I went in.

When she came to see me in the surgery she was all apologies. Sorry to come about nothing . . . probably just a strain . . .

'Sit down, Daphne,' I said, 'and let me decide what is wrong. Just take your time and tell me what's troubling you.'

Daphne complained about a lot of little things – her

eyes, and odd muscle troubles. She said, 'I sound silly, telling you all these things. I feel perfectly well. I can manage my work. The only thing is, I'm all wrong with my tennis. I don't know what it is. Do you think I'm just run down? I eat well and sleep well. Mother thinks it's just nerves, but there's nothing I feel nervous about.'

I examined Daphne and found that she had some definite neurological symptoms. Various things didn't work quite as they should and some of her muscle reflexes weren't equal.

'Well, Daphne,' I said, 'Mother is right in one way. Your nerves are upset but not in the way she means. Something has upset them, and I mean by that some of the nerve fibres in your body. I don't know what is causing it so we shall have to send you to a neurologist, who specialises in these matters.'

'What about my tennis?' Daphne asked. 'We have the club championship in a fortnight.'

I said, 'Well you mustn't play if you feel at all unwell or if your muscles don't work quite as they should. I'll make an appointment for you to see the neurologist. Report back to me a week after you have seen him. If in the meantime there are any other symptoms, come and see me. It's likely that all these little things you complain of will get better on their own but I mustn't take any chances with our potential Wimbledon champion; that's why I am making this appointment.'

Daphne got much better over the next two weeks and was well enough to win the Tadchester Ladies' Tennis Championship. By the time she saw the neurologist she hardly had any symptoms at all.

The letter from the neurologist was as I thought it would be. He wrote, 'This young lady shows definite signs of early disseminated sclerosis. She appears to be getting better, so for the present I would do nothing about it. If her condition should change, I should be pleased to see her again. I have told her that part of her nervous system has become inflamed, that it appears to be getting better, that if she is at all worried about herself to come and see you.'

I took the letter to Steve, my senior partner. He read it thoughtfully, then looked over his half-rimmed glasses and said, 'What are you going to say to her?'

'Well,' I replied, 'just the same as the specialist, that she has had an inflammation of a part of the nervous system and that it appears to be getting better.'

'Good,' said Steve. 'Over the years I have acquired great doubts as to whether there is a specific disease of disseminated sclerosis. Broadly it just means that a patient's nervous system, for no reason that we know of, has started to break down. The characteristic of this so-called disease is that it undergoes remissions spontaneously. For no known reason it disappears in much the same way as it starts. More often than not, the patients get completely better. There are, of course, some who don't and have a progressive deterioration.

'If you tie a label to people they consciously or unconsciously try to behave according to the description on the label. If you tell Daphne she has disseminated sclerosis, then always at the back of her mind there'll be the thought that she has a progressive disease. I believe these thoughts at the back of the mind are destructive, that they themselves help to actuate the disease.

'We come back to the vexed problem of what to tell patients, and when. I don't think you can generalise. I think you have to consider every patient individually and decide what you say to them after you have considered their particular situation alone. Sometimes I think we cripple people by telling them they have a certain disease. We do this, not always having the complete facts and thus the complete right to tell them.

'With the particular condition that Daphne has, the neurologist is right. She has some inflamed nerves that are getting better. That we should tie the label "disseminated sclerosis" on these symptoms is, to my personal belief, wrong.

'There are no true statistics about this particular disease, mainly because general practitioners are poor at keeping records. If someone disappears after being diagnosed, they don't enter the statistics, and the most common reason for their not reappearing is that they continue to be perfectly well. Unfortunately we base most of our records on people who don't do so well.'

He pointed to his file of patients' records. 'In there, Bob,' he said, 'I could find you a couple of dozen patients who have been diagnosed as having disseminated sclerosis. That's as far as the disease ever went with them. They've never known they were supposed to have had it, and they have gone on in perfectly good health for ten, twenty, thirty years, with no history of trouble. I wonder how they would have fared if I had told them the initial diagnosis. I may be wrong, but I doubt if they would have done as well. At the very least they would have always had to carry an extra worry.'

In my early years in general practice I leant heavily on Steve for his wisdom and advice. He was able to cover areas of patients' treatment and management that did not appear in textbooks. I was really an apprentice to a craftsman. Just over a century ago this was the way in which most doctors were trained. You could only properly learn your craft by working with and under a master craftsman.

When Daphne came to see me I confirmed what the neurologist had told her – that she had some inflamed nerves. When I saw her a month later, she was quite free of symptoms. Twenty-five years later, when she was looking forward to the birth of her first grandchild, she did not know that two and a half decades and eight tennis championships earlier she had been diagnosed as suffering from disseminated sclerosis.

CHAPTER 10

I was an active member of the Tadchester Round Table, a sort of junior Rotary Club. Candidates have to be under forty years of age to join, and the Table members are limited to one representative from each of the professions. This meant that we could have one doctor, one solicitor, one butcher and one school teacher, etc. as members.

We kept the rules fairly elastic and if there was more than one of any particular calling keen to join, we would stretch them so that there could be, for example, a general practitioner and an anaesthetist, a headmaster and a form master.

Tadchester Round Table met twice a month in a room

at the Tadchester Arms where they had a dinner, conducted their business, and usually had a guest speaker. They were a lively lot and were heavily involved in activities outside their meetings. These consisted mainly of various types of community service. They would arrange outings for such groups as the blind, mentally handicapped children, and old age pensioners. The rest of the time was taken up in charity fund raising. They took a major part in arranging Tadchester Carnival, as well as participating in it. They also staged a donkey derby during Carnival week. Their other money-raising activities were through such things as raffles, dances and motor rallies.

Tadchester had an active Round Table membership of thirty. This membership represented a good cross-section of everything that went on in the town. We had a banker, a butcher, a solicitor, a grocer, a timber merchant, a school teacher and a doctor, and so on. It would be hard to find any one area of Tadchester that wasn't represented by a Round Tabler.

The fortnightly meetings were pretty inebriated affairs and the guest speakers often came in for some fairly rough handling.

There was a speakers' secretary, who arranged our lecture programme. Although there were plenty of speakers available in the summer when the town was invaded by outsiders, in the winter we were thrown very much on our own resources.

The speakers' secretary arranged a series of talks where some senior member of the same profession as one of the Round Tablers was asked to come and talk about the other side of his life – his hobbies, his leisure pursuits, what he did to balance the exacting role of his work . . .

We had a fascinating talk on home movies with some home-made films illustrating it, by a senior bank manager; a talk on sailing by a senior solicitor, which wasn't too bad. It was only when he was finishing his talk that I remembered that it would be my turn to produce a senior member of my profession to speak in a fortnight's time.

I was very limited in my choice. Steve and Jack would never speak anywhere and Henry, once he had started speaking, was very difficult to stop. As for speaking myself, after the fiasco of the Cricket Club dinner I didn't think I would ever dare to raise my voice in public in Tadchester again.

There was nothing else for it. I approached Henry as my only potential speaker.

'What, lad? A talk on how doctors spend their leisure time?' (Henry always got things a bit wrong.) 'Delighted to, lad. Just leave it to me.'

With some misgiving I knew that I would have to leave it to Henry – he was a law unto himself.

Henry was late arriving for the meeting. I thought, for a time, he had forgotten, but he breezed in just after we had finished eating and in the middle of our business.

'Sorry I am late, lads,' he said. 'Just had an emergency at the hospital. All right if I start right away? I may have to shoot back there.'

Nobody ever dared to contradict Henry, not in Tadchester anyway.

Henry stood up and, without using notes or changing his expression, began his speech. I think it bears repeating:

'It is generally accepted that the doctor, whether surgeon or humble GP, is exposed to greater strains and responsibilities than his average fellow beings – the exacting toll of the operating theatre, where the saving of life is often dependent on the single skill of a particular surgeon, and general practice, where too often the only treatment required is the transfusion of the practitioner's own energy, the supply of which is not inexhaustible.

'To keep going in these exacting roles it is essential that the practising doctor has some wider interest and relaxation to distract, relax and refresh him for coming battles. In choosing his particular form of relaxation he has to be relatively selective. It is necessary that he is in a situation where he is not available to the medical demands of the general public and in a situation that will improve both his mental and physical health.

'Many splendid activities spring to mind -- camping, golfing, sailing, swimming, tennis, squash and badminton -- delightful sports which fill the criteria of availability and health improvement.

'For the non-sporting types there are chess, gardening, amateur dramatics, literary and art societies, television and the theatre -- a whole range of available activities. It is so essential to do, or belong to, something.

'The doctor, before making his choice of activity, should scrutinise with good clinical judgement his particular distraction to assess both the obvious benefits and possible less obvious disadvantages.

'Let us look first at camping --

'What better than the wide open spaces of camping, being close to Nature, rising by the sun and going to bed when it sets, no telephone, no distractions, at peace with oneself?

'But if it rains, then you are stuck in a tent with a muddy field to walk across. If it blows, you are hanging on to the pole for dear life to keep at least some covering over your head. If it continues to rain and blow, you arrive back from your relaxation with as much vigour as a survivor from a shipwreck.

'So perhaps this should not be recommended.

'Golfing? There is no doubt about the advantages of golf. It is a splendid feeling to beat your frustrations away on the golf course. A good round will put you in fine fettle, pull you out of any sort of depression that is bothering you, and you will return to the clubhouse feeling like a king.

'But if you have a bad round everything looks black. Not only do all your other troubles heap up on you, but your golf falls apart as well. More time is spent worrying and being neurotic about golf handicaps, swings, etcetera, than all the commonplace problems we have to deal with during our work. There is no worse depression than being off your game of golf. This depression will influence every other activity you participate in.

'So perhaps this should not be recommended.

'Sailing? The wind in your face, waves swishing across the bow, scudding along in a ten-knot wind, probably the most exhilarating sport there is. You come back a giant, bronzed, full of vim and vigour.

'But, if you have a boat, you have to maintain it. You must be prepared to spend as much time working on it as in it. You have got to find a place to moor it. Masts are always snapping and sails are always tearing.

'It is expensive. It is a worry. It is a commitment. It is time-consuming. Somebody might borrow your boat or, even worse, steal it. The work problem is so involved that it interferes with any other social invitation you may have.

'So perhaps this should not be recommended.

'Swimming? Probably the best all-round sport for general health and muscular trim and shape. The refreshment of the cool waves or the leisure of a tepid swimming bath relaxes you both in body and mind.

'But, of course, you could always drown.

'So perhaps this should not be recommended.

'Tennis, badminton or squash? The main benefits of these are that you can plan to spend a specific period of time playing them. You can book a court and thrash yourself round for an hour, dispelling the accumulated toxins of the sophisticated suburban life most of us now lead. A pint of beer and a shower afterwards and you are fit to face the world.

'But, if you are a busy doctor you can't maintain your general state of body fitness. Strenuous muscular exercise concentrated in one hour of violent activity brings the muscles out on strike. The more militant ones tear themselves off their attachments, protesting in the most effective way, crippling their owner and preventing him carrying out his normal everyday tasks.

'So perhaps these should not be recommended.

'We can now examine some non-sporting activities, starting with chess –

'This is a most stimulating exercise for the mind. You can set your wits and intelligence against somebody of just about, or just less than, your equal.

'But chess is usually played with a bad posture. And usually in a smoke-filled room. It can go on for hours. Your opponent may not speak. If you keep on losing, you get into the same state of mind as the off-form golfer, and your poor chess performances begin to influence every aspect of your workaday life.

'So perhaps this should not be recommended.

'Amateur dramatics? The main benefits of amateur dramatics are that you explore those unused parts of you that you feel have been wasted. Expressing yourself in a variety of different moods can only widen your depth of understanding. You can find a new dimension here which is both enriching and stimulating. It can enhance your community standing, where people recognise both your skill as a doctor and your talents as an actor.

'But it is difficult to spare the time to go to rehearsals. Swopping duties, getting somebody to stand in for you, and usually an epidemic breaks out the week of your performance.

'Amateur dramatic societies are plagued with intrigues, splinter groups and illicit love affairs. If you are not involved in them you will be asked to help to sort them out. In time most of your worries will be concerned with:

(a) the production;
(b) whether you can get to rehearsal; and
(c) how the hell you are going to sort out the nuts you are associating with.

'So perhaps this should not be recommended.

'Gardening has many benefits. Not only are you exercising in God's fresh air, but you are doing fundamental basic things – turning the rich earth, planting seeds, seeing them flower and fruit, and benefiting from the fresh foods you have grown. It has so many branches – vegetables, flowers, greenhouse products – that you can even specialise in one particular aspect. You become closer to Nature, fitter for your exercise, and better for the fresh foods you grow.

'But, once having got your garden to a certain state, you have got to maintain it. In time you don't run your garden, your garden runs you. You can't go away on holiday because someting needs cutting or something needs picking whilst you are away. All your hopes can be dashed by too heavy a shower of rain, too much sun, or just one night of sharp frost. Having achieved a standard you will find that you require every waking moment to maintain that standard.

'So perhaps this should not be recommended.

'Art societies? Literary societies? There are many societies dedicated to the Arts which always welcome a doctor as a member. He adds status to the society by virtue of his qualifications, he has a good intellect, he can give wider advice on most subjects.

'Involvement in some pure art interest, completely separate from the mundane worries of his medical practice, can be the one thing that keeps the doctor sane, keeps his balance and equips him better to deal with his everyday patients. However hard he is pressed, he knows he can always escape into this beautiful, abstract world of culture.

'But so many societies are controlled, run and composed of rather elderly ladies. So he won't get much mental or cultural stimulation there. Because he is a doctor and known to be a responsible citizen, they will try and shove some office – either secretary or treasurer – upon him. In a short time he will find that he is running the whole affair and he cannot stop. Without his guiding hand, the society would fold up.

'Having a live doctor as secretary or treasurer does save his fellow members having to go further than the weekly society meeting for medical advice. You can bet that the doctor will spend as much time dispensing medicine as he does organising visits to art galleries, literary congresses and poetry readings.

'So perhaps this should not be recommended.

'But a doctor must relax. He must get away from it all and into tranquil surroundings. What could be more refreshing than a straightforward hysterectomy on a cool summer's afternoon, surrounded by the highly qualified theatre staff who can anticipate every instrument needed? Cut off from the outside world, doing a job that has a beginning and an end, knowing nobody will disturb you, somebody will benefit, and relaxing in familiar surroundings with familiar people.

'This is highly recommended.

'For the general practitioner there is nothing to beat a snug surgery on a cold winter's evening. The regulars coming to pay tribute at his feet, to swop yarns over bottles of urine, makes the general practitioner feel wanted and necessary. At surgery he dispenses wisdom and comfort amongst people who depend on him, working again in familiar surroundings with familiar people. Most relaxing and refreshing.

'This is highly recommended.

'So, having permutated all the possibilities, there is a way for both surgeons and general practitioners to relax – providing of course they accept that they need their patients more than perhaps their patients need them.'

There was silence for a minute after Henry stopped speaking. Then, spontaneously, the whole Table were up on their feet applauding him.

Henry beamed, soaking in the applause, then as it died

down said, 'Sorry I won't have time to answer any questions, lads. I have to shoot back to the hospital.'

He took a quick swig from the nearest beer mug, then swept out of the room.

The inimitable Henry, who always got away with everything, had got away with it again.

CHAPTER 11

Carnival Week in Tadchester rivalled Christmas as the main event of the year. The abandonment, colour and gaiety may not have been quite up to *Mardi Gras* standards, but there was enough for Tadchester. To the locals it certainly felt very Latin and more than a little wicked, especially as the population was swollen by thousands of holidaymakers and day trippers who gave the old town an added air of bustle and fiesta.

The week was the second in August, and was virtually a public holiday. Any business not connected with eating, drinking or making merry came almost to a dead stop. Traffic ground to a halt as well: the main road to the quay was blocked off to site the huge West Country Fair which provided the focus for the jollifications.

The fair was one of the good old good ones: huge, old fashioned and with something for everybody. As well as the usual dodgem cars, a big dipper, octopus and ghost train, there were dozens of sideshows – stalls offering roll-a-penny, darts, shooting, coconut shies, candy floss, fish and chips, hot dogs and hamburgers – and a boxing booth. In addition there were half a dozen large tents that set the mouths of the Tadchester locals watering. There were cries of 'Come and see the only living mermaid'! There were shows that promised exotic Eastern fantasies. One claimed to have the only Elephant Man in captivity, and there was a special one called 'Scenes from Soho', in which several rather portly ladies semi-stripped to music from an old piano.

This last show used to drive the locals wild and was responsible for many proposals of marriage: the young men seemed to think that marriage was probably the only way they could get their fantasies realised. There were others, of course, who stuck to the traditional Tadchester proposal – 'Now that you are two months gone, hadn't we better start thinking about getting married?'

The busiest man of the Tadchester Week was Eric. Apart from the fair there were the West Country rowing races on the Tad, a business exhibition in the sports ground, athletics on the cricket ground for the children, a donkey derby at Sanford-on-Sea organised by the Round Table and, most important of all, the Carnival procession.

Eric and his chief electrician, Dennis, had to provide sound and music for every event. Eric didn't speak to me for the week that the Carnival was on. He had to lay two miles of cable along the bank of the Tad, so that there could be continuous commentary on the boat races. There had to be loudspeakers, music and microphones for whoever considered themselves God's gift to broadcasting at all the other functions.

After every Carnival there were always at least half a dozen young men who were modestly lapping up the praise of 'You were such a natural on the radio, surely you are meant for the BBC.' In actual fact two Tadchester boys became internationally known as radio and TV commentators. Part of their success was due, I am sure, to their training at the Tadchester Carnival.

Pam had taken a week off to enjoy her first Carnival. She had already had one week in June when she came down to start fitting up the flat we had rented from Herbert Barlow. The second week in August would be the remainder of her holiday entitlement, and on 3rd September she was giving up work altogether to have a few days off before our marriage on the 9th.

Pam worked for *Dalton's Weekly*, an advertising magazine. For some years she was the Query Department. The proprietors of the magazine were friends of her father's. I teased her that the real reason she was marrying me was that it would enable her to come and live by the seaside and avoid the terrible journey from Leatherhead to Clapham Junction each day.

Carnival Week usually brought good weather with it. Early on the first day everybody was up and about, sniffing the prevailing excitement. Hundreds of Tadchestrians and holidaymakers patrolled the quay looking for something to take an interest in. Eric had about two hundred volunteers to assist him in his riverside cable-laying. The fair people were still putting the final touches to the stalls and sideshows and the fair lads were sniffing out the local talent, usually successfully, and inevitably leaving me with a few heartbroken cases of gonorrhoea to deal with.

Pam loved every minute of the atmosphere. There is something special about communities like Tadchester: you belonged and were part of all that went on.

I was much involved with the Carnival procession. This was well supported by Tadchester and each organisation, shop, place of work had been hard at work on their floats for weeks. I was to be on the Round Table float. We were to go in drag as Miss Tadchester 1957. I had pinched from the hospital some rolls of stockinette normally used to line plaster jackets and Bob Lording, a local tailor, had made pink body stocking suits out of them. On top of these we were to wear bikinis borrowed from wives, friends and mothers. We wore bathing hats and, apart from the odd member with a beard or moustache, looked like very presentable females.

There seemed to be hundreds of floats, stretching for miles. In fact there were seventy-two, a record entry. We were surrounded by fairies, goblins, sailors, Tom Pearce and his grey mare, people on penny-farthings, wheelbarrows, pogo sticks and every other conceivable form of transport. Some of the floats were magnificent; there was one made entirely of flowers to represent a lifeboat. There was the Carnival Queen, Barbara Jacobs, a voluptuous wench, sitting on a lorry absolutely covered in tulips.

Gwendoline Jacobs, Barbara's elder sister, had been Queen the year before. The sexiest-looking girl I had ever seen, she had been a patient of mine and a great worry to me. She would send for me to call and greet me at the door in a bikini. When she worked on the Telephone Exchange she listened in to, and interrupted, my calls. She had made a final and unsuccessful bid to get me to propose at last year's Carnival Ball. Apart from a note saying that she was now living in London working in a strip club and that there was always a bed for me there if I ever wanted one, I had not heard from her since then.

Underneath it all, Gwendoline was quite a character. There was a twinkle in her eye beneath her open sexuality. Judging from the amount of bosom Barbara was showing, she obviously shared the dominant gene that Gwendoline had inherited.

The idea was that the procession would wind its way on a five-mile route through the town, giving the locals and the holidaymakers the opportunity of throwing money on to the floats. The charity this year was Tadchester Hospital where a new X-ray machine was needed.

First we had to be judged. There were about a dozen categories of float and about six prizes for each category, Best Turned Out, Most Original, Funniest, etc., so that in fact nearly every float received some sort of prize. This in no way reduced the meticulous standard of the judging, the judges consisting of the Lady Mayoress and three or four other ladies who were heads of the various women's organisations in the town, plus the Matron of Tadchester Hospital.

These poor unfortunate women knew that they had to live on in the community after the Carnival was over. Anything slipshod in their approach, or the wrong words of praise, could make enemies and lead to feuds that would last till at least next year's Carnival. In fact, it was difficult to get people to volunteer to judge. It had been suggested at one Carnival committee meeting that the judges should be appointed like members of juries, i.e., that names should be taken at random off the electoral list and anyone not turning up for duty should be fined.

With the record entry of floats the judging took literally hours. Although it was sunny in the late afternoon when judging started, by the time it had finished a steady and heavy drizzle had begun.

One foresighted member of the Round Table had installed a barrel of beer on our float. Waiting in the rain, we were able to match the dampness falling on our outsides by continually damping our insides.

It was all too much for Harry Robinson, the dentist, full of beer and having missed his lunch by working through in order to be free for the Carnival. Surrounded by willowy, boisterous, female-looking shapes, he became a bit confused and started to proposition Jimmy Millington, the local pork butcher. Jimmy, being beardless and moustacheless, with a bathing-cap clapped firmly on his head and his wet stockinette and bikini clinging tightly to him, looked exactly the right thing to Harry. That beer *must* have been good.

At last we were off. The crowds, having had to wait as long as we had, also seemed to have been refreshing themselves with beer. Whereas the children's floats got applause and money showered on them, our bedraggled lot was their target for abuse. The rain had made most of the stockinette body suits sag and they were beginning to collect in rings around our legs. A few bras had slipped, a few bathing hats had been knocked off and we looked a bit like refugees from a brothel being run out of town by the sheriffs.

Until we came round on to the quay the abuse had been mainly verbal. However, once we were parading in front of the row of pubs that lined the quay the abuse became more material. We seemed to have every sort of object coming at us from every angle; cauliflowers, apples, oranges, bread and a few empty beer cans. Being men of some mettle and being fortified by a couple of gallons of beer apiece, we did not accept these insults lightly. Everything that hit our float was thrown back indiscriminately into the crowd. I caught a glimpse of the Lady Mayoress removing cauliflower from her chain of office. Things were beginning to get ugly and the crowd began to surge towards our float with the obvious intention of taking it apart.

Police Sergeant Jenkins moved forward to make a barrier between the two lots of potential combatants. At this moment Bob Lording hit him full in the face with an ill-directed beer can and Sergeant Jenkins went down with blood pouring from his forehead. Seeing his condition, I leapt off the float to attend to him. I could see the cut was only superficial and that the fall had been aggravated by the sergeant's stepping on some wet cabbage. He was fully compos mentis, shouting, 'I saw who did that! I'll book you for that!'

The Round Table, sensing danger, started to shuffle about, changing their position on the float. There was no chance of anyone recognising anyone.

The crowd was silent and stunned at first. Then what started as a trickle of laughter steadily increased into a roar.

'Thank God,' I thought as I pressed my thumb on the bleeding point of the sergeant's face. 'Something has distracted them.'

I turned to see what they were laughing at. Couldn't be the float – that had disappeared into the distance. It was me! In jumping from the float, my strapless bra had slipped to my waist and the bottom half of my bikini had followed the path of the soggy wet stockinette and was situated somewhere around my knees. It was in this situation that I was bending over the police sergeant, pressing my thumb on his forehead.

The sergeant brushed my hand away, got up and, adjusting his helmet above his blood-stained face, went off growling, 'Bloody lot of nancy boys! Someone is going to pay for this . . .'

I was rescued by Pam and Gladys who, with tears of laughter running down their faces, pushed their way through the crowd bearing a raincoat and said, 'Come on, put this on and let's get you out of here.'

Just after we left, the drizzle turned into a downpour and the whole procession was abandoned in chaos.

Pam loved Carnival Week; Tadchester was alive and there was something going on all the time. We sat on the bank of the River Tad to watch the West Country rowing championship. Tadchester, being Tadchester, had two rowing clubs: the Reds and the Blues. It was much more important to beat the local opposition than it was to triumph over other clubs like Brixham and Torquay. The Reds won the championship with the Blues coming a poor third.

After the regatta we went for a meal with Janice and

Kevin Bird. Kevin was the farm manager for the de Wyrebocks and always kept open house for me. Janice looked a bit down during dinner and eventually, after a lot of probing, admitted that she had a stomach pain. 'Come on, Janice,' I said, 'let's get you upstairs and have a look at you.'

Janice was plump, in fact quite plump. She kept some of her contours down with various belts and supports. Kevin, watching her get dressed one morning, saw her put on some pants followed by a roll-on, followed by stockings and suspender belt, followed by some long johns.

'If you should by chance get raped today,' said Kevin, 'whoever does it deserves a medal.'

It took a while for Janice to disrobe, but eventually she lay on the bed presenting a vast expanse of white abdomen for me to have a go at. I wasn't quite sure where to begin.

'If your hands are cold,' said Janice, 'I'll scream.'

I turned away and washed my hands under the hot tap. When I came back to have a look at Janice's abdomen, things had changed. The broad white expanse now had a series of regular black marks running across it from the top right corner to the bottom left. I couldn't make it out. For some reason, Janice lay there giggling. When I looked more closely at the marks, they appeared to be some sort of muddy rubber stamp. There were several points on each mark, and by rubbing one of them I found I could remove the muddy-coloured substance to leave faint scratch marks underneath.

Before I washed my hands her abdomen had been spotless. I wondered if this could be instant shingles or some other rare condition.

'Janice,' I asked, 'how on earth did you get these marks?'

She burst out laughing.

'Oh Bob,' she said, 'while you were washing your hands, the cat came through the window, jumped on the bed, walked straight across my stomach then shot out through the door.'

I laughed with her, wondering why the cat should have walked across her stomach with its claws out; perhaps it was my hand-washing in the corner that had put it on edge.

I could find nothing amiss with Janice's stomach and she was fit enough to go with us to the fair in the evening. We were joined by Frank Squires, his wife Primrose, and Eric and Zara, and set off in high spirits to explore the attractions.

Kevin said, 'Why not pop in to the fortune teller, Janice, and have your stomach read? She might welcome a change from palms.'

We sampled most of what was going on – the dodgem cars, the big dipper, the octopus and a whole variety of things that went up and down and round and round.

'Now for the tents,' said Frank.

We had a good laugh at the Soho Strippers. The tent seemed full of youths who had attended me regularly for their acne. In the boxing booth we were greeted by Jack Dawson, the ex-hangman.

'Do you fancy a few rounds with me, doctor?' said Jack.

Jack, true to tradition, had spent the first half of Carnival Week knocking out all the booth professionals and was now employed to help them see the week through. He had few challengers and was a bit too big and strong for most of them. At one time he had been a contender for the professional heavyweight championship.

The Elephant Man was a disappointment. He had some sort of trunk, admittedly; a roll of flesh coming down from the middle of his forehead in a loop – but it was certainly not elephantine.

My medical curiosity was aroused, however. How did he get a loop of flesh like that? I decided to ask, and when the tent was quiet, walked over to him.

He put out his hand. 'Nice to see you, Dr Clifford,' he said. 'I hope you haven't forgotten me. I was under your care at St Chad's. I can never thank you for what you did for me. I've been able to make a steady living ever since.'

Suddenly I remembered. When I was the plastic surgery house surgeon at St Chad's we had a patient who had lost his nose through some congenital disease. The plastic surgeon had attempted to rebuild one for him. It was a complicated process. First the patient's upper arm had to be attached to his forehead. When the living pedicle of flesh had been established between arm and forehead, the part attached to the arm was severed and the severed end was then sewn into the area where the plastic re-moulding was to take place.

Charley Harrow, the Elephant Man, had had some trouble with the lower end of his pedicle graft. It should have taken root in the nasal area, but for some reason it didn't. Charley was due to have it re-stitched when he disappeared from the ward. How in his condition he managed to get out, we never knew. He certainly had no clothes in the ward and, to say the least, he was certainly not inconspicuous.

'When are you going back to have it all finished up?' I said to Charley.

'Only if the money dries up,' he replied. 'It's a good income. They aren't very keen on me when I go into pubs, but,' he said with a twinkle, 'it doesn't put the ladies off – they think I've got spares.'

The last tent of all contained the only living mermaid in captivity. Sitting on a rock in a tank was a half-naked girl with long blonde hair hanging down to her waist from where a plastic tail took over.

What did seem incongruous was that the mermaid was wearing sunglasses. And there was something familiar about her. Those bosoms – surely I had seen them somewhere before, but they didn't fit in with the long blonde hair. I stared and stared trying to make up my mind. Pam was always saying that I thought I recognised everybody. Anyway, I gave it up and after a nightcap in The Goat, we called it a day.

Next day, in the surgery, on my desk was a scented envelope and a letter in large childish handwriting. It read, 'Dear Dr Bob, Thank you for not giving me away. I had to dye my hair blonde when I knew we were coming to Tadchester. They tell me you are getting married soon. What a pity. Could you see me tomorrow at the fairground? My caravan is the blue one to the right of the big dipper. Please come. I'm in terrible trouble and I need your help.'

There were three large kisses at the bottom of the letter and it was signed *Gwendoline Jacobs* . . .

CHAPTER 12

The next day, after surgery, I drove my car to the fairground. The Carnival was over and the fair had lost all
the bustle and gaiety of the previous week. Stalls and
roundabouts were being dismantled and council workmen
were beginning to cart away the week's accumulation of
rubbish and refuse.

There were dozens of traction engines and lorries parked
all over the place with no sense of order and I could not
find Gwendoline's caravan. Eventually I stopped one of
the fairground hands and asked if he could point out Miss
Jacobs's caravan. He didn't seem to know her name.

'She is the lady in the tank,' I said, trying to be helpful.

'You mean our f . . . . . . mermaid,' he replied with a leer. 'She's parked out just beyond the fruit machine arcade, next to the big dipper.' He smiled knowingly. 'You're chancing your arm a bit aren't you, guv?'

Secretly I had been rather looking forward to seeing Gwendoline. She had always been quite a character, overtly sexual, but retaining a twinkle in her eye as if she were only really teasing and knew the rules as well as anyone else.

The insinuations of the fairground hand worried me. I began to smell trouble . . .

Gwendoline's caravan was in a poor state of repair, with the paintwork cracked and fading. The blue was no longer a true blue but had a sort of washed-out look about it.

Gwendoline opened the door to my knock. She said, 'Thank God you've come, doctor. Do come in.'

The poorly lit caravan was just as tawdry inside. There was an unmade bed at one end and a few broken-down chairs at the other. The small sink was piled with unwashed dishes. Gwendoline was wearing an old dressing-gown loosely held at the waist by a cord, loose enough for me to see that she wore nothing at all underneath. She wore sunglasses, as she had in the tank. Her long, dyed blonde hair tumbled down, unbrushed, over her shoulders and looked unkempt and out of condition. I felt very ill at ease.

'What can I do for you, Gwendoline?' I asked.

She shrugged her shoulders, then muttered, 'We'll have some coffee first.'

She turned to the sink, cleared away some of the pots and pumped some water into a tin kettle which she put on the gas stove. I tried to make light conversation, enquiring after her family and asking what had happened to her since she left Tadchester. She replied in monosyllabic grunts. My questions struck no sparks, brought forth none of the bubbling answers I expected. She stood with her back to me, watching the gas ring, her cigarette stuck to her lower lip as if it had been attached by adhesive. This was not the vivacious Gwendoline of twelve months ago.

The grunts gave way to no answers at all, and I abandoned my attempts at conversation. The whistle of the boiling kettle brought Gwendoline out of her reverie. She turned off the gas, wiped clean two mugs from the pile in the sink, put a teaspoon of instant coffee in each, poured in water from the kettle, added some milk from a bottle she picked out of the clutter, then came towards me with the steaming mugs.

She sat down facing me. Her loosely tied dressing-gown was half open and her nakedness looked somehow vulgar in the half light. We sipped our coffee without speaking. Every instinct in me was shouting 'Get up and get out of here!' Foolishly, I did not.

I broke the silence with my original question. 'What can I do for you, Gwendoline?'

Gwendoline didn't respond for a moment or two, except to put her coffee mug down on the dirty carpeting of the van. Then she got up, walked to the door and pressed a switch. The caravan was flooded with a harsh neon light from a tube in the centre of the ceiling. Gwendoline took off her glasses and slid her dressing-gown from her shoulders. It fell around her ankles.

I had my first proper look at her. She had aged twenty years since I had last seen her. She was unwashed, there were dirt rings on her legs and thighs. There were dark shadows under both eyes and her once-perfect breasts drooped above a distended pot-like stomach. This sagging body was framed by her dyed hair, hanging crinkly and unkempt. There were strange mottled marks on both forearms. She looked like some strange Macbethian hag.

Gwendoline had been queen of the castle in Tadchester, but London had obviously been too much even for her quite considerable resilience. She was a broken shell of the girl of last year. The Smoke had taken its toll.

The girl was obviously no longer in balance with herself. She had 'flipped'. And I had a big problem on my hands.

I repeated my question brusquely and professionally. 'What can I do for you, Gwendoline?'

She half simpered. 'I want to do a trade with you, Doctor Bob.' She smiled, edging towards me.

'What do you mean, a trade?'

'Well, Doctor Bob,' she said, 'you always had an eye for the girls, and presumably you've still got it. I need a fix. There's nothing loose in this bloody town. You are my only hope – you can prescribe anything you want. For God's sake – you can do whatever you like with me – and I mean whatever – but in return I want some heroin . . .'

The marks on her forearm now made sense – Gwendoline was taking heroin intravenously. Drug addicts were relatively rare at this time; if they *were* addicted, then it was to something pretty tough. Soft drugs were not abused then, as they were to become some years later.

'This is silly,' I said. 'You need some help. Let me fix up for someone to see you.'

I got up, heading for the door. Gwendoline, naked, stood in my way.

'Oh no you don't!' she snapped, and by now any pretence of pleasantry had gone. She snarled at me. 'A lot of people have seen you come into this caravan. I can ruin you in this town if I want to.'

'Don't be silly, Gwendoline,' I repeated. 'Let me help you. I have a friend who specialises in drug addiction. I can make an appointment for you to see him. You'll get nowhere by carrying on like this.'

I was now pushing against her, trying to get to the door. She clung to my arm and started to scream. I fought my way through, wrenched open the door, disengaged her hand and stumbled down the steps. She stood at the door, completely naked, screaming, 'Rapist bastard! I'll fix you – you see if I don't!'

Most of the fairground hands had stopped work on their dismantling and stood watching me as I made my way with as much dignity as I could towards my car. Nobody said a word, but I felt as if a thousand eyes were on me. Worse, I could still hear Gwendoline's piercing screams as I got into the car and drove away.

Now it was Question Time. How had I got into this situation? I had been foolish in that I had not registered the visit to Gwendoline in the surgery book, and the surgery didn't know where I was. I had to admit to myself I had secretly been rather looking forward to seeing Gwendoline. Vanity, I suppose.

I had read about other doctors in situations like this, but I had never envisaged that anything possibly like it could happen to me. For the first time I realised how vulnerable doctors were when they visited lady patients in their own homes.

I wondered if Gwendoline really would try to make trouble for me. Half the fairground staff had seen me leaving the caravan, with Gwendoline standing naked and screaming at the door. The fairground hand I'd asked directions from had half warned me. What a fool I'd been . . .

I called in at Eric's shop on the way to the surgery.

'Christ, what a mess!' he said. (Thanks a bunch, I thought. Nothing like a few comforting words from an old friend in times of trouble.)

'It's her word against yours,' Eric went on. 'But that's not the only point – if a hint of it gets into the press, as a doctor you're crucified whether you've done anything or not. I've had some of the same sort of trouble when I've been called to television breakdowns. I've found sometimes that it's the lady of the house, not the set, that needs rewiring. But I'm not a doctor, thank God, and I have my own language for dealing with these situations.'

I went back to the surgery in despair. I just didn't know what to do.

Gladys remarked, 'You do look down in the dumps today, Doctor Bob.' I raised as much of a smile as I could muster and went to my room where I sat thinking.

Whom could I talk to about this? It was laughable in one way but deadly serious in another. As Eric said – get a hint of this in the papers and, innocent as I was, they'd have me. I imagined the headlines:

THE DOCTOR AND THE MERMAID
'HE RAPED ME,' SAYS FAIRGROUND BLONDE

Steve, with whom I would normally talk over problems like this, was away on holiday. I was sure it would upset Pam, who was up to her eyes in wedding preparations. She would sympathise and stand by me, but practically she would not be able to advise. The situation would add yet one more worry to her list.

Henry Johnson would have laughed his head off. 'Just forget it,' he would say. 'She's a nut. Nothing's going to happen.' Henry had several times been put in the situation that I was in. He had just laughed it off, and that was that. But everything was like that with Henry.

I could not rid myself of this foreboding of trouble. Jean Hart, Jack's wife, was seriously ill in hospital, so I couldn't bother him. I was thrown back on my own resources and was frightened to discover how inadequate they were. I racked my brains. What could I do? Then I thought of Marion Cook.

Marion Cook was Tadchester's most prominent citizen. She was the town's first lady mayor, a JP, chairman of the governors of the grammar school, a member of a BBC advisory committee, and a *cordon bleu* cook. But above all else, this talented and tirelessly active woman always seemed to have time for people with worries and problems.

Marion was about the only person who would make herself cheerfully available for tiresome, tedious jobs like signing passports. She had been a great help to many of my patients in all sorts of emotional, economic and family upsets. I rang her and tentatively explained my problem. My story sounded very stupid as I told it over the phone, but Marion was instantly both compassionate and practical.

'Oh you poor thing,' she said. 'As if you doctors don't have enough to cope with. You must take this seriously, Bob: unbalanced people do unbalanced things. Now leave it to me. Come round for a cup of coffee at about eight this evening. I'll see what I can do.'

The fact that my problem was now shared, and shared with someone of Marion's stature, was a tremendous relief. I got through my day's work with half my mind still on the problem of Gwendoline, and duly reported to Marion at eight o'clock. She kissed me on the cheek.

'Come in and stop worrying,' she said. 'I have someone in the lounge I want you to discuss your problem with.'

Sitting in the lounge was the uniformed Inspector Harold, the head of the Tadchester Constabulary. Marion had been to work. It was difficult to believe that what had started off as a problem-free day was developing into a situation involving the town's mayor and head of police. Marion introduced us.

'Bob,' she said, 'perhaps you would tell your story to Inspector Harold. I have not discussed anything with him: I have just asked him round as a friend to give help and advice to another friend.'

Inspector Harold did not look in the least pleased to be there. Wearing his uniform was probably part of his protest. It would be difficult, nigh impossible, to refuse an invitation from the forceful Marion. She was so involved with everything that virtually everybody was dependent on her. Her word was, in fact, almost law. No head of law enforcement could possibly like that.

I told my story to Inspector Harold, feeling completely foolish. He sat perfectly still, his face expressionless. He made no comment until I had finished. With no attempt to encourage or reassure me in any way, he then said, 'A part of your story I already know. Strictly off the record' (he coughed and looked at Marion, embarrassed), 'Miss Jacobs called at the police station this morning to lay a complaint of physical assault and attempted rape against you. We know Miss Jacobs and we know you. The complaint was noted, but for our part we do not intend to take any further action.'

His face gave away nothing, but I remembered Eric's words in the morning: 'Once this gets about, however innocent you are, as a doctor you're crucified . . .'

I saw, or thought I saw, a sort of 'There's no smoke without fire' look behind the Inspector's lack of expression.

'What do you suggest I do?' I asked.

'There's nothing the police can do,' he snapped back. 'If you want to take out a civil summons against her, that is entirely your affair. It is not without its own complications and it's nothing to do with the police.'

He got up, ready to go. He was obviously dying for his supper and thought that all this was a terrible waste of time.

'You mean you can't help?' said Marion, in a steely voice which hinted that whatever functions she was going to patronise during her term of office, the Police Ball would not be one of them.

'I'm very sorry, Madam Mayor,' said the Inspector. 'There's nothing I can do. I have already exceeded my responsibilities by informing you of the complaint laid. If you'll excuse me, I will be on my way now.'

'He lacks the courage of his predecessor,' said Marion after she had seen him out. 'If old Inspector Watts had been here he would have sorted it all out in a jiff.'

I sat back in my chair, dazed. Things now seemed worse, not better – I had been reported to the police for attempted rape. Marion saw my concern.

'Do stop worrying, Bob,' she said. 'You have done

nothing. I'll have to sort this out on my own. Now you sit down in front of the television and relax. I'm going out – I'm going to lay this ghost tonight.'

She put on her hat and coat, and slipped out of the door. A few minutes later I heard her car drive away.

I sat in front of the television, not watching, with the sound turned down so that I would catch the noise of her returning car. I felt like a helpless child, with Mother going out to sort out my troubles.

It was an an hour before Marion returned. She was steely faced and tense – but obviously something had been done.

'Well, Bob,' she said, 'you can forget all about your little problem. Gwendoline will be off in the morning, the matter's closed. So forget it and stop worrying about it – and I mean stop *worrying* about it.'

'What happened?' I asked.

'What happened,' said Marion, 'is my secret. Let's say that this town appointed me as its mayor to ensure that there is justice and order in the community. Tonight I have been out in pursuance of that trust. Apart from that, the matter is closed.'

The traumas of that night, when I benefited so much from Marion's good offices, were the beginning of a long and valued friendship with her. The next morning, as she had predicted, the fair had gone, taking Gwendoline with it. It was a tremendous relief to me. I called on Marion with a bunch of flowers, feeling that this was the least I could do. I again tried to broach the subject of what had happened the night before. Marion looked stern.

'Bob,' she said, 'the matter is really closed.' Then she relaxed and said, 'One day, when you write your book, you will be able to put all this down.'

And now, as I write my book, I can pay tribute to Marion Cook, first Lady Mayor of Tadchester . . . and Woman Extraordinary.

CHAPTER 13

Two weeks after the Carnival I was called to see Janice Bird. Of all my friends she seemed to be the unluckiest with her health. She had been very ill the previous year when she was one of several people who were infected by eating diseased pork. From what Kevin had said on the phone, she was complaining of the same sort of symptoms.

The patients who had been infected by the pork all confessed to eating it uncooked, mainly by eating a pinch of raw sausage meat when spicing it. Surely Janice had learnt her lesson?

Things weren't too bad when I saw her. She was feverish and had a headache. As soon as I came through the door she said, 'Sorry to call you in, Bob. And before you ask –

I definitely haven't eaten any raw sausage meat.'

When I examined her I found that her temperature was raised and that she had several very large glands in her right groin. There were a few small glands in the left groin, and a few under each arm and in her neck. Apart from the glands in the groin her other glands didn't seem to be affected.

'I think you have glandular fever,' I said to Janice. 'I'll do a blood test to confirm it, not that it will make any difference; the condition will get better on its own. I can't say how long you are going to feel unwell, but it's likely to be at least a week and possibly several.'

I took some blood and called again in a couple of days. To my surprise Janice seemed completely recovered. Also her blood tests had come back negative to glandular fever.

My provisional diagnosis was wrong, but, as I said to Janice, I had to prove what she didn't have as a first step to discovering what in fact she did have.

The glands in her right groin were as big as ever. I examined the leg to see if there were any infected cuts that could be causing them, but it was quite clear and there was no obvious reason why she should have these glands.

'OK, Janice,' I said, 'you can get up and about, but I want to see you each week until these glands have gone down or disappeared.'

I subsequently saw Janice every week for four weeks. She was perfectly well but her glands still remained and I thought a couple of them were even a little bigger. I began to wonder if these were signs of something more sinister, so I made an appointment for her to see my physician friend John Bowler at the Winchcombe Hospital.

He rang me after he had seen Janice. 'I don't know what they are,' he said. 'I'll have to get one of my surgical colleagues to remove one and send it to Pathology.' Janice felt we were making an awful fuss, but we arranged that she should go in as a day case and have a gland removed.

A week later John rang again. 'It seems pretty good news for Janice,' he said. 'The gland is not quite typical; we think it's toxoplasmosis. This is a self-limiting disease and it will do her no harm. If the blood tests confirm it, then she can forget all about it.'

The blood tests unfortunately did not confirm this diagnosis and the pathologist at Winchcombe felt it was possible that she had a cancer of the lymph glands. He had found it difficult to establish what the gland was, so was sending slides off to St Bartholomew's Hospital in London for a further opinion. I made light of this to Janice, and anyway she felt so well that my continued fussing was all a bit of a nuisance.

The fact that Janice had a lump made all my other friends search round to see if they could find some of their own. On the same day I had both Lee – Joe Church's wife – and Frank Squires in to see me.

Lee had a painless lump in her right thigh. I'd never seen anything like it before. An X-ray of her leg was clear, so there was no obvious bone involvement, but she still had her lump. I thought it was most likely a muscular tear or a thrombosed vein, but I couldn't take a chance so I made an appointment for her to see the faithful John Bowler at Winchcombe.

Frank had a hard lump on the left side of his neck. I tried to hide my concern as I examined it. The lump was hard and fixed – it could be a sign of all sorts of nasty things. There was nothing for me to do but to bother John Bowler once again. I hoped he wasn't going to get fed up seeing all my lumpy friends.

John was on the phone to me after he had seen Lee and Frank.

'Bob,' he said, 'both of these could be nasty. I'll have to fix up for them to come in next week for biopsies. What's happening to you all in Tadchester – are you just trying to worry me to death?'

The day Lee and Frank were admitted to Winchcombe Hospital was my half day, so I went over to Winchcombe to keep an eye on them. The surgeon who was going to do the biopsies invited me to attend the operations and I went round with him for his last look at both Lee and Frank before he operated. He examined Lee's leg carefully. 'Just a torn muscle I think, my dear,' he said, 'we can put that right.'

'Frank is better off than I am,' said Lee. 'I can lose a leg— at least they won't chop his head off.'

The surgeon smiled. When we got outside I said, 'Thank goodness you think it's only a torn muscle.'

'It isn't all I think,' he replied brusquely. 'I think it's most likely that this is a very malignant kind of muscle cancer. We may, in fact, have to take her leg off.'

'You can't!' I said, horrified.

I hadn't even thought of this as possible and neither had Lee, in spite of her parting joke.

'If the biopsy shows it to be as bad as you think it is, then *she* must decide whether her leg comes off or not,' I said. 'The outlook is poor anyway. She mustn't be allowed to go to theatre thinking that she is having a muscle repaired and wake up to find she has a leg missing.'

'She won't do that,' said the surgeon. 'If it's necessary to remove her leg, we'll bring her round and discuss it with her before we proceed. Meanwhile I have an orthopaedic surgeon standing by.'

When Lee's leg was opened, the surgeon cut down and exposed a mucus-filled cyst. He removed the cyst, then snapped at the theatre sister: 'Send this for a frozen section and ask the orthopaedic surgeon to come up to the theatre.'

I protested again. 'You can't!'

The surgeon cut me short.

'A consent for operation has been signed,' he said. 'The only chance for this girl, if the cyst is malignant, is to remove her leg. This is my responsibility and my decision –

but of course we will do nothing radical until we have consulted her.'

We left Lee in the theatre with the anaesthetist, came out into the doctors' room and had a cup of tea and a smoke while we waited for the result of the frozen section. The wait seemed endless. I was thinking of how I would have to go and tell Joe that Lee had lost a leg. It was all too terrible to consider. At last came a call from the Path. Lab. No obvious malignancy on frozen section: a full opinion would be available in about a week.

'Thank God,' I thought. 'Whatever happens from now on, she'll at least have a say in whether she loses her leg or not.'

Frank's operation was without any of the drama of Lee's. The lump was bigger than first thought and the surgeon, after fiddling for about an hour, produced a round white object like a small potato from deep down in Frank's neck.

'I've never seen one of these before,' he said. 'Looks like a neuroma. It's attached to a nerve, anyway. It all looks quite harmless, but we'll have to see what the Path. Lab. thinks about it. Anyway, there's no reason why your friend shouldn't go home tomorrow, and we will let you know the final results in about a week.'

I had a restless week. Frank had lost his voice, either because of the anaesthetic or because they had to cut a nerve to get the lump out. It could have been the nerve that supplied the vocal cords, though the surgeon didn't think so at the time. They checked Frank's cords for movement after the operation and they all seemed quite happy about the way they moved.

Frank's wife, Primrose, said that it was the quietest the house had been for years. She was in no hurry for him to get his voice back.

I'd heard nothing from the Path. Lab. after seven days,

so I started to ring in each day, trying not to sound too concerned. Frank's potato, which I hadn't been very concerned about, now began to worry me. Each time I spoke to the technician at the Path. Lab. he would say, 'I'm sorry sir, we are still making further sections of the specimen; we have not made a decision yet.' There was still no news of Lee's cyst, and nothing had come from Bartholomew's Hospital about Janice's gland.

Joe, Kevin and Primrose would ring me each day on some pretext, then casually in conversation, as if it were of no consequence at all, each would say 'Is there any news yet?' They were obviously worried to death and there was little I could say to reassure them.

I made my usual daily routine call to the Path. Lab. This time the phone was answered by the pathologist and not the technician. I asked, holding my breath, if there was any news of Lee's and Frank's specimens.

'Yes,' said the pathologist, 'we have had difficulty in identifying Mr Squires' tumour; we've decided to call it a swanoma.'

'Is it malignant?' I asked.

'Oh no,' he replied. 'There's never been any suggestion that it could have been malignant. It's an unusual lump and difficult to put a name to.'

I could have thumped him for my ten days of needless worry.

'And Mrs Church?' I asked.

'Oh yes,' he said, 'another interesting case. A simple mucus-filled myxoma. If she's had one, she may have others here and there, but there's nothing to do about them – they are quite harmless.'

I could have wept with relief. Two down and one to go. If only I could get Janice's results through, life could resume some sort of normal pattern. It is so difficult treating friends, you tend to overtreat and it is difficult not to show your anxiety.

At last John Bowler came on the phone with Janice's

results. I held my breath. John chuckled. 'Bob, does Mrs Bird by any chance have a cat?'

'Yes, definitely,' I said, remembering the muddy scratch marks across her stomach.

'Well,' he said, 'she must take care in future. These glands show that what she is suffering from is cat-scratch fever. Tell her cat to keep its claws in in future.'

I sat down, exhausted. Three of my closest friends whom I was putting at death's door a fortnight ago were all completely clear.

We decided that Pam would give an after-lump dinner-party at our new flat. It wasn't completely furnished yet but there were enough chairs to go round. Pam produced a superb roast, the first meal she had cooked in Tadchester. Frank's voice was almost back to normal: it wouldn't be long before he was shouting orders to us, his slaves on the seine fishing-nets. Lee, who had still a slight limp, said, 'Bob, if my lump was a myxoma and they say I could have more, would that mean I've got myxomatosis?'

Kevin said, 'Well, you always did have rabbit teeth.'

It would be difficult to envisage a fictitious situation where three close friends should all produce some rare medical disease at the same time. I knew of cat-scratch fever but had never seen or even heard about swanomas and myxomas. I rang John Bowler.

'John,' I said, 'do you think I ought to go on a post-graduate course? I've never heard of conditions like swanomas and myxomas.'

'Don't worry,' said John, 'I've never come across them before either, but no more lumps for a bit, please – they can't all have happy endings.'

When I left medical school they had not warned me of the dangers from animals in general practice. Since coming to Tadchester, I had been attacked by pretty well every sort of domestic animal except the proverbial bull.

Mrs Chilcott was one of my nuisance patients. She was

always sending for me with some terrifying tale of illness. When I got to her house I would find her fully dressed and powdered, sporting three strings of pearls, and I would then have to listen to a monologue of how important her late husband had been, and all the important people she knew and the famous places she had been to.

She often forgot why she had sent for me. I recognised that hers was a cry for help; she was lonely and bored and I did not begrudge too much the time that I spent with her. It was as important as giving out pills or medicine. What I *did* begrudge was the guerrilla warfare conducted by her small Pekingese, Charles.

I am rather apprehensive about dogs. The dogs sense my feelings and this brings out all their nasty aggressive habits. Small dogs I didn't mind too much; I could usually block their attacks with my medical case.

Charles was different. I was completely on edge whenever I went into the house. He would launch his attack from behind settees, doors, chairs, anything that gave him some sort of cover. I never let my case out of my hand at Mrs Chilcott's. I knew that I would have to use it as a shield at any moment. I developed a technique of moving the case smartly towards Charles as he launched his attack, landing him a few fairly heavy bumps on the nose.

'Isn't he a marvellous house dog?' gushed Mrs Chilcott every time I fended off an attack. I longed to put my boot into this little monster, small as he was.

Mrs Chilcott sent for me one day. She was in bed with flu. She would leave the back door on the latch and see that Charles was safely restrained. 'Just let yourself in, doctor, I'll be in the first bedroom on the right.'

I made her my first call, purely to get it over with. Having let myself in, with case at the ready I stealthily walked to the first bedroom on the right, as Mrs Chilcott had directed. There was no sign of Charles anywhere.

Mrs Chilcott was sitting up in bed, powdered and

perfumed, still wearing her three rows of pearls on top of her nightdress. There was some preliminary talk about her condition, then I put my case down, got out my stethoscope and bent to listen to her chest. No sooner had my stethoscope touched her than out from under the eiderdown came hurtling the spitting, snarling Charles, determined to do me some actual bodily harm. He came out like a rocket, straight for my left hand. Fortunately, although I had put my case down I had unconsciously geared my reflexes and snatched my hand away just in time to miss his teeth.

Charles was unable to check his flight and sailed on, sinking his teeth into Mrs Chilcott's right breast. She shrieked – and the genteel manners and conversation that she had built up over the years were lost in a few minutes of the most blistering language that it has ever been my lot to hear. She gave precious Charles the belt round the rear end that I had been longing to give him, and shot him off the bed. This was a turning-point in my visits to Mrs Chilcott; it became quite a pleasure to go and see her. Charles, now broken-spirited, would greet me effusively whenever I called, and strenuously attempt to lick the parts that before he used to try and bite.

The Sunset Nursing Home, in Craven Hill Road, was quite different. This was a private house that offered accommodation to eight elderly ladies. They had a room each and were well cared for. The house rules, to qualify for admission, were that the patient must be ambulant, must be able to dress herself and mustn't be incontinent. Whenever I managed to get a patient admitted they seemed to behave well for a month, then go into a decline, take to their beds and become incontinent. It was to the great credit of the proprietors that they took all this in their stride and looked after their old ladies with affection and care.

I did not know how they were staffed dog-wise until one

day, visiting a patient there, I had to go in and see Mr and Mrs Reynolds who ran the Home. 'Come in,' they called, when I knocked on the door of their flatlet. I opened the door to see two gigantic Great Danes leaping off the settee to greet me and just had time to shut the door again before they reached it.

I was chided by the Reynolds. 'Oh, doctor, they wouldn't hurt a fly – they were only saying hello.' I had heard all this many times before when patients had shouted, 'Just ignore the dog, doctor, and come up.' It had cost me three pairs of trousers. I knew that the dogs by now were aware that I was scared of them, and however gentle they might be with anyone else, would vent any aggressiveness on me.

From then on, before each visit to the Home, I would ring up and warn Mr and Mrs Reynolds to shut the dogs away before I called. One day, I forgot to give my warning call, marched into the room of the patient I'd called to see, and started to examine her.

For some reasons, probably practical ones, the beds in Sunset House were very close to the ground. To examine my lady patient I had to kneel at the side of her bed. With my stethoscope in my ears I was oblivious to sounds outside. The first intimation that the dogs were not locked up was feeling hot breath on the back of my head and a large wet tongue starting to lick the back of my neck.

I dared not make a sudden move. These dogs were as big as horses. They could easily have picked me up by the scruff of my neck and shaken me. I conducted the most meticulous and thorough examination of a chest that I have ever carried out. For thirty-five minutes I listened carefully and intently to my old lady. All my movements were slow and deliberate so as not to arouse the monster that was poised literally a hair's breadth behind me. After what seemed an eternity, I heard the dog pad away. I got up stiffly, and my lady patient beamed.

'You are a marvellous doctor,' she said. 'Nobody has taken time and trouble like this with me before.'

In a fit of generosity one day I offered to do a visit for Jack Hart who was a bit pressed. I realised it was a mistake when I pulled up at a large gate which had written on it 'Beware of the Bull Mastiff'. There was no turning back. I hooted my horn just in case there was anyone about, but the gates were separated from the house by a two-hundred-yard drive and nobody came.

I slipped out of the car, pushed the gate open, then jumped back into the car. I left the gate open, hoping selfishly that if the bull mastiff was loose in the grounds it would take the opportunity of running out into the road. I drove up as close as I could to the front door of the house and looked round. No sign of a dog anywhere. I jumped out of the car into a corner of the porch, back to the wall and my case in front of me, and rang the doorbell. In the distance I could hear a muffled roar, which could have come from nothing smaller than a lion. I was let into the house, saw my patient who had been hurt in a hunting accident, then began to make my way down the stairs. As I reached the bottom, I heard a terrifying growling sound. There, framed in a doorway, was a twelve-year-old girl doing her best to restrain the biggest dog I had ever seen in my life. It could have eaten the two Great Danes for breakfast.

The girl was gasping for breath in her effort to restrain the great beast. She panted 'I would go as quickly as you can, doctor. Dinky doesn't like strangers and I don't think I can hold him much longer.'

I threw all dignity to the winds and was out of the front door and into my car in a flash. I determined never to volunteer for visits in unreconnoitred territory again.

It was not only dogs that tried to attack me. I was chased

by geese, butted by a goat, kicked by a donkey and had my finger bitten by a pet macaw. Cats, which I don't like, never bothered me; that is, they never actually attacked me. But because they sensed I didn't like them, cats always made a tremendous fuss, climbing all over me, depositing hairs all over my jacket, to the coos of their owners who would say, 'Oh, she's taken a liking to you, doctor. They can always tell a cat lover when they see one.'

I knew that whatever profession outside medicine I might have attempted, the one I would never have been able to contemplate was that of a vet.

The dangers from animals were not limited to their aggressiveness. Although I never caught anything from a pet myself, my patients seemed to be doing it all the time. I had one family of four, all down with pneumonia at the same time. I couldn't understand it; I had never heard of epidemic pneumonia. It was only on my second visit to the house that I realised what was happening.

The mother of the house greeted me with tears streaming down her face.

'Oh, doctor,' she said, 'all our parrots are dying. Do you think they have caught something from us?'

I went round the back of the house to an aviary in a shed. It was a pathetic sight. There were about two dozen dead and dying parrots on the floor. They were the root of the problem. It was the parrots that had infected the family, passing on a disease called psittacosis.

Hamsters and rabbits passed on all sorts of cystic worm infections and we even traced one source of dysentery to a tortoise. One of Henry Johnson's patients with a pet monkey nearly died of monkey-bite fever and one of Steve Maxwell's patients actually caught foot-and-mouth disease when there was an outbreak amongst the local cattle.

I said to Steve one day that I was coming to the conclusion that all pets were lethal and as far as I could see were harbingers of infection and disease.

Steve smiled. 'Well, Bob,' he said, 'I've never had much trouble with goldfish, but don't get too over-confident with them – they might easily give you a nasty suck.'

CHAPTER 14

Joe Church had become progressively restless. He was fed up with teaching and fed up with the confines of a small town like Tadchester – or, as he called it, Main Street.

He realised that he could never progress beyond being games master in a grammar school and that the job in Tadchester was as pleasant as he could expect anywhere else. He felt that his life had come to a stop. Apart from his fishing, rugby playing and other outside activities, life was just a tedious routine.

We used to debate this endlessly when I was round there for coffee or we were out seine net-fishing. I think that the scare of Lee's operation had brought him up with a jolt:

he felt that he had a whole life still to live and he was not making the most of it.

He pursued all sorts of different possibilities. He thought of going into business but had no capital, thought of other jobs but discovered he lacked the qualifications. Eventually he and Lee decided that the armed forces were the only answer – there would be travel, they would be under the protective umbrella of the Service, accommodation would be found for them, and there would be a new and wider range of people to meet and know. He hoped he might be a pilot. This sounded promising: a dashing extrovert like Joe would be bound to fit in.

There were endless comings and goings after he had made his decision. He applied, had his medicals and what seemed innumerable interviews, and was finally accepted by the Air Force as a potential pilot. As we filled in some of the forms together, in the space where it said 'station of choice' he put boldly in large capitals 'ANYWHERE IN THE WORLD'.

In the evenings, he would get out a map and pinpoint the places in the world where there were still RAF bases that he might get to. Singapore, Aden, Cyprus, Gibraltar, British Guiana – he imagined himself in all and any of these.

There was a round of parties, and one final super goodbye party at the Churches' the night before they left: Joe to report to an RAF station in East Anglia, Lee to move in for the time being with her parents in London.

I was very sad to see them go. They had been good friends, and Pam had looked forward to enjoying Lee's company again after the operation.

I took them to Tadchester station the next day, with piles of cases and boxes, and there was a tearful goodbye from Lee on the station.

'Wherever we go, Bob,' she said, 'we won't have a doctor like you.'

'Send us a postcard from Hong Kong,' I said. 'Best of luck.'

I felt that Joe was doing the right thing. Having become restless, whether it was right or wrong for him to make a move his restlessness would not be satisfied until he had made a change. His choice of the Air Force, what's more, did seem to hold everything he wanted.

Two weeks later I had a phone call from him. He was extremely depressed and down-hearted.

'How are you, Joe?' I asked.

'Awful.'

'You sound close. Where are you?'

'I'm at Winchcombe.'

'That's marvellous,' I said. 'Are you coming for the weekend? I can put you up on the settee in the flat.'

'No,' said Joe. 'You don't understand. I have been *posted* to Winchcombe. Is there any chance of you coming over to see me?'

Poor Joe. He had made this break to get right away from his surroundings – and of all the places had been posted to the Winchcombe RAF Flight Training School.

He sounded so depressed, I shot over to see him that evening. He was sullen and morose.

'Cheer up, Joe,' I said. 'This is a first-class training school and once you have learnt to fly, you may go anywhere.'

'I'm not allowed to fly,' said Joe. 'They found at my final examination I have some high tone deafness and some sinus trouble. I'm not allowed to do any flying.'

'Well, what are you doing?' I said.

'What do you think?' said Joe, 'The only thing I am able to do – they've signed me up as a teacher.'

There were no married quarters available for trainees, so Lee had to stay on with her parents in London. Joe was almost at breaking point. I went to see him several times and each time he was increasingly depressed. He explored all the avenues in the RAF that would take him out of

154

teaching, but nothing seemed to be going right for him.

'I'll see if I can buy myself out and come back to Tadchester,' he said the last time I saw him. He was being posted away for three weeks to some special drill course which they all had to attend.

When he came back he was a different person. 'I've made it!' he said, triumphantly.

'What? Air crew?' I asked.

'No,' said Joe, 'I've signed up as an RAF parachutist.'

'Rather you than me,' I said.

I lost touch with Joe after that, but some years later I saw him as the leader of the RAF parachutists' team. They were doing a free fall from some incredible height and joining hands in a circle before they opened their chutes and descended.

I wrote to him. From then on I had cards and letters from the places that he had hoped to go, like Cyprus, Singapore, and even one from Saudi Arabia where they had gone to give a free-fall display. He became quite a celebrity and was interviewed on TV.

Good for Joe, I thought. But I never forgot that crestfallen voice ringing up from Winchcombe.

He had set off bravely to conquer the world and been posted fifteen miles away. I am sure that if he had only asked to be posted to Winchcombe, that would almost have guaranteed that he finished up in Hong Kong.

The only comparable story to that of Joe's was an incident when Frank and Primrose were on holiday in Cornwall. They had been gone about five days when I bumped into them in Tadchester.

'Back already?' I asked.

'Back? Rubbish!' said Frank. 'We spent £3 each on a day's mystery tour – and this is where we have landed up. The place just won't let go of us.'

My patients continued to surprise and entertain me.

One bright-eyed schoolgirl, Penelope Shaw, came into the surgery with a very swollen stomach. She must have been at least six months' pregnant.

She asked for slimming pills to reduce her weight. I insisted on examining her first, and found that she was well and truly pregnant. I questioned her as gently as I could.

'Is there any chance that you could be pregnant?'

'Absolutely none,' said the girl.

I hesitated. 'Have you ever had intercourse?'

'Oh, yes,' she said. 'My boy-friend and I do it every Friday night after Youth Club.'

'Well, don't you think,' I said, 'that this carries a risk of your becoming pregnant?'

'Oh, no,' she said, very positively. 'We had biology lessons at school and I learnt all about having babies before I would let Jimmy anywhere near me. Our biology teacher said you could definitely only become pregnant if you slept with someone. There is no other way, and we have never ever slept together. Jimmy did get a bit dozy once, but I kept him awake. So you see, doctor, there is no chance at all of my being pregnant. I have never ever slept with anyone.'

There was a whole lot of gentle questioning to do. I had to see both sets of parents. The girl was only sixteen, and Jimmy seventeen, but in true Tadchester tradition they got married, had a fine baby, and made a real go of it.

Two years later I saw Penelope pushing a pram. She now had three babies to her name, all fat, healthy children. I guessed that since her marriage she must have started sleeping with Jimmy . . .

I had wondered often about the value of those biology lessons; I expect they are better than nothing at all, but I think the home is the place to learn about the birds and bees. Somehow school seems too detached and dispassionate. It is all a bit of a giggle, and the most inquisitive are often only too eager to do a bit of homework after this particular biology lesson.

In contrast to Penelope was Sandra Reeves, who was about the same age as Penelope. She burst into tears in the surgery as soon as she sat down.

'What is the matter, Sandra?' I said. 'Can you tell me?'

'Oh, doctor,' she said, 'I'm pregnant!'

'Well, how long have you been pregnant?' I asked.

'About six weeks now,' she said.

It did appear, on the surface, that she was better informed then Penelope.

'Did you not use any form of contraceptive?' I asked.

Sandra looked puzzled. 'I am not sure what you mean, doctor.'

'Will you explain to me what happened?'

Sandra, still in tears, stumbled out her pathetic little story.

She had been to a party during a period, and a boy kissed her. This is how she thought babies were conceived – being kissed during a period!

Poor Sandra. I had to give my own sex education lecture to her. I don't think she had slept since the fateful night, and was just about on the edge of a nervous breakdown.

I explained to her, in detail, the process of conception and birth – and it was a very relieved and smiling little girl who left my surgery.

Polly Davies was an unmarried mother, and proud of it. She had a huge, fat, sleepy baby, and I congratulated her on such a fine specimen.

I wondered quite how she managed to cope with a baby as she spent a fair amount of time in and around both The Goat and the Tadchester Arms.

'What do you do with baby when you are out?' I asked.

'Oh, he sleeps all the time. He is never any trouble,' said Polly.

I was a bit worried about her and asked Nurse Plank to pop in some time and just check that all was well.

A couple of days later Nurse Plank turned up at the surgery and showed me a bottle of brown fluid.

'What is that?' I asked.

'*That* is Polly Davies's baby's food.'

'Why is it so brown?' I asked.

Nurse Plank grinned. 'It's quite simple, and no wonder the baby is never any bother. Polly just puts a few spoonfuls of milk powder in half a pint of Guinness and the baby sleeps like a top. I think he is probably the youngest alcoholic in Tadchester.'

One of my favourite patients was Grannie Weedon. She had poor eyesight and lived in a cottage Up-the-Hill.

She had had some constipation trouble. After trying some fairly gentle medicine – which didn't work – I gave her some suppositories which I knew would do the trick.

When I called a few days later there was a disgruntled Grannie Weedon.

'Them things you gave me, doctor, ain't no good at all. You can have 'em back.'

This surprised me. The suppositories I had prescribed were pretty powerful.

'Were they no help at all?' I asked.

'Not a bit,' said Grannie Weedon. 'And they are uncomfortable too.'

I know suppositories are nasty, messy things, but had never heard them described as being uncomfortable.

'You had better let me have a look at them,' I said.

'Here you are,' said Grannie. 'You can take the rotten things away.'

She went to the cupboard and produced a small brown paper bag – full of 3-amp fuses! I could see my suppositories nestling, untouched, at the back of the cupboard. Grannie Weedon's eyesight was obviously not good enough for administering self medication. She was probably one of the few people who could truly say they had blown a fuse!

I had not thought when I saw my patients doing strange things and having strange beliefs that it was I sometimes who could be a source of entertainment and amusement to them.

It was brought home to me when John Denton, the fishing bailiff on the River Tad, came in one morning nursing a finger which looked as if it had been through a mincer. It was obviously very painful, but there was a broad grin on his face.

'What have you been up to now, John?' I asked.

'Just carelessness, Bob. Bloody pike. Makes me feel a right fool.'

John had been catching some big pike which were threatening his stocks of game fish.

'I've had two salmon in the past fortnight with chunks out of their sides,' said John. 'Pike bites. Their eyes are always too big for their bellies, are pikes', and they don't give a bugger what size fish they go for so long as they're lying still.

'Any road, I'd landed this big 'un, and I wanted to treat it gently so that I could hand it over in one piece to the Tadchester Angling Club for one of their lakes. I don't like using a gag* anyway; vicious bloody things they are – do more harm than good.

'So I used friendly persuasion and a few kind words while I was getting the hook out. Bugger me if I didn't pay

---

* A pike gag is a strong, v-shaped wire spring, with teeth at each end of the 'v', used to hold open a pike's mouth so that the hooks can be taken out without danger to the angler. It's a nuisance, however, can result in a dislocated jaw for the pike, and many anglers prefer to do without it.

attention for a second and the bloody thing had my finger. It spun round as well, while my finger was in its mouth: took the skin off like a Surform file.'

I shuddered as I thought of the lining of a pike's mouth: hundreds of needle-sharp teeth, and all pointing backwards so that anything which got in there had the devil's own job getting out.

But John was smiling again, and every so often, as I cleaned and dressed the finger, would give a suppressed chortle.

'Come on, John,' I said. 'Let me in on the joke. I'm always short of a few laughs at morning surgery.'

'Aye, all right then, lad. Mebbe I shouldn't, but it might be embarrassing for you one of these days. This bloody surgery needs sound-proofing.'

I thought for a second. What medical secrets could have been escaping through the solid walls and thick frosted windows of the surgery door? My God – Charlie Wainwright!

Charlie had been the patient before John. A gnarled Tadchester local, seventy-four years old, and deaf as a post. Like many elderly deaf people, he shouted at the top of his voice during normal conversation. And because he refused to have anything to do with hearing aids – his father and grandfather had never had one and he didn't see why he should break the family tradition at his time of life – anybody talking to him had to shout back.

Charlie had come to see me with a bad attack of constipation.

'I can't go, doctor!' he shouted. 'And I haven't been for nigh on a fortnight. Bloody agony it is. Hard as rock. I want some of that stuff you gave Wagger Martin last Easter. Soon shifted him, it did.'

'Yes, yes, Charlie,' I said. 'The first thing is for me to examine you.'

'Eh? Whatcha say?'

'I HAVE TO EXAMINE YOU. TAKE YOUR TROUSERS OFF!'

Charlie fumbled with his belt, strained at his flies, and then hit a snag.

'YOU'LL HAVE TO TAKE YOUR BOOTS OFF FIRST, CHARLIE! I yelled. 'And YOUR BICYCLE CLIPS!'

'Bloody 'ell. All I want is some o' that stuff you gave Wagger Martin. Went straight through him like a dose of . . .'

'YES, YES, CHARLIE. BUT I STILL HAVE TO EXAMINE YOU. JUST LIE DOWN THERE ON YOUR STOMACH WHILE I LOOK AT YOUR BACK PASSAGE.'

Charlie eventually negotiated his boots, bicycle clips, trousers and long johns and lay on the examination couch, still muttering about the stuff I had given Wagger Martin last Easter.

'First the good news, Charlie,' I said. 'Nothing wrong with you there. You haven't got piles.'

'Eh? Haven't got what?'

'PILES!' I screamed. 'YOU HAVEN'T GOT PILES!'

'I know that. I've got constipation. Some o' that stuff you gave . . .'

I got Charlie over on to his back and examined his abdomen. It was, as Charlie had said, as hard as rock.

'YES, CHARLIE. YOU CERTAINLY ARE CONSTIPATED. I'M GOING TO GIVE YOU SOME OF THE STUFF I GAVE WAGGER MARTIN . . .'

I didn't know that the whole shouted conversation was carrying to the waiting-room, and that the patients in there were convulsed with laughter and capping each other's bawdy remarks as poor old Charlie struggled back into his long johns, trousers, boots and, of course, bicycle clips.

Charlie had seemed quite surprised, and a little disappointed, that I gave him a prescription for the laxative instead of handing the bottle to him there and then.

I made three resolutions then. To talk old Charlie into a

hearing aid, to keep my voice down in future – and to have the surgery sound-proofed.

There was one consolation: I'd never seen, nor have I seen since, a chirpier lot of patients than those who followed Charlie that morning . . .

CHAPTER 15

On her pre-wedding visits to Tadchester, Pam had become
accepted and involved in the Tadchester community.
Our flat at Herbert Barlow's was now fully furnished and
in apple-pie order. It looked as if it was as anxious for us
to occupy it as we were to share it.

Pam had got to know and like my friends and we had
been invited out to dozens of dinner and cocktail parties.
The time just could not go quickly enough until she was
down with me permanently. We had been guests at the de
Wyrebock wedding, and Marjorie was now firmly Mrs
Charteris.

The night before her wedding her husband-to-be, Paul

Charteris, came to me in great distress. Would I look at his leg?

He slipped off his trousers to show a huge, blistered, inflamed area on the inside of his left thigh and some large, tender glands in his groin. I was puzzled about how it had occurred, and went carefully through his history, looking for clues.

He remembered that his leg had itched one night and he had scratched it. About three days later, this eruption had appeared.

Apart from his worries about getting through the actual wedding ceremony, they were booked on a Kenyan safari for their honeymoon, and he was terribly anxious to be fighting fit for both.

'It's almost as if you had a smallpox vaccination there,' I said.

'Oh, I have been vaccinated recently,' said Paul. 'But that was in my arm.'

The penny dropped.

'Let's have a look,' I said.

Paul took off his jacket and rolled up his sleeve. There was a red, swollen area extending over most of his upper arm. His vaccination had taken with a vengeance.

'It itched like hell,' he said. 'I'm afraid that I did scratch it the odd time or two.'

'What you've done in scratching the vaccination on your arm,' I said, 'is to get some vaccine in your fingernails. When you scratched your thigh you managed to re-vaccinate yourself: this second vaccination has become infected. There's one benefit out of all this, though: you stand no chance whatever of getting smallpox.'

'How long will it take to get better?' asked Paul.

'I'll give you some antibiotics and some cream,' I said, 'but I doubt whether it will be completely better before a week or ten days.'

Paul's face fell.

'Whatever you do,' I continued, 'keep it covered and

don't let anything rub against it.'

Paul's face fell even further.

'You are obviously very sensitive to smallpox vaccination. If you're not very careful, you'll have it all over your body.'

Like the true blue-blooded aristocrat he was, Paul took the verdict with a stiff upper lip, which meant pulling his expression back to its normal public school impassivity.

My thoughts flew to his poor wife-to-be, Marjorie. She had waited so long to get to the starting gate – and now that she was almost there, she was going to have to spend at least a further week in the saddling enclosure.

The de Wyrebock wedding was the great social occasion of the Tadchester year. There was a huge marquee on the lawn of the de Wyrebocks' house, and there must have been at least a thousand guests. Caterers had been brought down from London, and the cost of it all must have been tremendous. The champagne flowed freely and the caterers didn't stint the caviare.

Everybody seemed to be called Charles or Angela, that is when they were not calling each other *Daa-aah-ling*. Although it was high summer in the grounds of the Big House, it sounded like lambing time on the farm.

Mrs de Wyrebock was most gracious to me in spite of the fact that I was one of the few people wearing an ordinary suit. All the other guests, male guests that is, were in morning dress. I'd had no choice: I certainly couldn't afford to hire a morning suit twice and I had felt my best suit would be up to the occasion. The impending cost of my own wedding was about to leave me much less well off than my usual state, which was penniless, and on top of that we were booked for a honeymoon in Cornwall. What with the presents for the bridesmaids and everything, I couldn't see myself getting both ends to come within shouting distance of each other, let alone meet.

Paul Charteris conducted himself with great dignity

throughout the ceremony and reception. He must have been in great discomfort as he was towed round by Marjorie to greet each guest, but showed no sign of it, apart from the occasional well-bred wince.

Pam and I hardly knew a soul there, and scarcely anyone spoke to us. We made ourselves inconspicuous behind a hedge in the Italian garden, sat on a bank and ate our lobster salad and drank our champagne.

'This makes our wedding look rather teeny,' said Pam.

'Don't you worry,' I replied, squeezing her hand. 'They've just got quantity here. We have insisted on quality.'

She laughed.

I found that aristorcatic English blue-bloods in their morning coats and grey toppers behaved very much like rugby-playing medical students whenever there was a free bar. Before long our privacy was interrupted by elegantly dressed young men trying to find a place in which to be discreetly and elegantly sick. On our way back to the marquee, we saw a girl of about eighteen or nineteen, straight out of *The Tatler*, in a beautiful white lace dress, absolutely sparko, flat out on the ground behind a laurel bush while her escort tried in vain to revive her by fanning her with his grey topper.

Pam and I paid our respects to Commander and Mrs de Wyrebock and made good our escape.

The party went on all through the night. The following morning a lengthy procession of cars crept its weary way out of Tadchester, the occupants sitting stupefied behind the chauffeurs, trying to remember whether or not they had enjoyed themselves.

Apparently a bunch of the young bloods had gone down into the town for a midnight bathe in the Tad. They stripped to their underpants and splashed across the muddy flats into the water. Two of the girls who followed collected all the young men's clothes and put them in the ladies' public toilet, one of the features of Tadchester Quay.

After the swim there was nothing the young men could do but invade this very private territory. One stout lady holidaymaker, out later than she should have been, had called in to dispense with some of her evening's refreshments before going back to her digs. The sight of six wet young men in clinging underpants invading the Holy of Holies was a little too much for her, and she had to be carried outside and revived by the administration of some very expensive champagne.

During Pam's visits to Tadchester, I had driven her around the surrounding countryside as much as my free time had allowed. The country and coastline were magnificent, and as we went round we looked for a place where we would eventually like to settle. We reckoned that we would have perhaps two or three years in the flat at Herbert Barlow's. Then, hopefully, we would have saved enough money to buy a house.

There were many nice houses, but they were either too expensive or lay right in the path of the holidaymakers who came thundering down to Tadchester in their thousands every year. The summer traffic sometimes got so congested that it could take more than an hour just to cross Tadchester Bridge.

I took Pam to meet Reg Dawkins and his wife, Mary. For me, they were a regular every-other-Tuesday visit. Reg had an obscure disease which kept him confined to a wheelchair. Not a lot, medically, could be done for Reg – my treatment was to call in once a fortnight and share a bottle of his home-made wine.

I usually went there to get myself cheered up. In spite of his disability, Reg was always full of high spirits, had always some outrageous story to tell me. His home-made wine, which was his pride and joy, usually knocked me for six and I had developed a great respect for it. Reg had plenty of time to practise making his special brews and their potency was just something less than neat alcohol. I had warned Pam about their efficacy. After one glass she had learned for herself: she was bright-eyed and sparkling and much more talkative than usual.

'Would your intended like a glass of the dandelion?' asked Reg.

'No,' I said. 'She's got to develop a special stomach lining before she can cope with your stuff. I want to keep her alive at least until our wedding day.'

I changed the subject. 'Reg, if you had to buy a house round here, where would you choose?'

'Altriston, without a doubt,' he said. 'They still live in the Stone Age there, but it's a good village – and it's well away from the holidaymakers.'

'When are you going to take me there?' asked Pam.

'Not until after the wedding,' I replied. 'It's going to take us all our time to get home after Reg's wine.'

'Just one sip of the dandelion for you and your good lady,' said Reg, looking pleadingly at me and already pulling the cork.

'All right,' I said firmly. 'But just one.'

Pam was asleep by the time we got to the Harts', where she was staying. I woke her but she was giggly and drowsy. I had to go round to her side, open the door, put her over my shoulder in a fireman's lift, and carry her upstairs and put her on the bed, where she fell fast asleep again.

'Is Pam all right?' asked Jack Hart as I came down the stairs.

'Oh yes, Jack,' I replied. 'Just a little bit car-sick. Well . . . that, and a drop of Reg Dawkins's wine.'

Jack laughed. He knew the feeling.

It wouldn't be too long now before I no longer had to leave Pam in other people's houses, and then we would keep an eye open for suitable properties in Altriston.

*

The village of Altriston lies five miles inland and directly north-east of Tadchester. It is a compact village with a main street, a surrounding cluster of about fifty cottages, one pub, one post office-cum-store, and a pottery. It is dominated by the Manor House, which stands on some high ground overlooking the village.

Until just before the Second World War it was a feudal village, owned by and under the patronage of the Manor. When Lord Tyster, Lord of the Manor, died in 1937 the estate was split up and the villagers were given the option of buying their cottages.

Lord Tyster had ruled his domain with a rod of iron and laid down strict rules for the village and the villagers. All the cottages had to be painted in the same colours – green and yellow – and be kept in a state of olde worlde picturesqueness. The villagers were forbidden to cut the ivy which covered every cottage. In time the cottages almost disappeared under masses of foliage, which ruined the brickwork, harboured vermin and let in the damp.

During his daily drive through the village – when any villager not touching his forelock would be in danger of instant dismissal – Lord Tyster's evil eye would spot the merest trimming of the ivy, let alone any serious short-back-and-sides treatmeant.

On the night of his death, the villagers gathered at the Manor House to pay their last respects to their master. He died in the early evening: the church gave muffled peals of bells on his behalf, and the flags were flown at half-mast.

Respects paid, the villagers retired to their homes, but not to sleep. Through much of the night there was activity and noise, with torches flashing up and down the main street.

The morning sun broke on to a transformed village. There was not a leaf of ivy to be seen anywhere.

It was not only Lord Tyster who had dominated the village. His only daughter – Rose – had been an absolute tyrant. If a horse had not been groomed to her satisfaction, she would take out her riding crop and thrash the groom there and then. When any youth working on the estate reached his eighteenth birthday, so qualifying for the minimum agricultural wage, he would be sacked on the spot. And it would be Rose Tyster who did it, and took a delight in doing it.

At one time the practice used to have a branch surgery in the village, but it became uneconomical to staff and run and so was closed. Once or twice a month I did a round of visits in the village; anyone else requiring attention would leave a note at one of my regular calls. I would take prescriptions back to Tadchester to have them made up and the next day the carriers would take them to Altriston and leave them at the Post Office Stores where the villagers would pick them up with their shopping.

One of my regular visits was to Jack Wilson, a widower. I used to call once a month and check his blood pressure, then sit down and join him in a pot of tea. He was my local historian and I could – and sometimes did – sit and listen for hours to his tales of bygone days and the history of events in the village. He was a delightful, gentle man, and told his tales without any bitterness or malice.

'He was a great patriot, was Lord Tyster,' said Jack. 'When the First World War broke out, on the very first day he gathered all the estate workers together and ordered them to volunteer for the Army. It were terrible. My wife's late father were over age, and her brother were under age, but they both had to go, and they both got killed.

'There were thirty-three men from this village killed in t'First World War. It were highest rate for size of village in the whole country. There were only three killed in t' Second World War, so it just shows you . . .

'At that time, thank God, I didn't live in Altriston. I worked as a gardener ten miles away. This was my wife's village: I came here when I got married after the First War. I were in the Middle East fighting the Turks. We had a right do there. I left a lot of my mates behind in Mesopotamia. But I reckon I'd have left a lot more behind in France – or maybe stayed there with them – if I'd been with the lads Lord Tyster ordered out to get themselves killed.'

It seemed as if in those bad old days people lived out their lives in a cloud of injustice and ill-treatment. Freedom of choice, alternative employment and housing had been impossible to come by under Lord Tyster. The cutting of the ivy had symbolised a complete change of lifestyle: people would from then on be free to come and go, to own their own houses and no longer have to touch their forelocks when their lord and master went by.

But the days longed for and talked about most by the villagers were in fact those good old bad old days – when you lived under the protective umbrella of someone who took the ultimate responsibility for you and made the major decisions for you. It was Lord Tyster who paid the bills if anyone had to go to hospital for a prolonged stay; it was Lord Tyster who paid for the education of any village boy or girl who showed exceptional academic promise. People had long ago got used to and accepted this way of life for generations: for good or ill, better or worse, it was their inheritance.

'We were all pleased to see Lord Tyster go because we wanted to manage on us own,' said Jack. 'But we did not realise how difficult it was. We all knew our proper place. I did. So did my Dad and his Dad before him. It's all cars and television and washing machines now, but it'll be a long time before things are proper again.'

I think Jack was right.

For several years the pattern of life in this country did not change much. Suddenly, in a couple of decades between the wars, it was all different. But people were not flexible enough to change at the same speed, and many of the problems of today's society arise from the fact that the changes have been too swift for people to adjust properly.

Altriston had the best of both worlds: all the benefits of a small community without its disadvantages – once Lord Tyster was out of the way, that is. As the older people died, young people took over the cottages, and these tended to be young people from outside.

These new, younger inhabitants benefited by being part of an established rural community. They were able to join in such activities as the Flower Show, the Harvest Festival, the Nativity Play, and other long-standing communal events. As most of them worked away – many commuted to places like Winchcombe – they had interests outside the village which they brought back with them, and which widened the outlook of the community beyond its old insularity. There was a good balance of young and old, and a good community spirit. There were enough willing and fit hands to take care of and keep an eye on the not-so-fit.

The inevitable forces of change had destroyed the old order. (In Lord Tyster's case it was the one change which really is inevitable.) But the same changes which brought the young off-comers to the village in a strange way restored the pattern.

There was never any danger that someone in the village would be left for days unattended. Neighbours were neighbourly, and everyone was called on by at least one other person each day. The old order had given place to the new, but it still worked. And however efficient socialised medicine becomes, it will have a job to match up to the sheer efficiency and humanity of a small community looking after its own.

CHAPTER 16

As the summer wore on, most of my thinking time was
taken up by our approaching wedding. I had become so
preoccupied that I occasionally wrote the same medication
twice on the same prescription. I even wrote my new
address in the place where the number of tablets should
have been.

The wedding seemed to belong to everybody but Pam
and me. There were continual discussions about invitation
lists. Did we think that Auntie Enid would make it from
Maltby? Could we avoid asking Uncle Jim who always
got drunk and embarrassed people? We put down the
names of all the possible guests. They came to 320 – and

we had set a limit of 120. All the hours of building up the list had to be followed by hours of heart-breaking pruning.

Pam had asked Janice and Zara to be bridesmaids. That is, Janice would be a matron of honour and Zara (who was to marry Eric the month after us) would be a bridesmaid in the true sense of the word.

The artistic, creative Zara insisted that she would design and make the bridesmaids' dresses. Only too pleased to have one less job, we left it to her.

It was all go, and I didn't seem to have a spare minute. On my weekends off I rushed to London to my mother's or to Pam's parents at Leatherhead. When I was on week-end duty, Pam used to come down to Tadchester. I couldn't believe that other weddings were like ours. We had set up an organisation that involved enough planning to rival that of the D-day landing. We had to make decisions about choirboys, organists, church bells, wedding cars, wedding cakes, flowers and a hundred other things.

We had a long plodding interview with the vicar, or to give him his correct title, Prebendary.

Preb. Thomas was really concerned that we were quite familiar with the facts of life. He insisted on telling us in great detail about the birds and bees and was quite unimpressed that I had been involved with the delivery of babies as a student, house doctor and general practitioner for at least six years.

Pam's parents were marvellous. Her father, a tall, ascetic-looking engineer whose main love was horse racing, arranged a reception at the Bull Hotel which would not let him down in the eyes of his friends at the Eccentric Club.

Pam's mother, May, loved all the fuss and was determined to make the most of her only daughter's nuptials. She was a woman of great courage, having had major operations to both hips for osteoarthritis before the days when these operations were completely satisfactory. The operations were designed only to relieve pain and did not give the mobility that present operations do. May somehow overcame all her walking difficulties and wasn't going to miss a trick or be left out of anything. In spite of the great physical discomfort of getting about, she was here, there and everywhere, looking after present lists, dealing with florists, deciding how many relatives she could put up and where to fit in the ones she couldn't.

At the surgery there was a constant stream of well-wishers, and patients leaving presents. Gladys loved it all; you would have thought it was she who was getting married. She was the source of information to the world at large, received the gifts over the counter as if they were for her, and kept meticulous lists of whom I should write to and whom I should go and see. There was more surgery chat about the costume Gladys was going to wear at the wedding – she, was to represent the surgery staff – than there was about the bridal gown.

Steve was coming up for a few days to stay with relatives nearby, and Patsy and Henry Johnson were driving there and back in a day, with Jack Hart holding the fort until Henry got back to share the duties. I tried to imagine Henry in a top hat: it would make him about ten feet tall.

I had a bachelor night out in Winchcombe with Joe, Frank, Eric and Kevin, which almost ended in disaster. We had drunk almost all the Winchcombe hostelries dry, or that's how it felt, and on the way back I decided we must have some fish and chips to help soak up the beer.

We were on the main trunk road out of Winchcombe, a dual carriageway, with the two lanes separated by a wire fence. The fish and chip shop was on the other side of the road. I got across to the shop without mishap, bought my fish and chips and started to walk back with the newspaper-wrapped bundle which somehow seemed to upset my balance.

As I climbed the wire barrier to cross to the car in the lay-by, there was a sudden rush of wind. I didn't take much notice: I was too busy concentrating on walking steadily with my fragrant burden. When I got to the car I found Kevin, Joe, Frank and Eric white-faced and trembling.

'What's the matter with you lot?' I said. 'Can't you take your drink?'

'Get in, you silly bugger,' said Frank, 'and let's get off the road as quickly as we can. You were bloody nearly killed.'

Apparently when I was walking back, in my cups and concentrating on my fish and chips, I hadn't bothered to check whether there was any traffic. The rush of wind was a Jaguar car belting along at about 90 m.p.h. and which missed me by inches. The riotous evening came to a very subdued end after that.

Some years later I went to the bachelor night of the new junior partner we had appointed, Ron Dickinson. Having consumed a lot of beer at a lot of pubs, Ron appeared at the last pub with two rounds of champagne cocktails. In a few minutes we had all changed from being pleasantly merry to being completely drunk. Going home, Ron had in his car with him his best man, a young vicar friend who was to officiate at the wedding, and Ralph Upton, his father-in-law-to-be.

When they came to a Y-junction in the road, Ron declined the option of both the left and the right and hit the bank in the middle, bursting a tyre.

Nobody was hurt, but Stan, his best man and the young vicar were so full of booze that all they were able to do was to stagger out of the car and lie down on the bank, leaving father-in-law-to-be to change the wheel on his own. I often wondered what Ralph Upton, a local banker, thought as he changed the wheel – looking down at the insensible man to whom he was entrusting his daughter's future life.

I had had to go to Winchcombe to be fitted out with a

top hat and morning coat. Eric, who was going to be my best man, came with me. We both felt ridiculous standing in the mirrored fitting room in our tails, striped trousers and top hats.

'It's good practice for you,' I said to Eric.

'Don't you believe it,' said Eric. 'Zara is insisting on her own sort of white wedding. We are both going to wear some sort of white boiler suit. You know Zara. I haven't seen my outfit yet – I dread to think what it's going to be like.'

I went down to Leatherhead with Eric and Zara and spent my wedding eve at the Bull Hotel where the reception was to be held. My mother was staying there, as well as assorted relatives from both families. Uncle Bertie, my mother's brother, was acting as her escort, and kept us all amused.

Uncle Bertie was a great character who had had an amazing variety of jobs. He had been a dentist's apprentice in the days when dentists were apprenticed, a professional footballer, an electrician, a film studio engineer and manager of a grocery store. He had been a great man-about-town, a ladies' man, and there was a whispered story of his being married and leaving his wife on their wedding day. Although he was obviously never going to be very economically successful, he lived and enjoyed life absolutely to the hilt.

In my student days, when I was reluctantly doing some boxing, Uncle Bertie was one of my greatest supporters. Sporting crowds were the sort of company he loved. Boxing my heart out in some packed East End hall, I would hear his voice boom out from the back 'Come on the blond tiger!' I wasn't blond, and the last thing I could be called was a tiger, but it did distract the crowd from me. They were torn between watching my flailing inexpert arms in the ring and listening to Uncle Bertie's flow of wit from the back of the hall. He could have made a living as a stand-up comic in any company. Thankfully, he had promised to behave himself for the wedding.

I got to bed as early as I could but hardly slept. My mind was in a tremendous turmoil. What did it mean to be married? Was I ready to be? Was Pam ready to be? I eventually drifted off to sleep and woke early to a sunny day, with Eric looking sombrely at me from the door. He had a bottle of whisky in his hand, which he was offering me for breakfast. Eric had already had a couple of snorts. The duties of best man seemed to be worrying him more than mine as groom.

'I've got the ring safely here,' said Eric, patting his lower waistcoat pocket.

'Let's have a look,' I said.

Eric probed in his pocket for a few minutes, getting redder and redder.

'Christ, it's not here!' he said. 'There's a hole in my pocket.'

I put my finger into the lining of his pocket, and it went straight through a large hole. We felt along the front edge of his waistcoat and located the ring at its lowest point. We were able to work it along up through the hole in the lining, back into daylight again. Eric was sweating. I feared the wedding was going to be too much for him. He wasn't cut out for such heavy responsibility, and the early-morning whisky hadn't helped. We found another waistcoat pocket, made sure that it was hole-free, wrapped the ring in tissue paper and put it safely away.

'It's coffee for both of us,' I said to Eric. 'You'll be giving me a nervous breakdown.'

The wedding was to be at noon. At eleven o'clock the Johnsons arrived. Henry did *not* look ten feet tall in his top hat – he looked twelve feet if he looked an inch. Patsy looked as well groomed as ever. They had left Tadchester in the early hours and had driven straight through to Leatherhead. Well, they had *almost* driven straight through to Leatherhead . . .

Henry lived Up-the-Hill in a large house approached by

a long winding drive. Some time back, the local council had refused to come all the way up the drive to collect his dustbins. So, every week since, the dustbins had been put in the back of the estate car, driven to the end of the drive, deposited and left for emptying.

Henry and Patsy had started off for the wedding in the dark and hadn't inspected the car too closely, though Patsy had decorated the bonnet with one or two bows of white ribbon.

Henry was resplendent in a morning suit. Patsy in long pale blue dress with a huge floppy wide-brimmed hat. They were about fifty miles on their way when Patsy complained there was a smell of rotting food.

'Rubbish,' said Henry, 'we must have passed something.'

After a few miles Henry snapped: 'I guess you're right. There *is* a smell somewhere. We'd better go round and have a look.'

He stopped the car, got out, walked round the back, and there, in the space behind the back seat of the estate car, were two dustbins – filled to the top with a week's refuse.

'My God!' said Henry. 'We can't take these to the wedding.'

The ever-resourceful Henry drove on, until they came to a gang working on the road. He got out in his full wedding gear, as if it was the most natural thing in the world, went up to the foreman and asked if he could leave the dustbins with him for a few hours until he returned.

'Don't you worry, guv',' said the foreman, 'we will treat them as if they wuz us own.'

Somehow Henry kept his dignity as the grinning workmen unloaded the bins. He slipped a pound note into the foreman's hand, got into the car and drove on.

By the time Eric and I set out for the church it had begun to drizzle. We walked self-consciously up the aisle, sat in our places, and tried to interpret the noises as the church filled up behind us. Every two minutes Eric checked that the ring was still safely in his pocket. The church was brightly lit, and had been filled with flowers by the tireless May. It looked quite beautiful.

The huge double doors at the back of the church were continually opening and closing, and the murmur of voices increased as the church filled. Just about twelve o'clock, the time I was expecting Pam to arrive, I heard the doors open and shut once again. The murmur of the congregation that had hushed a little at the sound of the doors changed to a concerted gasp. There was a groan from Eric: 'Oh God, whatever will she make me wear at *our* wedding?'

I turned round.

Standing in front of the closed doors were Janice and Zara. They had obviously come in out of the rain to wait for Pam. The bright lights in the church acted as a spotlight on them as they stood framed by the dark oak panels.

Zara's bridesmaids' dresses were exotic creations of some floating gossamer-like material. The fittings must have been done in a very soft light indeed because, with the bright lights of the church and the dark background, the dresses were almost transparent. They were hardly visible at all – and neither girl was wearing a slip. From where I sat it looked as if Janice who, to put it politely, was on the plump side, was just wearing a spotted bikini bra and pants. The curvaceous Zara, who scorned things like bras, looked completely naked except for a brief pair of black pants that would have been banned on any Spanish beach. The bridesmaids smirked rather self-consciously at the impression they had made, having no idea how they made it!

Happily the scene was interrupted by Pam's entrance on her father's arm. She looked absolutely lovely – and, thank God, her long white dress and train were completely opaque.

The wedding ceremony went on as a sea of words and music. I seemed out of touch with the goings-on, and was conscious only of Pam holding my hand as I made my vows. Preb. Thomas was intoning away in a nasal voice and, after what seemed a relatively short time, he placed his hands on our heads. Lifting his voice above even his usual crescendo, he said: 'I now declare you man and wife.'

There was a short prayer, then we stood up and Preb. Thomas began to lead us to the vestry. Eric started to tug at my sleeve.

'Oh God,' I thought. 'He has flipped.'

Eric looked terribly agitated about something. Janice and Zara, seeing his confusion, took an arm each and swept him into the vestry, followed by my mother and Uncle Bertie and Pam's mother and father. The verger had the register open for us to sign and Preb. Thomas was putting everybody at their ease – everybody except Eric who was getting more and more agitated. He kept on trying to interrupt, squeaking, 'Excuse me! Excuse me!'

Eventually the rather irritated Preb. Thomas said, 'What is it, my man?'

'I've still got the ring,' said Eric in a hushed voice.

I was not on the spot when Lot's wife was turned into a pillar of salt, but Preb. Thomas must have given a pretty close imitation. He stood silently for a minute recovering himself. Clearing his throat, he said, 'I must deeply apologise to everyone. I have omitted part of the service. I will have to ask you to return to the church where I will bless the ring.'

We all trooped back into the church. The organ struck up a triumphant march and the congregation stood up, smiling. To everyone's amazement, instead of walking down the aisle we returned to our marriage positions. It was too much for the organist, or the organ, or both. The triumphant march stopped and the organ let out a wail like a deflating bagpipe.

I had not liked Preb. Thomas much so far, but now not only did I warm to him and pity him – I admired him. He left us standing at the steps and went up into the pulpit. There were tears in his eyes.

'Ladies and gentlemen of the congregation, bride and groom,' he said. 'In a lifetime's devotion to the Church I have conducted many hundreds of marriage services. I know the ceremony so well that I no longer use my prayer book during the service. Today, by not taking proper care, I have missed out the ceremony of the blessing of and giving of the ring. I trust that all of you – and God – will forgive me.'

There was a deathly silence in the church as he came down from the pulpit and blessed the ring. I placed it on Pam's finger and we all returned to the vestry. Most of the people there spent the time consoling Preb. Thomas rather than congratulating Pam and me.

Uncle Bertie, who looked as if he had had a few too many before the service, slapped Preb. Thomas on the shoulder and said, 'Cheer up, Vicar, you have given them a wedding that no one will ever forget.' It broke the ice, and we formed up to march down the aisle once more.

The organ, though a bit tentative at first, as if not wanting to be caught out twice, burst into the wedding march. The church bells began to ring. As we walked down the aisle the congregation was just a sea of smiling faces. We moved too quickly for me to put names to them; it all seemed a smiling, laughing blur.

Pam squeezed my hand as we reached the church door. When we got outside the rain had stopped and the sun was shining.

'Hello, husband,' said Pam.

'Hello, wife,' said I, looking into her smiling face.

We hugged.

Life was going to be different from now on.

POSTSCRIPT

There is the fable of the old man sitting outside a town, being approached by a stranger.

'What are they like in this town?' asked the stranger.

'What were they like in your last town?' replied the old man.

'They were delightful people. I was very happy there. They were kind, generous and would always help you in trouble.'

'You will find them very much like that in this town.'

The old man was approached by another stranger.

'What are the people like in this town?' asked the second stranger.

'What were they like in your last town?' replied the old man.

'It was an awful place. They were mean, unkind and nobody would ever help anybody.'

'I am afraid you will find it very much the same here,' said the old man.

If it should be your lot to ever visit Tadchester, this is how you will find us.

What Next, Doctor?

Illustrated by Nick Baker

For CLIFF PARKER
without whose collaboration, patience
and encouragement nothing would ever get done.

Contents

1	Rude Awakening	9
2	Back to Work	17
3	Surprise Pictures	25
4	Visitors	37
5	Fishy Business	43
6	The Little People	56
7	Pregnant Moments	64
8	Happy Families	74
9	Death of a Child	83
10	Soliloquy at Evening Surgery	91
11	Can't I go Down the Mine, Daddy?	96
12	Creatures of Habit	104
13	Sex and Side Effects	113
14	Loving Couples	119
15	Assorted Characters	131
16	Round in Circles	146
17	Moving House	154
	Postscript	160

I

Rude Awakening

I could hear a persistent knocking as I struggled to rouse myself from a deep sleep. My surroundings seemed strange, and in my half conscious state I couldn't work out where the knocking was coming from.

As I slowly surfaced I realised that I was in bed with Pam, that we were in an hotel in Cornwall, and that somebody was knocking at our bedroom door.

Then I remembered that Pam and I had been married the day before. We had motored through the night from Leatherhead in Surrey to the Carbis Bay Hotel at St Ives, Cornwall, arriving at three o'clock in the morning. We had ordered breakfast in bed for ten o'clock – our first breakfast together –

9

hoping the long lie-in would help recharge our batteries after the exhausting ordeal of our wedding and reception, followed by the slogging 300-mile drive down to Cornwall.

Having collected all these thoughts together, I was able to shout 'Come in!' to what had started as a tentative knocking and was now an exasperated hammering.

The door crashed open, and in walked an elderly, cross-faced, grey-haired lady, bearing a breakfast tray laden with coffee, boiled eggs, cornflakes and grapefruit.

'I've been hammering for hours!' she snapped. 'It's not good enough. I have had to walk up all these stairs – the lift isn't working. Fancy an old woman like me having to wait on young'uns like you. I've got arthritis, and the doctor says I shouldn't really be working at all.'

To prove her point, she limped across the room, and almost tipped the breakfast tray on our bed in transit.

'I don't know what young people are coming to nowadays,' she growled. 'Lying in bed till this time on a glorious day like this.'

We cringed self-consciously under the sheets.

The old woman grumpily put the tray down on a table at the foot of the bed. 'I hope it isn't going to be like this every morning,' she said as she stumped out. 'You want to get up and get out and get some fresh air.'

Pam and I lay in bed not talking, both very embarrassed. This was the first night we had ever shared a bed together, and to be attacked in it by a third party was something we hadn't bargained for.

We had looked forward to a long lie-in, and a leisurely breakfast. If we were not careful, this limping dragon was going to spoil it for us.

I got out of bed, collected the tray and put it down between us on the eiderdown.

'Come on, darling,' I said. 'Let's forget her and enjoy our first breakfast.'

We set out to make the best of it, but the coffee was cold, there was no sugar for the grapefruit, the eggs were hard-boiled, the toast was warped and snapped when we tried to butter it, there was hardly enough milk for the coffee, never mind the cornflakes, and after a few feeble attempts we gave up.

A breakfast as bad as this had not arrived by accident. Our chambermaid had deliberately made it inedible so that rather than face it in our room every morning, we would stagger down to breakfasts, however tired we were.

Pam had tears in her eyes. The first morning of our honeymoon should have been better than this. I put my arm round her. 'Never mind, darling,' I murmured. 'You've still got me.' (That's the kind of thing you can say only early on in a marriage.)

Then I remembered. 'Hang on,' I said, 'all is not lost.'

I rummaged in my case and came out with a long oblong box. This had been given to me by a patient, Simon Eggleton. Written on the box in bold letters were the words TO BE OPENED ON THE FIRST MORNING OF YOUR HONEYMOON.

We opened the box, and there was a huge magnum of champagne. Written on a card tied to it were the instructions –

THE ONLY POSSIBLE FIRST BREAKFAST FOR YOUR HONEY-MOON, DOC AND MRS DOC. DON'T DILUTE IT WITH TOAST AND MARMALADE, JUST DRINK IT NEAT, AS DIRECTED

'We can't drink champagne for breakfast,' Pam said.

'Rubbish,' I replied. 'It's just the thing.'

I walked across to the washstand and rinsed out the tooth mugs. I popped the champagne cork, and we sat in bed, mugs in our hands, looking out across the bay and toasting each other as Mr and Mrs.

'I think, darling, that Simon must have been in collusion with the chambermaid', I said, 'But for her breakfast we could have forgotten his present. I'm afraid I can't promise that breakfasts in future will be quite up to this standard, but I will do my very best.'

Pam giggled. A couple of mugsful of champagne at this time

11

in the morning, on an empty stomach, was perhaps not the way to get a sensible answer.

*   *   *

Simon Eggleton was unique in that he was the only man I have ever treated for serious frostbite in the middle of a Somerset summer. He had been unloading boxes of frozen peas from a refrigeration van without wearing protective gloves. His hands, cold at first, soon became so frozen that he did not feel a thing. It was only a couple of hours afterwards, when they started to thaw out, that his troubles began.

When I was called to him he was actually screaming with pain and the top two joints of his fingers on both hands were a nasty bluish colour. His pain was so bad that I had to give him an injection of morphia and send him to Tadchester Hospital.

We thought he was going to lose his fingers. They were severely frostbitten. Their colour did not improve and he was in constant pain. Frostbite being uncommon in Somerset, we had to ring London for guidance on the management and outlook for his condition. He was three weeks in hospital under intensive treatment.

It was a long and prolonged battle. Even after discharge from hospital he had to attend the out-patients department for treatment for several further weeks. His fingers survived but he was left with some permanent loss of sensation in all his finger tips. This was quite a handicap. It meant that he was unable to assess heat and was always burning his fingers in hot water or on stoves and fires. He was unable to feel when a cigarette had burnt down to the skin level and had two permanent burns on his first and second fingers.

There was a long legal battle over his injury and he was eventually offered £25 compensation. I encouraged him to stick out for more, supporting him with some very firm medical letters, and with my support he finally settled for £500.

Simon Eggleton sent me a book token for £15 for all my help, and had come round to the wedding reception with the box that made our breakfast.

* * *

I had met Pam a year before while on holiday with my mother. At first she had thought my young-looking mother and I were husband and wife – but when I was affectionately bringing Pam round after having knocked her over on the squash court, she realised I was not an unfaithful husband but an ardent suitor.

We had become engaged at my teaching hospital's New Year Ball, and had married in her home town of Leatherhead. After our fortnight's honeymoon Pam would return with me to the Somerset coastal town of Tadchester and start married life in earnest as the young doctor's wife.

I had been in Tadchester for two years by the time of our marriage, and was the junior partner in a group of four doctors. Tadchester (population 6,500 stands on the estuary of the River Tad, in one of the most beautiful parts of the Somerset coast. It is a market town, with some fishing, some light industry, and a great deal of farming. Six miles north is Thudrock Colliery, half of whose work force lives in Tadchester.

The town is split in two by the River Tad, and further split by the large hill which dominates one side of the river. The other side of the river is flat pastureland, stretching off to marshes and the sea coast. You are not just a Tadchester resident – you are strictly Up-the-Hill or Down-the-Hill. It had important social distinctions: the population Down-the-Hill tended to be made up of Haves, the population of Up-the-Hill tended to be the Have-nots.

We were the only general practice in the town, and in addition to our general practice duties took care of the local hospital. There were four partners, each with a special interest at the hospital. Steve Maxwell, the senior partner, had a special interest in medicine. Henry Johnson, the second senior, was the surgeon. Jack Hart, the third partner, was the anaesthetist. I, as the junior dogsbody, did most of the running around and was reckoned to be the expert in midwifery.

We practised from a central surgery Down-the-Hill, above which, before my marriage, I had a bachelor flat. There I fended for myself, living mainly on scrambled eggs and baked beans and suffering from a strange combination of malnutrition and indigestion.

* * *

Our wedding day had started disastrously. As the bridesmaids – Zara and Janice – entered the church, it was seen that their dresses were transparent. Both of them were unwittingly displaying most of their usually hidden physical charms to the congregation, bringing the colour back to the cheeks of all the male guests.

The day became almost a complete disaster when, as we were actually about to sign the register in the vestry, it was found that the vicar had omitted part of the wedding service. My best man, Eric Martin, was trying to draw everybody's attention to the fact that he still had not performed his one duty of handing over the wedding ring.

The wedding reception at the Bull Hotel, Leatherhead, passed as a blur. There were so many faces, so many congratulations, so many kisses that it was difficult to identify people individually. There were many of my friends from hospital days who I had not seen for some time, as well as the new friends I had made at Tadchester. There was a back-up of ancient aunts, uncles, nieces and cousins who had come from all over the British Isles, who only appeared at weddings and funerals, and tried to catch up in a few minutes with all the family happenings of the last few years.

With rugby friends from both Tadchester and London, and a free bar, the reception got steadily noisier. Zara and Janice in their revealing attire were surrounded by admirers and became so popular as the party became more inebriated that they retired to put on jumpers over their transparent wedding apparel.

This was like shutting the stable door after the horse had gone. Their uninhibited contours continued to make their points through their clinging jumpers. And the fact that they still looked as if they were naked from the waist down meant their jumpers had literally only halved their problem.

The wedding speeches eventually broke up the throng of the girls' admirers. The main speech was given by Mr Hogston, the father of Audrey Hogston, Pam's best friend almost from birth. He recounted Pam's life story from the Brownies onwards until she eventually met me. The Hogstons had been like a second father and mother to Pam and anybody marrying her had to pass their inspection. They were rugby enthusiasts and supported the Wasps, so the fact that I was a rugby player stood me in good stead.

Mr Hogston gave a very human, moving speech, with all the usual good wishes. He was followed by my Uncle Bertie, my mother's brother. Bertie was not on the speakers' list, but was always irrepressible on any social occasion. He was a great wit and should really have gone on the stage. As usual, with a few drinks on board, he got carried away and his stories and anecdotes became bluer and bluer. Eventually, my mother cut him short with a stage whisper 'Bertie! Behave yourself and *sit down*!'

The last speech was by Eric, my best man. He had to propose the toast of the bridesmaids. His was the shortest and most successful speech of all. He was half in his cups when he stood up and began, 'It is my duty to toast the bridesmaids . . .' He took one long, lecherous look at Zara (his bride-to-be, the chief and most uninhibited bridesmaid) and continued, 'I would much rather eat both of them untoasted', then sat down to a thunderous ovation.

Pam and I walked round together receiving our guests, talking to friends and relatives, having drinks. We cut the cake to boisterous applause, were photographed, and then at last the time came for us to go away and change. Returning in our going away clothes, somehow we struggled through confetti storms to reach my bedecked Morris Minor. Kisses, more kisses. Good byes, good byes, good byes. Then at last we were away. I stopped round the first corner to remove all the boots, saucepan lids, and bottles that were tied to the back of the car. Then off on our 300 mile drive to Cornwall.

We knew that we had a long and tedious drive ahead of us, most of it through the night, but we were full of beans. We had had a lovely wedding, and we knew that we had two uninterrupted weeks ahead of us. We also knew that whatever time we arrived, we could have a long lie-in and a lazy breakfast in bed the following morning.

2

Back to Work

I had always loved the St Ives area of Cornwall. When I was a medical student the hospital's rugby fifteen came to St Ives every Easter to play against the surrounding towns. We stayed in a different hotel every year, not because we were trying to find the best, but because one visit was the most any hotel would put up with. Next year there were always no vacancies.

In my last year as a medical student we had finally exhausted the St Ives hotels and booked in to the Carbis Bay Hotel, three miles out of the town. It was there that Pam and I had come to spend our honeymoon. I had taken some risk in choosing this area. When I was playing rugby I was young and fancy free and there could well be one or two young ladies who'd remember my amorous advances after the end of some rugby club dance in St Ives.

Pam was patient enough to let rugby be part of our honeymoon and we went to Camborne to watch them play a touring side – Roslyn Park – and watched St Ives in their bloody local battle with their rivals, Redruth.

We had a delightful, wonderful fortnight. The weather was kind to us. We wandered round the tiny cobbled streets of St Ives, sat on the quay to watch the fishing boats come in, and explored the almost empty beaches that ran along the coast to the east of St Ives.

Apart from our initial brush with the chambermaid, the service at the hotel was excellent. We could not have wished for anything better. All too soon the fortnight was over and we were packed in my Morris Minor en route for Tadchester to start work as Dr and Mrs Clifford.

Starting married life in Tadchester and sorting out all the presents was like the early days when I first arrived in the town, with leather patches on my jacket and the impoverished look of a newly qualified doctor. I thought then that all the gifts which were showered on me – food, chickens, eggs, loaves of bread, bottles of wine, boxes of chocolates – were in gratitude for my services. It took me some little time to realise that I looked as if I was unable to afford a square meal. There was method in my patients' madness. Having at last got a live doctor, they were going to do their best to keep him that way.

It was the same with a lot of the wedding presents. Fortunately we kept a strict list of what we received from patients, together with their names. We nearly had to develop a card index system. It was well worth doing. Over the next two years, when anyone rang Pam when I was on duty, their requests for a visit would usually be prefaced by, 'Oh, I am Mrs Jones of Mountain Ash Farm. We gave you a vase for your wedding present. It's a tall one with a spiral bottom. I hope Doctor won't be too long in coming.'

The doctor I followed into the practice had only been there briefly for a couple of months when he was sacked because he wouldn't work hard enough. He was one of the first young doctors to take part in the general practitioner training system and he had come into practice with one or two preconceived ideas. These included not seeing more than eight patients a day and putting his car away at five o'clock at night. This did not go down well with my hard-working partners.

Even though his time in the practice was short, Dr Smith still made his mark and was remembered afterwards as the doctor who hypnotized the patients. Having hypnotized one patient, he found at the end of the therapy that he was unable to get her out of her trance. He had to send her to hospital with a diagnosis of 'hypnotic trance – unable to bring the patient

18

round'. That alone was a good enough reason for him to leave Tadchester.

Dr Smith had followed the famous Dr Cooks, who had worked so hard and conscientiously that he set himself standards he could not keep up. He got so involved with patients and their troubles that he would get bogged down with his work and be unable to cope with the volume of it. He emigrated to Canada, hoping to make a fresh start but, being the sort of man he was, he would in no time at all have recreated the situation he had left.

The first home for Pam and myself was a first floor flat in a three-storey house Up-the-Hill. It stood on its own in about a quarter of an acre of garden. The large ground floor flat was occupied by Americans who were tenants of the owner of the house. We were sub-tenants of Herbert Barlow, who rented the top two floors and lived alone in a room on the top floor.

Herbert Barlow was one of the most remarkable and memorable men I have ever met. He was a writer and a man of the theatre. He revelled in the fuss of our settling in and was happy to take messages and to receive graciously the presents that poured in for us. He was a great help when a patient came with a gift. If Pam or I met them, it was sometimes difficult not to ask them in, and once in many of them would have happily stayed all day. Being received by Herbert, with his polished and gracious theatre manners, made them feel they were being treated as very special people.

At one time or another, Herbert had stage managed every London theatre. He had been a script writer in France before the war and had come back into the country to manage the Tadchester repertory theatre. After a break-up of one of his marriages he had devoted his time to play writing, hoping to restore himself to the position that he had once held in the West End. When you knew him well enough to get past the flamboyant stage gestures and flowery language, the man underneath was one of the finest men one could meet, a man of considerable courage and of great personal integrity.

Our week of settling in after our honeymoon passed very

quickly. Almost before I could realise it, I was off to do my first surgery as a married man. It was nice to know that I had my own personal telephone operator when I was on call, that when I came home from work there would be a meal and a welcome waiting for me – and that my routine of eggs or beans on toast was gone for ever.

Apart from the domestic comforts, being married did help to make life in general practice easier. Before I was married there was the tendency to be treated by the older patients as if I were a little boy, by some women patients with female problems with embarrassment and hesitancy, and by my partners – God bless them – as the young lad who was always available because he hadn't the family commitments that they had.

I walked into the consulting room for my first surgery. Gladys, the senior receptionist, was waiting. 'Come on, Dr Bob,' she said, 'the honeymoon is over. Back to work.'

On my desk were piles of hospital letters, medical journals and advertisements from drug houses, which had accumulated during the three weeks that I had been away. It looked comfortingly familiar.

Steve Maxwell came in just before I began to tackle the twenty or so patients, whose names were jotted down on a list before me.

'Nice to see you back, Bob,' he said. 'We've missed you while you have been away. Now don't forget you are a doctor and a married man now, and you are married to your wife and not the practice.'

Steve was probably the wisest and best man I have ever met, and was always able to put his finger on the point of any issue. Many doctors had become so involved with their work and its demands on their time that their marriages had suffered. There was an air of wistfulness about the kindly Steve when he spoke to me in this way. He had always been a bachelor, and he was very firmly married to general practice and his patients. Over the years there must have been many girls who'd set their cap at him, but Steve, being Steve, and knowing himself probably better than any of us would ever know ourselves, realised that there was something in him that would stop him from being able to divide his time equally between a wife and his practice.

I couldn't see that Pam and I would ever have problems in this situation, but I don't expect any young married doctor and his wife, setting out as we did, felt that they would either. I would never be as good a doctor or as wise a man as Steve. It was so good to know that he was keeping an eye on us as a couple, not just me as a doctor-partner. It was a privilege to be able to work with such a man.

* * *

My first patient in my first surgery as a married man was Sam Hardcastle. Born in Leeds, exiled in Tadchester, Sam was one of those short-measure conversationalists.

A strange habit among Yorkshiremen, and one which I've noticed in myself now and again, is not finishing the end of a sentence. Whether it's a manifestation of Yorkshire thriftiness, I don't know, but next time you meet a Yorkshireman, listen out for it.

My diagnosis of Sam's ailments was done more by thought reading than by analysis of the spoken word.

Sam would sit down and say, 'Morning, Doctor. I've got a pain in me . . .'

'Leg?'

'No, it's more like me . . .'

'Arm?'

'No, I've just told you. It's more like along me . . .'

'Back?'

'It wouldn't be so bad if it were. You fixed that last time. No, it's a bit more towards . . .'

Eventually, by following Sam's gestures, I would locate the pain. The next thing would be to establish its nature.

'Is it a sharp pain, Sam?'

'No, it's more like a . . .'

21

'Is it constant? There all the time?'

'No. It's more what you might call . . . It sort of comes and . . .'

'Goes?'

'Hey, that's it! Exactly.'

During one visit I couldn't resist talking back to Sam in the same way.

'Eh, Doctor,' said Sam, 'I'm having a bit of trouble with me . . .'

'I see. With your . . .'

'No. With me . . .'

'Not your. . . ?'

'Yes. Especially in the middle of the . . .'

'During the . . . ?'

'That's it. Gives me terrible cramps in me . . .'

'Oh dear. Does it ever spread to your . . . ?'

'Yes. Gives me gyp, it does.'

'But you've never had it in your . . . ?'

'Not so far, no.'

'Well that's not so bad, I shouldn't worry, Sam, unless it spreads to your . . .'

'Eh, d'you think it might?'

I couldn't contain myself any longer, and burst out laughing. Sam looked bewildered for a moment, then the penny dropped.

'Hey, Doc, you've been kidding. Having me . . .'

'On?'

'That's it. Having me on. Cheeky young . . .'

'Bugger?'

'Bugger . . .'

After that, Sam always made sure he got his story organised and rehearsed before he came to surgery. But after the diagnosis proper we would go into our taciturn Yorkshireman routine for five minutes just for the laughs. Often I'd start:

'Eh, Sam, I aren't half having some trouble with me . . .'

'By heck, that's worrying. Does it ever come out in . . .'

'No, it's more what you might call . . .'

'*Is* it? Have you ever considered having it . . .'

22

WELCOME BACK, DOCTOR BOB!

'No, no, Sam. I'm much too attached to it for that. Had it all me . . .'

'As long as that? Think yourself lucky, young man. I've known fellers whose has dropped off first time out . . .'

This would get quite Rabelaisean until in the end I would reveal that I was talking about the exhaust on my car. Sam and I would part with tears rolling down our cheeks. And for both of us, it was a tonic more effective than all the medicines I could prescribe.

*   *   *

Most of the patients who came to surgery that morning had really come to congratulate me. For once most forgot their ills. They seemed to come mainly to be reassured that I hadn't changed now I was married, and things would be as they were.

The slave driver, Gladys, anxious to bed me down in work straight away, had arranged for me to do a long comprehensive

23

medical insurance examination at the end of my surgery. I groaned when I looked at the insurance form. It was the most comprehensive examination that I have ever been called on to do by any insurance company.

My patient, a rather plump, red-cheeked man of forty-three, seemed to have come in determined to enjoy every minute of it. Nobody had ever taken such an interest in his body before. I had to examine eyes, ears, nose, teeth, chest, abdomen, back, limbs, and every orifice that was available to me.

I had to push tubes up him, down him and across him, wherever there was an aperture to enable me to.

At last I finished my tedious and drawn out examination. 'Thank you,' I said to the eager figure on the couch. He had withstood all my pummelling and prodding with a cheerful look on his face. I left him in the cubicle to get dressed, and sat down at my desk to complete his insurance form. I completed it and noticed there had been no movement from behind the curtains since I left the patient, and wondered if he was suffering some reaction to the indignities he had been exposed to.

I gingerly put my head through the curtaining round the couch, and there was the patient, naked except for a pair of socks. He looked up, smiling, and said 'WHAT NEXT, DOCTOR?'

3

Surprise Pictures

There are two routes in and out of Tadchester. The main road from Winchcombe follows first the estuary of the River Trip, turns almost at right angles in the village of Stowin, and runs alongside the estuary of the River Tad into Tadchester.

The other route runs westward from Tadchester Bridge to the small town of Dratchet, about eight miles away. The Dratchet road follows the River Tad right into Dratchet itself.

Three miles out of Tadchester on this route, the river ceases to become tidal. Below this point, in the tidal waters, the fishing rights are free and open to all. Above this point, in the non-tidal waters, both banks are marked off in closely guarded sections for the expensive lease of salmon fishing rights.

It is difficult to say which is the more beautiful of these two approach routes. Each has a character of its own, and contrasting scenery. On the Winchcombe road, you are almost in contact with large expanses of water all the way, with beautiful and changing views of the estuary. The Dratchet road runs through some beautiful countryside, undulating tree-covered hills, and has views over the quiet and gently flowing Tad.

A small railway runs from Tadchester to Dratchet, parallel to the road on the other side of the river. Tadchesterians have always complained that they were cut off from the world on two sides by the sea, and on the other two sides by the railway.

There was a very indifferent train service from Tadchester to

Winchcombe, and a slightly better service from Winchcombe to the outside world: from Winchcombe you could get main line trains to London and various other major cities. The line to Dratchet carried few passengers but was important commercially: a special type of clay was mined in Dratchet and goods trains transported it to the Midlands.

When in later years Dr Beeching axed some of the peripheral train services, the passenger service from Dratchet to Tadchester was closed, but the clay trains were still allowed to chuff their way through to Winchcombe on their way north.

Dratchet was a self-contained community with its own doctors, a small hospital, and a small nursing home, fiercely proud and independent. It tried to have as little to do with Tadchester as possible. Our practice tried similarly to have little to do with Dratchet. There was not much point in a doctor driving eight miles from Tadchester when medical services were there at hand.

There were three single-handed practices in Dratchet, and two of them were real oddities.

Dr Barza settled in Dratchet when there was no real practice to come to. In order to make a living he would take on patients anywhere, never mind the distance. He was quite elderly and lived with his sister. Although based in Dratchet he had patients not only in Tadchester, but in Winchcombe and all over the place. I would be coming back from a visit late at night and see him visiting in Tadchester, and at eight o'clock in the morning would sometimes see him doing routine calls.

There were all sorts of tales about him, some of them true. It was said that it was one of his practices to say to a patient with a headache, after a brief examination, that he had a cerebral tumour. He would say, 'You have come just in time,' and give him some tablets – privately of course.

Two or three months later, after some expensive treatment, he would pronounce his patient cured. You could safely say that there were more cured cerebral tumours in Dratchet than any other place in the world.

The other eccentric Dratchet doctor, and the best known and

most loved, was Dr Knight. Dr Knight's first love was a bottle of whisky. There is something about doctors who are addicted to alcohol. Patients adore them. They make any excuse for them when they are incapacitated by drink, and always say, 'My God, what wonderful doctors they are when they are sober.'

Perhaps people assume that alcoholic doctors are the most sensitive and human of all. That they know what life is really all about, and feel that the only sensible thing to do is to kill the pain with drink all the time.

Dr Knight met his come-uppance when in Tadchester one market day he had too much to drink at the Tadchester Arms and the landlord refused to give him any more. Infuriated by this impertinence, Dr Knight jumped into his car and drove to the police station to report the landlord. Of course he was accused of being drunk in charge of a motor vehicle and eventually disqualified from driving for a year. For that year he had to have a man to drive him around – and this enabled him to drink even more.

There were many stories about Dr Knight and his boozing. The hospital secretary, visiting his home after some hospital Christmas function, was offered a drink of whisky. 'There were only five of us,' he said, 'but a third bottle had to be broached to complete the pouring of one round.'

Dr Knight was a great advertisement for the staying power of alcohol. He was still running his general practice at the age of eighty, and was still the well-loved and well-respected general practitioner. The patients used to say 'Our old doc. will go on for ever, and will never need embalming. He has been completely pickled for the last thirty years.'

Although we discouraged patients living in and near Dratchet from joining our practice, it was very difficult to strike off patients we had looked after for many years and who moved out there.

Doris and Bill Slewman, husband and wife, were two such patients. They had had one of the roughest, dirtiest old farms Up-the-Hill, about five miles from Tadchester. Now they had moved to a dirty, tumbledown cottage, six miles west of

27

Tadchester, in a field two miles to the east of Dratchet. It had no amenities, such as running water or inside plumbing, and Doris, who'd worked all her life and was now getting on, reckoned she'd at last earned a sit down.

Although I was called to the cottage many times over many years, I never ever saw Doris move from her chair. She used to sit there, looking out through the door over the fields, with a small clay pipe clenched between her teeth, and an old battered radio playing at her side.

I had some evidence that she did move occasionally. One day I sat down in a chair next to her, only to discover when I got up that the seat of my trousers was decidedly damp. Doris had so determined to rest and put her feet up when they gave up the farm, that now she wouldn't even leave her chair to go to the toilet.

Somehow she lived on, refused any medical care, became steadily more odoriferous as the years went by. She reluctantly agreed for the district nurse to give her a wash once a week, and lived on to a great age. In spite of the fact that she sat in a pool of her own product most of the day, she never ever got a bed sore.

The one luxury the Slewmans had in the cottage was a telephone. This was needed for Bill's calls to the doctor. Bill was unlike Doris. Whereas she had no difficulty in passing water, which was obvious from the state of the saturated chairs, Bill's problem was that from time to time he 'got stuck'.

Men who get stuck, who cannot pass water, have to have their prostate gland removed. Once you have inserted a catheter and emptied the bladder, the bladder will block off again unless the gland is removed, or so I was told as a medical student. Bill's case defied the teaching. After his bladder had been emptied, he would often manage to remain unblocked for two or three months.

Bill, who had to be intermittently unblocked for several years, suddenly changed to not blocking off at all, and wandered around wetting everything as if he was (in fact he *was*) carrying his own personal stream around with him.

'You've got to do something about it,' said Doris from the depths of what I suspected was her own urine-soaked chair. 'We're going to be washed out of the house.'

I was at a loss to know what to do. On one occasion I had to dissuade Bill from putting a clothes peg on his offending member. In despair, I went to consult Neville Jackson who ran the Tadchester chemist's. I asked if there was anything on the National Health that might help this situation.

'Yes,' said Neville. 'The best buy, that is the best give away, is a portable male urinal.'

He fished behind the counter and brought out a thing that looked like a pair of gun holsters with a balloon in front and a tube leading off to another balloon below. It really was a most ingenious piece of plumbing.

I took it straight round to Bill and between us we strapped it on him. He had to insert himself into a tube that led into a bag through which another tube passed to a further bag that had a strap to go round his ankle. The whole apparatus was fixed on by a combination of rubber and webbing, and was anchored firmly by a belt round the waist.

Bill thought it was marvellous. He said 'When I'm int'

29

market, doctor, all I've got to do is to stand by the street drain and open me bottom tap. Nobody will know what I'm doing.'

It worked like a charm. Bill was very happy with his new device. I only wished there was one that his wife could have worn. But you can't win them all.

* * *

I only knew general practice or, in fact, medicine, after it became nationalised. Although the nationalised branch of medicine had been going for a few years by the time I went into practice, patients hadn't fully explored all its possibilities. They were still testing and trying this new unbelievable toy which was all theirs for absolutely nothing. Some felt that they now employed doctors and treated them very much in that way. Many, particularly the well-off, accepted the National Health Service as a great blessing – free universal medicine for all – but still expected to get private and personal treatment. The doctor must understand that they were rather different.

Steve Maxwell said that in the old days there were those who paid, those who were always about to pay, and those who never paid at all. The commonest delaying tactic was 'Oh, we will be killing a pig in the next week or two, and will settle up then, Doctor.'

The semi-rural area in which the Tadchester practice was situated benefited to some extent by these changes. So many people in the farming community were used to paying in kind at Christmas. After the inauguration of the National Health Service, their doctors still received a tremendous amount of produce – drink, chickens, turkeys and geese. The farmers who had always paid bills just couldn't believe these medical services were for nothing.

For the patients who never ever paid bills, the abundant munificence of the National Health Service was overwhelming. So many things could be obtained for nothing if you knew how. These included plastic anklets which could keep the feet warm in winter; elastic stockings, both full length and below the knee

—these could either be nylon yarn for the winter or fine nylon for the summer; hernia trusses; corsets, both boned and unboned; plastic knickers; surgical brassieres and any amount of cotton-wool. Lengths of gauze substituted very well for net curtains. False teeth, glasses, wigs and hearing aids were all standard. There were various ancillary services such as aids for getting in and out of your bath, special elevated seats for toilets, and extra food for special diets. Also available was extra money for special heating and insulation where the patient's medical condition required a warm or draught-free atmosphere.

It was no surprise to me when Fred Bowen came to the surgery. Fred had had chronic asthma and bronchitis for many years. He was not a severe case, but he was to a certain extent handicapped by recurrent chest infections, especially in the winter. He came to the surgery looking relatively well, and his request was not for medicine.

'It's like this, Doctor,' he said. 'When I goes up from the lounge to me bedroom; the cold air in me bedroom makes me lungs go into spasm and I can't get me breath. If you gives me a letter to take to the Social Security, they will put a gas fire in me bedroom and help pay the bill.'

Always happy to take the least line of resistance in these cases, I dutifully gave Fred his chitty. As he was leaving the consulting room I noticed some big, round object hanging from his hand by a strap.

'What's that?' I asked.

'Oh,' said Fred, 'that's a crash helmet.'

'Whatever do you want with a crash helmet?'

'Well,' said Fred, a bit sheepishly, 'I have just bought meself a motorbike. I get a bit breathless climbing these hills.'

I exploded . . .

*　　　*　　　*

Fred's motorbike didn't last long, and for some reason he didn't get his gas fire installed. His chest got progressively worse and he had to spend quite a lot of time at home. He was too breathless to get out, particularly when he had one of his recurrent infections.

When I called one day I noticed him painting with poster paints in an exercise book. This was a great surprise to me as I had never had the highest opinion of Fred's application. I found that he had about a dozen exercise books filled with carefully executed primitive paintings. They had a special quality all their own. Although by some standards they could be judged as childish, they obviously illustrated what the artist meant to show. A house was a house even if it was out of proportion with the rest of the landscape; a tractor was a tractor; a car was a car, even though a dog in the same picture could easily be as big as the car. I knew nothing about painting, but felt that Fred had some particular quality in his work and that, as a therapy at least, he should be encouraged.

'I wish I could have some lessons,' said Fred. 'I've always wanted to paint in oils.'

We had in Tadchester a very well-known artist, John Floyd. He was successful in that he had seven children whom he managed to send to private school, two houses and a gallery, all of which he supported by his paintings. He was one of the few successful, or at least economically successful, painters that I have met. Many of his more important works were exhibited in London.

I asked if he would come and cast an eye over Fred's work and perhaps give him some instruction and encouragement.

When he had seen some of Fred's paintings he said, 'I can't instruct him. I wouldn't dream of interfering with what he does. He is a natural, primitive artist of the highest calibre. I'll just show him a bit about oils, but I wouldn't dream of trying in any way to give him instruction.'

So, with the encouragement of myself and John Floyd, Fred started to do one or two oil paintings on canvas. There was something very engaging about his work. We encouraged him to enter some paintings for the exhibition by Tadchester artists at the Humber Memorial Art Gallery, situated in the park just off the Tadchester Quay.

Tadchester had an art gallery which was much better and much larger than one would have expected for a town of its size and situation. Charles Humber had been a successful son of Tadchester, who had made money abroad, come back and built the Humber Art Gallery as a memorial to himself.

For two weeks in the summer the Tadchester Art Society, a very snooty, tight little circle of people, held its own exhibition at the gallery, when paintings by the members were put on show for possible sale. Non-members too were allowed to submit paintings for consideration, and the successful paintings were exhibited in a room set aside specially for the purpose. With our encouragement, Fred entered four. Two, with pressure, were very reluctantly accepted by the Art Society and were hung in the gallery. In the exhibition catalogue one was priced at £5 and the other at £7.

Fred, his wife and his daughter, all bursting with pride, went down every day hoping to see the red stamps on the paintings which would indicate that they had been sold.

With two days of the exhibition still to go, neither of Fred's pictures had been sold. I started to worry. I knew that Fred needed the encouragement of a sale to involve him seriously with painting. John Floyd had stressed that Fred must persevere with his particular style to develop his quite exceptional talent.

Then I made the mistake of doing what is so easy to do as a GP – of trying to play God. Being so pleased that through my perceptive, artistic intuition I had discovered an artist, I couldn't let it stop there. I anonymously bought the less expensive of the two paintings. I couldn't have it delivered to my house, so I rang up my old friend Bob Barker, who kept the bookshop at Sanford-on-Sea, explaining the situation, and asking would he mind if the picture were delivered to him.

Bob chuckled. 'Playing God again,' he said. 'It will land you in trouble one day. Yes, I can put it away in a corner of the shop somewhere, particularly somewhere I don't have to look at it.'

So it was arranged that the painting should be delivered to

Bob Barker's bookshop.

The Bowens were overcome and bursting with excitement that one of Fred's pictures had been sold. They pestered and re-pestered the Art Society committee to find out who had bought it. Eventually they managed to drag out from one of the officials that the picture had gone to Bob Barker's bookshop at Sanford-on-Sea.

They gleefully told me their story when I next visited them. I had to appear surprised, and congratulated Fred.

Fred now really got down to work with a will, and was soon producing a painting every other day. I had to examine them all and make comments on his latest product every time I called.

There was an air of success and happiness around the house, and I was pleased with myself that a lot of this was due to my efforts.

It was my habit once a week, or at the very least once a fort-night, to slip away from my work to Barker's Bookshop and spend some time with dear old Bob, who kept a small box of cigars in his desk drawer for my visits. We explored whole areas of literature together, and put the world to rights. It was an as-sociation I treasured, and a man for whom I had tremendous admiration. When I visited him a week after the art exhibition, I had a welcome that for the first time was less than cordial. Bob was, if anything, a bit grumpy. He looked at me, nodding over his glasses.

'Good afternoon, God,' he said. 'I don't want to get mixed up in your good works again.' And with a twinkle in his eye he told me he had had to call into a shop in town. It happened to be the butcher's. His wife was picking up the meat and he was idly gazing out of the window when a young woman came round the counter and asked if he was Bob Barker. When he confirmed that he was, she almost got on the ground to kiss his feet. She was apparently Fred Bowen's daughter. With tears in her eyes, she told Bob Barker how much difference his buying her father's painting had made to all their lives. What a fine, won-derful man he was, and how generous and perceptive. No adjec-tive was too extravagant for her to use in his praise.

'You see what you let me in for,' he said. 'Now here is £5. I couldn't possibly accept the painting for nothing. I have got to pay for it, having all this goodwill heaped on me. I hate the bloody painting and have hidden it behind the cupboard. So just keep me out of any further of your projects please Dr Bob.' (With both of us being Bobs, my name was always given a handle by Bob Barker, close friends though we were.)

Bob Barker had no malice, and his bad temper was only pretence. We had a good laugh over it. It was a lesson to me. It is so easy being clever, playing with people's lives.

Fred Bowen did stick at his painting. He began to sell pictures here and there, entered more local exhibitions. In all he perhaps sold seventy to eighty paintings, enough to cover the cost of materials, his canvases, paints, brushes, and to bring the family a small amount of money. Not enough to make any real difference to his life style, but enough to buy a few small comforts and give him some standing.

Fred's painting gave him pride and a place in the community. After being a nonentity for many years he was now a somebody. The height of his artistic career was reached when Western Television screened an art summer series each week, showing on the programme the work of an artist from the west of England. For one week Fred Bowen's paintings were shown – a different painting each night – as the work of an established West Country artist.

Over two or three years Fred reached heights of achievement that one would never have thought possible. He did this in spite of ill health. He never had a lesson. He was never internationally famous, but before he died, he'd sold about a hundred paintings. The most he ever got for one was £40, and the majority sold for about £10 or £15. But what was important was that he changed from being a nobody into a somebody.

The chest condition which had bothered him for so many years had begun to throw a strain on his heart. Eventually his heart could cope no longer. About six months after his paintings had appeared on television, he died. But he did not die as Fred Bowen of 63 North Street, Tadchester. He died as Fred

Bowen, the well-known artist, whose paintings had been shown on television. There is no better accolade in this day and age than to appear on television.

Over the years Fred had given me some of his paintings, which I kept, telling him I expected that one day they would be worth a great deal of money. And I noticed, although I never mentioned it, that the painting that Bob Barker had so unwillingly bought was placed in a prominent position in his shop soon after the television appearances of Fred's other paintings. Even wise, dear old Bob was as susceptible to conversion by the media as anyone else . . .

AS SEEN ON TV
(AND BOUGHT BY GOD)

4

Visitors

Pam settled down very happily in Tadchester. As we were by
the sea, we had an unending stream of visitors. We were surprised how popular we had become with friends in London now
that we lived and could provide accommodation for them in the
glorious countryside and seaside of Tadchester and Sanford-
on-Sea.

Younger friends loved to go seine net fishing with us in the
surf at Sanford-on-Sea. There was something fundamental and
satisfying about wading through the breakers, tugging a net and
catching one's own food: certainly a contrast to London life.

Pam explored all the Tadchester shops with her friend Zara.
Zara always had an eye for a bargain and knew all the little out-
of-the-way places where the best things could be had. As well as
the shops there was the huge covered pannier market to which
the country people brought such assorted produce as fruit,
vegetables, preserves, pickles and flowers.

We were fortunate that we lived next door to Fred Derrigan.
Fred had a smallholding where he grew vegetables, and a few
glasshouses where he grew tomatoes, raspberries and strawberries. He was a big, stoical man, and wicket keeper in one of the
village cricket teams. He kept us constantly supplied with vegetables. I am sure that they were at a reduced price. Anyway
Pam found that housekeeping was cheaper than she thought it
would be.

It was Pam who called me urgently to see Fred one morning. 'Come quickly,' she said. 'I think Fred's dying.' Pam had still not yet got used to people with medical conditions.

When I reached Fred he certainly looked in a bad way.

'I feel as if I am going to die, Doc,' he said. 'I have a tremendous pain in my side, it's the worst I have ever had. The pain is really terrible. It goes down into my left testicle.'

Fred was in obvious distress. As I questioned him further I found that he'd been passing water more frequently. He really did look a sorry sight. I examined him, and could find nothing wrong, except that he was a bit tender in his left testicle.

'Well, Doctor?' said Fred as I finished my examination.

'I think, Fred,' I said, 'you've got what we call a ureteric calculus. This means a little stony crystal is trying to pass down the tube from your kidney to your bladder. It is one of the most painful conditions there is. I shall want a specimen of urine from you, and I shall want you to look to see if you pass any bits of gravel. I'm going to give you an injection now that not only relieves pain but also relieves the spasm of the little tube that's got the crystal in it and helps to pass it along.'

I explained that the most common cause of these stones was oxalic acid crystallising out in the kidney, and the kidney trying to pass the crystals down to the bladder. This is more common in hot climates where there has been excessive sweating and the urine becomes concentrated, but if you eat a lot of fruit which contains oxalic acid, like tomatoes or strawberries, it is much more likely to happen. Sometimes the crystals form without there being any apparent outside factor.

'Look out for stones, Fred,' I said. 'And if the pain gets very bad again, give me a ring. Drink plenty of water and bring in a sample tomorrow. If you should start passing blood in your water, don't worry: it often happens in this condition.'

Fred called me during the night, in absolute agony. I had to give him an injection of pethedin. The next day he was up, perfectly fit again. His urine sample showed some blood cells in it, but no sign of infection.

I saw no more of Fred for two days after my night visit until

he came beaming into the surgery with a small jagged crystal in his hand.

'Here it is, Doc' he said. 'I've laid an egg. Is that it now?'

'I think so,' I replied. 'What we have to do now, Fred, is to have a special x-ray of your waterworks just to see if there are any other stones left that might be blocking off your kidney. Some dye will be injected into your blood stream and pictures taken of the dye as it passes through your kidney down the tube from the kidney to the bladder. It's called, if it's any help to you, an intravenous pylogram.'

After his x-ray Fred came to the surgery for the result. It was quite clear.

'I must say, Doc,' said Fred, 'I had been bashing the strawberries a bit. I've grown them under glass this year and have been eating them all the time. You know what my wife is saying now – "People who work in glass houses shouldn't grow stones".'

After Fred's kidney incident we found that our vegetables got even cheaper still. He almost gave us our tomatoes and strawberries for nothing. This was a tremendous help to Pam as the summer came along, when we had even more visitors coming to see us and the seaside at the same time.

* * *

Two of our first visitors in our new home were Herbert and Margaret Hodge. Herbert had had a stroke and was unable to

39

drive, so I drove across to Hastings to fetch them.

Herbert and I had struck up a friendship from appearing together on a TV show when I was down the coal mines just after the end of the war. It was a topical magazine programme and I got a telegram to ask if I would appear. I am still trying to work out why.

When I first met Herbert he was in the peak of his achievements. He was a taxi driver who'd become a very well-known writer and broadcaster. He had written several books including *A Cockney on Main Street,* about his adventures in America where the Ministry of Labour had sent him lecturing during the war, and other books about the cab trade.

His life read like a book. He'd come from a poor, but scrupulously honest background. After his mother died, he had gone steerage with the insurance money to Canada by cattle boat. In Canada he had worked on the railways, as a lumberjack, and as a firefighter in the timber forests. He had then come back to England, worked in a garage, and progressed to become a cab driver and chauffeur.

Sitting in the cab ranks, he began to scribble, and his first articles were accepted for magazines like *Cab Trade News.* Then he wrote two plays, *Cannibal Carnival* and *Where's that Bomb?* These were political plays performed at the Unity Theatre, and were subsequently taken up and performed by the Oxford and Cambridge Dramatic Society in England and the Harvard and Yale Dramatic Society in America.

A big, heavily built man, Herbert was one of the most fundamentally honest men that I have ever met. He took up any new experience, shook it like a terrier and explored it to a degree. After our first meeting he took me to a cab shelter, a wooden shed with a steaming stove in the corner. There, sitting jammed among the cabbies, I learnt some of their terminology – a new cab driver was a butter boy, for instance – and all about the gruelling examinations they had to go through on the geography of London streets before they could pass as a London cabby.

One of Herbert's books *It's Draughty up Front* was autobiographical: the title came from the fact that the cab driver had to sit at the front, uncovered and exposed to the elements. In this book Herbert described his life outside his work and his various stages of exploration and education.

He began in his late teens by being caught up with religious fervour, exploring one denomination after another, and finally giving this up in order to become a communist. He went from communism to fascism, joining Mosley's Party, gradually getting disillusioned with it, but not until he had stood as a Mosley candidate in the East End against Clement Attlee.

He then became an ardent and potentially lifelong socialist and was absolutely thrilled when the first post-war government was Labour. He said somehow it all seemed too good to be true. He wondered whether all their wonderful socialist ideas would work. In his latter life he considered that they hadn't.

He said, 'I hate to confess it, but now that I have a little bit of money, I worry about it, whereas I was never worried about it before. If anybody classified me now, I expect I am a conservative.'

Herbert's literary achievements steadily grew and he became a well-known figure, both as a writer and broadcaster. He wrote three major hard-back books: *Cab Sir?*, *It's Draughty up Front*, and *A Cockney on Main Street*. He'd had both his plays produced, he started doing radio for a magazine programme called *London Town*, and his broadcasts on London were used in commonwealth schools to teach children about London. He wrote a great number of articles for various magazines and journals and was approached by *John Bull* magazine. He was asked by them to come and see them, but kept on putting it off. Eventually they offered him £5 expenses to go and see them, and this resulted in Herbert writing a thousand-word weekly column: a friendly, philosophical column which ran for a period of about ten years. In the meantime he had also become the theatre and film critic for *John o' London's Weekly*.

A couple of years after I met him he had his first stroke. I think what had happened was that Herbert had written himself out. He was so honest that if he had written something once, then he couldn't write it or use it again; he had to find fresh material each time to put fresh ideas forward. Over ten years it is very difficult to find fresh ideas for a column every week. I think that he had exhausted himself completely, mentally and physically. As well as his column, which took most of his time and energy, he was lecturing for libraries and at one time did some two-way transatlantic broadcasts with Alistair Cooke.

The fresh air of Tadchester seemed to revive him. He seemed to have more use in his paralysed limb – he even drove my car for a while – and he went back after a holiday all fired to write. But it was as if nature had said, 'You've done all you can; there is no more writing left in you.' As soon as he had started to write again he had a further stroke which prevented both writing and typing.

Round about this time Radio Luxembourg did a *This is Your Life* programme about Herbert, and in lieu of a fee presented him with a tape recorder. This meant that although he couldn't write, he could speak into a tape recorder. For some years up until his death we carried on discussions and arguments on the tapes.

His was a friendship that I valued greatly, and I was heart-broken that it had to end so soon. But he was one of several cases that I came to see in my years in practice; when someone had given all they had to give, their body stopped them from doing any more. If Herbert had written anything else it could have been only repetition of previous works and he just wasn't this sort of animal. I took the best, or what I thought the best, of the hundreds of philosophical workaday articles like *To Doubt is to Discover* and put them away. I hope that one day I might be able to bring them out and that somebody might be interested enough to give them a second reading.

5

Fishy Business

I was always glad to bump into John Denton, the River Authority bailiff on the Tadchester end of the River Tad.

Born and raised in the industrial North, in an atmosphere he described as three parts sulphur dioxide and four parts muck, he had opted for the country life after his wartime army service and eventually finished up in Tadchester.

Big, bluff, boozy, gregarious, he was a dedicated bailiff and angler and the scourge of the local poachers. Patient as a saint with youngsters or inexperienced anglers, he took no nonsense from anybody trying to pull the wool over his eyes; especially the superior county types who, as he so delicately put it, got on his bloody wick.

He came into surgery one morning in the summer with a bandaged finger.

'Mornin', Bob,' he said. 'How are you?'

'All the better for seeing you, John. But I'm supposed to be asking the questions. How are *you*? And what have you done to your finger?'

'Bloody mink,' he said.

This was John. He seldom needed my professional services, but when he did it was always for something bizarre. The first time I treated him was for the removal of a salmon lure which a clumsy pupil had managed to hook very firmly into John's giant rump.

'Mink?' I said. 'Of course. There's a lot of it about. You're the tenth case of minkitis this morning.'

'No, Bob, I'm not kidding. Took a mink out of a trap this morning and the little bugger nearly had my finger off.'

He unwrapped the bandage. The top half of his finger gave a passable imitation of freshly minced steak.

As I cleaned and dressed the wound, or rather wounds, and prepared an anti-tetanus injection, John told me the story.

The banks of the Tad were plagued by mink, wild mink augmented by cross-breeding with escapees from the local mink farm. Beautiful animals, they ranged in colour from black to golden brown, and some of the fully grown males were almost the size of an otter.

They gave John a lot of problems. Incredibly fast, fierce and vicious, they wreaked havoc among the water birds and the fish. More than a match for the normal natural predators, they were also prolific breeders. Without John's intervention they would have ruined the balance of wildlife along the river, let alone the fishing.

John kept their numbers down with shotgun and traps. The trapping was done with humane catch-'em-alive traps. Instead of drowning the mink inside the traps, or shooting them through the bars with a .22 pistol, John preferred to take the catches to the mink farm. There, those with unsuitable pelts would be painlessly gassed. Those with marketable pelts would stay for a short but happy life of non-stop eating until they grew to full size.

The mink farm manager was happy to do this: it eased his conscience about the inevitable number of escapees which were constantly adding to John's problems. John was happy: the mink were put down painlessly, and he made a bit of beer money from the sale of the pelts. There was even a market for odd-coloured or unmatchable pelts as fun furs in the local gift shops.

'Any road,' said John, 'I had this mink in the trap this morning. A big 'un. And a lovely colour. I didn't have my leather gloves with me, and like a fool I took it out to put it in a sack

44

barehanded. Thought I was used enough to 'em by now. Know all, know nowt, me mam used to say.'

John waxed lyrical about the qualities of mink. Beautiful, voracious, aggressive, fearless, passionate as lovers and devoted as parents.

'There was this pair in the spring,' he mused. 'Courting. Doing this funny little dance, running round and round each other, making all sorts of loops and twirls, getting faster and faster. All happening on the bank, with the morning sun making their coats shine like polished gold. They went faster and faster and faster, moving closer to each other all the time. And then they clutched each other in this sort of embrace for the actual mating . . .'

'Oh, that's beautiful, John.'

'Then I shot 'em. Pair of 'em. With one barrel of me twelve-bore. Broke me heart. But what a way to go . . .'

* * *

John's tales of fish and fishermen made me decide to take up the sport. As a boy, of course, I had tried the bent-pin-and-string techniques, but boxing and rugby took over in my early teens, girls took over in my later teens, and from then on my leisure time was fully occupied.

I fancied game fishing – fly fishing for salmon and trout – with all the mystique which seemed to attend the pursuit of these two fish. But John said, 'Nay lad. You'll start where you ought: with coarse fishing. You'll learn to use a rod properly, learn how to read a water, learn how to use cover. And then you can move on to the fly.'

Coarse fishing didn't sound right to me. Certainly I had heard many of the tweedy game fishermen sneering at coarse anglers.

'Take no notice,' said John. 'Coarse doesn't mean *coarse*. There are techniques in coarse fishing which are much more refined than half these tweedy buggers could use. There are hooks so small you can hardly see to put the bait on, and line so fine that it's almost invisible.'

He explained that the origins of the word *coarse*, applied to fish, were obscure. As far as he had been able to discover, the word came from the old phrase *in course*, which meant in the normal run of things, ordinary, i.e. every freshwater fish except salmon and trout.

John was a true angler, an all-round fisherman for whom every fish had its own special magic, and every technique its own special application. He had no patience with the 'dray flay mob', as he called them, who brayed every evening in the Tadchester Arms about the delicate art of fly fishing being the only occupation for an officer and a gentleman.

'See him,' he said one night, indicating an elderly man in sober tweeds, quietly drinking in a corner of the bar. 'Ex-colonial governor, he is. Can run rings round these bluffers with any bait you like. Pulled out a salmon last year which was damn near the record for the river. Yet he's as happy as Larry going for pike and carp as well. If anybody wants advice, he'll give it. Otherwise he keeps himself to himself, probably for fear of bursting out laughing. He's spit better fishermen than this lot before breakfast.'

'I say, Denton,' brayed one of the chinless wonders. 'We're trying the pool at Robbins' Reach tomorrow. What do you think of our chances?'

John bristled. He was paid as a bailiff, but the terms of employment did not include having the handle left off his name. With a great effort of self-control he turned calmly to face his questioner.

'If you can catch fish,' he said quietly, 'you'll be all right at Robbins' Reach.'

'Ah, thank you, Denton. Hear that, chaps? We should do well tomorrow.'

'Don't know why I bother,' muttered John. 'Sarcasm's wasted on this lot. Tell you what, Bob. Tomorrow I'll show you two fishermen at opposite ends of the scale. Then you'll begin to see what I mean.'

*   *   *

At six next morning I joined John at the gates of the fish farm. The farm bred trout for the restaurant trade, and both trout and coarse fish for periodic stockings of the river. Running the farm was part of John's duties.

Trout which had grown beyond the optimum restaurant size, or those which were surplus at any given time, were put into a stock pond. Anglers were allowed to fish the pond for a moderate fee, and were restricted to a brace of trout each.

John led the way to the stock pond. In the middle of the pond stood the archetypal trout fisherman: waders, tweed jacket, creel over his shoulder, short-handled net looped in his belt, a tweed hat festooned with trout flies, and swishing a rod back and forth over his shoulder as he paid out line.

He looked up as we approached.

'Ah. Morning, Denton.'

'Another of 'em,' muttered John. 'Ignorant buggers.' Then, 'Morning, Colonel. How's your luck?'

'Not too good, I'm afraid. Little devils playing hard to get this morning. Still, a bit of sun on the water and I'll have the blighters.'

'I'm sure you will, sir,' said John. 'No more than two, mind.'

'Dammit, man, what do you take me for?' bellowed the Colonel.

'A bloody idiot,' said John quietly as we turned away. 'Ex-Indian Army, that one. Pride of the Bengal Prancers. Comes here every year, done up to the nines, and fishes the stock pond with a dry fly. Won't use anything else.'

John explained that a dry fly floats on the water, and is only effective on gin-clear runs at certain times when natural flies are hatching.

'He's fishing a pond of murky water. A bloody sight murkier by the time he's finished wading all over it. And for trout which have been hand fed on bloody great protein pellets and wouldn't know a dry fly if they saw one. He'll fish it every day for a week, catch nowt, and then complain in his club that fishing in England has never been the same since we lost India. But he knows that nobody but a bounder would use anything else but dray flay.'

'What would you use, John?'

'Small spinner. Big, heavy, wet fly. If nobody was looking, a bloody great lobworm.'

'Why if nobody was looking?'

'Against the rules. Too easy. We like the customers to get their money's worth. And two trout in five minutes is hardly cricket, what? Come on, lad, and I'll show you the other kind of fisherman: the real one.'

We approached the bank of the Tad.

'Take it quietly from here, Bob,' whispered John. 'Follow me, single file, and don't step on any twigs.'

We crept up to the bank and peered from behind some foliage.

'There he is,' hissed John. 'Dead opposite on the other bank.'

'I can't see anybody,' I whispered.

'Exactly. That's a real fisherman. Now watch this.'

He cupped his hands to his mouth and bellowed:

'Out of there, you little bugger – I can see you! I'll be over in my boat in a minute and tan your backside! Go on – out of it!'

There was a scurry in the undergrowth on the opposite bank, a glimpse of a tousled head of sun-bleached hair, and the flash of two fresh-caught fish strung by the gills. Then silence. And not another movement.

'He'll go far, that lad,' said John. 'Tommy Thompson. Best little poacher for miles.'

'What will you do about him?'

'Nowt. That's the rules. He's a lucky lad, growing up in the country. Goes ferreting for rabbits. Got a little terrier for rats. And a rod that's no more than a hazel twig with six feet of line on the end. See those fish he had? Trout. Good 'uns.

'With lads like that, the rules are that I make a lot of noise and they clear off.'

'And I thought you were a hard man.'

'I am that,' said John. 'Hard as bloody putty . . .'

*　　*　　*

48

My fishing career was due to start on the first day of the coarse fishing season: June 16th. For a couple of weeks beforehand, John loaned me a set of tackle and gave me some lessons on dry land in the field behind his cottage.

He taught me how to assemble the rod from the top joint downwards; take it apart from the bottom joint upwards. How to 'sight' along the rings of an assembled rod to make sure they were all in a straight line. How to cast, first with a centre-pin reel – the 'wheel' type – and then with the more sophisticated fixed-spool type. He had me casting both for distance and accuracy, using weights but no hooks on the end of the line. Though I say it myself, I became pretty good at both. He taught how to 'strike' – how to lift the rod with a smart wrist action to set the hook in the fish's mouth, yet to do no more than that to avoid damage to the fish.

John even taught me how to play a fish, with himself as the catch. With the end of the line in a gloved hand – the fine nylon could cut like a knife into bare skin – he would lumber about in imitation of the fish's diving and turning movements and bellow instructions.

'Keep the rod up – up, you silly bugger! Now give it line! Now turn its head at the top of the run . . . sidestrain! Drop the rod tip and turn it! Now bring it back towards you . . . even pressure . . . steady as she goes . . . Now the landing net . . . into the water. Always fish to net, never net to fish. Right . . . net in the water – now bring me in. Gently . . . I'm knackered, but I still might kick at the last knockings. Gently . . . over the net –' and here he would clomp one of his size ten wellies into the landing net '– and hup!'

All this would have looked silly enough if anybody had been around to watch it – and certainly the cows in the field looked pretty bewildered by it all – but it was nothing to John's lessons on approaching the water.

I had to assemble the rod away from the bank, and leave it behind while I took the big wicker fishing basket down to 'set out my stall', as John put it. The approach to the water was done at a crouch, keeping below the skyline, using cover in front

49

of me and behind me, and in one or two exposed places even in a commando crawl.

This looked ridiculous – and on one occasion came as a great shock to a courting couple – but it was necessary if one was not to frighten the fish away. Fish can see a surprising distance above the surface, can register bright colours or flashes of light and will shy away at sudden movements, unfamiliar objects on the skyline, or shadows. So clothes had to be drab, movements slow, and posture low.

'Looks daft, Bob,' said John. 'Let's face it – it is daft. But we're *stalking* the fish. They're not very bright, but they survive by clearing off at the first sign of anything they're not used to. The best kind of fisherman is the one you don't see – like the lad we chased off the other week. And don't forget: the fish can *feel* vibrations very keenly. So tread softly. Don't go clumping about in your bloody great boots.'

Setting out the stall meant unpacking the gear from the basket, placing rod rests gently but firmly into the bank, putting bait tins and bags of groundbait within easy reach, staking out the keepnet in the shade, and assembling the landing net before any thought of fishing.

'Never forget that, Bob,' said John. 'Always assemble the landing net first, no matter what fish are moving, no matter how excited you are. I've lost count of the loonies – and even experienced fishermen – who have had a damn great fish on and then had nowt to land it with.'

* * *

June 16th was traditionally the time for tench. John didn't tell me, but a week before he had dragged a v-shaped path through a bed of weed in the river. Every night for that week he had thrown groundbait into the cleared swim. So unless I did something horribly wrong, I couldn't fail. But, as John said later, 'There's no start like a good start, Bob. And there's nowt better to start with than tench.'

The magic of that misty summer morning is still with me. Just the tip of my float was showing above the almost still water of a gentle green eddy. The only movement was that of a vole which fussed across to the bank, climbed out, shook itself, had a scratch, and then ambled off without even noticing the presence of the two humans. A robin perched cheekily on the end of my rod, then hopped down to filch a couple of maggots from the bait tin.

Nothing happened. Nothing . . . Until, 'Here they come, Bob. See those bubbles . . .'

In several parts of the cleared swim rose dead straight lines of tiny bubbles.

'Feeding tench,' whispered John. 'Always thousands of tiny bubbles in straight lines. With bream you get fewer bubbles, but bigger. And wobbly. With carp, bigger bubbles still. And with both of them, clouds of mud. But with tench, dead straight lines of . . . eh, watch your float, lad . . .'

The tip of my float had trembled ever so slightly.

'Give it time,' said John. 'Tench are fiddlers. Be ready, but there's no rush. It'll pick up the bait and lift the float. Then the float will lie flat on the surface. Then it will slide under. When it slides under, strike . . .'

After what seemed an age of trembling and fiddling, the float rose in the water. Then it keeled over and lay flat. Then it slid gently under . . . strike!

No amount of theorising can prepare you for the thrill of a real fish, especially such a fish as a tench, whose broad, powerful tail gives it a remorseless forward thrust. No fireworks, such as you get with pike or trout; no darting, jagging fight; no head-shaking leaps out of the water . . . just a steady, seemingly unstoppable thrust.

Thanks to John's previous instructions, and to his whispered 'Don't panic. Keep your rod up. Turn him at those weeds . . .' I kept in contact with the fish and eventually drew it over the landing net. Hup! And there it was . . . a magical, green-bronze, compact bundle of muscle with an eye of African gold.

I had six tench that morning. No spectacular weights, as I learned later – each around the three and a half-pound mark – but to me they were the biggest and most beautiful fish in the world.

The only thing I wasn't keen on was their slime: thick, glutinous and plenty of it. John told me of the legend of the Doctor Fish: that pike were supposed not to eat tench, in return for being allowed to rub their wounds against the tench's healing slime.

'Do you reckon that's true, John?'

'Couldn't say, Bob. If it is, the pike I've opened up can't have spent much time listening to old wives' tales . . .'

* * *

Since then I have caught every kind of freshwater fish, but I can remember only one other first: my first salmon.

John initiated me into spinning and fly fishing for trout later that summer. By autumn I was eager for a salmon, but John told me to be patient and wait until the next year's spring run.

'Too close to spawning, a lot of 'em,' he said. 'Your first salmon should be a clean fish.'

So, one evening early in March, came a 'phone call from John.

'When are you free this week, Bob?'

'I've a surgery tomorrow morning, but I'm clear in the afternoon.'

'Couldn't be better. Try to get to the cottage about half past one. Might be able to put you in touch with a salmon. Don't worry about the gear. Right?'

'Right.'

John was waiting outside the cottage when I arrived, a rod already assembled and baited with a spinner, a metal lure with vanes which revolved round a central pivot, and armed with a wicked treble hook.

'Right, Bob,' he said. 'We won't hang about. The run's well under way now, and there's one feller I've had my eye on since yesterday. He's been jumping about cleaning off his sea lice, and he's been resting up in the narrow pool below the bridge. He won't stay there much longer, though, so we'd better go and say hello.'

'Thank you very much, John,' I said, eyeing the nine-and-a half-foot rod with what must have been ill-disguised disappointment. 'Will this rod be big enough to hold him?'

'Oh, yes, Cleverclogs,' he said. 'You've been watching them show-offs with the twelve-footers. We'll take no notice. This rod's plenty long enough – and if this feller takes you past those trees on the bank you'll be damn glad you've only got nine feet of it to worry about.'

The salmon was lying deep, in the middle of the pool and facing upstream. I could just about see the dark shape, with the occasional glint of silver, in the spot where John was pointing.

'Right,' said John. 'Cast upstream, and bring the spinner back across his nose and past him. More than likely he won't budge for the first few goes, but then he'll get annoyed. Go on, lad – get stuck in.'

Spinning back downstream can be tricky, because you have to reel in faster than the current to get any movement in the spinner and to stop it sinking right to the bottom and possibly getting snagged. But I managed it, once, twice, three times, bringing the lure towards the salmon – or at least towards where the salmon was lying, because it was impossible to concentrate on the lure and see the fish at the same time.

Four times . . . five and – bang! The line tautened and the rod tip bent like a bow.

'Got him!' shouted John. 'Strike again for luck.' (I hadn't actually struck – the salmon had done it for me – but I knew what John meant.)

I struck into what felt like a rock. There was a pause.

'Keep the line taut, but be ready to give some!' shouted John.

Then the rock moved, shunting upstream at a speed which had the line running out from the reel at a frightening rate. Then it stopped.

'Take in the slack,' shouted John. 'Keep contact. And be ready for him to turn.'

Turn it did, charging downstream towards me this time, making me crank like mad to take up the slack line. The fish went downstream past me, with the current to help its bulk, and I just managed to turn its head before it reached the broken water at the tail of the pool.

Up and down and across the fish went, with the danger of a broken line at every turn, every shake of its head. Three or four times it leapt clear of the water, and I remembered John's instructions to drop the rod tip as the fish fell back. I was really glad to be in charge of only a nine-and-a-half-foot rod. A twelve-footer would have been bound to hit the trees on the bank above me.

The fight seemed to last for hours. My arms were aching from playing the fish, my eyes aching from straining to see the line where it cut the water in an attempt to forecast the fish's next move.

'How long does this go on for?' I yelled.

John looked at his watch.

'I reckon it's a fifteen-pounder,' he said, 'and you can usually reckon on a minute to the pound. Won't be long now.'

After a couple of minutes he shouted, 'Come in, number fifteen – your time's up!' and stepped into the shallow water by the bank with a tailer, a wire noose on a short handle.

He was right. By now the fish was fairly beaten, and I was able to manoeuvre it upstream towards John.

A dip with the tailer, a double-handed snatch – and there was this beautiful, yard-long, streamlined silver creature thrashing on the bank.

John knelt on it swiftly and with a 'clunk' administered the *coup de grâce* with one blow of the priest.

I staggered over, my arms shaking and my knees like jelly. Proud as I was, a dreadful sense of anti-climax set in.

'It's so beautiful,' I said. 'Seems a pity it's ... it's ...'

'Dead?' said John.

'Yes.'

'Much better that way, lad. Otherwise you'd have a hell of a job keeping the bugger in the oven ...'

6

The Little People

Living in the Tadchester area were several characters who were
so small in size that it made me sometimes wonder whether
there was once a race of small people in Somerset.

Whether or not it was some aboriginal strain in the local
ethnic mixture, whether there really was once a race of tiny folk
in Somerset, I don't know, but there certainly were several very,
very small people among the inhabitants. They weren't dwarfs
and didn't appear to have been stunted by any dietary defects.
They were just perfectly formed tiny folk.

The first two I met really gave me the willies. I called at a cottage right off the beaten track. A beautiful place with a well-
tended little garden, a yellow-tiled roof and wistaria growing
up the side and spreading across under the eaves.

Beautiful as it was, there was something strange about it.
When the door was opened I found myself saying 'Good
evening' to empty air, and was answered by a voice which came
from somewhere just below my waist. It was a tiny, very tiny,
old lady, wrinkled like a dried apple. She was very old but spotlessly dressed in an old-fashioned long frock and apron, with
bright and very brown eyes.

'Oh,' I said, recovering myself. 'I'm Dr Clifford. I've called to
see Mr Fletcher. Am I speaking to Mrs Fletcher?'

'That's right, Doctor,' she said in a thin piping voice. 'Do
come in.'

Sitting by the fire in the living room with a shawl around his shoulders was a little old man. A tiny old man. When he stood up to greet me he was about an inch taller than the tiny old lady.

The room was full of normal-sized furniture but it looked giant-sized against the elfin frames of the two old people. It was really eerie to see them moving about amongst enormous chairs, an enormous table, and an enormous grandfather clock which filled the room with its loud tick and rattled the teacups with its chime.

Strangest of all, however, was the creature which sat opposite the old man in front of the fire. It was a cat, but the biggest cat I had ever seen. Almost like a tiger. A yellow creature that watched me through enormous and luminous slanting green eyes as I examined the old man's chest.

'How old are you Mr Fletcher?' I asked.

'Eighty-one,' he replied in the same fluting voice as the old lady.

'He's eighty-one,' echoed the old lady, proudly.

'And you are looking well on it,' I said. 'Nothing wrong with you, Mr Fletcher, that keeping warm and dry won't put right. I'll give you a prescription for some linctus to help clear your chest. Take a tablespoonful three times a day.'

The old man nodded.

'You'll make sure your husband takes it won't you Mrs Fletcher?' I said.

'He's not my husband,' piped the old lady. 'He's my son.'

The grandfather clock whirred and struck the hour with a resonance which by rights should have shaken the windows out.

Eighty-one and her son! I must leave, I thought, before I turn into a pumpkin.

I took one last glance behind as the old lady closed the door. In front of the fire still sat the enormous yellow cat, grinning at me. The Cheshire cat was alive and well in deepest Somerset!

As I fastened the garden gate in the neat and freshly painted white fence, I realised what was odd about the cottage. It was the Gingerbread House! I drove back to Tadchester as quickly as I could and downed a large scotch in the Tadchester Arms. Imagination, I told myself, nothing more. But I still shiver every time I think about the little cottage, with two tiny people and the enormous yellow cat . . .

*　　*　　*

Another tiny person I treated was Ranger, the cowman. Nobody knew Ranger's other name, not even Ranger. He had no birth certificate and didn't know how old he was. With his permission I entered him on the records as John Ranger, but all he had ever been was Ranger, and had been for as long as even the old-timers could remember.

I was talking to Kevin Bird in the Tadchester Market one day – Kevin conducted most of the cattle auctions there – when we were interrupted by Josh Palmer, a local farmer. Palmer had a superb dairy herd and was reputed to have a lot of money, which he was also reputed to be very loath to part with. He came up and said, 'You the doctor?'

'One of them, yes,' I said, taking an instant dislike to him. 'My name's Clifford.'

'You'll do,' said Palmer. 'Better come down tomorrow and look at Ranger. He's took badly. Coughing all over the place. Can't have that when there's milk about. Dozy little tyke, can't hardly get out in the morning, either.'

'Who's Ranger?' I asked.

'I thought everybody knew that. Me cowman. Little feller. Lives in the bottom field behind me farm. Fourways Farm, over towards Winchcombe.'

'I'll call in the morning.'

'Right. See you do.'

'Look here,' I started, intending to give a short, sharp homily on manners. But Palmer had abruptly turned his back and walked away out of the market.

'Don't let him upset you Bob,' said Kevin. 'He's always like that: even worse on market days when he has to sell some of his milked-out cows. I'm just off to see what I can do for him. Take care. We hope you and Pam will come round at the weekend and have something to eat.'

As I turned to go I bumped into John Denton the River Authority bailiff.

'Hey up, our Bob,' he said in his broad Manchester accent. 'You look as if you've swallowed a quid and found a tanner. What's the matter?'

'Nothing, John. I've just had the pleasure of meeting Josh Palmer.'

'Him? Miserable old bugger. Wouldn't give you the snot from his nose. What's he been up to?'

I explained and asked John about Ranger and where exactly he lived.

'Poor little feller,' said John. 'A nice enough lad, but not the full shilling. Lad! He's more like a bloody gernommy. Tiny little bloke he is, Palmer's cowman. Knee-high to a shit bucket. He can do anything with them cows, bulls an' all.

'He saved Palmer's life one day when that big bull of his pinned the old sod to the shippon wall. Just walked under its nose, got hold of the ring in his little hand, stood on tip-toe and sang into its ear. Bloody *sang*, at a time like that. Any road, it worked. The old bull calmed down and walked back with Ranger to the stall quiet as a lamb.

'Palmer was all right, apart from a couple of cracked ribs, and for once in his life he dug into his pocket. Raised Ranger's wages he did, on the spot. Just as well – given time he'd have thought better of it.'

'That's something in Palmer's favour anyway,' I said. 'What did he raise them to?'

'Seven and six a week.'

'What? What was he getting before?'

'Seven shillings.'

'John, you're kidding.'

'There's plenty in here will tell you the same,' said John. 'Bloody slave labour that little fellow is, and he's worth three ordinary cowmen. But, as I said, he's not full muster. Got a screw loose somewhere and he's grateful to Palmer for giving him a roof. Scared he'll lose it if he upsets the old bugger.'

'What is the roof John?' I asked, 'So that I'll know what to look for tomorrow. A cottage?'

'Cottage?' shrieked John, as he fell about laughing. Then he shouted across to some of his cronies having a cup of tea and a bun at the mobile tea stand. 'Ranger! Doc's on about Ranger. Wants to know if he lives in a cottage!'

The cronies and everyone else within earshot fell about laughing, and John bellowed above the din, 'Cottage be buggered! The poor little sod lives in the back of a lorry!'

Backward and feudal as some parts of Somerset were, I just couldn't believe that a man could be kept in conditions worse than those of the animals he tended, and paid a pittance which would scarcely feed a dog for a week.

The next morning I discovered that it was true. In the bottom of the field behind Fourways Farm stood an old lorry, wheelless and jacked up on four piles of stones. The back of it was covered by a tarpaulin. Inside I found Ranger.

What looked like the body of a seven-year-old child lay on a pile of sacks, covered by some more sacking. The face was obviously that of an elderly man but it had the strangely young look of the simple minded. From the tiny body came staccato bursts of coughing, and wheezing attempts to suck air into the lungs.

A very brief examination was enough. Ranger had pneumonia and pleurisy. I said, 'Ranger, you need somewhere drier and warmer than this if you are going to get better. I will arrange a ride to hospital for you. You will have a nice warm bed and nice kind nurses to look after you.'

'No, no!' wheezed the little man. 'My cows! My cows! Who'll look after my cows?'

'Mr Palmer will look after them while you are away, Ranger. And it won't be for long. If you stay like this you will make the cows poorly, and you wouldn't like that would you?'

'No. But what about my home? It'll be here when I get back won't it? Master won't let anybody else live here will he?'

'No, Ranger,' I said, looking around at the clammy tarpaulin which constituted the walls of the home. 'He certainly won't. I'll see to that.'

I drove back to the nearest telephone box and arranged for an ambulance to take Ranger to the Tadchester hospital. I didn't want to ask for the use of Palmer's phone, assuming he had one. Ranger must be got away quickly out of the old villain's clutches. He was taken to hospital just in time: another twenty-four hours and he would have been filling a very small coffin.

As it was, he made steady but good progress. I saw him most days in the ward in the hospital. He was a great favourite with the Sister and the staff. John Bowler, the physician from Winchcombe who came over from time to time, cast a specialist eye on him and took some fluid from his chest which speeded his recovery. It was not long before he was out and about walking round the ward, pushing the tea trolley, and being treated as benevolently by the other men in the ward as if he were a little boy. He loved hospital – he never conceived that life could be as pleasant, as warm, and as comfortable as this – but he still hankered after his cows.

In the meantime I had not been idle on his behalf. What I

61

should say is that others had not been idle. I put the word out to a few chosen friends like John Denton, Kevin Bird and Joe Church. Ranger would be far better off with another job, a decent roof over his head and a living, if modest, wage. Within two days there were offers of jobs from four farmers, two with cottages thrown in. This was not generosity on their part: Ranger had the reputation of being the best cowman for miles around.

Ranger took a great deal of persuading. He was terrified of Palmer and dreaded some revenge, not to mention being almost grief-stricken at the thought of parting from his beloved cows.

Mrs Bemrose, the local social worker, talked gently to Ranger for some hours spread over several days. She assured him that Palmer was powerless to take any action against him. She drummed into him all the benefits of the jobs which were offered. She made him realise that he would be paid money he found hard even to imagine, and finally gave the little man some sense of his own worth. Ranger accepted a job with the farmer whose herd most closely resembled Palmer's, and there was a snug little cottage to go with the job.

Mrs Bemrose acted swiftly, getting an order from the Council Health Department declaring the lorry unfit for human habitation, so that Palmer could not enslave another poor soul as he had done Ranger. She also contacted the local Rotary Club who stocked the cottage up with secondhand but serviceable furniture, and by the time Ranger was discharged from hospital he had a fully equipped home to go to. It was beyond his wildest dreams.

I drove Ranger home from hospital to the cottage myself. The farmer's wife had a hot meal waiting for him. The farmer, a gruff but kindly man, greeted him warmly.

'When you're fit, Ranger,' he said, 'I'll show you round the farm and you can get to know the stock. But there's no hurry. Get fit first and let me know when you would like to start.'

'I've got my boots on, Master,' said Ranger, pointing to the child-sized wellingtons on his spindly legs. 'If it's all right with you, I'll just finish this food first.'

From then on Ranger never looked back. The farmer got more than his money's worth out of him. The dairy and the shippon (cowhouse) were always spotless, the milk yield increased and sickness amongst the herd dropped almost to nothing.

For the first time in his life Ranger had a home which was warm and dry, and he kept it scrubbed and tidy. The little man had come into his own. But not before time . . . and no more than he deserved.

Pregnant Moments

Hovery was the most famous beauty spot in the whole area. It was a village which lay at the foot of the cliffs and which could only be approached by a very steep, pebbly road. The road wound in and out through cottages and you thought, as you walked down it, that at each corner you would reach the bottom. When you eventually did reach the bottom, you found you'd walked much further than you originally intended. For some of the older holidaymakers it was too much, and every year we had several coronaries among the people attempting to walk back up the Hovery hill.

At one time supplies were taken down to the harbour by donkey or sledge. It wasn't until later years that another track parallel to the main village street was hacked out along the cliff face, enabling a Landrover to ferry supplies and some of the less fit holidaymakers.

Hovery was really out of the practice area, but one or two patients still hung on and demanded our services as they did in Dratchet.

In days gone by, the Hovery people had lived in a small, inbred community and had a high incidence of mentally retarded children. Mongolism was very common in and around the area. I had a great affection for the mongols, those sweet, gentle children who would never grow up and who never became aggressive. Whenever I was called to Hovery there would always be several of them scampering around trying to help carry my bag.

Many of the farms around Hovery assimilated a mongol child, whether their own or somebody else's, into the family. The children helped with small tasks round the farm. Some could milk the cows, chop wood, and do other simple jobs, and they added a useful complement to the families that had taken them in. The very location of the farms on which they lived protected them from the more sophisticated society outside where they would have found it difficult to cope.

* * *

Two new friends who had joined our circle in Tadchester – Philip and Joan Gammon – bought a cottage on the Hovery road, about five miles out of Tadchester itself.

Philip had taken up a post as games and physical education master at Tadchester Boys' Grammar School, and Joan taught the same subjects at Tadchester Girls' Grammar School. Philip had taken the place of Joe Church, one of our closest friends, who'd gone off to join the Royal Air Force. We missed Joe and his wife Lee, but Philip and Joan couldn't have been better replacements.

Philip was a keen naturalist. He had a couple of acres of ground around his cottage and started a sanctuary for birds of prey. He became an expert – one of the few in the whole country – on the care and keeping of these birds. Sick and injured birds from all over were brought for his medical care. On two or three occasions, with a little help from me, he even got birds x-rayed at Tadchester Hospital.

Philip and Joan had been living in their cottage for about a year when Joan became pregnant. It was her first pregnancy and it was taken for granted that I would look after her, as I looked after and delivered the babies of all my friends. Although I was pleased to do it, and would have been offended if I hadn't been asked, it was always more of a strain looking after people with whom you were friendly, related, or close in any way. The very nature of the relationship was such that it wasn't quite so easy to make clear, or anyway dispassionate, judgments.

Happily, Joan had no trouble with her pregnancy at all. She was very fit, she was pleasant natured and easy going, and the confinement was to take place in the small bedroom up the sharply winding stairs of their cottage.

As she was a friend I gave her all those little bits of extra attention. I took her blood pressure a bit more often, tested her water a bit more often, and kept a closer watch generally like the fussy old hen that I was always accused of being. Nurse Plank was to be the attending midwife. It was always a great comfort to me when she was there: she did all the work and I was happy just to obey her instructions.

All seemed set for a happy and straightforward delivery. I called round to see Joan on a Wednesday evening, checked her blood pressure, and checked that her water was clear. She felt fine, but was beginning to get twinges of pain.

'I think this is it, Joan,' I said. 'I have the feeling you are going to give me a disturbed night.'

At three o'clock in the morning there was a call from Philip. I arrived there just in time to pretend to assist Nurse Plank in the very straightforward delivery of an eight-pound girl. I was pleased to get the birth over because I did tend to worry about pregnancies. All was absolutely fine. Mother fine, baby fine, after a successful confinement at home. This was just how childbirth should be.

I was back home by eight o'clock to tell Pam the news, and we were almost as pleased as they were. Pam called in to see Joan during the morning and took her some flowers. Philip was busy writing out funny cards to announce the birth of the child.

At two o'clock in the afternoon as I was starting surgery, Gladys came racing in.

'Quick! they want you urgently at the Gammons'.'

Gladys never panicked unnecessarily. When she said you had to go quickly, then there was no doubt it was urgent.

66

Gladys was one of the best sifters of cases that I ever met. She could distinguish the important cases very clearly from the ones that were less so.

Obviously something was wrong. Phil was a very level-headed person, not a panicker, and a message like this meant that something pretty awful must have happened.

As I drove as fast as I could up the Hovery road to their cottage I permutated all the things that could be happening to Joan. I thought that she could be bleeding or had something worse, like a cerebral haemorrhage. Or the baby could have choked.

I broke all personal speed records in getting to the cottage. I raced up the stairs, and there was Joan in bed, unconscious, grey in the face, and looking desperately ill.

'Oh my God,' I thought. 'She's had a cerebral haemorrhage.'

Joan suddenly started to twitch and went into a fit. She needed an injection before she eventually stopped convulsing.

Phil was almost as ashen as Joan. I sent him off to phone for an ambulance and just sat there by the bed, counting the minutes until the ambulance arrived. Joan's condition didn't change much. She looked grey, her lips looked blue, her face looked swollen and her breathing was stertorous. The baby was fine, crying lustily from its cot in the corner.

At last the ambulance arrived. We then had to get Joan down the stairs. The local ambulance men had a kind of canvas sling that we slid under Joan to carry her downstairs like a parcel. The winding stairs of the cottage, which had always seemed fun and full of character, now presented terrible problems. We at last got Joan, still unconscious, into the ambulance and it rushed off to the maternity unit at Winchcombe.

Although the couple were by now my closest of friends, I breathed a sigh of relief that the responsibility of looking after Joan would be in somebody else's hands. The maternity unit at Winchcombe hospital was new, and I knew that Joan would have the best possible care.

I just could not think what could be wrong. I'd never had any situation like this before, and I still had a terrible fear that Joan had a brain haemorrhage, though it was a rare occurrence in young people.

It also looked a bit like a pregnancy fit. One of the main reasons an expectant mother attended a doctor in those days was to see that the blood pressure didn't come up, and that there was no protein in the urine. These were signs of what was called toxaemia of pregnancy, which might progress into an eclamptic fit. Such a fit was a great worry before midwifery became more sophisticated, and better drugs became available.

But Joan's condition had come about *after* the baby was born. I'd checked both urine and blood pressure only the night before and they were perfectly normal.

I rang the hospital later in the day and was told that Joan had what they called a *post-partum* eclamptic fit. This meant that she had a fit related to pregnancy, but *after* the birth of the child. I didn't even know that this could happen.

I came back to the surgery and made for the great tomes on midwifery in Steve Maxwell's room. I pored through them and eventually, in one American volume, I read that there had been a few reported cases of *post-partum* eclamptic fits. I took it as a reflection on my learning.

In my early days of practice at Tadchester, any doctor you met would tell you horrifying tales of ladies with toxaemia of pregnancy lying dangerously ill in darkened rooms, away from any noise that might start them off in a fit. Once the baby had been born and removed from the mother the toxaemia of pregnancy finished. It was thought that it was some sort of mother's allergy to her own baby. It was a rare condition before baby was born. It was a very, very rare condition *after* baby was born. Trust one of my friends to produce it, I thought.

Joan had a stormy time, was unconscious for a couple of days, but in a week was fully recovered, full of beans, home with a healthy baby and with a guarantee that there would be no after effects. It was a tremendous relief to see her home and well again.

*   *   *

I had been anxious for Joan's confinement to be on time for an ulterior motive. Kevin Bird, Janice, Pam and I had booked a cabin cruiser at Oxford for a week's holiday on the Thames. I couldn't have gone if Joan had been late, or hadn't recovered from her illness so soon.

We'd all been rather hard pressed at the practice and I badly needed a holiday. We called in to see Joan before we left. She was her old natural self, sitting up talking animatedly. It was with great relief that we packed up our car with Janice and Kevin and motored off to Oxford to pick up our cabin cruiser at Folly Bridge.

I love the Thames. As a schoolboy, I and a group of friends used to hire camping rowing boats. Five or six of us would pile into one of these boats and tear away downriver, trying to break all rowing records during the day. At night we would spread canvas over the special hoops on the boat, roll out mattresses, and sleep in the bottom. It was a bit like a floating covered wagon. We'd do our cooking on the bank, and we had the river to wash in.

It was really all good boy scout stuff, and I loved every minute of it. I vowed that one day I'd do it in comfort in a cabin cruiser where there were such sophisticated things as lights, a cooking stove and somewhere to wash.

So this was to be our holiday. We pulled in to our car park just by Folly Bridge to find our craft moored at the bottom of some steps by the bridge. It looked, to put it kindly, a little bit dilapidated. There were lots of superb looking craft around. Ours was by far the oldest and most battered. We immediately called her the *African Queen*.

'I'll be Humphrey Bogart,' I said to Pam, 'and you can be Katharine Hepburn.'

The holiday with Janice and Kevin was in very early May and we'd brought along plenty of warm clothes with us. Janice in particular had boxes, cases, coats, even a fur coat. We had to unload these from the car, deposit them on the towpath and then drive the car off to park it in the boatyard.

Our stuff on the towpath – huge mounds of cardboard boxes

and various items of clothing, particularly Janice's – almost blocked the right of way. The college eights were coming down to row and they were terribly amused to see this great pile of equipment, enough for a good-sized safari. They launched their boats by the side of us, and offered to take the girls with them for nothing.

Somehow we got everything aboard and packed after a fashion. The next problem was how to turn round in the cabins. There were two two-berth cabins, with bunks either side of a central gangway. There was a small stove and sink at one end and a large Calor gas cylinder perched on the back of the boat. A battery was charged from the engine and there was electric light, or so we were told.

Having loaded up, we went back to make our final checks with the boat office and to pick up maps of the river. There was an urgent OHMS envelope waiting for us.

My heart sank. We both so needed a holiday, particularly after the strain of Joan's baby. Could this mysterious envelope contain something to spoil it?

I opened it. Out came a long sheet of printed paper which I couldn't understand at first. Then the penny dropped: it was a notice of prosecution for taking underweight fish out of the sea.

We used to trawl the beaches at Sanford-on-Sea with a seine net and never queried the size of the mesh, which was the same as the commercial fishermen used. All of us shared the net – Janice, Kevin, Eric, Zara, Joan and Philip. Why suddenly pick on me? And how had they found me at Oxford? I was a bit worried because I had twice taken some sea trout out of the sea, but to my knowledge I had never taken undersized fish.

Pam could see I was worried and said, 'Oh, darling, surely it can't be bad news? Not just as we're starting this holiday?'

I turned the notice over. There was a funny drawing of a man and his wife and a tiny baby. Written underneath it was, 'Have a good holiday, and just leave those little tiddlers be – Philip and Joan.'

'The wretch!' I thought, laughing with relief. 'Just wait till I get back home.'

We pushed off from Oxford with the boat laden almost to the gunwales. It was cold and there was a slight drizzle. We were glad that we had all our warm clothes with us. The forecast was that the weather was going to be even colder still.

We only went a few hundred yards downriver on our first night. We practised circling the boat and getting used to all the problems of stopping, starting, and turning it round. We moored at the side of the bank, went to a pub for dinner, and came back into this cold, smelly boat. We put all our clothes on to keep us warm – and woke up sweating in the morning to find the sun blazing down on us. The sun shone for a whole week. All the mass of clothing that we had brought with us stayed where it was until the holiday was over.

I had brought a pair of rugby shorts with me just in case the weather improved. These and a pair of gym shoes were all I wore. I'd also tucked away a pair of legged bathing trunks. Kevin borrowed these and used them as shorts. The girls had light clothes and Janice had a very revealing bathing costume.

These were virtually the only clothes we wore for the whole week.

Our boat truly lived up to the name *African Queen*. It seemed to break down almost every other mile along the river. We somehow managed to struggle down to Abingdon, Goring, Pangbourne and Sonning. Each time we broke down, some fresh new mechanic from the boat company would appear, take one look at the boat, say 'Good God! Is this thing still running?'

Although they were a terrible nuisance, our stops, the cups of tea and the laughs we had with various mechanics all seemed part of the holiday. The enforced stops made us spend a longer time in areas that we would not normally have given much time.

Pam's parents came up from Leatherhead and met us at the Swan at Goring for lunch. At Abingdon we had dinner with Joe Church and his wife. Joe was posted there to the RAF Parachute Training School. We took them for a trip down the river after dinner.

None of us was very nautical. Kevin and I took it in turns to take the wheel and we used the girls as slaves to jump out and moor us tight into the bank as we went through locks.

Only once did the girls each have a go at steering. Pam insisted on taking us in to the Swan at Goring. Heedless of our advice she approached the quay going at full tilt. She meant, she said later, to put the brake on when she got there. She hit the jetty with such a whack I am sure she pushed the hotel back three or four feet.

Janice decided to do her steering along a canal lock. She got distracted and started to head for the bank. Some workmen sitting on the side eating their lunch saw the boat approaching at speed, dropped their sandwiches and ran up the bank. It was the only time I have seen men chased by a boat. Kevin and I were almost helpless with laughter. Janice got us lodged half way up the bank. It took all our efforts and those of the workmen – whose panic was now over – to get us afloat again.

The crazy incidents were just part of the whole delightful week. With the unexpected brilliant sunshine, the uncrowded river, the plentiful wildlife, it was often enough to sit and watch the world go by.

It was marvellous to wake up in the morning and sit in the cockpit of the boat, with bacon and eggs frying, surrounded by swans. Then in the daytime, to wander slowly through the locks and explore the riverside towns. Henley, Wallingford, Maidenhead and Marlow . . . they each have their special memories now.

Pam had brought with her Jerome K. Jerome's *Three Men in a Boat*, and we went to many of the places his characters had visited.

Too soon, as with all good things, the holiday was over and we were on our way back to Tadchester, fit and bronzed, with a whole heap of unused luggage. We said goodbye to our boat, which now sat forlornly on the side of the quay. We'd cursed it and sworn at it, but in the end had got very attached to it. I think it was probably the boat's swansong. It was so decrepit that it could not have stayed afloat much longer: we must have been pretty well the last people to use it. Over the years we had many river holidays, but never ever caught sight of it again. At least I can say now, when the conversation turns to boats, 'Yes – reminds me of the time I was aboard the *African Queen* . . .'

8

Happy Families

Soon after returning from our river holiday with Kevin and Janice, I began to worry about Pam's health. Her appetite began to fall away and she was not at all interested in going out.

She had always been prone to car sickness but now she was sick even on short journeys, and once or twice I found that she'd been sick and hadn't told me.

It is very difficult as a doctor to treat your own family and I imagined a whole lot of fearsome conditions. It must be cancer or tuberculosis or something like that: it wouldn't be anything simple, I was sure.

Pam refused to go and see Steve Maxwell, saying 'I'm sure it will pass. I'll work it off.' However, a couple of weeks went by and she didn't work it off. She felt awful particularly in the mornings, was hardly eating at all, and was gradually losing weight.

I'd promised not to mention her illness to my partners but now, realising how poorly she was getting, she reluctantly agreed to let Steve Maxwell see her. Steve was round in an hour. I realised why his patients were so devoted to him: just to have him in the house was a great comfort. As soon as he had opened the door, I knew that everything was going to be all right.

He went up to the bedroom where he examined Pam and listened to her history, then came down to me. He had a half smile on his face which I thought was unlike him when a patient, especially Pam, was so obviously ill.

'Before making a complete diagnosis we'd better just check Pam's water,' he said, 'but I don't think it's too much to worry about.'

How often had I said this to patients before, thinking I was reassuring them? If Steve said it wasn't too much to worry about, it probably meant that there *was* something to worry about, and I was one of the world's greatest worriers.

It took two days for the test on Pam's urine to come back, and Steve called me in to his surgery that morning. I was full of anxiety when I went in.

'My diagnosis is confirmed,' he said, 'and I'm surprised that a bright young medical rising star like you didn't think of it straight away.

'Pam's condition is quite curable. I don't know quite how long her symptoms are going to continue, particularly her sickness. But from my estimation, in about seven months' time she will be completely cured of anything to do with this particular problem – although she might have new responsibilities and extra things to take care of.'

It didn't strike me for a minute what he was trying to tell me, and then I realised – Pam was pregnant. Whereas with every woman patient of childbearing age I would have thought of it straight away, I had missed the obvious when it came to looking after my own wife.

Pam took it all in her stride after her initial sickness, which ended after about twelve weeks. She went her full nine months and went conveniently into labour one Saturday afternoon when I was off duty. I took her over to Winchcombe and she was delivered by lunchtime the next day.

Steve had thought it not a good idea for her to be looked after by one of the partners. He said, 'It's so difficult when you are making medical decisions about people you know very well, particularly people whom you work with. Your judgment can be impaired by the emotional involvement.' Happily, as everything turned out, no judgments were really called for.

I was having lunch with Kevin and Janice, and our old friends Frank and Primrose, when we heard the news that Pam had given birth to a seven and a half-pound boy. We dashed over to Winchcombe and there was Pam looking as if she had been a mother all her life, with a sort of horrible pink bawling thing – Trevor – nestling in the crook of her arm.

Life changed when Trevor came home. I had to get used to damp nappies and interrupted nights, but we fared better than most. Trevor was one of the most docile, placid and self-contained babies I had ever met. As he grew older we would put him in his play pen and he was perfectly content to sit and watch the world go by.

When Trevor was three years old, Pam began again to have the symptoms of sickness and loss of appetite. This time I was able to make the diagnosis without calling for a second opinion – Pam was pregnant again.

Whereas her pregnancy with Trevor had been smooth, with this pregnancy she had all sorts of upsets. There was a false alarm that she was going to go into labour early. The date on which she was expecting to be delivered came and went. Another week passed, and then a second week, and we were beginning to despair.

On my Sunday off, we took the car out and went for a ride along one of the bumpiest tracks we could find in the practice – and by two o'clock the next morning Pam had started in labour.

We had nobody to leave Trevor with, so we wrapped him up in the back of the car for the ten-mile drive to Winchcombe. The atmosphere in the car was tense: Pam was gritting her teeth through the contractions, and I was hunched, grim-faced, over the steering wheel. There was a strained silence which was suddenly broken by the piping voice of Trevor saying, 'We haven't had swede for lunch lately, have we?'

At this, Pam and I both roared with laughter. It took away all the tension and the worry of getting her to hospital in time. We toyed with the idea of calling the new arrival 'Swede', but we didn't think we'd get away with it.

We arrived at the hospital at five o'clock in the morning, and

were met by a grumpy, breathless midwife who examined Pam while I waited.

'You doctors are all the same,' the midwife said to me after the examination. 'Rushing in with your wives before they have started in labour. She'll be hours yet – she hasn't even begun. The best thing *you* can do is go home.'

Crestfallen, I took Trevor back home. I couldn't go to sleep. At quarter past six the phone rang and the grumpy midwife was on the line.

'What's the matter?' I said, alarmed, thinking that at the very least she was ringing me to tell me to bring Pam home again.

'You've got another boy,' she said.

'You told me she wasn't in labour,' I said.

'Oh, the enema I gave her brought it on,' said Mrs Grumpy, determined not to be caught out.

And so Paul was born.

*　　　*　　　*

Of all the things in my life, I cannot think of anything more important, or which has given me more pleasure, than my children. Pam and I have been lucky that the children have always

77

got on well together and always been extremely fond of each other. Trevor welcomed his new little brother home joyfully. He was going through the three-year-old's passion for hats – almost a fetish – and spent many happy hours putting hats on the new arrival. A baby brother was a live, moveable object on which he could place any one of his collection of hats and admire them from his customary Buddha-like position.

Whereas Trevor had been quiet and docile, Paul was noisy. He had us awake at night, worried the life out of us, and was completely different in nature. Though they were so different, they were complementary. Trevor was hard-working, devoured books, and read anything he could lay his hands on from the earliest age. Paul was about as unacademic as it is possible to be, never read anything and lived in a world of dreams with a virile imagination. Strangely, he was always meticulous in the care of the equipment of whichever sport in which he was going to represent England at the time, whether it was cricket, hockey, or football.

Having children of my own gave me a much greater depth of understanding of the problems that women had with their babies, and the problems of the babies themselves. Before I became a father, I had nonchalantly advised mothers how to cope with a baby who cried at night, a baby who was constipated, a baby who wouldn't take its food. Dealing with my own children was another problem altogether, and I was always asking Nurse Plank what was the right thing to do.

Nurse Plank had taken care of Pam and both boys as soon as they had come home from hospital. She was an absolute godsend. I wished I could have kept her in the house. Despite all my experience and my supposed knowledge, if either of the babies wasn't crying I was always poking in the cot to see if they had stopped breathing. If either *was* crying, I was always rushing in to see if anything was wrong.

Pam had made friends with a widow, Margaret Buck, and her daughter Sally. Sally was about four years older than Trevor and behaved like an elder sister towards both boys. Over the years, Margaret and Sally became part of the family. Margaret, the ever-generous, came on many family holidays with us. We used to pull her leg about her habit of walking round with her handbag open, eager to pay for everything that was going.

Just a few months after Paul was born, Zara, Pam's other close friend, had her first baby, Nicholas. The extrovert Zara had had a quiet wedding. Whether she had been put off by our wedding, or the fact that it was her dress design that led to the bridesmaids' see-through dresses, I don't know, but she abandoned all ideas of a large wedding of her own. She had threatened Eric with all sorts of fancy weddings, including one at which he'd have to wear a white suit and a white top hat, but one day they just slipped off on their own to a register office and came back married.

*   *   *

Pam and I went through most of the heartbreaks that other parents experience on seeing their children first go off to school. From the back window of our house we could just see to the yard of the primary school, which lay to one side of Fred Derrigan's smallholding. On Trevor's first day I caught Pam at the bedroom window with tears streaming down her cheeks.

We both looked together into the school yard and there was a group of boys playing. Standing on the outside hopping on one foot, wanting to join them but not knowing how to, was Trevor, all on his own.

'Come away, darling,' I said. 'He'll settle in in no time' – trying to hide the fact that I was feeling very choked up myself.

The first day at school of one's first child is so traumatic. In the past I'd reassured mothers and patted them comfortingly on the head, not understanding why they were getting upset. The children were just going off for the day and they'd be back in the evening. Having it happen to one's own children was a very, very different proposition. Although I'd always examined children with care, I examined them with even more care once I had children of my own.

*   *   *

When Paul was quite young, Pam decided to resume her amateur stage activities. On one of the first dates we ever had, I had to go and see her performing as a maid with the Fetcham Players, a company from near Leatherhead, very much on a par with the Tadchester Drama Society.

Pam would pop off two or three nights a week to rehearsals in Tadchester. She would get my evening meal ready and leave it in the oven if I wasn't back in time. I was quite happy about it all and glad she was taking part in the town's activities. Apparently her experience in Fetcham counted very highly in Tadchester and she was to play the lead in the next production. Things went well until four weeks before the opening night, when Pam came down to breakfast feeling poorly. There were two large tell-tale swellings behind her ears.

'Look Bob – whatever's happened to me? Am I allergic to something?'

'No,' I said. 'I'm afraid you've got mumps – you ought to be ashamed of yourself.'

Sometimes infectious diseases play strange tricks. Among the young mothers in Tadchester that year there was an epidemic of mumps. Although Paul and Trevor were often in bed with Pam in the early morning, and I am sure many of the other children at Trevor's school were in their mothers' beds, none of the children caught mumps. But many of the adults did, and they were very poorly with it.

So Pam, with her stage production looming, was confined to the house and feeling very ill. Margaret Buck came over to help as often as she could, despite the fact that she was frightened of catching mumps herself.

'How long will I take to get better?' Pam kept on asking, worried at the prospect of letting the whole drama company down.

I didn't look after her myself, but left it in the hands of Steve Maxwell. After two weeks, he allowed Pam to get up, but not to go out. With the production now only a fortnight away, the Society was desperate, so it was decided that rehearsals would be held in our lounge. We had quite a large lounge which opened on to a dining room, separated by a huge hanging curtain. Although it didn't make an ideal setting, the players could rehearse and make a show of drawing the curtain back and presenting their play.

Herbert Barlow, who always swore that he wouldn't have anything to do with amateurs, came along and helped them with their direction and lines and advised them about scenery.

Steve said Pam would be fit enough to leave the house and actually appear in the play the following week, but she would have to continue rehearsing at home almost to the last minute.

With rehearsals going every night for two weeks, I had to fend for myself when I came in in the evening. The house was full of strangers. I would go into the kitchen and find the odd person lifting the lid of the pan in which I was trying to cook a meal, just to check what I was having for dinner.

I breathed a sigh of relief when at last the drama society left the house. I had Pam to myself for a whole Sunday – and then she disappeared for a whole week, appearing first at the Tadchester Hall and then at the Plaza Cinema, Winchcombe.

I went over on the last night with Gerry and Bill, Pam's father and mother, who were looking at houses in the area and staying in Winchcombe. I had to watch Pam embraced, a bit too lovingly I thought, by her leading man who I recognised as a bearded clerk from the Surveyor's office at the town hall.

'She was only the Town Clerk's daughter,' I thought grimly, 'but she let the Borough Surveyor.'

I only hoped for his sake the bearded clerk didn't turn up at my surgery with a boil to be lanced.

Pam finished the play's run triumphant. She'd been a great success in the part, and there were demands for her to appear in the next production. But the whole five weeks had left me an exhausted wreck. I didn't know whether I could stand any more of it.

'Pam,' I said – as we got to bed after a party with the cast, at which everybody had gone round kissing everybody and calling everybody *Darling* – 'it's all a bit too much for a simple GP. I vastly admired you in your first two productions – Paul and

Trevor – but I can't be certain that I am quite as delighted with this latest production.'

'Oh, goody,' said Pam. 'You mean we should concentrate on more children?'

9

Death of a Child

For the first two or three years after the birth of Paul, life was at its best. I couldn't remember there ever being a better time. I cannot recall anything bringing more joy than having children of my own, and watching them grow up.

Pam's father, Gerry, retired. He and Pam's mother, May – who for some reason we always called Bill – came to live at Winchcombe. They were always prepared to come and babysit or look after the children when we went away on holiday.

Bill was a marvellous person. She was crippled with arthritis, always in pain, and had had two major operations on her hips. This was before the days of artificial hip replacements. In spite of her pain, she was never down in spirits and was a wonderful help to Pam with the growing boys.

Gerry settled down in this new area, fishing, shooting, and occasionally dragging me out for a game of golf.

Herbert Barlow would also babysit for us at any time. He acted as an uncle to the two boys. After a series of marriages, Herbert had lost touch with his own children and my boys took the place of the family he used to have.

He was a great asset to the household. He made toys for the children and was instrumental in getting Paul to start walking by making him a wheeled contraption with which he could propel himself round. As well as making household furniture, Herbert was a skilled tailor – a legacy of the days when he stage managed in the theatre – and would make dresses for Pam and shirts for me from offcuts of material he picked up in the market.

With the children and home secure, we were able to take a marvellous holiday with Janice and Kevin Bird.

My Morris Minor, the first car that I had owned, I had run into the ground. It was like losing an old friend but I was very proud of my new A40, with its Italian-designed body, the first of its kind in Tadchester.

We loaded the A40 to bursting point and drove to Newhaven. There we watched my precious car being swung by crane on to the boat, to pick it up at Dieppe and then drive down through France and Spain to a villa we had hired in Loret del Mar.

Knowing that we would be staying in the villa for most of the holiday, we had taken the bare essentials, and had a hilarious time camping on the way down.

I had left Kevin to equip us with a tent, and at our first camping site I saw it for the first time. It was a small, square, ridge pole tent, spotlessly white, somehow typically British, and to emphasise this had a Union Jack sewn firmly on its side.

The sleeping arrangements were quite hysterical. The four of us could just squeeze into the tent, lying side by side. There was no slack space to be taken up. If one turned during the night, it meant we all had to turn. Janice and Kevin were going through one of their heavier periods at that time and could muster about twenty-eight stone between them.

The French and other Continentals on the camping sites, with all their sophisticated camping gear, used to look in amazement as four people rolled out of this tiny tent. Through the day they watched every move that we made in total disbelief. A Frenchman with a tent opposite ours used to eat his meals outside with his eyes glued on us. He would shovel food into the corner of his mouth furthest away from us so that his feeding hand never interfered with his vision. Once he became so engrossed that a forkful of food finished up in his ear.

Kevin and I, early one evening, decided to go fishing. We asked the girls for the stale bread we knew we had, for bait, to be

84

told that it had already been thrown away. Followed by the startled eyes of our conscientious watcher opposite, Kevin and I walked to the waste bin, fished out a loaf of bread, and walked back to the tent. Our onlooker's eyes nearly dropped from their sockets. *Les pauvres Anglaises!* Obviously things in Britain were worse than he'd suspected.

When we returned from our fishing trip we found Janice flaked out on an airbed outside the tent with Mediterranean tummy. Our faithful Briton-watcher was nodding his head knowingly. That's what happens when you start eating bread you have picked out of the dustbin . . .

Our villa in Loret del Mar was luxurious and terribly cheap, as were food, wine and cigars, particularly cigars. I could buy six large ones for a shilling.

Loret at this time was a small Spanish fishing town, with new hotels only just beginning to appear. We had a marvellous holiday, swam in the Mediterranean, cooked barbecues in the garden of our villa, and stocked ourselves up with local leather produce – shoes, slippers and handbags – and filled all the empty spaces in the boot with bottles of wine for the journey home.

We went back via Paris, camped the last two nights in the Bois de Boulogne, and had a day's sightseeing around that magical city.

We split up in Paris, each couple going their own way. Pam and I went to some art galleries and up the Eiffel Tower with just enough money left for what we thought would buy us a small meal. Pam was dying for a cup of tea. It turned out to be the price of the small meal we had so looked forward to. All we had to eat for the day was an omelette that we shared between us.

It was obvious that we weren't as clever with our money as Janice and Kevin. When we came back to the tent in the evening to rejoin them, we had to listen to their description of the three marvellous meals they had eaten that day, which included oysters, steaks, wines and gateaux. It was too much for me. I sprang on an old crust of French bread lying in the corner of the tent and devoured it. This time I really was *le pauvre Anglais*.

We returned from our holiday bronzed and happy, and picked up the boys from their grandparents. They had had such a good time they were almost loath to come away. We came back to our flat to find that Herbert had not only a meal ready for us, but had filled the house with flowers. Life was really beautiful.

Back in Tadchester we saw a great deal of Eric and Zara. Eric and I both fancied ourselves as cooks. We used to take it in turn to produce exotic meals, with Pam and Zara sitting back happily enjoying our various culinary efforts.

We went fishing on the beaches with Frank and Primrose, and introduced Phil and Joan to this new art. I was very heavily involved with the Round Table and all their festivities, carnivals, parties; there didn't seem a minute to spare. Life was full and I couldn't wish to live in a better place, surrounded by better people. I got on well with my partners and enjoyed both the practice and the hospital work. It was a glorious summer that year and we spent as much time as we could on the beach and in the sea. It looked as if the good things would go on for ever. But I was to learn . . .

*   *   *

Amongst my medical duties I shared the emergency anaesthetics with Jack Hart, week in and week about. Henry Johnson made himself available to do the emergency surgery practically all the time; just occasionally he allowed one of the Winchcombe surgeons to deputise and give him a night off.

I was called one weekend by Henry to the hospital to give an anaesthetic in an emergency operation. 'A bad one here, Bob,' said the gruff Henry. 'You may need Jack Hart to give you a hand.'

Jack and I shared the emergency anaesthetics but whenever there was a difficult case we worked in tandem. Two pairs of hands were better than one if somebody was very ill and drips and intravenous transfusions had to be put up.

I went to the hospital straight away, and was shown a delightful three-year-old, golden-haired boy. He was obviously very ill, with acute appendicitis and peritonitis. He was in a very poor condition and it was going to be a fight to get this little lad through.

It was part of the duties of all of us to give anaesthetics when required, but none of us was fully trained as a qualified anaesthetist. Each year I used to go back to my teaching hospital to do a couple of weeks of anaesthetics to keep me up with the latest trends, but there was always the possibility that there might be some technique that I didn't know.

This used to worry me, but Jack Hart was always a great comfort. He'd been giving anaesthetics for many years and had never had any trouble.

The anaesthetics available for children in those days were very limited, and consisted mainly of a mixture of chloroform and ether. We didn't have all the wonderful new relaxant drugs that are available now.

This little mite was all togged up ready for his operation. He looked like a little golden-haired elf. As we came to him (and it was the only time it ever happened to me in medicine) he put his arms up and said, 'Can I kiss you, Doctor Daddy?' Jack and I both had to be kissed by this little chap before we could start the anaesthetic.

The boy was very ill all through the operation. Henry, working quickly, removed the offending appendix. He was stitching up when the little boy collapsed and began to behave in a way that I'd never known an anaesthetised patient behave before.

He started to convulse. It was a very muggy night and the theatre was hot, so we began to cool him by spongeing him down. His condition deteriorated and we started all the procedures available for the resuscitation of a collapsed patient. I put a tube into his lungs and began mechanically to respire him. Although I could keep him going, he didn't appear to improve. Henry rang for the consultant anaesthetist from

Winchcombe to come over, and we continued with our respiring.

Slowly the little boy began to respond. His colour improved, but he was not able to maintain his breathing without help. I was very relieved when the consultant anaesthetist from Winchcombe arrived and took over the whole situation.

He changed the tube that I had put into the lungs for a bigger one. As he did so, the little patient collapsed again. We couldn't find his pulse and the colour drained from him. We tried all the methods of resuscitation – cardiac massage, oxygen, injections – to no avail.

The little patient died.

I couldn't believe it. This was the appealing, golden-haired elf who, only an hour earlier, had insisted upon giving me a kiss.

Life from this point on became an absolute nightmare.

I had to go and break the news of the boy's death – he was an only child – to his parents. Though I broke the news to them as gently as I could, it was naturally all too much for them. They ran screaming round the room, howling dementedly like stricken animals. It was some time before I was able to get them to take a sedative, and the only effect that had was to change their howls of grief into deep, painful sobs.

Over the weeks, I had to give the parents as much support as I possibly could. Daily I grieved, not only for the little boy, but for the parents, and for myself. This was the sort of thing that happens only to other people.

The post-mortem examination revealed that the little boy had died of ether convulsions. This is a situation that usually happens only in the tropics and would never happen in this day and age with such different anaesthetics and modern techniques.

I had to go through the harrowing ordeal of a coroner's court, give evidence, and look after the distraught parents when the hearing was over. The verdict was that death was brought about through natural causes and no blame was put on the doctors. On the contrary, we were praised for our efforts. But that was small consolation . . .

I could not get over the death of the little boy. I began to question myself, to question medicine, and was prepared to tell my tale of woe to anyone. All the time the memory of those screaming parents horrified me.

I somehow got through my work. I used to come home and sit staring into space, or leafing through the *British Medical Journal*, looking for jobs. I hardly spoke to Pam and ignored the children who, sensing something awful had happened, kept quiet and went off to play out of sight whenever I came in. I just didn't know how I was going to get through this one.

Henry Johnson called me into his surgery two weeks after the death.

'Bob, lad,' he said, 'I want you to anaesthetise a case for me this afternoon. And I want you to anaesthetise for me regularly for the next few weeks.'

I realised what he was trying to do, but the thought of it terrified me.

As he said he would, Henry called on me for every anaesthetic case that came in. Each operation was an absolute agony for me. I would sit by the bedside after the patients had been returned from theatre, waiting until they became conscious again. Every anaesthetic I gave was a nightmare, but I had to sit it out and sweat it through.

Always Jack Hart was somewhere in the background, stepping in and keeping an eye on things. And there was always Henry Johnson saying, 'Come on, lad. You're doing fine.' But after every successful operation the old grief returned.

It was Steve Maxwell, my senior partner, who finally got me on my feet again. All the way through he had been a comforting, reassuring presence. He had shared my duties with the bereaved parents, giving the special comfort that he exuded from his own personality.

'Bob,' he said, 'the time has come to be firm with you. You've had your agonies, but we all have them. Henry has to suffer the loss of a patient perhaps once a month – a patient for whom he has done all he can to keep alive. Some things are beyond us and we have to accept them.

'You have nothing to reproach yourself for. You have to get up and about again, and live normally. It's not fair to Pam, the patients, your children, or the practice.'

It was the first time I had heard Steve speak sternly, if that is what it could be called. It really shook me. I mumbled an apology.

'Forget it,' he said. 'Just get out and get on with your work. Try and get back to being the happy man you were before this happened.'

Steve's talk was a tremendous help. With time, I slowly got back into the swing of things. But I never enjoyed anaesthetics again. Eventually, as Winchcombe Hospital grew, more full-time surgeons were appointed and their full-time consultant anaesthetists were in attendance. One of these anaesthetists had to spend half his time at Tadchester and after twelve-months I was able to give up anaesthetising.

But as long as I live I shall never ever forget the small golden-haired boy, who reached out and said, 'Can I kiss you, Doctor Daddy?' just before I was to put him to sleep, into a sleep from which he was never going to wake . . .

Soliloquy at Evening Surgery

The death of that child had shattered me almost irrevocably.

For months I went over and over again in my mind the sequence of events of that dreadful day, tracking back over every detail of the operation in an attempt to discover if and where I had made a mistake. I think that subconsciously I *wanted* it to be my fault. Taking the burden of guilt might be some kind of atonement, even some sort of reparation to the parents for the agony of their grief.

I was within an ace of giving up medicine altogether, of going back down the coal-mines where I had served my time as a Bevin Boy, of going into retreat, of becoming a missionary: of doing any one of a dozen things which would take me away from this awful and awesome area of responsibility and allow me to pay at least some of the debt I felt I owed.

But, being as critical as I could of myself, my colleagues, the equipment and the procedures of the operation, I could not lay blame. It was literally a million-to-one chance. There was the combination of warm, muggy weather, a little-known side effect of ether, and a constitutionally susceptible patient. With hindsight, it appeared that the child might well have reacted the same way, whatever the weather. But then there was no way of telling. And now there was no way of knowing.

It is a rare general practitioner who is unaffected by death, familiar as it becomes over the years. The loss of a patient – even of one whose illness is obviously terminal, or whose life has run well beyond its allotted span – is a personal loss. Afterwards, there are always the self-doubts, the silent questions. Could I have done more? Could I have spotted the signs any earlier? Dare I have risked one of the new drugs whose possible adverse effects were not yet proven?

In the professional life of every GP there is always at least one death which shakes him to the roots of his being: a death totally unexpected, and often inexplicable, of someone who had every reason and every right to live.

I have not laid the ghost of that child, nor ever will. What I *have* been able to do, with time, is to come to some sort of terms with it. Some sort of terms, too, with the whole of my medical work.

It is easy for a general practitioner to feel depressed. He has a strenuous working life, with a high responsibility factor, spent entirely in contact with sick people. His company is sought only by the unwell. If somebody is happy, healthy, coping, achieving or being successful by any definition at all, he does not seek out his doctor.

In his blacker moments a GP can see himself living in a half world in a half light, populated by ailing, inadequate and often hopeless people. In a seemingly endless stream, these people come along and raid his own physical, mental and emotional reserves, which by the end of the day are almost always near to exhaustion anyway.

Often, at the end of an evening surgery, I will spend a few quiet minutes mentally soliloquising, recapitulating on the day and getting things back into perspective.

A great help in dealing with a pompous, arrogant or aggressive patient whose personality is threatening to overwhelm the whole consultation, is the advice given to me once by an uncle: imagine him sitting on the toilet. Suddenly, this loud, overbearing, perhaps nasty piece of work, is reduced to human scale and I can concentrate on the real issue of what ails him.

If I am treating a nice character, a good character, an honest, hard-working, cheerful or creative one, I can think beyond the actual treatment to the life-style of the patient, and feel glad that I am making some contribution to its comfort or continuance. When I am injecting the piles, say, of an artist – be he writer, painter, sculptor, musician or singer – I think of the joy of his art, not of the sordid job of the moment.

Faced with the piles of a character towards whom I feel antipathetic – one of the pompous, arrogant or aggressive ones perhaps – I am faced simply with piles. These I treat competently, professionally and gently. But one third, perhaps even two thirds, of my mind is metaphorically looking out of the window.

During the mechanical procedure of treatment the saving third of my mind is busy in my garden, mending my seine fishing net, casting a spinner across the nose of a lurking salmon, making a golf shot or composing a speech for a Rotary dinner.

Now and again I get some really bad hat as a patient and I wonder why I am taking all this trouble. A wife-beater, perhaps, with fibrositis of the right shoulder. I treat him, make him well – and for what? To be fit enough to beat his wife again?

According to the Hippocratic Oath, of course, I should not be asking questions like this. But now and again even Hippocrates must have wondered what it was all about.

Many patients do not come for treatment of a physical ailment, even if they have managed to produce a physical or psychosomatic condition as the excuse. They come because they want to be told what to do. They have reached a point of stagnation or unease in their lives and they want advice. The cause of the unease can be almost anything – money, sex, marriage, career, life-style – and often they themselves do not know. But they feel uneasy and they come along in the expectation of a magic formula which will solve the problem.

Even if they are not sure of the question, they want an answer. I don't know the answer. They don't know the answer. Possibly there is no answer. But I am expected to give it.

The common denominator of such patients is that they lack direction. All I can do is to point them in one. It may not be the direction in which they want to go. Often it has to be a short term direction, such as just clearing off for at least forty-eight hours to a place they have never visited before. But any direction is better than none. It breaks the pattern in which they have become trapped. It gives them a view from the outside of their own condition and surroundings. It breaks the inertia in which they have been sitting perhaps for years. It gives them some momentum. They are on the move again. And once on the move, they are much better fitted to find a direction of their own.

*　　　*　　　*

So often I sit there after evening surgery, checking on my own bearings, adjusting my own direction.

I have no authority, other than that which my medical skills command. I have no wisdom, other than that which I have acquired slowly and often painfully over the years. I have no sincerity – no, perhaps that's not quite fair.

I feel the lack of sincerity when I have to make tactful pronouncements about a condition which is self-inflicted. I cannot tell patients that they are suffering from whatever because they are idle, greedy, self-indulgent, neglectful or weak willed. I cannot say to an overweight woman, convinced that the trouble lies in her 'glands': 'You are fat because you are greedy. You eat too much. Eat less. And get off your backside and do some work for a change.' I have to be diplomatic, couch the diagnosis in phrases which would do credit to an ambassador, and break the terms of the cure more gently.

Often I have to tell an outright lie about a condition: perhaps a cancer which may or may not respond to treatment, but with the knowledge of which the patient would obviously not be able to cope. This is not really insincerity: it is tailoring the revelation to the mental or emotional resilience of the patient.

For some of the time I *can* be sincere. I can tell a patient straight, and without beating about the bush, what is wrong and what the treatment will involve. Patients such as these – and sometimes one has to be almost a mind reader to judge – do a lot to restore one's faith in humanity.

94

But for much of the time I look upon myself as an insincere Solomon, reaching into the reserves of my energy, doling out handsful of my own substance in an effort to keep people on the move. I realise that with some individuals the limit of. my achievement is to assist them over a stile, knowing that my help will only last until the next stile. If they can't get over that one unaided, they'll be back again for another piece of me.

However much I would like to, I cannot swim around the great lake of life supporting people in the water. All I can do is to throw lifebelts to some who look as if they might drown.

Sometimes the soliloquy takes all sorts of odd turns. I can recognise quality in people, but am not articulate enough to name it. I believe that hard work is the salt of life and that without it everything would lose its savour. Some days I seem to know all there is to know, but most days I know nothing at all.

So it goes on, in those few precious minutes of quietness after evening surgery. The thinking is often not logical, seldom conclusive, but it does help to loosen the grip of tension and blow away the mists of depression.

In recognising tension and depression after a gruelling day's work, I am naming the villains. Once named, they lose their power. I begin to recognise in the people of the day all sorts of qualities I had not noticed before, and they rise in stature as the recognition dawns.

Slowly my equilibrium returns. And by stepping on the jumble of my thoughts, climbing over the mental and emotional debris of an exhausting day, I have risen a plane. I can once again see the beauty and purpose of all things. And leave the excreta of my mind behind.

I I

Can't I go Down the Mine, Daddy?

Thudrock Colliery was to close. The announcement in the *Tadchester Echo* came as a tremendous blow to the town. Most of the Thudrock work force came from Tadchester and formed a sizeable part of the working population.

The original shaft of Thudrock had been sunk in 1905 and the pit had continued to produce coal uninterruptedly for more than fifty years. Now the coal was getting more difficult and more expensive to get out and the National Coal Board decided to close the colliery.

The closure was to be phased over a period of six months. Although people had felt for some time that this was likely to happen, although there had been lots of coming and going by high officials in the Coal Board, nothing had actually been said and now the whole community was stunned.

There were still a few old-timers who could remember the days before the mine was there, but for the vast majority it had always existed as an essential and integral part of the area. The pit buses used to travel the six miles to and from Tadchester Market Place every hour. I had held a surgery at Thudrock ever since I came to Tadchester, and with the mine closing this small, primitive outpost of medicine would be closing too.

It was interesting that all the miners I ever met, both at

Thudrock and during my own mining days, said they hated coal mining and would do anything to get out of it. Now that the pit was closing, however, it appeared that coal mining was the only thing most of them wanted to do.

I had been a Bevin Boy just after the end of the war and had worked on the coal face for two years. Although the conditions were indescribable and the work extremely hard and difficult in the most uncomfortable surroundings, mining had a dignity and sense of adventure about it, and I would consider coal face workers much in the same way that I do mountaineers. They are fighting the elements, pitting themselves against Nature. The coal face was only as safe as the worst workman on it, and there was a unity and comradeship among coal face workers of the kind found only among men in hazardous callings.

There was little alternative employment in Tadchester. In the rather short summer season, various jobs could be found in the holiday industry, but in the winter there was no other real basic industry for men to work at. On the individual, personal level it was bad enough to see a huge collier having to change from hacking away at the coal face to selling ice-cream or tending deck-chairs on the front, but for the town it was a major disaster. There were protest meetings, suggested sit-ins,

97

letters to the MP, and a campaign conducted by the local paper. Finally one of the complicated Government inducements to industrial firms was offered for the Tadchester area. An electronics factory opened near the coal mine. Just after work started on the site, one of the big international chemical companies decided that there was still some life in the slag heaps that surrounded the village of Thudrock and Thudrock Colliery, and put forward plans to build some huge works to convert the slag heaps into plastic. Apparently Thudrock slag had special qualities that slag heaps at other collieries didn't have.

Over a period of two to three years, both the electronics factory and the plastics factory were in full production. The electronics factory employed more women than men, but the plastics factory employed more people than had ever worked down Thudrock Colliery. But something had gone from the area. The ruggedness of the local miners seemed to disappear when they went to work in clean clothes, some wearing collars and ties. That, coupled with the decline of the fishing industry — only two boats still fished out of Tadchester — changed the character of the area and it became more suburban.

These changes didn't affect the farming community. The farmers were a sturdy, independent lot, and I got to know many of them in the Tadchester Market through my friend Kevin Bird, who was employed by a firm of agricultural auctioneers.

Kevin had been originally farm manager to the de Wyrebocks. Commander and Mrs de Wyrebock had presided over a large house and a huge estate. On the death of Commander de Wyrebock, Mrs de Wyrebock moved away to live with her daughter and son-in-law. Her daughter, Marjorie — whose teeth were almost as large as those of the horses she rode so well — was one of the problems, emotional and medical, that I had to cope with in my earlier days in the practice. I was lucky to escape the altar, the fate that Marjorie had in mind for me.

When the estate was broken up it was bought up by some huge London farming consortium. Kevin didn't relish the prospect of working for someone else on a farm he had managed for years, so he looked around for another job. He was soon snapped up by one of the local agricultural auctioneers and did most of the auctioning in the Tadchester Market.

The cattle market was situated down near the riverside. It had been built since the war, and had well-designed stalls and comfortable accommodation for sheep and cattle. Its one big disadvantage was that it was away from most of the pubs. The old market had been near the pannier market in the upper part of the town. There was a large square which was half pannier market, half cattle market and surrounded by shops and pubs.

I don't think that the publicans minded the moving of trade: in fact the effects were barely noticeable. Tadchester got so crowded on market day that it was hardly worth taking your car into the town. By the time the farmers and traders had walked to the pubs from the new market they were thirstier than they were in the good old days when they could step from the market straight into the pub. Anyway, no-one grumbled.

The farming community had always steered clear of the mining community, and when the colliery closed they each still went their separate ways. Very few of the colliers looked for jobs in farming. Although they had complained for years about the horrors of working underground, they'd got so used to it that the thought of working out in the open didn't appeal to them.

The only times the farmers and miners really got together were at the point-to-point meetings. The local farmers' point-to-point race meetings were held in the spring and late autumn. It was traditional for the colliery to shut down on the first Monday in May and the first Monday in October, and the two days were real festive occasions. The October holiday was also timed to coincide with the Tadchester Agricultural Show.

The Show was held later than most agricultural shows but for some strange reason always was blessed with good weather. If you wanted to make sure that your holiday week had good weather, you timed it to coincide with Tadchester Agricultural Show. But if you went away on holiday you missed the Show and that – along with the annual Tadchester Fair, Rowing Regatta and the Cattle Show – was an annual event no Tadchesterian would miss.

There were equestrian events at the Agricultural Show and some of the best riders in the land took part. One or two locals had reached the top in this particular sport and one from near Dratchet had actually been in the British 1948 Olympic show-jumping team.

I had to take Henry Johnson's place as Medical Officer to the Agricultural Show this year. Henry had been asked by the Town Council to be Mayor of Tadchester for one year: a great compliment. Normally only Council members were elected Mayor under some order of seniority. This particular year the rival factions in the Council both put up a man. Neither would accept the other's choice, so it was decided to go outside the Council and Henry was chosen.

*　　*　　*

With Henry Johnson as Mayor we were short handed in the practice and decided to engage a locum. We found a retired army medical officer who had spent most of his days practising medicine in East Africa.

Dr Jumbo Edwards was a huge man in his late sixties. Somehow he fitted himself into a huge old Humber car which was crammed with medical samples, bottles of medicine, cases, cardboard boxes and a whole variety of other odds and ends.

He became noted for his two favourite questions. As well as exploring somebody medically, he would ask for the spelling of a set of difficult words. They were so difficult that apparently only about two per cent of the population got them right in their first attempt. Jumbo also had a standard question he liked to ask farmers, which was: 'Are a cow's ears in front or behind its horns?'

If a patient was not too ill and had time on his hands, struggling through the spelling was quite fun. With the question about the cows' horns and ears, he had a fifty per cent chance of getting it right. But I began to have complaints. There were patients who were gasping for air with pneumonia, whose lips had turned blue and who thought their last moment had come – and who, instead of being given oxygen or a penicillin injection, were submitted to a spelling test.

One farmer's wife said, 'There was my husband, nearly at death's door. He'd had a coronary and we were waiting for the ambulance – and Dr Edwards kept on asking which was in front on a cow's head, the ears or the horns. My husband couldn't answer – he was almost unconscious. Why couldn't Dr Edwards go and look at a cow and find out for himself?'

While we were being helped out by Dr Jumbo, part of Tadchester Bridge fell away and was out of action for three months. This cut the town in two and separated the westward part of the town from the world in general. By car you could get to the other side of the river only by doing a twenty-five-mile detour round country lanes through Dratchet, but you still were allowed to walk across the bridge. So the practice hired a car to keep on the Up-the-Hill side of the bridge. We left our cars on the Down-the-Hill side then walked across to use the other car.

One day when Dr Jumbo was on duty, he was called Up-the-Hill to see some cases. The first was a patient who lived in a cottage at the far end of a wood yard that stretched for a mile along the banks of the Tad. It was quite close to the bridge so Jumbo spurned the use of the car on the other side. It would have been difficult to get his six-foot-two, eighteen-stone frame into it anyway. He set off in the rain with his case in his hand. The wood yard seemed to go on and on. It was raining heavily, Jumbo wasn't as young as he used to be, and his case got heavier with every step.

By the time he got to his call, Jumbo was soaked through and exhausted. The patient he had called to see had to rub him down, dry his clothes, give him tea and brandy, get out his own car and drive him to the other two visits on that side of the river.

It was too much for poor Jumbo: he was in bed for a fortnight with a chest infection. Reluctantly he resigned from his locum and went back to do a three-month spell in the sunnier climes of his beloved East Africa. We could all imagine him out there, still asking silly questions about cows' ears – and setting tricky spelling problems in Swahili.

* * *

We were fortunate enough to get as a replacement a young, newly qualified Oxford running blue, called Ron Dickinson. He stayed on after Henry's term of office, becoming junior partner and increasing our number to five.

The plastics factory had brought more labour into the town and the practice had expanded to the extent that we needed an extra pair of hands. Steve Maxwell had indicated that he didn't want to do quite as much as he used to do, and had begun to cut down.

Ron Dickinson was one of the most athletic men I have ever met. He was always bouncing about, involved in every athletic pursuit that the local area had to offer. He would run with the harriers, play rugby, cricket, sail, swim, water-ski and play squash. If he was ever missing, a quick ring round the local sporting establishments would soon find him.

It was disconcerting in later years, when we'd built a house just outside Tadchester by the river, to look out of the window and see Ron go by on his water skis. Pam would look at me quizzically.

'Who's on duty?'

'Oh, Ron,' I'd say. 'I think I must have said I'll stand in for him.'

* * *

Henry made a magnificent job of Mayor. He was always a good speaker: in fact the difficulty usually was in stopping him speaking. The one problem was that, at over six foot, he was taller than most mayors. Although some of the regalia had to be made for him, Tadchester couldn't fully re-equip him for just one year, so some of the mayoral garb was a bit short in the sleeves. The beaverskin hat worn traditionally by the Mayor – a remnant of Tadchester's ancient link with the Newfoundland cod trade – was far too small for him.

Henry flagged a bit towards the end of his year. He was still doing some work at the surgery and some operating at the hospital. Seeing him looking pale at the end of surgery one day, I enquired what the matter was.

'Sauterne and bloody chicken, lad,' he replied.

Henry had worked out that of the 220 dinners he had been to during the year he had Sauterne wine and chicken at 120.

Young Ron fitted well into the practice and had the same problems as I had with lady suitors when I first arrived in Tadchester. Most of his admirers seemed to come down from London, whereas mine had been local. After a couple of years of struggling to maintain his independence he succumbed and married Jeanette Upton, a delightful daughter of one of the local bank managers.

Although Steve Maxwell had said he was reducing his work, he still came in every Sunday. He decided that as he was reducing his work he ought to reduce his holidays. So he took a fortnight's less holiday than we did and he now lived outside Tadchester with old Dr Watts and his wife. Dr Watts had been the senior partner before Steve.

Dr and Mrs Watts had a few acres of ground that Steve used to work on with all sorts of modern agricultural devices. He never seemed to want to go too far away on holiday. He used to say that he would plant his potatoes in his first fortnight's spring holiday, and spend the second fortnight of his leave in the autumn digging them up. He always remained the same selfless smiling Steve, and looking after his potatoes was all the leisure activity he ever seemed to want to do.

We were all invited with our wives to Henry's final mayoral banquet. Ron, still single at this time, and by far the junior member of the practice, was full of beer at the end of the lengthy speeches. It seemed that anybody and everybody remotely connected with the mayoral office in the town had spoken. Then Ron got up, staggered towards Henry, clutching a brown box, and said, 'A special remembrance present Mr Mayor, from your junior partner.'

Henry opened the box with some embarrassment – and found two unplucked chickens, tied carefully round a bottle of Sauterne . . .

I 2

Creatures of Habit

I would not have missed for anything my weekly philosophical chats with Bob Barker at the bookshop at Sanford-on-Sea. He had great wisdom and most times I visited him he would take up a subject and then would explore it.

One day, as usual, his smiling face looked over the desk at me.

'Coffee and a cigar, Bob?' he said – he had obviously been waiting for me to come – and launched forth with today's subject: 'Creatures of Habit'.

'I've always marvelled at the part habit plays in people's lives,' said Bob. 'So many people have a daily, weekly, monthly, annual rhythm which it would be unthinkable to break. More than a few even set the rhythm in advance, planning out their lives over the foreseeable future, listing how every penny is to be spent, where they are going for their holidays, when they are going to change the car, what they will do when the children leave home, and where they will retire to. Their life is patterned out completely before them.

'To some extent it's like the man who learns to drive a bus round a particular route. He knows that from then on he can do this route for the rest of his life, and the only thing he has to do is to keep his nose clean.

'This,' said Bob, 'horrifies me. Take away life's unpredictability, take away all the surprises, know exactly what tomorrow will bring, and what have you left, except a long long yawn? But

I must admit that a lot of people like it that way and seem to prosper on it even if they never are the life and soul of the party.

'When disaster strikes such people they react in different ways. Some refuse to believe that their ordered pattern could possibly be interfered with. You have a situation, say, where the husband comes in and says, "Darling, bad news. The cat's dead." The wife replies, "Impossible, she's only five years old." "Yes," says the husband, "but the lorry didn't know that."

'Other people finding themselves faced with something which was not in their forward planning just go to pieces. It is as if some central nerve has been cut and all the other parts of their life pattern can do nothing but flop around in an uncoordinated and quite bizarre way. Others just ignore any kind of disaster and go on as if nothing had happened. For some it's a life saver, for others it's a bit like the chap whose bicycle had been stolen from outside the house. He was so used to it being there that he rushed out that morning, leapt gaily into the saddle and fell flat on his face.'

I went along with Bob only so far.

'Come off it, Bob,' I said. 'Most people have to find a formula for survival. They form a habit pattern so that there is something they can depend on: they are just not of the disposition to cope beyond a certain area and they are wise living within the confines of their own limitations. Habit is their stabiliser.

'Housewives, for instance, get into a routine while the children are young, feeding, washing, shopping, cleaning, and cooking. This routine is very necessary for the orderly functioning of the household. When circumstances sometimes change, the routine can be hard to break. I have known wives who, for months after the children left home, went on cooking the same amount of food for meals. It resulted in a lot of waste or a great increase in the weight of the parents. Or even chronic indigestion or constipation for both husband and wife.

'At this stage, with their habit broken, people will often produce some medical infirmity. It is a true and real one and it provides something to hide behind. The whole basis of such an illness could possibly be self-induced and I think more and more doctors should treat the whole patient rather than treat the disease: the disease is probably a reflection of the person's situation and state of mind, economic circumstances or whatever.'

Old Bob chuckled. He said, 'I remember our neighbour Lucy Parker was due to go on holiday with her husband and baby son. She had washed, ironed, packed, got everything ready for departure. When the taxi arrived outside the house the breakfast pots had not been washed.

' "Come on," said her husband, who in fairness to Lucy had not done a lot to help. "If we don't leave this second we'll miss the train to Winchcombe and there isn't another to London for hours."

' "I can't leave this house," said Lucy, "until these pots are washed," completely forgetting that the object of the exercise was to get away for a well-earned rest.

' "Look," said her husband, "you get in the taxi with the lad and get the driver to put the cases in. I'll wash the pots and lock up and come out to you."

'Lucy did this, fretting in case her husband didn't wash up properly, but they got away in time to catch their train. That evening in London they decided to have a leisurely stroll up the Mall from Admiralty Arch to Buckingham Palace, then wander in St James's Park and feed the ducks.

'Lucy, with the boy in the pushchair, set off up the Mall at a brisk trot. The husband, who'd been admiring the legs of some Scandinavian girl tourists, suddenly realised this and chased after her.

' "Where are you rushing off to?" he panted. "I don't know," said Lucy – and nor did she. She was so used to rushing round the shops at home, full pelt, that a leisurely stroll now called for a great deal of conscious adjustment.

'However, the holiday did have its effect on Lucy and when she returned home she was a great deal more relaxed. But the tension returned as soon as she opened the kitchen cupboard to make a cup of tea. There before her eyes was a stack of unwashed pots, covered after a fortnight with a green mould and grey fur!

'Her husband had taken the rational man's way out. The holiday was the first priority, the pots didn't matter – so he'd shoved the whole lot dirty into the cupboard and shut the door.'

I followed Bob's story with one about the young husband of a patient of mine. I called him Jack so as not to break any confidences, though Bob didn't know him anyway.

Jack had been brought up in the old tradition of being waited on hand and foot by the womenfolk of the family. As a youngster and as a single man he had never done a stroke of work at home, nor had his father or his brother. When they arrived back from work they ate their meal and stretched out in comfortable chairs in front of the fire.

Mother and sister washed up, brought the coal in – stepping over three pairs of legs to reach the fire – did the ironing and mending, made the supper, and did all the other dozens of things which have to be done.

Jack got married and, although his wife was working full time, assumed that things would remain the same. His wife would lay out his clean clothes in the morning, cook breakfast, wash up, dash off to work in a panic. All Jack ever did was read the morning paper and ask for a cup of tea.

Jack's wife then became pregnant but carried on working. She worked half an hour longer than Jack every day and consequently arrived home after him. One Friday evening in winter, when she was almost seven months pregnant, it snowed heavily. That day she did the week's shopping, scurrying around in her lunch hour and picking up the rest of the food after work. She walked a long way up the hill in a blizzard, aching with cold, and weighed down with two enormous shopping bags.

Meanwhile, back at home, Jack was huddled over a one-bar electric fire with a cup of tea. The fire in the hearth needed lighting, but this was not his job. When he answered the door Joyce stood there, unable to move another step. Seven months pregnant, she was chilled to the bone, aching with fatigue and covered in snow. All she could do was burst into tears.

'Don't just stand there sniffling,' said Jack. 'Where the hell have you been until this time? I've been sitting in here an hour freezing to death, and dying of hunger.'

When Joyce came to see me next morning, I asked her to send Jack along to the afternoon surgery. Jack was in before the end of the *morning* surgery — Tadchester United were playing at home that afternoon, and he wasn't missing the match for anybody.

I kept the lecture short and simple, and direct. Jack was amazed. It had never occurred to him that he could be treating his wife badly at all. From then on, apart from the occasional lapse, he was much more considerate and I like to think that I nipped at least one Andy Capp in the bud.

* * *

When I'd left Bob and got on my rounds I thought of many of the other strange creatures of habit who were patients. There was Arnold Bishop, a bachelor, whose Saturdays always followed the same pattern. He would rise early, clean his tiny flat, eat his breakfast, then start his perambulations.

The round was always the same. First: Tadchester covered market. There he would savour the sights and smells of the fruit, vegetables, fish and meat and perhaps buy something for his tea.

Next: Tadchester Museum. After browsing among the exhibits he would go to the toilet: (a) because it was time, (b) because he had a special fondness for the marble and brass fittings of the Tadchester Museum Gents.

Then a promenade up the High Street, mainly window shopping at the antique shops and browsing in the secondhand book shops. At each shop he would spend exactly the same amount of time as he had done every Saturday for years. When shopkeepers saw him approaching in his slow, abstracted way, they would check their watches and adjust them if they did not correspond to Arnold's regular time of arrival.

A wander through the graveyard of Tadchester Parish

Church and a reading of some of the more interesting tomb-stones was followed by a visit to the church itself. A few minutes were spent in silent prayer, followed by an inspection of the brasses.

Then would come Arnold's pub crawl: four pubs in meas-ured succession and a chat with a different set of cronies – but always the *same* different set of cronies – in each.

In each pub, too, he had a different kind of drink. Lager in one, beer in another, red wine in the next and gin and tonic in the last. What this did to Arnold's constitution I shudder to think, but his constitution was also almost certainly a creature of habit, and well able to cope.

What puzzled me was that between the third and last pub, Arnold always took a peculiar route. He would pass the last pub, walk right to the end of the High Street and stand there for five minutes outside the petrol filling station before walking back to make his last call and savour his gin and tonic.

One day when he came to the surgery with his annual stomach upset and very bad sunburn, I asked Arnold about his dog-leg progress to the last pub.

'Ah yes. Of course, my dear chap,' he said. 'Before your time on that site used to stand a delightful hostelry called the

109

Plough, and it was my custom to call there before doubling back to the Dog and Partridge. A few years ago by some fiendish act of chicanery, it was bought up, its licence revoked, demolished, and that monstrous filling station built on the site. I suppose you could call it a sentimental journey . . .'

For a couple of weeks one winter, Tadchester Market was closed for alterations. It completely wrecked two of Arnold's Saturdays. The following Monday morning saw him in my surgery, edgy and twitching, and asking for something for his 'nerves'. Arnold's survival depended on routine.

Even more bizarre than his routine at home were the reasons for Arnold's annual stomach upset and sunburn. During the war, the only interruption in Arnold's life, he'd spent two years with the RAF in Libya. Every year since he'd taken a fortnight's holiday in the same town in which he was stationed, staying in the same hotel in which he was billeted, laying about on the same beaches that he laid about on as an airman.

Arnold did not like Libya, he did not like the people, he did not like the hotel, and couldn't stand the food or wine, nor was he fond of swimming in the sea or lying about on the beach. His skin was sensitive and any exposure to sun brought it peeling off his shoulders. But at least he knew what he did not like.

He knew that he would complain about the same things that he complained about every year, argue with the same hotel

110

manager. He knew also that his stomach would be dreadfully upset and that his sun-burned skin would cause him agony. If any man ever knew where he stood it was Arnold Bishop, Creature of Habit . . .

*   *   *

Among other extreme examples of creatures of habit were some of the local freshwater anglers, who were nothing if not set in their ways. A tributary of the Tad, the Dipper, was notorious for its unpredictability as an angling river. Some years there would be no fish caught in it at all, and on 'good' years a few sickly and stunted specimens would be pulled out, to be marvelled at by the regulars on the bank.

The anglers on the Dipper were real regulars who had fished it for years with appalling results, yet who refused to move down to the rich pickings in the Tad itself. 'The Dipper Dafties', John Denton, the water bailiff, used to call them.

During his first year as bailiff, John tried telling them that the water was not worth fishing, but the answer was always the same. They'd fished that river, man and boy, and enjoyed every minute of it; there were bigger fish in there than ever came out, and they were blowed if they were going to join the once-a-year fair-weather fishermen on the Tad.

Please yourselves, thought John, and after that he changed his patter. As he checked the fishing tickets of the old boys and listened to their miserable record of non-catches, he would give a knowing wink and say, 'Ah yes. The fish on this river don't give themselves up.' This pleased the old boys no end. The bailiff knew what they knew. To catch anything in the Dipper you had to be something special, and one day patience and skill would be rewarded.

The problem with the Dipper turned out to be pollution, seepage from some old mineworkings near the headwaters. By the time the water mixed with that of the Tad the pollution was dilute enough to have no effect. But on the narrow Dipper it was a killer.

Eventually, the source of the pollution was traced and dealt with, and the fish started moving up the Dipper again. The regular anglers pulled in some real beauties for a whole season and boasted in the local pubs with many an 'I told you so'.

By next season the word had got round, and the banks of the little river were crowded with strangers. In spite of their big catches the old boys grumbled that there was barely space to cast a line and that their once beautiful banks were being covered with all sorts of litter, that things weren't what they used to be, and never would be again.

From late autumn to early spring, there was almost continuous rain, interrupted only by massive snow falls just after Christmas. The Dipper was scoured by a succession of flash floods and all the fish and most of the vegetation were swept down into the Tad.

When the waters finally subsided the pollution had returned. Floods had broken the seals on the mineworkings and the Dipper was back to normal – not a fish to be had. Through the whole of its length the regulars had it all to themselves again, and they sat there day after day with seraphic smiles on their faces, literally happy not to be catching a thing.

They were like so many of us, particularly as we grow older. We like things predictable, don't want things to change. There's probably a little bit of Arnold Bishop in all of us . . .

13

Sex and Side Effects

Apart from its being a prerequisite of the continuance of the human race, sex has always seemed to me a delightful way of communication and I am grateful for the fact that it's here to stay. But it is surprising how many complex problems it brings to the door of a country practitioner.

Whether the problems are more common in a country practice than in town, I don't know, but I feel that in town people probably have more enlightened attitudes towards – and more access to – the sophisticated side of physical communication between people.

Sex, as mankind's most powerful instinct, is bound to bring problems, but the problems are often not with the instinct or the act itself. Rather do they tend to arise from the deviation of the drive or ignorance of the function. A frightening aspect is the number of people who spend years thinking they are abnormal – perhaps out of ignorance, fear or the result of a repressive upbringing – when all they have is a healthy sex drive which they do not understand or for which they have no outlet.

Joshua Verity was a well built young man, dark-haired and good looking, but he had problems.

'Animal appetites, Doctor,' he whispered, glancing round the consulting room in case anyone was listening behind a filing cabinet. 'That's what I've got.'

'What form do they take?' I asked. 'Over-eating?'

'No, animal appetites. You know – *lust*. Lusts of the flesh. *Women*.'

He said the last word with a shiver.

'How old are you?'

'Twenty-one.'

'And when did you first start noticing these appetites?'

'About five years ago, two years before I went into the army for my National Service.'

'And what form did they take?'

'Thoughts. Wicked thoughts. All about women. And dreams, even worse. Dreadful things started to happen in the night. Awful.'

'Nocturnal emissions?'

'Pardon.'

'Wet dreams?'

'Yes, yes. But I couldn't stop them. I couldn't tell anybody. My parents are members of the Apocalyptic Brethren.'

So that was it. Brought up in a very strict religious sect which had strange views on the most normal of happenings. Poor kid.

'Tell me,' I said, 'what happened when you went into the army? Didn't that change your views?'

'Evil! Oh, it was evil. You've no idea. The language. The behaviour. And the films they showed us about what would happen. Horrible!'

I felt a twinge of sympathy. Films on the danger of VD shown by the army to young men were enough to put anybody off sex for life.

'Did you have sex while you were in the army?'

'Of course not. I would have had to answer to my parents and the church elders when I came back.'

'When you came back, what happened?'

'I couldn't settle at home, especially with the guilt I felt about my appetites. So I left. That was about six months ago. Now I'm in digs in Tadchester and I've got a job.

'I tried group therapy, that didn't work. They tried to get me to confess all sorts of things. They talked to me about libidos and ids and things I couldn't understand.'

'Do you have any friends?'

'Not in Tadchester. No.'

'Girl friends anywhere?'

'No. I can't even talk to girls. My animal appetites overcome me, and I can't speak.'

'Can you dance?'

'No. Dancing is forbidden among the Apocalyptics.'

I had to take a chance.

'Right, Joshua,' I said. 'There is nothing wrong with you except a strong sense of guilt, and a lack of normal social relationships. Your animal appetites are nothing more than a normal young man's sexuality. You are, in other words, just plain randy.'

He looked shocked at first at the bluntness, then an expression of pure relief flooded his face.

'Really?'

'Really,' I said. 'Now what I want you to do is to put yourself into circulation. There are several social clubs in Tadchester. You can get a full list of them from the library. Join one, join several, get yourself moving about among people. Force yourself to talk to them. Above all, listen. You've been drawn in on yourself for too long, now you owe it to yourself to relax a little. Have some fun and make friends.

'Tell you what, on your way out have a chat with Jill, the receptionist. She's a member of one or two clubs and she can advise on what might suit you best. Jill's a girl, I know, but you are asking her on my behalf, not yours. Doctor's orders. No need to feel shy – now off you go.'

It was perhaps wicked of me, but if anybody was to help the boy on his road to normality, it was Jill, my healthily sexed young receptionist at evening surgery. And it worked.

I saw no more of Joshua. But a few months later Jill said, 'Jossy sends his regards, Doctor.'

'Jossy, who's Jossy?'

'You know. The holy man. Or former holy man. You know what they say about convent girls once they're let out? That's nothing to what's happened to old Jossy. If I want to see him

EX-HOLY
MAN
—
ANIMAL
APPETITES
—
QUEUE
HERE

now, I've almost got to book an appointment.'

Well, it may not have been medicine, but my God, did it work . . .

*　　*　　*

Ignorance, though in a slightly different form, was the problem of a sweet and innocent young engaged couple who came to see me. They were worried because they knew very little about the mechanics of sex and reproduction, and were to be married in a month.

This was way back in the days when sex education at school was skimpy and any child who missed one particular biology lesson could be left in ignorance of everything except what he or she picked up among the sniggers in the school yard. It seems like another age now, but it wasn't really so long ago.

I got them to call back after evening surgery, gave them the basic sex education talk and recommended a manual for newlyweds.

Twelve months later the young wife, Sheila, visited me again.

She was pregnant.

'I see the instruction manual worked all right then,' I joked.

'Oh yes, Doctor, but we did have trouble the very first night. Jim kept having to turn back to page 34 to see if he was doing it properly.'

She realised what she was saying, broke off and blushed deeply.

'Don't worry. More couples than you have had the same trouble,' I said.

'Just one thing worries me, Doctor.'

'What's that then?'

'Are we *really* supposed to do it every night?'

It turned out that husband Jim, once having discovered the knack, had grown really keen on sex and dedicated himself to his art unstintingly. I muttered something about moderation in all things, mutual respect for each other's feelings, and one or two other stock answers. It is difficult to mediate in another couple's love life, especially when oneself is young and newly married.

Sheila passed out of my care for a while into the round of antenatal clinics, relaxation classes and finally to the maternity ward of Winchcombe Hospital where she produced a fine baby.

Jim came to see me two days after the baby was born.

'Excuse me, Doctor' he said, blushing. 'How long is it before I can, we can, start . . . er . . . trying for another family?'

I looked at him, this shy, innocent youth of twelve months ago.

'At least six weeks,' I said.

His face fell.

I thought how different, yet how alike, the two young men were. Jim, the sweet innocent who had had to take his instructions from a book, had turned into a seven-nights-a-week sex machine. And Joshua was the one who had complained about his animal appetites . . .

*   *   *

A really pathetic case was old Norman Singer, the local dirty old man, who'd been convicted a couple of times for offences against young girls. Nothing really vile: the poor old lad wasn't capable of it. But it was certainly upsetting for the girls, and dangerous for Norman if ever his paths were to cross those of the fathers.

He was brought in by Geoff Stansfield, the local probation officer, after being charged with yet another offence.

'I'd like you to look at old Norman,' he said. 'Everybody's yelling "Dirty old man! Hang him!" That kind of thing. But I've spent a lot of time talking to him. He seems quite rational and I am wondering if the problem is something physical, something outside his control.'

I gave old Norman a thorough examination. One or two tests produced odd results, so I referred him to the consultant neurologist at Winchcombe Hospital.

There it was discovered that Norman had some kind of obstruction which was pressing on a nerve which gave him sexual urges of almost uncontrollable magnitude. He was admitted to hospital as a matter of urgency, where a simple operation removed the obstruction.

The operation was quoted by the defence at his trial and Norman was given a conditional discharge. The condition was fulfilled to the end of his life. Norman never molested another child.

I often wonder, when I see cases reported in the more lurid Sunday newspapers, whether if more probation officers followed a case through as thoroughly as Geoff Stansfield, more pathetic old men like Norman might be saved from living their last years in shame or behind bars.

14

Loving Couples

I spent more time than enough in surgery trying to sort out other people's marital problems. So many people came in with so many horrific stories – infidelity, ill-treatment, you name it – that I really began to fear for the future of the whole institution of marriage. Then I came across Mick and Alice, and my faith was restored.

Married fifty years, devoted and loving, Mick and Alice never had much money and never let it bother them. The ideal couple. I asked Mick for the secret of their success. 'A bloody good row at least twice a week,' he said. 'Clears the air something lovely.'

Marital relations became a little strained when Mick retired from his job driving a van for the Tadchester Carpet Service. Alice had a full-time job working for the Tadchester Hospital Canteen and still continued to go out to work.

Mick used to wave her off from the window, a hot mug of tea in his hand, as she trudged off to work through snow, slush, rain or hail.

One night Alice had had enough and combed through the Situations Vacant columns in the *Tadchester Echo*.

'Here you are, Mick,' she said. 'I've found you a job.'

'Give over, woman. I'm retired,' he said.

'You *were* retired,' said Alice. 'Get yourself down there first thing tomorrow and don't wear that flat cap. It's a disgrace.'

'What job is it?' asked Mick.

'Funeral parlour. Driver and pall bearer.'

'Bloody hell.'

'Never mind bloody hell. I'm fed up of going out in all weathers with you standing there with a mug of tea and a silly grin on your face. Besides which it's not good for you to be loafing about all day.'

And so started one of what Mick called the week's bloody good rows.

Next morning, however, Mick set out immaculately dressed in his best suit, overcoat and boots and wearing a velour trilby instead of his favourite flat cap. He even put his teeth in. He was a credit to his loving wife who brushed him down and straightened his tie. Naturally he got the job.

Mick was a bit on the short side and it was a shock at first to see the hearse with Mick's nose underneath a peaked cap just clearing the dashboard. The hearse looked as if it was being driven by an invisible man.

After three weeks Mick came to see me. 'Pulled a muscle in my back I think, Doc,' he said. 'Those flaming coffins weigh a ton. And if there's somebody inside like Sammy Thomas' (the local heavyweight whose corpulence was the cause of his death) 'I've got to shove like mad to stop the thing tilting over and falling on me.'

The problem was that Mick's lack of height made it impossible for him to rest the coffin on his shoulders. To reach the shoulder height of the other pall bearers he had to push upwards with the flat of his hand taking all the strain on his arm and back. I laid him off work for a few days and asked him to mention the problem to the funeral director and the other pall bearers to see if there were any solution.

Next week Mick was back. 'I've done the other side in, Doc,' he said.

'But . . .'

'I know. This you'll never believe.'

'Go on – surprise me.'

'Right,' said Mick. 'I did as you said. Asked if there was a way around the problem of me being so little. They were all very nice and they said yes, change over sides and take the leg end of the coffin. Leg ends are always lighter you see. It worked a treat for a couple of days, carrying on my good side with not much weight.'

'Then what happened?'

'A legless ex-serviceman. Heavy chap. By the time we got to church he'd slid to my end of the coffin. Had to shove like hell to keep him on an even keel and now I'm dicky on both sides.'

That night I called in at Mick's house on my rounds and had a quiet word with Alice. She went through the Situations Vacant columns again and next week Mick was working as a lollipop man outside the local school. With that responsible but not too strenuous job, honour was satisfied all round. Mick had the time to take on a small allotment, providing Alice with fresh vegetables and flowers and giving her considerable pride in her little husband whenever he carried off prizes in the Allotment Society Shows.

*　　　*　　　*

The Golden Wedding celebrations of Mick and Alice ran true to form. They were both staunch Roman Catholics and had given freely of their time and labour. St Malachy's, the Roman Catholic Church, was the youngest of all the religious institutions in Tadchester. It had to fight with innumerable Free Church organisations that had sprung up in the times of John Wesley: Congregationalists, Baptists, as well as the firmly entrenched Church of England and a great number of other, what for a better term could be called, minor religions, such as Christian Scientists, Jehovah's Witnesses, Salvation Army, Seventh Day Adventists, Bible Readers, Gospel Turners, and other sects with obscure names that came and went. Father Daly was the first Parish Priest for St Malachy's and had been in the Church for forty-eight years. Mick and Alice had been married in Winchcombe, but had attended St Malachy's ever since its consecration.

Father Daly decided to give them a surprise for their Golden Wedding and ask them to attend church for a special mass. The special mass was for *them*, and the lovely old couple finished it in tears.

After mass, Father Daly asked the congregation to come round to the church hall for a cup of tea. When they got inside it was more than tea. Tables were laid for a meal. The hall was festooned with bunting and a large placard read 'Happy Golden Wedding, Mick and Alice'. That did it. The tears started again and Mick and Alice saw their food only in a blur.

After the meal, Father Daly gave a speech of congratulations and good wishes. He told of all the help that Mick and Alice had given to the church and the Roman Catholic community in Tadchester. He spoke of what an example their marriage was, what an example they were to everyone present, and what a credit they were to the community. Then he sat down. Alice and Mick sat there with the whole assembly shouting, 'Speech! Speech! Speech!'

Mick by this time was feeling distinctly uncomfortable. To protect himself against the cold in the church he had turned up in his usual winter worshipping outfit: woolly vest and long-johns, woolly shirt, pullover, waistcoat, jacket, overcoat and trousers. He sat down to the meal wearing the lot.

'Take your cap off! Have some respect!' Alice hissed through her tears.

The central heating in the hall was very efficient and Mick was sweating profusely by the time Alice got up to make her speech of reply. Perhaps the heat made him a little tetchy, because twice he interrupted Alice to contradict her on some memory of the past.

'Do that again,' she hissed, 'and I'll fetch you one.'

Mick did it again and Alice fetched him one – a swift clout across the head with her handbag.

The congregation loved it. They rose to their feet applauding thunderously, shouting, 'More! More!'

When Alice finished her speech, Father Daly gave a nod. Somebody switched on the record player in the corner. The hall was filled with the strains of 'Take a Pair of Sparkling Eyes'.

'Ee, Alice,' said Mick.

'Ee, Mick,' said Alice.

The old couple got up, tears running down their cheeks, to take the floor for an anniversary dance. It was a tune which was played by the band in the park when Mick proposed all those years ago, and Father Daly had got to hear of it.

There were beads of sweat on the brows of relatives in the congregation in case Mick had forgotten. But he hadn't, and the old pair celebrated for once without a 'bloody good row'.

*   *   *

Another long-term relationship, but this time as far from marriage as it was possible to get, was that of Major Hawkins and Charlie Sloper. Major Hawkins was everything that his name implied. Tall, erect, brisk in speech, though slowing down in action, well groomed, silver haired and moustached, dressed in tweeds, brogues and always carrying the walking stick with which he had gone over the top several times in World War One.

Charlie Sloper was the complete opposite. The local poacher and ne'er-do-well, diminuitive, smelly, incredibly dirty. Bets had been made in Tadchester about what colour he would be if he ever washed. But the event never happened to settle it. He dressed in a set of holes held together by smelly tatters and the occasional safety-pin.

As a lieutenant, Major Hawkins had been Charlie's platoon officer in the trenches. Charlie, being Charlie, was never out of trouble in the army, and the Major grew sick of seeing his grimy face among the morning defaulters. During an attack, however, so the story went – though nobody had actually heard either man tell it – the Major was blown into a flooded shell hole and would have drowned if Charlie had not jumped in after him and held his head above water until the stretcher bearers arrived.

During the First World War, people from the same community were often in the same army unit. This was particularly true of the village of Altriston just outside Tadchester where the patriotic Lord Tyster had volunteered the whole of his work-force, gardeners, groomsmen on the first day that World War One broke out, and Altriston lost thirty-three of its sons killed in the first world holocaust, all in the Somerset Regiment and most on one dreadful bloody day on the Somme. Altriston had the highest casualty rate of any other comparable village of its size in England. As Bob Barker said, the tragedy of our losses in the First World War was that we lost the cream of English manhood, that the best and ablest volunteers went out there first and were decimated.

The Major and Charlie, both from different walks of life, would have been amongst the first to go abroad. Although they had the comfort of familiar faces around them when they served, they also had the horror of seeing friends and relatives being killed.

Charlie and the Major were both survivors, each in his own way. They'd fought battles to rank and personality during the war, and they fought a running battle of personalities in the later years of their lives. Both basically lonely men, they spent a lot of time in the Tadchester Arms. Strangers who didn't know them thought they hated each other and feared the worst as arguments raged in the public bar.

The choice of location was interesting. These two saw each other twice a day for mutual and ritual insults and the public bar was always the venue. The Major, though accepted and loved by the roughnecks in there, looked distinctly out of place. He really belonged in the saloon among the tweedy county types. Charlie was not allowed in the saloon on the grounds of offending the customers, frightening the horses and generally contravening the germ warfare clauses of the Geneva Convention. So the Major chose the public bar.

It would start as soon as he walked in.

'Here comes Colonel Bogey!' Charlie would shout, and follow it up with a few bars of that well-known military air.

'Ah, Sloper, you squalid little man,' the Major would reply. 'Is that you? I thought you'd be out in the garden blending with the compost heap.'

'Piss orf,' Charlie would reply, the riposte chosen most frequently from the Sloper repertoire of stinging wit.

For an hour or more they would insult each other. The Major's public school accent and studied delivery contrasted strongly with Charlie's wild and obscene utterances.

'Sloper by name and Sloper by nature,' the Major would say. 'Never around when you were needed, always sloping off somewhere. You shouldn't have been drummed out of the army. You should have been fumigated out.'

'Piss orf,' Charlie would reply and follow up with a sophisticated raspberry.

It was worse when they had any real and immediate bone of contention.

*　　*　　*

Charlie was a natural scavenger. Folk would look out of their bedroom window first thing in the morning and see a diminutive dark shape going through the shrubbery. They would come down to discover that the hens hadn't produced as many eggs as usual, or that there was a gap in their row of cabbages. Sprout plants were bereft of the buttons that only yesterday were there and ready for picking and there were half a dozen holes in the ground where yesterday there were carrots.

Charlie had kept his army haversack, by now incredibly old, filthy, greasy, and an affront to the Major. The haversack was always full of loot.

One autumn day in the public bar, Charlie rummaged around in the haversack and handed the Major an apple.

'James Grieve that is,' he said. 'Lovely variety, marvellous eating.'

'Ah, yes,' said the Major. 'Delicious. Curiously enough I've got a James Grieve at the bottom of my garden: only a young tree as yet, but it's got enough apples on it to make the picking worth while. I'll have some this evening. Thank you very much for yours, Sloper. Very civil of you, for a change.'

When the Major went out with a basket to harvest his crop

that evening he found only four apples left on the tree. The public bar resounded to accusations and indignant denials, threats of lawsuits, fisticuffs, and pistols at dawn. The Major couldn't prove anything and eventually subsided like a rumbling volcano. Only to erupt again when Charlie, on his way out, tossed him an apple and said, 'Here – have another . . .'

Money was the next bone of contention. One foggy night in the Tadchester Arms, Major Hawkins said, 'Reminds me of the time I lost a whole pocketful of money.'

'Piss orf,' said Charlie. 'You never 'ad a pocketful of money.'

'I'll thank you to keep a civil tongue in your head, Sloper,' said the Major. 'Indeed I had. Seventeen shillings and fourpence, if I remember. I must admit I was a little the worse for wear at the time, having attended the Regimental Dinner from which you were conspicuously absent by popular request. I stopped at the seat at Victoria Corner by the edge of the common. Just to get my breath back and take fresh bearings, you understand.

'When I stood up I lost all the loose change in my trouser pocket. Infernal hole must have crept up on me. Tried to find the old akkers, but in the dark and fog, and all that tussocky grass and stuff, couldn't find a penny. Overnight it snowed heavily, kept snowing for ten days and by the time the stuff had melted there wasn't a penny to be found.'

'How long ago was that?' asked Charlie.

'Good ten years.'

'Going to say,' said Charlie, 'that seat's not been there for five. Vandalised. By vandals, they say. Shoot the bloody lot of them I would.'

By next evening there had been a great deal of scuffing about in the tussocky grass and gorse around the site of the bench at Victoria Corner. In the public bar of the Tadchester Arms Charlie was busy breathing on a collection of assorted coins, and rubbing them vigorously with his off-black handkerchief. The Major came in and after the usual exchange of insults ordered his usual half-pint of bitter.

'On me,' said Charlie.

'Steady on, old chap!'

'I insist.'

'As you will. Most grateful.'

'How much did you say you lost at Victoria Corner all them years ago?' said Charlie.

'Seventeen and fourpence. Why?'

'Either you was mistaken or you was robbed. I could only find eleven and ninepence.'

'You blackguard!' exclaimed the Major. 'Return that money at once!'

''Ow do you know it's yours?' asked Charlie. 'More than you have emptied their pockets at Victoria Corner. All them courting couples for a start must have lost thousands. Treasure trove this is. Anyway shut your row – you've got a half-pint out of it.'

Truth to tell, the Major was not as well off as he seemed. After World War One he went back to a steady but poorly paid job in an estate agents and stayed there until his retirement. True, he now had a detached house with a reasonable bit of garden all paid for and in good condition. But he had to do his share of scrimping and scavenging to keep it going. Especially to please his wife who had married him as a dashing young hero and now thought that perhaps he hadn't made as much of himself as he ought.

*　　　*　　　*

The log was the last big argument. The Major had a fireplace which would take logs and there were logs in plenty in the woods around the common. After every high wind the place would be littered with rotten branches and fallen trees. In would go the Major with a length of rope and a ripsaw, muttering to anybody passing, 'Nothing like the old log fires, eh? Nothing like sawing your own: keeps you fit, what?'

He would drag the log home with the rope and put it in his woodshed to dry out sufficiently for use.

One day he came across a beautiful log, left behind from a tree which had been felled by the local council as dangerous.

The council had carted the tree away, but had left a great limb in the undergrowth. The Major trimmed it as best he could, tied a rope around it and tried to drag it away. It wouldn't budge. Dusk was falling and he could not have sawn up the log before dark. He managed to roll it into a hollow, covered it with bracken and left it.

That night in the Tadchester Arms he told Charlie of his find and of his cleverness in concealing the log, to be sawn up later. Next morning he arrived with his saw, and his log was gone.

Lunchtime at the Tadchester Arms that day was quite an event. The Major went for Charlie with his walking stick, using it as if it were a sword. Charlie used his own knobbly stick as if it were a quarterstaff. The two went at it out of the public bar and around the garden for twenty minutes, by which time both had run out of puff and called a halt.

Never once did Charlie admit taking the log, but John Denton gave the game away a few weeks later. He told me about meeting Charlie at first light struggling to tie one end of the log to his ancient bicycle and how he had given Charlie a hand to carry it home.

'For God's sake, John, do me a favour and don't mention it to anyone else,' I said. 'I almost had two coronaries on my hands over that log. If the truth gets to the Major I am going to have a corpse on my hands. A dirty little smelly one.'

Four or five years later when the log incident had passed into local folklore, the Major collapsed in the public bar and was taken to hospital. Little Charlie followed the ambulance on his bicycle, leading the Major's dog on a long piece of string, and sat for hours in the waiting room until a Matron with a keen sense of smell ejected him.

Diagnosis on the Major was difficult. It was more a combination of small ailments than one big specific one. Old age for a start, with some nerve and tissue degeneration, poor circulation, a piece of shrapnel which was still moving about his body and occasionally blocking things, and a heart prone to stutter now and again.

He was sent home in a fortnight with strict instructions: plenty of rest, no excitement, no smoking and strictly no drinking until further notice.

It is probably uncharitable to say that this was the chance Mrs Hawkins had been waiting for. She now had her husband all to herself, away from the friends and habits she had so long disapproved of, and she kept him virtually a prisoner in his own home.

Charlie went round to see the Major once only. Mrs Hawkins's nose wrinkled with distaste when she opened the door. She allowed Charlie upstairs only on the understanding that he didn't stay too long. He stayed more than long enough. From his haversack he produced a bottle of scotch, the result of a collection by the public bar regulars. He and the Major swigged great gulps of it in tea cups and by the time Mrs Hawkins came up to investigate, they were both roaring drunk.

That did it. Out went Charlie, never to return. From then on none of the Major's cronies was allowed across the threshold. For six months the poor man saw nobody but his wife. Only one concession was made to Charlie. He was allowed to walk the Major's dog twice a day. There was no contact with the house.

The dog was tied to the gatepost for Charlie to pick up and Charlie tied it up there again on his return. After six months the Major was able to venture out, not too far at first, but gradually a reasonable distance until that distance stretched to the Tad-chester Arms.

He walked into the public bar and it was as if he had never been away. He and Charlie moved straight into the mutual insults routine and Charlie demonstrated to the Major how much his dog had improved under the Sloper training course. Charlie had taught the dog to carry beer mats from one person to another. He sent one over to the Major. The Major wrote on it, 'Thanks for everything, you squalid little man,' and sent it back by return of dog. Charlie sent his reply on the mat. It said, simply, 'Piss orf'.

The two old enemies, the two best of old friends, were back in business . . .

15

Assorted Characters

Since the turn of the century, Tadchester had had its own prize silver band. Over the years its fortunes fluctuated, depending on how much the town council of the time was prepared to finance it, and on the ability and industry of the bandmaster who happened to be in control over any particular period.

It was certain that the band reached its peak just after World War Two under the influence of the bandmaster, Leighton Evans. It won competition after competition, and even played at the Albert Hall in London in a national competition.

Leighton was a Welshman from the valleys who had been invalided out of the coal-mines with silicosis. He put all his Welsh fervour into his love of music and the Tadchester silver band was his pride and joy. With the baton in his hand he was an absolute tyrant. He spared nobody at practice. The bandsmen (and particularly the town's junior band) were terrified of him. But he cajoled, threatened, encouraged and inspired them to musical heights far beyond their normal capabilities.

In addition to his musical capabilities, Leighton was the most accident prone man that I have ever met. At one time or other he had broken twenty-three bones in his body. Later he developed severe rheumatoid arthritis, which drastically limited his mobility, apart from causing a lot of pain and discomfort, and finally developed cataracts in both eyes.

He had tremendous courage and somehow survived all his

incredible medical conditions, was much more alive than most, highly intelligent, and a tremendous ally.

We developed a great friendship. We both had mining in common (I had had my two years down the mines as a Bevin Boy at the end of World War Two) and had a language of our own. When I visited him, we had a marvellous repartee. I would say, 'Bloody miners. Its all featherbeds down the pits nowadays.'

'Bloody doctors,' Leighton would reply. 'They have so much money now, they are having to bury it in tins in the garden.'

Mrs Evans would make us a cup of tea and we would sit talking – coal mines, socialism, the town council – and generally putting the world to rights. Leighton was an ardent socialist, very articulate about his beliefs, and a great fighter for social justice. He was also a good business man. He always knew of bargains, somewhere where you could get musical instruments for half price, a place in Wales where you could buy men's suits from the factory for a quarter of the market price. He was always bright, never depressed, and it was almost impossible to stop him talking.

His first medical condition was silicosis. It was not too bad, but prevented him from working underground, and made him very prone to chest infections.

Leighton's salary as bandmaster was not sufficient to maintain him, so he made up the deficit by doing a part-time job with one of the timber merchants who operated from Tadchester Quay.

His first accident there was when some timber fell on him, crushing both his feet.

After innumerable operations, he finished up by having to have both his ankles fused. This relieved some of the pain but meant he had two stiff, unbending ankles.

He then developed rheumatoid arthritis. His hands and fingers became twisted and he could no longer play musical instruments. His knees became swollen and fixed, to be followed shortly by the same condition affecting his hips, limiting his walking to a few shambling steps with a walking frame. This was in spite of all the modern drugs, including Cortisone, that were available.

'This won't do, Doctor,' said Leighton. 'I have to get walking again.'

I sent him to every specialist I thought might help him. There were various operations which gave some relief, but his fixed knees and hips seemed at an impasse.

Then a new orthopaedic surgeon was appointed to Winchcombe, with new techniques and appliances. At first Leighton was given metal hinges in his knees, then he had hip replacements on both sides. Before you could have imagined it possible, there was Leighton walking round the town with a stick, and driving his car to brass band concerts.

He had invested the compensation for both his silicosis and his leg injury and was able to live comfortably, if not extravagantly. He and his wife had a house in Stonehouse Street, on a steep road leading down to Tadchester pannier market. He had known days of extreme poverty in the depressions of the thirties, was penny wise, and was determined that his two children should have security. His daughter married a successful engineer. His son, Owen, as well as winning the national solo trumpet crown, passed his matriculation and got a good job with the Inland Revenue. In his later years, Leighton said proudly, 'I never thought, Doctor, that I would have two grandsons at a public school and two granddaughters at a private convent.'

'You always were a bloody capitalist at heart, Leighton,' I said.

His reply would not have been repeatable at chapel in Tonypandy.

* * *

I asked Leighton's advice about music education for Trevor and Paul. I would have liked them to have played an instrument. What did he suggest?

'Send them to me,' he said. 'You want to start them on the cornet. In a brass band you start playing tunes early, so you don't lose interest, and you do it with a lot of mates.'

'How old should they be when they start?' I asked.

'Eight years old,' said Leighton. 'Send them to me when Trevor is eight.'

Soon after Trevor's eighth birthday he and Paul, who was then five, would be met by Leighton from school and go back to his house for tea and for Trevor's instruction on the cornet. Before each lesson they had to have a traditional Welsh tea. On their first visit Mrs Evans, in as musical a Welsh voice as her husband, said, 'What would you boys like?'

'What is Owen having?' asked Trevor.

'Beans on toast,' said Mrs Evans.

'Beans on toast, please,' said Trevor. If Owen ate beans on toast, they were obviously a great aid to trumpet playing.

'What about you, Paul?' asked Mrs Evans.

As far as food went, Paul knew exactly what he wanted.

'Egg and chips, please, Mrs Evans.'

Whatever Paul's activities, then or since, egg and chips have been the fuel and inspiration.

This became their Friday evening nourishment. Every Friday for ten years Trevor and Paul would go to tea with the Evanses, Trevor to have beans on toast and Paul to have egg and chips, and Leighton would talk and instruct them both about music.

Trevor joined the youth band and eventually graduated from the cornet to the trumpet. The only time he doubted Leighton's wisdom was when, following his advice, he and a group of boys from the band spent forty-eight hours at an army camp to see whether they would like the idea of becoming army bandsmen. Trevor hated it. He loved his creature comforts and reveille at 0600 hours, with a cold shower and drill, was not his idea of musical fun.

Leighton made Trevor into a proficient trumpet player, good enough to fill in for local orchestras, and a tremendous asset to the jazz club when he went to university. And Trevor formed a great affection for him.

When Trevor went on holiday after we, the family, had moved away, it was always with Leighton that he went to stay.

When I last saw Leighton I broke the news that Trevor, who by now had two law degrees, had given it all up to go to drama school.

'I knew he would do something like that,' said Leighton. 'Six months after he had started his law school he said to me, "Leighton, there seems to be one law for the rich and one for the poor. I don't know if I like that".'

'Had you been indoctrinating him, Leighton?' I asked.

'No, boyo,' said Leighton. 'I taught him music. Somebody else taught him law . . .'

* * *

Leighton was still as bright as ever, with seven or eight more operations under his belt, the latest being for cataracts in both eyes. He still managed to get about with two elbow crutches, and was as full of vim, vigour and courage as anyone.

'Did I tell you about my latest accident?' he said.

'No,' I replied.

'Well,' he said, 'I was given a lift to the Institute, got out of the car, and fell down a bloody hole in the road. I couldn't attract anyone's attention until a motorist saw my sticks in the road and came looking to see what was wrong. I was real shaken up. He helped me up and I managed to walk into the Institute, but I couldn't make it home; somebody had to run me back.

'I was in bed for a fortnight. I could hardly move my leg, my chest and arm hurt, and the wife had to lift me on to the potty.

'I was getting worse, and in the end I had to send for the doctor. He got me straight into hospital and they x-rayed me: broken pelvis, three broken ribs and a broken arm. No wonder I wasn't walking properly.

'I was in hospital for three months, came home, and then a week later I started coughing. Coughed up about two pints of blood.

'Back into hospital, blood transfusions and antibiotics. Now, thank God, I'm back out on my feet again. They said it was my old silicosis.'

He continued, 'It was funny in hospital the last time. This young lad of a doctor came to examine me and said, "What is wrong with you, Mr. Evans?"

'Not a lot,' I said. 'You will find my ankles are fixed solid, I have got metal hinges instead of knees, both my hips have been replaced and I have got silicosis. Now it hurts down below, my arm and chest hurt and I'm coughing up blood.'

The young lad said, "We shouldn't keep you in the ward. I think we'd better take you straight to the museum".'

Leighton was irrepressible. He survived all his major medical catastrophes by sheer spirit and determination. Half of what he had had would have killed most people. He brought the gift of music to Tadchester and instilled the love of music in my boys. Leighton would always battle on until he dropped, and dropping was only a transient time until he picked himself up again. I was proud to have him as a friend.

*   *   *

Tadchester was too small for Harry Walters, but he made little effort to get out of the place, perhaps because as a youth pleasurable things came too easy. Strong, athletic and good looking, he concentrated at school on girls instead of exams. Though he had a good brain, he ended his schooldays with nothing to show for it.

Called up for National Service he enlisted in the Grenadier Guards, hoping to see action in Korea or in one of the minor wars Britain was engaged in at the time. His battalion, however, stayed at home.

Life in the Guards was certainly no rest cure. But though he saw plenty of action with au pair girls in darkest Chelsea and once led his squad in a mock night attack on Salisbury Plain, ambushing a flock of sheep instead of the Scots Guards, he did not get the testing his restless mind and tough physique craved for.

He returned to Tadchester after his service even more restless. He had tasted London life, and Tadchester High Street was not exactly the King's Road. After two or three years of drinking, fighting and wenching he married, got a steady job and settled down. At least he settled down as far as someone like Harry Walters could.

Two years after his settling down I was called out to treat him twice in the same evening. The karate craze had come to Tadchester and Harry was one of the first to enrol in the club. At a party at his home one night, well-oiled, he insisted on demonstrating how to break a plank in half with one blow.

Either he hadn't quite mastered the art, or the plank was thicker than he bargained for, and he broke his hand very badly.

Harry's wife phoned me. After one look at his hand I drove him down to Tadchester Hospital. He was supported on the back seat by one of his mates so that he wouldn't fall over and do any more damage.

I had to call out my surgical colleague, Henry Johnson, to come and put the hand straight. We could not give Harry a general anaesthetic because of the amount of booze he had on board. Using local anaesthetics, Henry had to deaden the nerves that supplied the hand before putting things straight. He completed the setting job by enclosing the lower arm in plaster of paris.

Harry lived not too far from me so I drove him back home, where his anxious wife took over and steered him through the carousing guests upstairs to bed. Half an hour later Harry's wife phoned me again. She'd got him in his pyjamas, supporting the plaster with a sling, and put him to bed. The party was still going strong downstairs, however, and Harry didn't want to miss any fun. Over he rolled, fell out of bed and dislocated his shoulder.

Concussion was the next thing I treated him for. He came home from work one summer evening when the neighbourhood children – by now he had two young boys of his own – were playing Batman and charging about in capes and improvised batmobiles.

'BATMAN!' he yelled, spreading out his jacket, and jumped

clear over a five foot fence in some form of western roll. He landed on his head and was just coming round when I arrived.

The children thought it was marvellous fun. 'That was great Dad, do it again,' his eldest boy was saying. 'Yes, Uncle Harry,' chanted the neighbours' children. 'Please – just once.' His reply was not one of those recommended by Dr Spock.

Harry's right hand came in for a lot of damage one way or another. One of his boys was once badly knocked about by a big boy at school.

'There's only one way to settle this,' Harry said to his son. 'No matter how big he is, hit him first – like this'. So saying, he spun round and aimed a fearsome blow at the living room door. His fist went straight through the panel. It took me some time to get the splinters out and strap up the dislocated fingers and torn ligaments.

Fire drill was next. There had been a kitchen fire along the road. Thankfully nobody was hurt, but Harry decided to give his boys an object lesson on how to escape from a burning house.

'Say you are standing at the top of stairs like this,' he said, watched from below by the wide-eyed boys who knew their father had the answer to everything. 'The hall is clear, but the whole staircase is alight. What do you do?'

One of the lads volunteered, 'Climb out through the back window.'

'Rubbish! No time for messing about. What you do is this.'

With a 'Hup!' he vaulted over the banister rail at the top of the stairs and plunged down into the hallway below. Or he would have plunged if his hand had not slipped on the banister. It jammed between two of the rails, pulled him up sickeningly short, and left him dangling in mid-air.

'It's a wonder your hand is still on the end of your arm,' I said as I strapped up, splinted and bound it. 'You're at an age now where you should be learning a bit more sense.'

'You're right, Doc,' he said. 'You're not wrong, you're dead right. From now on you are going to see a change. You are now looking at the new Harry Walters.'

The new Harry Walters turned out to be not all that much different from the old one. He came in one day looking harassed.

'I don't know, Doc,' he said. 'I think it's my nerves. Perhaps it's the quiet domestic life I'm leading. Perhaps it's family responsibilities. But I keep getting butterflies in my stomach, my hands tremble, I wake up in the middle of the night worrying about my job, the bank manager, the mortgage, the electricity bills and all that sort of stuff. And I get up in the morning absolutely whacked.'

I gave him a course of mild sedatives and warned him, 'Go easy on the booze. These pills and draught bitter don't mix.'

'Sure, Doc. I've been cutting down lately.'

During the next fortnight I kept hearing disturbing stories about Harry's behaviour. He was barred from three pubs in the town after fights. One evening coming home from work in his car he hit one of his brick gateposts and demolished it. A week later he demolished the other. Then he announced to his family that he was going off into the moors above Tadchester to go back to nature and live off the land for a while.

Off he went in his car singing *Born Free* at the top of his voice. He was back shortly after nightfall complaining that there was nowhere on the moors where he could plug in his electric blanket.

I was mulling over his antics during a lull in the evening surgery and thinking that perhaps I would call on him, when I was saved the trouble. The next patient was Harry himself. A little glassy-eyed and not in a good mood.

'Here, Doc,' he said, banging the plastic pill container on my desk. 'You can have the rest of these bloody things back. I've not been right since I started them. In fact I reckon you have given me the wrong prescription.'

'Now then, Harry,' I said. 'Simmer down. I've heard of one or two of your little adventures lately, and obviously something is not agreeing with you.'

'Too right. It's those bloody pills.'

'Remember that I warned you about drinking, and you said you were cutting it down.'

'Correct, but you can't rush these things. I've been doing it gradually.'

'How much do you drink a day?'

'Not a lot. Perhaps three or four pints at lunch time, and at night perhaps seven or eight.'

'And then you worry about the bank manager, the mortgage, and the electricity bills?'

'Yes. Ah . . . er . . . Well I've got to have some relaxation.'

'I'll keep these pills, Harry,' I said, 'and won't prescribe any more. You stick to your sedatives, and until you really cut down on them, I'll stick to mine.'

During the five minute chat which followed, I suggested tactfully that Harry might consider joining Alcoholics Anonymous. He seemed to consider this an excellent idea, and went out whistling.

It's strange what curious blind spots people can have: odd bits missing from the jigsaw of knowledge which most of us have in our day-to-day information banks.

I met Harry in the street a fortnight later. He came out of the Tadchester Arms.

'How's it going?' I asked. 'Did you do anything about my suggestion?'

'Oh, yes,' he said. 'But they wanted me to stop drinking. What kind of an outfit is that?'

'What kind did you think it was?' I asked.

'What its name suggested. Alcoholics Anonymous. A private drinking club where you didn't have to give your name.'

In spite of his eccentricities, or perhaps because of them, Harry was a very likeable character. Even the neighbours he upset or punched could not stay out of friends for long. He went his merry, boozy, erratic way of life, living up to his motto of 'Sod 'em all' until his boys were well into their teens. And then he changed.

Part of it might have been switching his job. He went to work one morning to be greeted by some petty quibble from his boss.

'That's it!' he exploded. 'You can stick your job!' and jammed a wastepaper basket over the boss's head.

He went from there to the labour exchange, and by some fantastic stroke of fate walked straight into another job, out of doors, which suited him right down to the ground. By this time one of his boys was working, and his wife was free to take a job of her own, so money was not a problem.

Another reason for the change might have been an impromptu karate match between him and his eldest son, now a strapping seventeen-year-old. Harry misplaced a kick which caught the lad in a very sensitive spot, and to a seventeen-year-old a very precious one. The lad lashed out in pain and temper and laid his father unconscious on the hearth rug. Perhaps Harry then realised that nobody can remain invincible for ever.

The final reason for the change, or perhaps a result of it, was his sudden passion for gardening. For years he had neglected the garden, paying the boys a few shillings for pushing the mower around once or twice a year. Then one day he bought himself a complete kit of gardening tools and started digging furiously. Within a week the whole garden was turned into a vegetable patch, dug, manured, hoed, raked – the soil was rich and friable, so there was no waiting for frost to break it down – and planted with all kinds of seeds. All his spare time from then on was spent in the garden. The pubs saw him only occasionally at weekends, and then he usually turned up in his gardening clothes, making time just for a couple of quick ones.

'My, my,' I said one day as I admired the profusion of healthy, tidy and edible greenery, 'you have made a grand job of the garden.'

'Yes,' he said with a wry grin. 'Makes you spit, doesn't it? But even Peter Pan had to come down to earth some time.'

*   *   *

Two of my patients had each lost a leg – one in a riding accident, and one by an anti-personnel mine during the war. Each had adjusted to his handicap in a totally different way. Though they did not know it, they were neighbours. And the adjustments they had made were to lead them into a bizarre confrontation.

Edward Murdock was a successful chartered accountant, with a large and flourishing practice. He lived in a mock Tudor house at the top of the great sweep of ground which rose up the hill from the banks of the Tad.

Always an active, vigorous man, his passion was riding. He rode to hounds, rode in local point-to-point races and show-jumping events. Almost every spare minute he spent in the saddle. One day, as he was hacking home from a hunt, a lorry rounded a corner on the wrong side of the road and spooked the horse. The horse shied and threw Murdock under the wheels. His leg had to be amputated from the thigh, and his riding days were over.

Eventually he took up shooting. His grounds were large enough, even though strictly speaking he might be breaking the law. There was enough small wild life around – crows, pigeons, squirrels, rabbits, even the occasional stray deer – to provide him with targets.

From then on nothing on his land was safe. Even one or two

of the local cats finished up dead by mistake. And when the natural game ran short, he started raising pheasants and partridges, releasing them when they were grown, and blasting the daylights out of them.

One far corner of Edward's land adjoined the back garden of a local painter and sculptor, Leslie Barnes. The two pieces of land, so dissimilar in size, were separated by a natural copse. Indeed, so well separated were the two that the owners had no real idea who was on the other side. Murdock knew that someone with a relatively small garden lived there. Leslie knew that somebody with pots of money and land to match, lived on the other side of what he regarded as 'his' copse.

Leslie was an animal sculptor and painter of extreme skill and sensitivity, and he used as his models the many animals and birds which used his garden as a sanctuary. Leslie would harm no living thing, and despised anybody who did, especially if they did it for sport.

He had not always been so caring and gentle. In his youth, before the war, shooting had been his one passion. All his spare time had been spent with a gun in his hand and he would shoot anything that moved.

He was quite happy in the army. It was but a small step from shooting animals to shooting people, and the ethics of it never bothered him.

One day, towards the end of the war in Europe, he found himself in Austria. The German troops had retreated, there was no action for miles, so he took himself off with his service rifle into a forest which abounded with deer.

He was a natural hunter, and it was not long before a stag was kicking on the ground about fifty yards away. Leslie started towards it to give it the *coup de grâce*. Halfway across the open ground there was an explosion and he was lying there, one leg gone and the other badly shattered.

The next ten minutes or so were an eerie experience. He lay there apparently doomed to bleed to death, facing a stag which was also bleeding to death. He had failed, he thought, as a hunter. He had not killed the stag outright. It was still kicking, and in pain. So he dragged himself painfully on his stomach, took careful aim, and put the stag out of its misery. Then he turned over, bound a handkerchief tightly round the stump of his leg, and started to drag himself out of the wood.

Luckily for him a patrol heard the shot and came into the wood to investigate. Leslie's life was saved. But his leg was not.

Discharged from the army with a disability pension and a tin leg, he tackled his problems completely differently from Edward Murdock. He had known real pain for the first time in his life, realised it was the kind that he had been inflicting for years on living creatures, and decided to cause no more pain to anything.

He came to Tadchester, bought the small cottage by the Tad with a garden which ran up to the copse, and started on the animal painting and sculpting by which he eventually was to earn a living and some small fame.

Before long his garden had become a miniature wildlife sanctuary. Birds of all kinds, squirrels, rabbits, badgers, deer, and the occasional fox used to appear and eat the food that he left out for them. If he appeared, the creatures were in no hurry to move away: they seemed to sense that he meant them no harm.

One particular fox he grew very fond of, and it grew fond of him. Though it would not actually eat out of his hand, it came close enough for him to throw it scraps of meat. It would sit there and eat while Leslie watched.

After its morning meal one day the fox slipped back into the copse. Five minutes later there was the sound of a shot from Murdock's land, and the fox re-emerged in Leslie's garden with half its side blown away by shotgun pellets.

Leslie sank onto his knees, the metal joint in his leg squeaking. The fox put its head on his lap, as though it were a faithful housedog, and died.

There was a crashing about in the copse and Murdock appeared at the boundary.

'I say! You there!' he shouted.

In his sculptor's smock Leslie looked the archetypal peasant.

Murdock *was* trying to re-assert himself so that would explain, if not excuse, his apparent rudeness.

'You seen anything of a fox?'

Leslie lifted the bloodied form from his knee.

'This it?'

'Ah, yes. Mine, I think.'

Murdock climbed stiffly over the boundary fence (by now he too had been fitted with an artificial leg) and strode towards Leslie who, with the aid of his walking stick, was struggling upright.

It was the walking stick that laid Murdock unconscious across the fox, and which also did considerable damage to Murdock's ribs as he lay there. Leslie took up Murdock's gun, broke the expensive thing in half against a tree. Then he phoned the police.

I treated Murdock at his home. He was raving and threatening to press all sorts of charges. I explained about Leslie's disability and he calmed down.

Leslie visited him the next day, stayed for a long talk, and thereafter the two got on reasonably well. They never became close friends but they were sensible enough to live and let live, and they were helped by the realisation that someone else had the same disability.

'What frightened me,' said Leslie when he came into the surgery one day for treatment for chafing on his stump, 'was my reaction after I had laid Murdock out. There was a cartridge still left in that gun and my finger had actually taken up the slack on the trigger before I remembered the deer in the woods all that time ago. Just goes to show how thin the line is between . . .'

'Between?'

'St Francis of Assisi and Attila the bloody Hun,' he said. 'See you, Doc. Be good.'

16

Round in Circles

I had to go to London to attend a two-day postgraduate course at a chest hospital. These courses always caused me some disquiet. Obviously it was important to keep up with the latest trends of medicine but usually, in learning the new advances, I was shown the deficiencies and dangers of the old techniques and apparatus that I was using.

This applied particularly to my hospital work. I would learn that only the new super deluxe electrocardiogram gave proper recordings, and the particular machine I was using at the time was not only no good, but dangerous.

Having absorbed all the new and valuable information I would then have to go back to Tadchester and use my old equipment: apparatus that had never let me down and which, before the course, I would have trusted with my life. Now I used it with the worry that not only was it no good, it was lethal. I knew also that I had no alternative but to go on using it: it would be at least ten years before the latest advances reached Tadchester.

Happily, medicine tends to go round in circles and by the time the new equipment and techniques had reached Tadchester, the circle had been almost completed. It was the new machine that was now held to be faulty and they were using something very like my old machine as the most wonderful and latest advance.

This cycle of thinking affected almost all areas of medicine. In later years in the National Health Service it was decided to shut all the small hospitals and build more large ones. So one by one all the cottage hospitals like Tadchester were closed down and huge structures catering for thousands of patients erected all over the country.

Just before, or just as, the last small hospital was shut down, some senior bureaucrats had a wonderful idea. These huge healing palaces that they'd built didn't work all that well for the patient who needed hospital care but didn't need too specialised treatment. Why not a community hospital so each community had its own? Where elderly patients and others not requiring major surgery or medical treatment could be looked after by the people of the community that they lived in? Where their general practitioners could keep a day to day eye on them? Where they wouldn't take up the more expensive beds in these bigger highly specialised hospitals? Cottage hospitals – what a splendid idea.

So as soon as they had closed all the cottage hospitals down they started building new cottage hospitals again. I am sure the bureaucrat who thought up the idea got knighted for his brilliant and original thought.

*   *   *

I had to spend two nights in London for the course at the chest hospital. Pam had a lot of home commitments and could not come with me, so I was to stay with my old friend Albert. We had both been Bevin Boys together at Dinnington Colliery in 1945–46. I had worked on the coal face but Albert had opted to be a pit pony driver – much the more hazardous of the two jobs. His strong, overfed and underworked pony used to give him the most hair raising time.

After leaving the mines, Albert had started up in a modest way as a jeweller in Birmingham. He had prospered and had moved to London to be closer to Hatton Garden. We had kept in touch, mainly at Christmas, but had seen each other only intermittently over the intervening years. It seemed a good opportunity to renew our acquaintance and I wrote to ask if he could put me up for one night. He and his wife replied with the most welcoming invitation.

I didn't realise how successful Albert had been until I approached his house in one of the more expensive parts of Hampstead. I turned into a gravel drive in this most expensive looking area and drove up to a large Georgian house. As I drove up I could hear the baying of dogs . . . and one of my big fears had always been of large dogs.

Albert and Mary came to the door to greet me. My first question was, 'You've got some dogs?'

'Yes. We'll let them out in a minute. They won't bother you – just stand still until they get used to you.'

My heart sank.

'Now!' shouted Albert. A manservant opened a door, and out bounded two snarling Alsatians. They came up to me, looked me over and sniffed me up and down. After what seemed like hours they left me alone and went about their business.

'It's all right. You can move now,' said Mary. 'They just like to get to know you. Jenny, the small one,' – Jenny looked huge to me – 'is my favourite, and Rover, the big one, is Albert's. We have so many diamonds in the house that we have to have some protection.'

During my stay I was very wary of these dogs. The fact that the dogs knew I was terrified of them didn't help. Once in an unguarded moment, when I walked in part of the house unaccompanied by Albert or Mary, the dog sitting nearest let a low rumbling noise from its throat. It sounded like the lowest note of an organ. I retreated slowly – and backwards.

'They're marvellous dogs,' said Mary that evening after dinner. 'We've had so many robberies here that we just have to have some form of security. Thieves broke in up the road and held the houseowners at gunpoint. They tortured the dog until they told them where the valuables were, and then killed it. But theirs was a little dog – I can't imagine a burglar subduing these two, even with a machine gun.'

148

The evening and the meal they gave me were delightful. Albert and Mary were really good and old friends – Albert was Trevor's godfather – and he and I had a marvellous evening reminiscing about our days down the mines.

It so often happens that one's best friends live at a distance, and one never seems able to find time to get to see them. There just aren't enough days in the year.

After a long evening full of reminiscences, brandy and cigars, we went to bed. The two dogs slept in huge baskets outside Albert and Mary's room. We had wined and dined well and I went to bed in a happy, relaxed state and slept soundly.

I was awakened in the early hours by my body telling me it wanted to get rid of the excess fluid I had taken in during the evening.

I opened the door to go to the bathroom. As I did so, two low pitched growls emitted from the baskets outside Albert and Mary's door. As I stepped closer both these growls increased in volume and I imagined the huge snarling jaws in the darkness of the corridor.

I went back to bed, thinking I would just have to hang on somehow until morning. I stuck it for another hour and realised nature was going to win this battle. I mustn't be foolish about two dogs, I told myself: they'd been quite friendly. I opened the door boldly and took two steps down towards the bathroom. Immediately both dogs leapt snarling out of their baskets. I ran back into the bedroom and shut the door.

I was bursting. I had to choose between having a ruptured bladder or my throat torn out by the dogs. I was in total despair . . . until I looked in the corner of the room and saw the sink with the two shiny taps. I walked across, turned on one of the taps loudly to drown any other noise, and in a few minutes had relieved the situation. There was now no need to face the hazards of a journey to the bathroom.

I didn't tell Albert and Mary of my adventures during the night. Friendship can only be stretched so far, and the beautiful furnishings and fittings of the house didn't quite fit in with my communion with the bedroom sink.

I was spending the next night in a London hotel with toilet and bathroom en suite, so even if there had been a wolf pack roaming the corridors, I wouldn't have any problems getting to the toilet.

※　　　※　　　※

On the second day of the postgraduate course we were introduced to a machine, then a new invention, that measured one's breathing capacity. By blowing into this machine you could tell how efficient your personal breathing apparatus was. Called a peak flow meter, the machine was designed for assessing the progress of people with chronic chest disease.

The bearded intellectual professor who introduced the machine explained that it gave the answers to all questions on breathing, and stressed how important it was to disregard the patients' views on how they felt at any particular time. This was a great surprise to me. Certainly a new method of approach.

The professor said the patient might have taken a preparation for his breathing that made him feel better, but the peak flow meter could show in fact that his breathing was worse. On the other hand, he said, the patient might take a preparation for his breathing that made him feel worse, and the peak flow meter could show that he was in actual fact better. So one should disregard the patient's opinion and rely purely on this machine.

I envisaged a situation where I could be with a patient and not have one of these machines handy, and neither I nor the patient would be able to tell whether he was better or not.

My next-door neighbour at the lecture, an old rugby colleague – at postgraduate courses one always bumped into several old mates – whispered, 'I see. You're better when you feel worse and worse when you feel better. Why didn't I think of it before . . .'

Many years later I attended a course at the same chest hospital. There was a new generation of professors and lecturers, whose wrinkled brows and balding foreheads showed how intellectual they were. They thought that they would tell us general practitioners about this wonderful new discovery they had made.

'We have found,' said their spokesman, 'through our studies of patients with chest diseases over the years – and it is very important for all you chaps to remember this – that what the patient says is important. If a patient says that he is feeling better, then he probably is. By the same rule, if your patient says he is feeling worse, then it is quite probable that he is worse.'

I was sorry that my old rugby colleague who had sat next to me at the original lecture wasn't there for some comment.

Thinking had gone full circle in yet another branch of medicine. How profound, how intelligent, how learned were our tutors, and what a gem of wisdom I could take back to Tadchester with me. Let's get it right, now: if a patient said he felt worse, he was probably right, and if he said that he felt better, there was a good chance that he was improving. What an advance in medicine! And as yet nobody has produced another machine to disprove it . . .

* * *

It was strange being in London again after so many years. Having forty-eight hours there made me realise how much I appreciated living in Tadchester, being part of a well-defined community and having a part to play in that community. London was so impersonal and seemed to have changed a great deal since the days when I had been a student there. It was noisier, there seemed to be more cars, people appeared less polite, and of course everything was much more expensive.

I took my cases from the hotel to the hospital for the last day of my course so that I could get away, immediately after the last lecture, on the first available train to Tadchester.

I caught a taxi from the hospital to the station. I was cross-questioned by the taxi driver.

'You a doctor, Guv?' he asked.

'Yes,' I replied, expecting to be asked to make a diagnosis for some obscure condition on the spot. Instead, I got the taxi driver's life history.

He'd been driving a cab for forty-two years. 'In fact,' he said, 'I'm the only dead cab driver still driving.' He claimed he was the only man in England walking around with his own death certificate in his pocket.

'It was like this, Guv,' he said. 'My mother had a hard time with me when I was being born. When I was pulled out eventually I didn't breathe, so they left me on one side. The doctor had to attend to mother. Then he had another look at me and said, "He's not going to do anything," and wrote out a death certificate on the spot.

'One of the neighbours wouldn't have it, and kept dipping me in and out of tubs of hot and cold water. Eventually she got me breathing. I was a sickly baby at first but grew up to be a perfectly healthy lad, played games and was keen on athletics.

'It was only when I went up for army service during the war they told me that I'd only got one lung. This was why I was so sickly at birth. One of me lungs hadn't opened, but me other lung grew to fill the whole of me chest. If they hadn't told me, I'd never have known. Anyway they wouldn't let me in the army, so I had to spend the war driving around in the blitz.

Probably much more dangerous than going to the front.'

'Have you ever thought of telling the Income Tax authorities you are not alive?' I asked him.

'Yes, Guv. I did once, and they said if I was dead I couldn't have a licence for me taxi. They win every time.'

We pulled up at Paddington Station. I got out and looked up at the departure board. It was somehow reassuring to see the notice that a train was due to depart for Taunton, Winchcombe and all stations to Tadchester and Dratchet.

I was on my way home. There was somewhere I belonged.

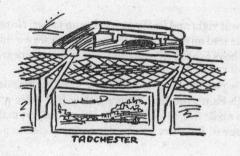

TADCHESTER

17

Moving House

Trevor was eight and Paul was coming up to five. No other child had appeared on the horizon and we felt that we would settle for the two boys as a family, although we would have dearly loved a girl.

Pam's parents, too, would have loved a granddaughter. Through Pam's brother, Thomas, they had three grandsons: our two made five, and they felt a girl would just make up the complement. But there was no sign of any impending new arrival.

As the boys grew bigger we were beginning to burst out of the seams of Herbert Barlow's flat. We looked round for a suitable house to buy. There was one in Altriston that we'd set our hearts on and got as far as putting a deposit down. We thought all was settled when the old lady from whom we were buying suddenly upped the price by several hundred pounds. This put it way beyond our reach. We had very bitter thoughts about the old girl, and started again from scratch. There didn't seem to be anything that we could afford within a reasonable distance. Then Kevin came to the rescue by offering a plot of ground by the river's edge, half way between Sanford-on-Sea and Tadchester.

This was almost too good to be true. His firm were selling off part of a larger estate. Not only did this threequarters of an acre have a marvellous view of the estuary, it was also full of different types of pine trees, part of a much larger garden and estate. The late owners, over several generations, had collected the most beautiful assortment of trees from all over the world. The new owner who was selling off part of the land was very particular to whom he sold: happily a doctor was to his taste and we were offered the ground very cheaply.

We had not ever thought of building and I had no idea how to begin, though we would obviously have to knock one or two of these beautiful trees down to get a house in at all. The land was on a steep gradient and I began to wonder whether it was possible. I also doubted whether I could afford architects' fees to survey and plan a house for us on this land.

Through Eric we managed to get the architect from the town and country planning office who'd do a bit of surveying and planning for people in his own time at a very much reduced rate paid in cash. Thumbing through a magazine we saw the plan of a house on a hill. We liked the look of it and our architect adapted it for us. He couldn't supervise the building, but we'd got the best quote from a builder patient whom I knew would be meticulous in his craftsmanship.

It was so exciting watching the house grow. First of all a bulldozer found a path through the trees, and only had to knock one or two down. Then it flattened a plateau that would not only enable us to build a house on it but would allow for an area in front where cars could turn, and which looked straight down over the estuary.

We turned the original house plan upside down so that our dining room and lounge and kitchen were upstairs, looking out over the estuary, and we went downstairs to sleep.

The house wasn't very big because we hadn't much money. It was terrifying to see a wheelbarrow almost filling a room that was going to be a bedroom.

Herbert was very sad to see us leave the flat, but had managed to let it to some retired theatre people who would be just his cup of tea.

At last the day came for us to move. Most of the stuff we moved in a van from Eric's shop. Kevin's father produced a

larger van to take our bigger furniture, and we did all the
moving ourselves.

We loved our new house. It was really a house to be retired in.
Through my lounge window I could watch the tide ebb and
flow along the estuary. I could see the fishermen row up and
shoot their nets in the river below the house. I could watch the
wild birds and see heron standing on the bank fishing. Unfortunately I still had to work hard and didn't have enough time
to stand and stare, but I never ever tired of the view.

I started to cultivate part of the garden. It was wild and full of
thorn bushes where there weren't trees growing. Roy, Kevin's
brother who worked for Somerset farmers, brought along the
latest rotovators and cultivators and beat up the ground for me
so that I would have a good start.

I bought a small dinghy that we moored down at the bottom
of the garden. Unfortunately when the tide was out there was
almost a quarter of a mile of estuary mud to walk across to
reach the actual river. .

We went up river for picnics and down river for fishing. It was
three miles down the river to the mouth of the estuary. We were
very enthusiastic at first but having once or twice lost our wellingtons in the mud, we only went out when the tide was right
and the weather was right. The times when both these things
were right and I was off duty and I wasn't wanting to do any-

thing else, got fewer and fewer. But the thought of having a boat there if we wanted to use it was a tremendous boon.

We bought a little Cairn terrier, Susie. Trevor and Paul and Susie were in their seventh heaven in this new house. Racing up and down the river bank, fishing, following rabbits. There was something to do from dawn till dusk.

The only thing that had marred the move was that, just after we moved in, Pam's mother became unwell. After a lot of persuading she went into hospital to have some investigations. She had an operation and it was found that she had a widespread malignant disease. There was some chance that she might recover, but it was a very small chance.

Pam took the news of her mother's ill-health badly and started being unwell herself. I thought that this was probably in sympathy with her mother, but then I realised that she was ill in her own right – in fact she was pregnant again.

Pam took the news of both her mother's illness and the pregnancy very badly. She was terribly upset. Her mother was such a courageous person, always full of vim and vigour, adored and loved by her grandchildren, and had a special language with which she could talk with them. Trevor in particular played games with her for hours on end.

Pam realised that she was going to be occupied with her pregnancy during these last months of her mother's life when she would have liked to be able to devote all her time to her.

We had built the house for a family of four. We'd only been in for four months when we were having to knock down walls and rearrange things because we had to have a nursery for the baby which we hadn't anticipated.

As Pam's pregnancy progressed so did the general health of Bill, her mother, deteriorate. We were very lucky with our friends. Margaret Buck in particular took Pam and Bill as much as she could under her wing and did what she could for both of them. Bill got steadily worse and was admitted to hospital in the last month of Pam's pregnancy.

It was thought that she would be well enough to be allowed out of hospital for Christmas and Margaret Buck invited us all to stay with her. It was an awful Christmas. Everybody tried to be cheerful, but it was so terribly depressing seeing such a brave spirit as Bill going so painfully downhill. Gerry, her husband, could hardly hide his grief and there was no way we could console him. Pam, now so near the birth, was so depressed that her beloved mother was obviously going to leave her soon.

I do not know how we would have coped without Margaret Buck who looked after us all and remained cheerful throughout. She had lost her own husband some years before and appreciated what we were all going through.

We had to get Bill back to hospital as soon as Christmas was over. We were able to get a side ward for her in Tadchester Hospital where we knew we'd be able to keep her comfortable over the last few days of her life. Pam who had been in poorer health during this pregnancy than with either Paul or Trevor, was at the lowest I'd ever known her.

I visited Bill in hospital two or three times a day, and she was obviously deteriorating fast. I called in to see her one Saturday, obviously near her last. Pam wasn't certain whether she was in labour or not, but was too unwell to come up to the hospital. Bill took my hand.

'Never mind, Bob,' she said. 'Take care of Pam. I'm sorry I won't be alive to see the little girl.'

These were the last words she said to anybody. She died peacefully that night.

In the midst of all the worry and trauma of fixing up a funeral and making all sorts of other arrangements, Pam went into labour and was sent into Winchcombe Hospital. Her other labours had been quick but this one was prolonged and she was making heavy weather of it. She was still in labour on the Wednesday morning of Bill's funeral. I couldn't not go to the funeral. I knew Pam would want me there, and there was nothing I could do at the hospital. The staff wouldn't want me near the place.

I went with Gerry to the funeral and sat next to him, trying to comfort him as best I could. Poor Gerry: his wife was being buried and his only daughter was in hospital having a difficult labour. Life for him seemed full of bitterness and pain. He and Bill had been happily married for over forty years and there just didn't seem much to look forward to.

Towards the end of the funeral service I heard footsteps at the back of the church. I half turned round and saw Henry Johnson, my partner, creeping up the aisle of the church. He sidled along the pew behind me, reached forward between Gerry and myself and whispered in a loud voice (poor old Henry was incapable of speaking softly) 'All's well. It's a little girl, and Pam's all right.'

I saw Gerry's features brighten and it was as if a cloud had been lifted from above my own head.

Life was going to be different from now on.

Postscript

There is the fable of the old man sitting outside a town, being approached by a stranger.

'What are they like in this town?' asked the stranger.

'What were they like in your last town?' replied the old man.

'They were delightful people. I was very happy there. They were kind, generous and would always help you in trouble.'

'You will find them very much like that in this town.'

The old man was approached by another stranger.

'What are the people like in this town?' asked the second stranger.

'What were they like in your last town?' replied the old man.

'It was an awful place. They were mean, unkind and nobody would ever help anybody.'

'I am afraid you will find it very much the same here,' said the old man.

If it should be your lot to ever visit Tadchester, this is how you will find us.